CONFINEMENT

CONFINEMENT

THE HIDDEN HISTORY
OF MATERNAL BODIES
IN NINETEENTH-CENTURY
BRITAIN

JESSICA COX

First published 2023

The History Press
97 St George's Place, Cheltenham,
Gloucestershire, GL50 3QB
www.thehistorypress.co.uk

British Library Cataloguing in Publication Data.
A catalogue record for this book is available from the British Library.

ISBN 978 0 7509 9857 4

Typesetting and origination by The History Press
Printed and bound in Great Britain by TJ Books Limited, Padstow, Cornwall.

Trees for LYfe

Contents

Praise for *Confinement*

'Illuminating, provocative, and so engaging. Cox's history of motherhood is revelatory about a past that resonates powerfully today. This important and timely book is written with great intellect, grace and empathy. I cannot recommend it enough.'

Helen Cullen, author of *The Truth Must Dazzle Gradually*

'*Confinement* is a long overdue contribution to nineteenth-century history. It's astonishing to consider that while women's bodies have birthed the world, so little attention has been paid to the realities of the maternal body of the past. This is an important, fascinating and frequently shocking read.'

Bernardine Evaristo, author of *Girl, Woman, Other*

'This new book offers us a rare glimpse of the maternal experiences of Victorian women. It encourages us to reflect on the rights, responsibilities and restrictions of the birthing body, and how they have been and continue to be debated, challenged and subject to change.'

Sarah Fox, historian and author of *Giving Birth in Eighteenth-Century England*

'*Confinement* finds the life thrumming inside original Victorian court documents and medical reports; inviting the reader to experience the past in perfect authenticity. Cox anticipates the modern reader's questions and answers them with sensitivity to modern mindsets and grace toward Victorian ones. *Confinement* is a thoroughly researched deep-dive into Victorian maternity that even the most casual paddler can access and enjoy.'

Therese Oneill, *New York Times* bestselling author of *Unmentionable: The Victorian Lady's Guide to Sex, Marriage and Manners*

'This is a brilliant, original and deeply researched book. Jessica Cox's writing is both erudite and engaging, and brings to the fore a subject that has too long been omitted from the historical imagination. *Confinement* is sure to interest scholars from a wide range of disciplines as well as the general reader.'

Prof. Emma Griffin, author of *Bread Winner: An Intimate History of the Victorian Economy*

'Compelling and compassionate ... A fertile study of women's history and a real labour of love that is long overdue.'

Kate Lister, author of *A Curious History of Sex*

'*Confinement* is a powerful work of history. Each chapter is thoroughly researched and carefully crafted, guiding the reader through each aspect of the book. Cox's great skill here is the way she weaves evidence into analysis. We see pregnancy and childbirth as it was experienced in the nineteenth century, through the touchstones of her own contemporary experiences of motherhood.

This is a wide-ranging book, capturing the stories of babies in palaces as well as workhouses. Confinement is full, informative, and deeply moving.'

Claire Lynch, author of *Small: On Motherhoods*

'Compelling, compassionate, and powerful, Jessica Cox's *Confinement* uncovers the moving and fascinating history of maternal bodies and experiences in the 19th century. Meticulously researched and elegantly told, *Confinement* is a necessary and vital work of historical recovery. A beautiful book.'

Elinor Cleghorn, author of *Unwell Women: A Journey Through Medicine and Myth in a Man-Made World*

For Keir, Tam, and Effie – with love.

Acknowledgements

This book has had a long gestation, and throughout its labour and delivery, I have incurred many debts. I must first thank Laurie Robertson at Peters Fraser + Dunlop, whose support and enthusiasm for this book from its early stages has been incredible. Thanks also go to Amy Rigg, Simon Wright, Rebecca Newton and Laura Hunt at The History Press and to PR consultant Angela Martin for their guidance and help during the publication process. I extend my thanks to the various archivists who helped with my research, including those at Tyne and Wear, Northumberland, Durham, and the Gladstone Library. A work of this kind is inevitably indebted to scholars and researchers who have gone before – particularly so in this case as much of the work was written during the pandemic when access to archives was heavily restricted. I must single out the scholarship of Emma Griffin and Joanne Begiato in particular, which introduced me to some wonderful sources on pregnancy and childbirth. I am lucky enough to work with some brilliant colleagues, whose support made it possible for me to find the time to write this book. Particular thanks go to Katrina O'Loughlin, Emily Horton, Emma Filtness, Iman Sheeha, Claire Lynch, Helen Cullen and Meretta Elliott. Huge thanks also to Kenn Toft, for gin and distractions when needed. For advice and encouragement at various stages, my thanks go to Emma Butcher, Vicky Holmes, and especially to Sarah Fox, who read and commented on the draft manuscript. During the writing of this book, the North Sea and the most amazing group of women kept me (mostly) grounded – thank you, mermaids! Love and thanks as always to Mum and Dad, for proofreading, help with childcare, and a thousand other things. Most of what I do would not be possible without the support of my incredible husband, Murray, who picks up the kids, the slack, and the pieces on a regular basis, and to whom I am forever grateful. Finally, my thanks to the three little people whose arrival was the starting point for this work: Keir, Tam, and Effie. This book is dedicated to you.

Introduction

This book begins not in the nineteenth century, but in the twenty-first: in September 2016 in a hospital in Northumberland. I have just been admitted, heavily pregnant with my third child. I am ten days past my due date, and my waters have finally broken, but contractions have not started. Concerned about possible traces of meconium in the waters, a sign that the baby is in distress, the midwives treating me decide to induce labour. I am hooked up to various machines, and contractions soon begin. But there is a problem. With every contraction, the baby's heart rate is dropping. Doctors are worried, and the decision is quickly taken to perform an emergency Caesarean. Within minutes, I am in surgery, and shortly afterwards the baby is born: kicking, screaming, and healthy – to my immense relief. I have lost a lot of blood, but doctors decide a transfusion is not necessary. We are discharged the following day, and I am sent home with strong painkillers and anti-clotting medication to aid my recovery.

My daughter's birth was the starting point of this book, which examines the experiences of women through pregnancy, childbirth, and the postnatal period in nineteenth-century Britain. Her arrival – in circumstances which proved dramatic, though not, ultimately, traumatic – led to a collision of two parts of my life. As a Victorianist and a mother, I began to reflect on the difficulties experienced by women in childbirth at a time when medical assistance was limited, and in some circumstances dangerous. It quickly became clear that one – perhaps both – of us would not have survived this birth in the nineteenth century. The operation that saved my daughter's life was rarely performed in Victorian Britain on account of the high risk it posed to the life of the mother at a time when preventing haemorrhaging and infection was often impossible.[1] Today, around 25 per cent of births in the UK are via Caesarean section, but the options for women 200 years ago were more limited: allow the labour to progress naturally in the hope of a positive outcome, or intervene with a view to preserving the mother's life. That of the child was considered less important: healthy women could go on to have more children, whilst even a healthy baby still had to survive the precarious years of early infancy, at a time when childhood diseases were widespread and often untreatable. Consequently, procedures such as embryotomies, involving the surgical destruction of the baby in the womb in order to enable extraction in cases of difficult deliveries, were still routinely performed for much of the period. Delayed labour, and particularly births involving medical interventions such as the use of forceps, carried a significant risk of infection for which treatment was extremely limited. Maternal mortality remained a very real risk, with around 1 in 200 births resulting in the death of the mother.[2] The blood loss I experienced was manageable, but for many nineteenth-century mothers it was not, and haemorrhaging was a key cause of maternal mortality. Furthermore, whilst my daughter and I were cared for by the NHS, access to medical assistance during childbirth in nineteenth-century Britain varied dramatically and was principally dependent on social status and income. The positive outcome in my case speaks to 200 years of progress in obstetrics and maternity care, as well as in medicine more generally.

These reflections gave me pause for thought. Early motherhood for me – as for so many women – at times felt overwhelming. Pregnancy, childbirth, and breastfeeding frequently left me feeling physically exhausted. The shift to mother required a profound re-evaluation of my sense of identity, and felt, on occasion, like an emotional rollercoaster, in which love, anxiety, frustration, and exhaustion battled for prominence. Each time I returned to my work as a lecturer following maternity leave, I struggled with the sense that motherhood had simply drained away my capability to perform this role. On occasion, I felt I had to reconsider my previous casual dismissal of Victorian arguments around women and work: that women's biological functions meant that they were not suited to the professions. Fortunately, such thoughts correlated strongly with sleep deprivation, and were gradually dismissed as my children began to sleep for more than a couple of hours at a time. Nonetheless, motherhood changed me in ways I had not anticipated. Such feelings are not unusual: motherhood *is* an overwhelming, life-changing experience. For nineteenth-century mothers perhaps even more so: both infant and maternal mortality were considerably higher; pain relief options during childbirth were limited; and women were likely to have a larger number of children. In addition, there were few choices available for women who found themselves unhappily pregnant; unmarried motherhood carried a significant stigma, and the workhouse was often the only solution for women struggling with poverty and a lack of family support. Today, women in Britain can access support for their mental health during pregnancy and following childbirth, albeit with services under significant pressure, but in the nineteenth century, such help was extremely limited, and there was little recognition of the possible after-effects of a traumatic birth – at a time when a traumatic birth was statistically far more likely than today. And against this backdrop was the pervasive idea, perpetuated by nineteenth-century social, cultural, and religious discourses, that motherhood represented women's 'destiny'.

Between 1801 and 1901, the population of Britain grew from around 10.5 million to almost 37 million. This dramatic increase has frequently been discussed in relation to industrialisation and urbanisation, but rarely with reference to the *maternal* labour behind it. These figures represent millions of birthing women, many thousands of whom lost their lives in the process, and all of whom will have experienced motherhood on a personal, individual level. Yet the maternal experiences of women in nineteenth-century Britain have been largely unrecorded, lost, or overlooked. Pregnancy is notable by its absence in the art and literature of the time; the pregnant body is a reminder of female sexuality, and therefore typically concealed in public discourses. Childbirth is both a messy and often a private experience,[3] so explicit accounts from this period are relatively rare – surviving primarily in medical literature and hospital archives. The oral tradition of sharing birth stories which likely existed between some women has, inevitably, not been preserved. This, then, is a history which is mostly undocumented, often absent from the archive, and, where this is not the case, generally unexplored. In a century of dramatic social and political reform, rapidly advancing technology, and cultural endeavour – of progress, but also deep social inequalities – the maternal experience is deemed largely insignificant. For mothers, though, then as now, such experiences were often momentous, transformational life events. In reconstructing these women's maternal histories, this book reveals much not only about nineteenth-century motherhood, but also about medicine, (pseudo-) science, class, and gender roles, and rewrites the maternal body back into history.

During my pregnancies, particularly my first, I read through the advice offered by countless books, magazine articles, and internet forums on pregnancy and childbirth; some of it based on medical knowledge and understanding, some on personal experiences. Sometimes helpful, it was also, not infrequently, confusing and contradictory, and at times formed part of wider ideological beliefs around motherhood. In this respect, it echoed the multitude of advice books available to the nineteenth-century mother – particularly in the latter decades of the century, following the rapid expansion of the literary marketplace. The appetite for this type of literature expanded dramatically at this time, and by the end of the period, countless works on almost every aspect of motherhood were available. Many such works sold in their tens of thousands, and the advice they contained was widely circulated: one of the most popular works for mothers, *Advice to a Wife*, sold in vast quantities, running to dozens of editions between the 1840s and the close of the century, and exerting some considerable influence on expectant and new mothers. Such texts were directed primarily at the middle-class reader, but having the time and money to afford such things did not necessarily improve women's maternal knowledge. Then, as now, the advice offered could be contradictory, and, paralleling today's online world, it was partly responsible for the spread of misinformation about pregnancy, childbirth, and infant care. Many of these works were written by men claiming medical expertise, and, at a time when women's access to education was limited and there was a reluctance to discuss publicly the reproductive functions of the female body, the guidance contained therein would have been difficult for the reader to dispute. Often the contents of these works invoke wider ideological discourses around gender and motherhood, reinforcing some of the commonly held assumptions about women's capabilities and roles, with many promoting an idealised, unrealistic vision of motherhood. Male-authored advice literature did not provide a platform for women to tell their own stories of pregnancy, birth, and motherhood, but it does offer a window into the information women were given about maternity, and the various culture pressures to which they were subjected.

Today, there are multiple forums for women to explore their own stories and experiences of maternity, from online spaces to social and community groups. Shortly after giving birth to my first child, I attended my final NCT class. We had met several times already, and this final class was an opportunity to meet the babies and compare birth stories. Though my experience was (thankfully) fairly mundane as far as childbirth goes, it was a story I came to share over and over. Prior to my first child's arrival, I consumed the birth stories of others – those of friends, family, and strangers on internet forums – in an attempt to understand the experience I would shortly undergo myself. Following the somewhat more dramatic arrival of my third child, I began to realise the importance of these narratives as a way of working through our own experiences, of understanding their significance and the impact they have. Years later, discussions of motherhood with friends and acquaintances still include references to the stories of our children's births, so significant are these experiences. They are passed from mothers to daughters, from long-experienced mothers to mothers-to-be, from new mothers to midwives and doctors, between friends comparing notes on everything from pain levels to postnatal recovery. They serve an important function: transmitting knowledge, validating our experiences, enhancing our understanding – not only of the medical aspects of childbirth, but of its emotional impact as well. In nineteenth-century Britain, opportunities for women to hear and tell birth stories were much more limited. Public discourses – including advice literature, for much of the period – typically avoided references to the details of childbirth. The information passed from mother to daughters was often circumspect at best; and there were generally very limited opportunities for women to discuss birthing plans with medical professionals before giving birth. These silences had potentially grave consequences: some women gave birth with no or extremely limited understanding of what it actually involved, and for women who experienced difficult or traumatic births, there was little opportunity to work through these experiences retrospectively. More broadly, there were few opportunities for women to discuss their hopes, fears, and anxieties relating to pregnancy, childbirth, and motherhood. The term 'confinement' in the nineteenth century referred to childbirth and the period immediately following, during which time women were typically confined to their beds, but it reflects, too, the wider social and cultural confines that were imposed on women: the expectations to which women were subject in respect of motherhood; the restrictions placed on the pregnant, birthing, and lactating body; and the lack of opportunities to discuss and understand the experiences of pregnancy and childbirth. This book is an attempt to give voice to those experiences, to uncover and piece together the birth narratives hitherto obscured, which, in turn, represent the many millions of stories lost entirely to the mists of time. Whilst the maternal experiences of women in nineteenth-century Britain contributed to the transformation of maternity care for the generations of women who followed, their individual stories are rarely heard, yet these are, like those of mothers today, important and valuable.

This work, then, is an account of those women's experiences of pregnancy, childbirth, and breastfeeding. It begins with women's experiences of fertility and infertility, examining the lived experiences of those women who struggled to have children and those who, with little control over these matters, gave birth to large numbers of babies. It considers women's experiences of pregnancy, which differed greatly depending on social status and circumstances. I explore at length varied experiences of childbirth itself, including in relation to maternal mortality, infant loss, and maternity care. The desperate situations of women experiencing unwanted pregnancies are examined in a chapter which looks at abortion, abandonment, and infanticide. The final two chapters consider women's postnatal experiences, including postnatal depression, puerperal insanity, breastfeeding, and wet nursing. I look at women's own accounts of their maternal experiences in letters, diaries, and memoirs, as well as medical and advice literature, newspapers, journals, and fiction, and attempt to uncover the lived experience of the maternal body in nineteenth-century Britain. I consider the experiences of public figures, such as Queen Victoria (mother of nine children), alongside those who lived more obscure lives in which maternity was a defining feature, tracing maternal histories from the royal palaces to the workhouses. For women of the royal family and other prominent public figures, there is a wealth of archival material: letters, diaries, newspaper reports, and medical notes. From these, we can reconstruct their experiences of motherhood, often in their own words. Details of the maternal experiences of women at the other end of the social scale – the multitudes of women who gave birth in one of Britain's many workhouses, for example – are scarcer, and in particular there is a lack of material produced by the women themselves.[4] A significant number of those women who inhabited the workhouse at various stages of their lives were illiterate, and those who were not were unlikely to have the resources, time, or reasons to write about their experiences. There were deep divisions between rich and poor: the Victorian period in particular is marked by entrenched class hierarchies, which in turn gave rise to deep social inequalities. These divisions are often reflected in women's experiences of pregnancy, childbirth, and motherhood. Unplanned or unwanted pregnancies could be devastating for any woman, but poorer women faced the added challenge of limited financial resources, and were more likely to find themselves unable to support a family. They were also less likely to have access to sanitary surroundings, pain relief, and medical care – or to supportive partners, let alone servants, to assist them. Unwanted pregnancy impacted women in different ways, dependent on class status, but any woman engaged in sexual relationships could do little to prevent pregnancy, with their being considerable opposition to and ignorance around the use of contraception (though some did employ contraceptive methods effectively).[5]

The stories and accounts in hospital, workhouse, and asylum archives, as well as newspaper reports, medical journals, and court, census, and parish records, enable us to garner some insight into the lives of poorer women, as they negotiated fertility, pregnancy, maternal loss, childbirth, and motherhood. Their lives are less clearly detailed in the historical record than those of their more privileged counterparts, and their identities are often obscured: hospital and workhouse archives might include a name and age, but often little further information, making them difficult to trace, whilst published case studies generally exclude even these basic details. For those women in slightly less precarious positions, there is a significant amount of material to explore, in the form of working-class autobiographies, for example, many of which were written and published in the twentieth century but look back to the late Victorian period. Whilst these often only contain, at most, passing references to the maternal experience, they nonetheless provide significant insights into the lives of these women. One particularly useful source from the early twentieth century is a collection of letters from working women written in response to a request from the Women's Co-operative Guild in 1914 for information about women's experiences of childbirth and motherhood. Almost 400 women responded, and many of the letters detail their maternal experiences in the late nineteenth century, and talk candidly about pregnancy, miscarriage, abortion, childbirth, and infant loss. The particular value of these letters lies in their capturing of the voices of women who often struggled financially and were frequently forced to work throughout and shortly after their (often many) pregnancies. Such sources enable important comparisons to be drawn between the maternal lives of those at the poorer end of the social scale, and those more privileged lives.

In examining the experiences of women from across the social spectrum, this book contributes to an increasing body of work on 'history from below', moving away from those histories which focus exclusively on the middle and upper classes (proportionally a minority of the population in nineteenth-century Britain).[6] If social histories of this period have focused predominantly – until relatively recently at least – on the middle and upper classes, they have also concerned themselves principally with the experience of Britain's white population. Consequently, such histories (along with film and television period dramas which all too often, certainly until the last few years, have tended to feature exclusively white casts), give the impression of an almost entirely white British population. This is misleading: whilst Britain's ethnic minority population was, of course, significantly smaller in the nineteenth century than it is today, it was, nevertheless, diverse. Britain has a long history of migration, and in the nineteenth century there were thousands of people of – amongst others – Indian, African, and Chinese descent living in the UK.[7] My aim was to make this book as representative as possible, to discuss the maternal experiences of women from a broad range of backgrounds, but uncovering the lives of Britain's ethnic minority mothers in the nineteenth century is difficult. Life writing – memoirs, diaries, letters – makes limited reference to these experiences. Hospital, asylum, and workhouse records contain few allusions to ethnicity, and the same is true of published medical case notes. The census did not explicitly include ethnicity until 1991, which means there is no reliable way of identifying people of colour born in Britain based on the extant historical records. Newspaper archives do provide occasional information in this respect (though often using racist terminology), but it is piecemeal and difficult to locate. Whilst the archives provide some information about the lives of people of colour living in Britain at the time, their histories of pregnancy, childbirth, and motherhood remain largely elusive, and consequently, with some exceptions, the stories discussed here are either focused on white women, or those of unknown ethnicity.

The central remit of this book is to shed some light on the maternal experiences of women from all backgrounds in nineteenth-century Britain, but the availability of materials inevitably means that some groups and figures receive more attention than others: as a consequence, the aristocratic classes – almost exclusively white – are overrepresented both in this work and in the wider historical record; it is inevitable, therefore, given her long reign, and the wealth of surviving letters, journals, and other records, that Queen Victoria and her family should feature prominently.

The royal family, of course, had access to all the trappings associated with wealth and status, but whilst this conferred certain privileges in respect of motherhood, it was not always a guarantee against the dangers and risks of pregnancy and childbirth. Money could not purchase protection from infection, medical negligence or ignorance, or unforeseen complications. Whilst the births of Queen Victoria's nine children were, on the whole, uncomplicated and all of her offspring survived both birth and infancy, other members of the royal family were not so fortunate. Eighteen months before Victoria herself was born, her cousin and heir presumptive to the British throne, Princess Charlotte of Wales, gave birth to a stillborn son, and died shortly afterwards from internal haemorrhaging. Almost twenty years earlier, the only child of Charlotte Princess Royal, a daughter, was stillborn. Although stillbirths and infant mortality were considerably higher than today, this did not mitigate the grief of mothers who lost their babies. Many others, rich and poor, suffered complications during childbirth which threatened the health and well-being of mother and child, and sometimes left long-lasting physical and emotional consequences. The birth of Victoria's first grandchild, the son of her daughter the Princess Royal (also named Victoria), was difficult: the baby was breech, and although he was eventually delivered alive, the nerves in his left arm were damaged, leaving him with lifelong injuries. In 1871, another of Victoria's grandchildren, the son of the future Edward VII, was born prematurely, and died the following day. Princess Helena, Victoria's fifth child, lost a baby son only a few days after his birth, and, following a subsequent pregnancy, delivered a stillborn son. Helena's sister-in-law, Maria

Alexandrovna of Russia, wife of Prince Alfred, also gave birth to a still-born son – born prematurely in October 1879. Wealth and status, though, did offer some protection at a time long before the National Health Service provided state-funded maternity care for all. The medical support Queen Victoria received during her confinements was fairly typical of the upper and middle classes in nineteenth-century England, with physicians paid to visit and treat patients at home. Predictably, the doctors who attended Victoria were considered the very best in the field, and this was reflected in their fees, which were beyond the reach of most of the population at the time. The wealthier classes were paying for experience, reputation, medical training, and qualifications – the latter not guaranteed at a time when regulation of medical practitioners was limited.[8] Both of Queen Victoria's doctors belonged to the Royal College of Physicians, an important indicator of expertise and experience, although limitations in medical knowledge as well as negligence on the part of some doctors meant women were not necessarily better off when attended by medical men. Poorer women with limited income might give birth with only the support of family members, neighbours, or friends, summoning medical assistance only if complications arose. Midwives were less expensive than doctors – mainly due to the fact they often lacked formal qualifications – and thus typically attended mothers from the poorer classes. The reputations of midwives suffered extensively in the nineteenth century, in large part a result of the ongoing medicalisation of childbirth, which brought it under the control of the male medical practitioner, and the denigration of female practitioners by the medical profession and popular culture – the latter epitomised by Dickens's Mrs Gamp in *Martin Chuzzlewit* (1844) (see figure 10). It wasn't until later in the century that women were able to access formal midwifery training, but even without qualifications, many practising midwives provided women in their communities with an invaluable service.

There were alternative options available for those women who could not afford to pay for medical care during childbirth in the form of charitable and (very limited) state provision. Lying-in (maternity) hospitals, several of which were established in Britain in the eighteenth century, were typically philanthropic institutions offering medical care during and after childbirth for poorer women.[9] However, several of these, including the British Lying-in Hospital in London and the Newcastle Lying-in Hospital in north-east England, catered only to married women, and thus would have been inaccessible to unmarried women. Whilst most women throughout the period gave birth at home, expectant mothers attending one of the increasing numbers of lying-in hospitals in Britain or one of the many workhouses established in the wake of the 1834 Poor Law Amendment Act could expect, in theory, to receive some medical care, but this was often limited. Many doctors and obstetricians supplemented their income from private practice – or indulged their philanthropic inclinations – by attending patients in these institutions. One of Queen Victoria's physicians, Charles Locock, continued to act as consultant-physician to the General Lying-in Hospital in London even after he was appointed First-Physician Accoucheur to the Queen,[10] and key figures in the field of nineteenth-century obstetrics were attendant physicians at the various lying-in hospitals, drawing on their experiences there in their published works on pregnancy and childbirth.[11] Respectable doctors also held positions at some of the large number of workhouses.[12] Nonetheless, standards of maternity care in the workhouse were often poor, and in some institutions downright dangerous. The workhouses catered to society's poor in general, and were not specifically designed or equipped to deal with expectant mothers. Whilst qualified medical men did sometimes attend birthing mothers in the workhouse, the lying-in wards themselves were usually staffed by unqualified attendants – sometimes even other inmates – and were frequently unclean and cramped, resulting in increased maternal and infant mortality rates. The quality of the medical provision within the workhouse was not the only issue; as reports of multiple cases demonstrate, there was no guarantee that pregnant women attending these institutions would be treated with compassion or respect.

Some improvements in medical care for those applying for poor relief came about with the passing of the Metropolitan Poor Act in 1867. This resulted in the establishment of separate asylums for the sick in London's districts – removing infirmary care from the workhouses themselves. It also established a framework for the employment of trained nurses to treat the sick, and marked an important step forward in the reform of the laws and policies which impacted the lives of society's poor. The Act was the result of various campaigns by reformers, writing in medical journals and bringing the issue to the attention of parliament. *The Lancet* ran a series of articles on the distressing conditions in London workhouses, and Dr Joseph Rogers, medical officer for the Strand Workhouse, testified in

1861 before a House of Commons select committee on conditions in the workhouse. His description of the nursery ward at the Strand Workhouse highlights the dire circumstances in which some women gave birth:

> [The nursery] was a wretchedly damp and miserable room, nearly always overcrowded with young mothers and their infant children. That death relieved these young women of their illegitimate offspring was only what was to be expected, and that frequently the mothers followed in the same direction was only too true. I used to dread to go into this ward, it was so depressing. Scores and scores of distinctly preventable deaths of both mothers and children took place during my continuance in office through their being located in this horrible den.[13]

Rogers' account also indicates that the presence of a trained and conscientious medical officer did not necessarily improve the experiences of – or outcomes for – birthing women in the workhouse. Many of the midwives who often attended the workhouse would not have received formal training but were nonetheless often very experienced. Unless complications arose, it was entirely likely that the medical officer would not be called upon to attend women during childbirth; indeed, he might be forbidden from doing so by the matron or attending midwife, who effectively controlled access to the birthing room. Although limiting women's access to medical assistance contravened the regulations governing workhouses, Rogers suggested this type of gatekeeping was common practice.[14]

The latter half of the century witnessed significant improvements in maternity care, experienced – in varying degrees – by both rich and poor.[15] Whilst poorer women might receive improved care under the amended poor laws, wealthier women who could afford such 'luxuries' could take advantage of the increased availability of pain relief during labour and childbirth. In addition, women across the social spectrum stood to benefit from an increased understanding around the spread of infection, which helped to reduce cases of puerperal fever – sometimes spread by unhygienic medical practices, and a major cause of maternal mortality. However, whilst these developments in obstetrics and maternity care brought benefits, the continuing medicalisation of childbirth throughout this period also increased the potential for complications in certain circumstances: infection spread more easily in lying-in wards and hospitals, where beds were often close together, and doctors went from one patient to another with little regard for hygiene practices such as handwashing (until the later decades of the century). Obstetric tools such as forceps might increase the baby's chances of survival, but they were also often responsible for inflicting significant damage resulting in ongoing physical problems for mothers. The perforator and crotchet, used to perform embryotomies, remained relatively widely used throughout the century, with destructive operations carried out in cases where the mother's life appeared to be at risk (see figure 9). In some instances, there was evidence that the baby was already dead, but in others these procedures were performed regardless, as it was deemed preferable by most medical men to preserve the life of the mother at the expense of the child if necessary. Whilst the mother's life might (though not always) be saved by such interventions, they were often painful and extended, as well as deeply traumatic, procedures. The increasing use of chloroform from the mid-nineteenth century offered the possibility of less painful births – it was used by Queen Victoria, amongst many others – but it was not without risks to both mother and baby. Women still also had to negotiate fertility issues, unwanted pregnancies, the physical effects of multiple pregnancies, as well as the general ailments of pregnancy and childbirth and its after-effects. Even in straightforward cases, the physical demands of pregnancy, childbirth, and breastfeeding could be overwhelming, and traumatic births were far more common than today. The after-effects of these could be significant, potentially contributing to the development of what we would now recognise as postnatal post-traumatic stress disorder; asylum records for patients suffering from what was generally termed 'puerperal insanity' to some extent bear witness to this.

Whilst women had to contend with widely differing levels of maternity care, they also had to negotiate often deeply entrenched social and cultural attitudes towards motherhood. These varied from the idealisation of the mother in discourses around 'respectable' married women, to the demonisation of the figure of the unmarried mother, to concern around levels of reproduction amongst the poorer classes, and anxieties about the potentially damaging effect of work and education on women's maternal role. Such discourses shifted considerably as the century progressed, but nonetheless, these attitudes towards and discourses around motherhood had the potential for significant psychological and material impact.

The women's histories included in this book span the length of the nineteenth century, and in some respects there are clear continuities in their stories – as well as parallels with our own contemporary moment and the experiences of mothers today. The examination of the maternal experiences of women across the period, side by side, highlights these continuities, but perhaps potentially obscures the dramatic changes that took place throughout the century. Whilst there are points of similarity in women's experiences of pregnancy, childbirth, infant loss, breastfeeding, and childrearing between 1800 and 1900, there are also significant differences, reflecting the changes that took place over the course of this transformative century: women giving birth in early nineteenth-century Britain lived in a radically different world to those in the late Victorian period – and these differences necessarily affected the maternal experience. Medical knowledge and practice changed and developed as the century progressed; attitudes towards and debates around women, the family, and sexual behaviour also changed; and the legal context – especially in respect of women's rights – shifted considerably. In turn, these changes gave way to even greater transformation in the twentieth century, in which the establishment of the welfare state, the formation of the NHS, and the introduction of legislation around maternity rights laid the foundations of women's experiences of maternity in Britain today. Although the stories in this book are not arranged chronologically, nonetheless the shifts that took place over the course of this century form the backdrop to the women's stories and experiences discussed here.

For many women throughout the nineteenth century, maternity proved a trial. For those who experienced motherhood, it was frequently a central aspect of their lives, whether for good or bad. In this context, it seems surprising that the maternal stories of nineteenth-century women have been largely overlooked until relatively recently, particularly in light of the continuities that emerge with the contemporary maternal experience. Whilst there have been momentous improvements in maternity care, and in maternal and infant mortality rates, there remains a cultural silence around issues such as infertility, miscarriage, and abortion, which echoes that of the nineteenth century.[16] Over the course of the period, women's maternal experiences contributed to significant developments in medical understandings of pregnancy, childbirth, and its associated risks. In this respect, they were at the heart of the improvements in obstetric and midwifery care that began in the nineteenth century and continued throughout the twentieth and twenty-first centuries, eventually leading to greatly improved maternity care for women in Britain today. Furthermore, when the experiences of nineteenth-century mothers are brought to light, we find in the everyday, ordinary, mundane details of their maternal journeys voices which speak to our own understanding of motherhood and its attendant emotions. And amidst the myriad of harrowing accounts of pregnancy and childbirth, we also find moving descriptions of maternal love and bonding. This book is an attempt to uncover the maternal voices from the past which have been largely forgotten, overlooked, or dismissed as insignificant. Of the millions of women who gave birth over the course of the century, this work, inevitably, provides only a small snapshot. Surviving letters and diaries belong predominantly – though not exclusively – to middle- and upper-class women: those with the time, education, and resources to record their experiences. The details of the maternal experiences of poorer women, those with limited education, or whose lives were so dominated by work and family that they did not have the time to write are often available only through others: in the case notes from the lying-in hospitals which catered to these women, and in the medical literature on midwifery. In these cases, others speak for them – and those that do frequently consider only the medical perspective, rather than women's emotional experiences of childbirth and its after-effects. It is through our own understanding of maternal love, of grief, and of trauma that we may come to appreciate something of what they endured.

1

(In)Fertility

But I now, but I now –
Seared by the high God's scorn –
Lives that will never come to birth
Body of me has borne.
Harriet Monroe[1]

In October 1870, Queen Victoria announced that her fourth daughter, Princess Louise, was engaged to be married to the Marquess of Lorne, the eldest son of the eighth Duke of Argyll. Shortly before the wedding, the Queen wrote to Lorne's father, informing him that her daughter was 'barren'.[2] Rumours have long persisted suggesting that a few years prior to her wedding, Princess Louise gave birth to an illegitimate child.[3] One of Louise's biographers, Lucinda Hawksley, speculates that complications during this alleged birth had left the Princess infertile – a perceived stigma and source of shame for women in nineteenth-century Britain, particularly those amongst the wealthier classes who were frequently expected to fulfil their 'duty' and produce an heir. Whatever the truth may be, Louise's marriage to Lorne did not produce any children. This was in stark contrast to the experience of her mother, who evidently would have preferred to have had fewer children had she been able to prevent some of her many (nine) pregnancies. Prior to her wedding, Victoria recorded a conversation with Lord Melbourne in her journal, in which he declared: 'The measure of married happiness is to have a great number of children,' 'which,' she writes, 'I'm sure I shall never think; that is the only thing I dread'.[4] Her admission

here, recorded in a private journal, is at odds with widely held perceptions of women's role and 'duties' at this time, and, as the monarch, many
amongst not only Victoria's own family but also the wider public would
have hoped for the safe arrival of more than one heir in order to secure the
line of succession. Her fears proved to be well founded – to the delight of
the nation, if not the Queen herself. Victoria's first pregnancy occurred
shortly after her wedding to Albert in February 1840, and she was deeply
unhappy about this, despite the need to produce an heir to the throne (and
with a succession crisis still within living memory). In a letter to her grandmother following the realisation that she was pregnant, she wrote:

> It is spoiling my happiness; I have always hated the idea, and I prayed
> God night and day for me to be left free for at least six months, but my
> prayers have not been answered, and I am really most unhappy. I cannot
> understand how one can wish for such a thing, especially at the begin-
> ning of a marriage.[5]

Her first child, Victoria Princess Royal, was born at Buckingham Palace
in November 1840. Less than three months later, the Queen again found
herself pregnant, and within less than four years she had four children.
Her resentment at her numerous pregnancies remained in evidence many
years later. Shortly after Victoria's wedding to Prince Frederick of Prussia
in January 1858, the Queen wrote to her. She had heard rumours that
Vicky was pregnant, and was pleased to discover these were unfounded:

> I cannot tell you how happy I am that you are not in an unenviable
> position. I never can rejoice by hearing that a poor young thing is pulled
> down by this trial. Though I quite admit the comfort and blessing good
> and amiable children are – though they are also an awful plague and
> anxiety for which they show one so little gratitude very often! What
> made me so miserable was – to have the first two years of my married
> life utterly spoilt by this occupation! I could enjoy nothing – not travel
> about or go about with dear Papa and if I had waited a year, as I hope
> you will, it would have been different.[6]

Given Victoria's views on the difficulties of frequent and numerous pregnancies, it is somewhat surprising that she allowed her daughter to marry

at the age of only 17, by doing so increasing the likelihood of her producing a large family (which indeed she did – eight children). The best
way to have ensured her daughter was not 'pulled down' by the 'trial'
of pregnancy at a young age would have been to delay her marriage.[7]
In another letter written in 1858, Queen Victoria referred to the 'miseries and plagues' which she endured for the first years of her marriage
to Albert.[8] She made clear her views on women who produce excessive
numbers of children, despite her own position as a mother of nine: 'I positively think ladies who are always *enceinte* quite disgusting; it is more like
a rabbit or guinea-pig than anything else and really it is not very nice.'[9]
Her letters attest to the fact that she was unable to prevent her pregnancies, despite her evident desire to do so. Queen Victoria's and her daughter
Princess Louise's differing experiences of marriage and maternity reflect
the fact that for most women of the time, fertility was frequently as much
a matter of luck as a matter of choice. Women who found themselves
unable to conceive were left with few options, at a time when there was
little understanding of the causes of infertility and medical solutions were
limited. In this respect, maternity acted as something of a social leveller:
rich as well as poor could experience fertility problems, and money could
not provide a cure.

For many women, as now, fertility was as much of an issue as infertility.
At various points of our lives, many of us are forced to confront the issue of
our desire – and ability – to bear children: the notion that you spend your
twenties trying not to conceive and your thirties trying to fall pregnant
is familiar to many. Many of us are fortunate, today, to benefit from reliable contraception, recognition of our agency when it comes to pregnancy
and motherhood, and dramatic improvements in treatments for infertility.
There were various reasons why nineteenth-century women had little control over their fertility. Marital rape was not criminalised in the UK until
1991, so married women could not legally, until then, refuse to engage
in sexual relations with their husbands. Many women had limited or no
knowledge of how to prevent pregnancy. In any case, reliable methods of
contraception were little practised, and women were generally reliant on
their husbands being willing to employ these.[10] In addition, the use of con-
traceptives was strongly discouraged in some quarters. One work on the
subject, entitled *The Moral and Physical Evils likely to follow practices intended
to act as Checks to Population* (1878), argued that the use of contraception

rendered sexual relations an act of 'conjugal onanism', which it declared a 'moral crime', proposing that 'It is destroying in the beginning what, under God's blessing, might have matured into a living soul, and proved a blessing to humanity.'[11] Arguments in favour of limiting the number of children produced within a marriage frequently highlighted the tendency towards large families amongst the poorer classes. Stereotyping of the poor in some quarters depicted them as the irresponsible producers of large families that they could not afford to support, and the homes of the poor as dens of immorality, with parents spending their meagre income on gin rather than food for their children. Attitudes such as these partly informed the eugenics movement in the late nineteenth century. Elsewhere, though, there was little concern for the large number of poor children; one opponent to contraception argued that although larger families were more common amongst the poor, 'as the children of the indigent are generally less long-lived, they cannot be said to increase population'.[12] Infant mortality is here problematically positioned as an alternative to the use of contraception, with no recognition of the fact that mortality rates might be reduced if family size decreased, or indeed of the emotional distress that inevitably resulted from the death of a child. Instead, there are echoes here of the notion of natural selection: survival of the fittest. Charles Darwin himself, like many others, suggested that the use of contraception would encourage immoral relations. In 1877, Annie Besant and Charles Bradlaugh were prosecuted after publishing a book by American writer, Charles Knowlton, which contained information on contraceptive methods. Darwin (father of ten children) was asked by Bradlaugh to testify for the defendants, but refused, stating his opposition to the use of contraception: 'I believe that any such practices would in time spread to unmarried women & wd destroy chastity, on which the family bond depends; & the weakening of this bond would be the greatest of all possible evils to mankind.'[13] In another letter on the subject written to George Arthur Gaskell, another ardent advocate of birth control, Darwin asked, 'If it were universally known that the birth of children could be prevented, and this were not thought immoral by married persons would there not be great danger of extreme profligacy amongst unmarried women[?]'[14] Such views were not unusual, and if ideological reasons held no sway, both ignorance and convenience undoubtedly contributed to some men's reluctance to employ contraceptive methods as well.

Inevitably, given the public furore around works such as Knowlton's, most advice books aimed at married women were silent on the subject of contraception, or even explicitly condemned the use of methods intended to prevent pregnancy. One notable exception to this was physician Henry Arthur Allbutt's *The Wife's Handbook*, first published in 1886. This short work, aimed primarily at the wives of working men, provoked controversy for its inclusion of a chapter on preventing conception, and was also far more explicit than most other advice books on the subjects of pregnancy and childbirth. As a consequence, the General Medical Council judged Allbutt to be 'guilty of infamous conduct in a professional respect' and his name was removed from the medical register. In his defence, published as a preface to later editions of the book, Allbutt argued that his work would give the poor married woman 'the means by which she can keep from the workhouse by having only as many children as she can bring up in comfort'.[15] However progressive this might seem, among Allbutt's list of contraceptive methods were many that were utterly ineffective. These included: sitting up and coughing after intercourse; avoiding sex 'from five days before the monthly flow till eight days after it' (a period which for most women would not include ovulation, when the chances of conceiving are higher); withdrawal (effective, Allbutt notes, but not recommended as it can be 'hurtful to the nervous system in many persons'); injecting a mixture of alum and water into the vagina following sex; inserting a sponge soaked in tepid water or quinine into the vagina before sex; and the use of 'French letters' (condoms). He also mentions the practice of taking 'arsenic and other drugs in small doses daily, to lessen male sexual vigour and thus produce impotence', but advises against this as, although effective, it will come at the cost of 'irreparable ill health'.[16] Allbutt's work, and the controversy surrounding it, point to the difficulties involved for women in obtaining reliable information regarding the prevention of pregnancy. Misinformation on this subject continued to appear in publications aimed at married women well into the twentieth century; a work on family health published in the 1950s, which sat on my grandmother's bookcase, advised that the safest time for marital relations in order to avoid conception was in the middle of a woman's cycle.

Ignorance about contraception and no legal redress against marital rape notwithstanding, abstinence – the most reliable way of preventing pregnancy – was not something to which many couples would readily agree.

Many women had no desire to abstain from sexual relations, despite the stereotypes later perpetuated about the Victorians in the twentieth century. When Queen Victoria was advised by her doctor against having any more children following the birth of her ninth child in 1857, she allegedly asked, 'Can I have no more fun in bed?'[17] The fact that Victoria did not experience any further pregnancies in the period between Beatrice's birth in 1857 and Albert's death in 1861 (when she was aged 42) suggests the couple may have practised some form of contraception.

In the late nineteenth century, methods aimed at preventing conception became more commonly used. Suffragette and socialist Hannah Mitchell was one of those in favour of employing such methods – in theory and in practice (she had only one child herself):

> although birth control may not be a perfect solution to social problems, it is the first and the simplest way at present for the poor to help themselves, and by far the surest way for women to obtain some measure of freedom. I had seen many pretty, merry girls who had married on a small wage, and whose babies had come fast, turn into slatterns and prematurely aged women.[18]

Whilst there was a marked decline in fertility in the late nineteenth century, large families were still a common occurrence throughout the period. The experience of Mary Jonas, the wife of a furniture maker from Chester, was nevertheless unusual: over the course of some twenty years from the late 1830s, she gave birth to thirty-three children, including fifteen sets of twins. As for so many other women of the time – both rich and poor – it is unlikely that Mary had much say in determining the size of her family.

Despite the fact that fertility was, in many respects, beyond most women's control, discourses around marriage and motherhood nonetheless positioned both childlessness *and* excessive fertility as in some ways problematic. In *Advice to a Wife*, the author suggests both states pose a risk to women's mental and physical health – although excessive childbearing within marriage is perceived as preferable to none:

> There are two classes of wives most liable to hysteria, namely those who have had too many children, and those who have had none at all [...]

[O]f the two, the childless wife is far more liable to hysteria, and to many other diseases, than is the prolific mother.[19]

Married women, then, were encouraged to fulfil what was typically perceived as their biological destiny – to produce children – but in some instances, as shown here, they were also blamed for producing excessive numbers of children, yet their maternal narratives remained largely beyond their control.

Infertility

In an article which appeared in *The Lancet* in 1866, medical statistician William Farr estimated the number of childless families in 1851 at around 1 million.[20] However, it wasn't until 1911 that the Census for England and Wales included a question on the number of children born within a marriage, making estimates of the number of childless marriages more accurate. The 1911 data suggests 16.6 per cent of wives were childless – although of those married for more than ten years who had wed before the age of 25, the figure was only 5.2 per cent.[21] Today in the UK, approximately one in seven couples experience problems conceiving, though IVF in particular has transformed the prospects of infertile couples, with a success rate of treatment approximately 1 in 3 for women under the age of 35.[22] Of course, infertility was not the only explanation for a childless marriage in the nineteenth century. As awareness of contraceptive methods increased in the latter decades of the period, this raised the possibility that couples might remain voluntarily childless. Infant mortality – still troublingly high at the close of the century, despite declining over the preceding decades[23] – might also leave couples childless. One of the respondents to the Women's Co-operative Guild in 1914 had suffered one miscarriage, two stillbirths, and lost two children to whooping cough within a week of one another, leaving her childless.[24] A large number of children might provide some reassurance in this respect, but this was not necessarily a guarantee against childlessness. One extreme example of this is the case of Rebecca Town, from Keighley in Yorkshire. She married her husband, Benjamin, in 1828, and over the course of the next twenty-three years bore him thirty children, but only one appears to have survived beyond the age of 3.[25] At the time of both the 1841 and the 1851 census (the latter conducted shortly before her death), she appears to have been living alone with her husband. For some involuntarily childless women, infertility was not the problem, in so far as they were able to conceive, but were unable to deliver children alive – suffering multiple miscarriages and/or stillbirths. In some instances, the latter were the result of deformation of the pelvis, often caused by rickets, making it impossible for them to deliver without the employment of destructive operations (craniotomies or embryotomies), as one obstetrician writing in the mid-nineteenth century observed:

> Melancholy are the reflections, where a woman has a very much distorted pelvis (and such women have usually wonderful aptitude to conceive), that there should be little, if any, chance of preserving the lives of their children; and yet, in the course of practice, I have in several instances been called to the same woman in five or six successive labours, merely to give a sanction to an operation by which the children were to be destroyed.[26]

The living conditions of the poor rendered many of them more susceptible to conditions such as rickets: an inadequate diet and lack of access to sunlight (a problem for those living in densely populated city slums and those working long hours indoors) increased the chances of developing rickets, and thus of problems during childbearing. Poverty, then, in a multitude of ways, could have a devastating impact on women's maternal experiences

The feminist and author Olive Schreiner also experienced childlessness as a consequence of infant loss. She gave birth to a daughter in 1895, but the child only lived a matter of hours. Subsequently, she suffered a series of miscarriages. In a letter to her brother some years before this, she commented on the figure of the childless woman: 'There is something sorrowful to me in the thought of a woman passing through life without children [...]. I think there is always something sad in an instinct crushed out.'[27] Writing to another correspondent two years later, she stated:

'To me sexual union to which there is no child born is like a statue left unfinished.'[28] Two years before her marriage (at the age of 38) to Samuel Cronwright in 1894, when motherhood must have appeared an increasingly distant possibility, she wrote: 'The only thing that makes me sad in thinking I shall have to live all my life alone is the thought I shall never have a child.'[29] Her marriage and subsequent pregnancy offered the possibility of motherhood, but ultimately she was left childless.

Allbutt, in *The Wife's Handbook*, warns women against conceiving if they have experienced previous problems during pregnancy and childbirth: 'if a woman has once suffered from any disease or affection either during pregnancy or at the time of labour, or in the first three weeks after delivery, which affection is produced by these conditions, she should be very careful not to have any more children.'[30] Regardless of the circumstances, at a time when prevailing gender ideologies perpetuated the view of motherhood as women's 'destiny', for women desirous of a family but unable either to conceive or deliver, childlessness was as emotionally distressing as it was physically distressing. Women who did not desire a child were also often subject to significant pressure regarding their fertility. One case study, included in a work on sterility in women, highlights not only the pressures women faced to produce a family from husbands but also from doctors. In 1880, one Dr James Beresford Ryley apparently treated a 26-year-old woman suffering from infertility. She had been married six years but had no children. Ryley's unsettling analysis was that:

The consummation of marriage had gradually grown from an act of indifference to one of repugnance, and latterly to feelings of loathing and pain. She did not desire any children herself, but her husband did so exceedingly and the relations between them on these several accounts were getting more and more strained and unhappy.[31]

Ryley claimed to have performed an operation which resulted in the cessation of the pain the patient had experienced, and ultimately in her becoming pregnant. He wrote:

to crown the whole proceeding, in six months after the operation she became pregnant, and in due time brought forth a strong healthy child, who became the means not only of developing that beautiful instinct of maternal love which is innate and lies dormant in the heart of every properly constituted woman, but of winning back the affections of a husband whose early love was being slowly alienated by a series of domestic circumstances over which she had no control.[32]

This account is disturbing for several reasons. It appears to evidence women's experience of marital rape in the nineteenth century: the patient's response to sexual intercourse is 'repugnance', 'loathing and pain', yet it is clear that relations with her husband continued. It also undermines the validity of women's choices around motherhood: her assertion that she does not desire any children herself is effectively dismissed – interpreted as mistaken, and the 'instinct of maternal love' constructed as 'innate'. The account thus highlights the marital, medical, and cultural pressures women faced, and their limited control over both maternity and fertility. Other works – both advice and medical literature – seek to reinforce this message, sometimes employing religious arguments to make their case. *Advice to a Wife*, quoting from Genesis, reminds the reader that 'It was ordained by the Almighty that wives should be fruitful and multiply,'[33] and suggests 'It is an unnatural state of things for a wife to be childless.'[34] It also emphasises that women must be healthy in order to bear children, likening them to a fruit-tree: 'It is as impossible to have fine fruit from an unhealthy tree as to have a fine child from an unhealthy mother.' The unhealthy wife 'either does not bear children – she is barren – or she has frequent miscarriages – "untimely fruit" – or she bears puny, sickly children, who often either drop into an early grave, or, if they live, probably drag out a miserable existence.'[35] It proceeds to offer advice on idleness, dress, walking, exercise, and other factors the author deems significant in maintaining women's health in preparation for motherhood.

Both this and Ryley's works seek to establish the authority of the medical man in relation to (in)fertility, despite limited medical understanding of the issue at this time. The case study cited by Ryley is fairly typical of nineteenth-century medical literature on the subject of female infertility. Much of this was written by medical men and detailed their own experience in treating these women, so perhaps it is inevitable that we find plenty of cases of infertility being 'cured' by doctors. *Advice to a Wife* suggests that 'A large majority' of infertile wives 'might be made fruitful' with the correct treatment.[36] The author writes, 'a childless wife can often, by judicious treatment, be made a child-bearing one. Few things in this world are impossible.'[37]

The reality for many women, though, was very different, and there was often no miracle cure. For those women unable to conceive, identifying the cause of, and offering viable treatment for infertility was, at best, difficult, and, in many cases, impossible. Then as now, a failure to ovulate was likely a major cause of infertility (today, this is estimated to be a significant factor in 40 per cent of women experiencing fertility problems). The absence or irregularity of the menses may have provided an indicator of the problem for nineteenth-century doctors (Ryley, for example, identifies 'scanty menstruation' as indicative of a fault with the ovaries),[38] but there was little they could do to stimulate ovulation. Sexually transmitted diseases were likely another significant factor in both male and female infertility. Indeed, the government was concerned enough with this problem and its possible consequences to attempt to legislate to try and stop the spread of venereal disease (in garrison towns in particular) – through the Contagious Diseases Acts of 1864, 1866, and 1869.

Despite limited understanding of infertility, both medical literature and advice manuals offer a variety of 'solutions' to the problem and identify a range of causes. Whilst some of these are physiological, women's behaviour is also frequently perceived as a potential factor. Pye Henry Chavasse, author of *Advice to a Wife*, suggests that a childless marriage may be the consequence of constant 'visiting', 'late hours', and 'gadding out night after night' during the first months of marriage: 'How many homes have been made childless – desolate – by [such behaviour]?' he asks.[39] Advice such as this appeared to require women to police their behaviour if they did not wish to impact their ability to become mothers. There was also a commonly held assumption that a couple's failure to produce children was likely a consequence of female, rather than male infertility. This is highlighted in one medical work from the late nineteenth century which notes that 'occasionally impotency may exist in the male. This is of such rare occurrence, however, that it may be looked upon almost as phenomenal.' Significantly, the author notes that 'when it does occur, it can generally be traced to the effects of some previous gonorrhoeal or syphilitic attack'.[40] Nonetheless, he concludes that 'If pregnancy does not follow marriage within a reasonable time, there must of necessity, in the majority of cases, be present some unhealthy condition of the generative organs of the female.'[41] Women's bodies were thus frequently constructed as the root cause of infertility within marriage. The inaccuracy of this assumption is plainly demonstrated by a number of accounts which point to male, rather than female infertility. A medical qualification is not necessary to decipher some of Chavasse's misdiagnoses, including one case from 1839, in which a woman remarried following the death of her husband. The first marriage had produced no children, but at the age of 50, within twelve months of marrying again, she gave birth to her first child.[42]

Chavasse suggests a luxurious and indulgent lifestyle may in itself be the root cause of infertility. He writes: 'Riches seldom bring health, content, many children, and happiness; they more frequently cause disease, discontent, childlessness, and misery.'[43] If a marriage did not produce children within the first two years, he suggests the wife 'commence to live abstemiously on fresh milk, butter-milk, bread, potatoes, and farinaceous diet, with very little meat, and no stimulants whatever; let her live, indeed, very much either as a poor curate's wife or as a poor Irish woman is compelled to live,' for these women 'generally have […] large families.' He concludes:

> It is not the poor woman that is cursed with barrenness – she has often more mouths than she can well fill; but the one that frequently labours under that ban is the pampered, the luxurious, the indolent, the fashionable wife; and most assuredly, until she change her system of living to one more consonant with common-sense, she will continue to do so.[44]

Here as elsewhere, it was women – and frequently their lifestyle choices – who were associated with infertility within marriage in nineteenth-century Britain.

The solutions proposed by nineteenth-century medical literature to treat female infertility appear at best unlikely to produce any improvement, and at worst potentially dangerous. Bell, for instance, suggests various means of treating the alleged causes of female infertility, several of which include the application of harmful substances. One treatment recommended involves cleaning the uterine canal, before applying iodised phenol to the uterus, 'which application is followed by the introduction of a tampon saturated with the glycerine of alum and boracic acid solution'. This procedure is to be repeated over the course of a number of weeks.

Bell suggests this treatment should result in 'complete recovery in the course of two to four months'.[45] He claimed to have employed a similar approach in the case of a 28-year-old woman, 'Mrs K', who was suffering from painful periods and excessive clotting. In this case, the application of the solution-soaked tampon was accompanied by the administration of a pill containing zinc and extract of conium – the latter a toxic substance which can cause birth defects. The woman was treated in this manner for a period of four months, after which time, Bell recorded, 'She became pregnant, and was delivered at the full time of a well-nourished child.'[46] Undoubtedly, some women did, against the odds, fall pregnant after several years of infertility, though perhaps not necessarily as a consequence of the questionable treatments available. Robert Lee cites one such case from 1841: that of a woman who after many years of marriage delivered her first child at almost 50 years old. He reports that 'she had been married fifteen years without ever becoming pregnant'. After a protracted labour, she was successfully delivered by forceps with 'neither mother nor child sustain[ing] the slightest injury'.[47] Her experience anticipates that of Jane Spencer, Baroness Churchill (Lady of the Bedchamber to Queen Victoria). She was married to Francis Spencer, Baron Churchill for some fifteen years before producing the only child of the union, a son, at the age of 38. Unexpected pregnancy following years of apparent infertility is not uncommon today; around one in four couples experiencing unexplained infertility for three years will conceive naturally.[48] The reasons behind this are not fully understood, pointing to the fact that whilst understanding of and treatments for infertility have improved dramatically, there remain gaps in our knowledge which mirror those of the nineteenth century.

For many women, though, there was no happy ending to their struggles with infertility, and fulfilment had to be found in a life without children. In 1859, Louisa Beresford, Marchioness of Waterford, found herself a childless widow following the sudden death of her husband in a hunting accident. The marriage had lasted seventeen years but produced no children. Though much of her correspondence appears to have been destroyed, surviving letters suggest she found consolation in both religion and art (she was a painter and artist's model associated with the Pre-Raphaelite movement). In one such letter written towards the end of her life to her niece, the Countess of Pembroke, she gives a brief insight into her feelings: 'To me, without children, without [my] own family, a gift was given to be used – not only for self, but in some measure for the setting forth of ideas which I have no eloquence to speak of, and that it might sometimes express what must otherwise be sealed up.'[49] Despite her art, it is evident her lack of family was a source of sadness for Lady Waterford. In another letter, she wrote: 'I am entering old age, and trying to make the best of it, but it is not a happiness unless one had children and grandchildren, and then it might be very nice.'[50] Elsewhere, she reflected on the 'grey' of her childless life, writing to a friend recently parted from her children: 'With happy comforts of dear children, these great sorrows must come, but it is better than the grey level of having no home ones to care for. I think the deep joy and sorrow is best, though the most trying.'[51] Involuntary childlessness was often a source of enduring pain, in spite of religious and other consolations. Even today, women who are involuntarily childless describe feelings of shame, as well as grief, and in the nineteenth century, when ideas of womanhood and motherhood were more closely intertwined, and opportunities for women beyond marriage and children so much more limited, these feelings were undoubtedly heightened. Queen Victoria made passing reference to the emotional distress that accompanied childlessness for some women in a letter discussing Princess Marie Leiningen, who had been married to Victoria's nephew, Prince Ernest, for three years without producing any children: 'Poor dear Marie, she does cry a great deal – but that is from nervousness and fretting so much about not having children!'[52] In fact, the marriage did eventually produce two children, but evidently the five years between the wedding and the arrival of her daughter was a time of concern and distress.

Whilst childless marriages were sometimes the subject of gossip and speculation, the issue of infertility was also co-opted by certain commentators for ideological purposes – in particular, by those opposed to the higher education of women and the entry of women into the professions. Perhaps the notion of a problematic relationship between women's intellectual pursuits and childbearing has not entirely dissipated, albeit it is now framed slightly differently: at the start of my academic career I was warned by more than one professor against having children, as this would 'inevitably' damage my career prospects. In the nineteenth century, proponent of social Darwinism Herbert Spencer was one of those to sound a warning over the education of women in relation to its potential impact on their fertility: 'absolute or relative infertility is generally produced in women by mental labour carried to excess'.[53] Another work on the subject notes that 'great culture in a man does not unfit him for paternity [...] For women, on the contrary, exceptional culture will infallibly have the tendency to remove the fittest individuals [...] from out of the ranks of motherhood.'[54] As with those discourses which point to possible behavioural causes of infertility, these voices position women as partly responsible for their own fertility. Such messages were inevitably absorbed by some women, yet it was not always possible for women to adjust their lifestyles – particularly poorer women who sometimes had little choice but to work in strenuous and demanding jobs throughout their pregnancies. One woman whose children were born in the late nineteenth century explains how long hours working in a factory, and subsequently in the home, during her pregnancies impacted the health of her babies, causing, she believed, infertility in three of her daughters:

> The first part of my life I spent in a screw factory from six in the morning till five at night; and after tea used to do my washing and cleaning. I only left two weeks and three weeks before my first children were born. After that I took in lodgers and washing, and always worked up till an hour or so before baby was born. The results are that three of my girls suffer with their insides. None are able to have a baby.[55]

In aristocratic families in particular, there was frequently an additional pressure on women to produce children, and thus an heir, in order to pass on titles, land, property and wealth, and to continue the family name. Perhaps the most famous struggle to produce a legitimate heir in nineteenth-century Britain arose following the death of Princess Charlotte and her stillborn infant son in 1817. Their loss removed two heirs to the British throne, and left her father, who was to become George IV in 1821, with no direct heir. Indeed, at the time of her death, Charlotte was the only legitimate grandchild of George III, and thus a succession crisis loomed. Charlotte's uncles, William (later William IV) and Edward, married shortly after her death in an attempt to produce the elusive heir. William's wife Adelaide gave birth to a daughter in March 1819, but the baby died shortly afterwards. A stillborn child followed later the same year, and another daughter in 1820, who lived only a few weeks, was followed by stillborn twin boys in 1822, leaving

Adelaide involuntarily childless, and Victoria – born to Edward and his wife in 1819 – heir to the throne.

An infamous case from the 1870s arising from the failure to produce an heir was that of Lady Annie Louisa Gooch. As with many aristocratic families, Lady Gooch was under pressure to produce an heir – specifically a son – for her husband. Her only child having died in infancy, and failing to conceive another, she embarked on a plan to secure a newborn infant and present it as her own. Her actions landed her in court after she was charged with having 'unlawfully combined, conspired, confederated, and agreed together to palm off on Sir Francis Robert Sherlock Lambert Gooch [...], as his own child, born of the body of the said Lady Gooch, a strange child, with intent to defraud and deceive'. During the period prior to acquiring the baby, Lady Gooch had told several people that she was with child and disguised her figure so as to appear pregnant. She visited London's Foundling Hospital, and from there was referred to a nearby Infants' Home – 'a refuge for deserted mothers and their children'. There, she was given a baby boy, who appeared to be two to three weeks old. Her husband, though, already suspicious of his wife, had allegedly employed detectives to watch her, and was unconvinced by the attempted deception, instigating the court case in consequence of her actions. Lady Gooch's desperation for a child appears to have been motivated not only by the desire for the continuation of the male line and the securing of her husband's wealth. In testimony given in court, surgeon James Worthington, who had been consulted by Lady Gooch, stated that she had informed him that she had initially believed herself to be pregnant, and on discovering she was not, was afraid to tell her husband, fearing 'separation and [...] unpleasantness'.[56] Lady Gooch's fears of the possible consequences resulting from this discovery were not unreasonable: separation threatened permanent damage to a woman's reputation, and would potentially leave her impoverished. Lady Gooch's actions appear to have been partly motivated by a fear of her husband dying and leaving her with insufficient means on which to live. An heir would ensure she was financially protected in the event of his death. As with many other women in nineteenth-century Britain – both those anxious for a child and those who wished to avoid motherhood – Lady Gooch acted out of desperation. The case was dismissed on the grounds that she was not in her right mind, but as one newspaper report noted, 'the position of Lady Gooch in the future,' as a consequence of the damage to her reputation resulting from the widely publicised court case, 'will be of itself a punishment more than commensurate with her folly.'[57]

With motherhood the expected outcome of marriage in nineteenth-century Britain, the possibility of infertility was a source of much distress and anxiety for some women. One Victorian diarist, Kate Russell, the Viscountess Amberley, became a mother without too much trouble, but wrote of a friend whose marriage had not yet produced any offspring: 'She is very anxious to have a child indeed. She was married 6 months before I was & not begun yet – She said she envied me my boy.'[58] Infertility was undoubtedly a source of bitter disappointment for some couples, although first-hand accounts of the experience from the nineteenth century are rare. Passing remarks, such as that made by Lady Amberley of her friend, provide the briefest glimpse of the difficulties encountered by couples whose marriages did not result in offspring at a time when there was significant social pressure – on middle- and upper-class couples in particular – to reproduce. Some twenty years prior to Lady Amberley's offhand comment, we find a similar reference in a letter from her father to her mother, again in reference to friends of the family: 'The Castlereaghs arrived here last night, she still pretty and graceful but [...] I am afraid they are disappointed at not having any children.'[59]

With successful and reliable medical solutions to the problem of infertility unavailable, adoption offered an alternative solution for childless couples. There was no legislation around adoption prior to the twentieth century, therefore all adoptions were necessarily informal, and adoptive parents had no legal claim to the child. This also meant that adopted children had no automatic rights to inheritance, and so adoption as a solution to the problem of passing on land, titles, and wealth was potentially problematic (particularly in the case of entailed estates). For some parents, it was preferable for the wider world to believe an adopted child was their own biological child, and several reports in the nineteenth-century press attest to this – as well as in some cases to the legal entanglements resulting from attempts to conceal a child's true origins. On occasion, this deception extended to the adoptive father. Such cases often illustrate the desperation of women unable to bear children of their own. Wilkie Collins depicts this situation in his 1857 novel, *The Dead Secret*, in which a servant, Sarah Leeson, gives birth to an illegitimate child after her lover dies suddenly before they are married. Her mistress, who has been unable to bear children herself, claims to be the mother of the child, deceiving even her husband, who raises the girl as his own after his wife's death, unaware of her true origins. As sensational as the plot seems, it mirrors dozens of stories which appeared in the pages of Victorian newspapers in which women, like Lady Gooch, unable to have children themselves, attempted to purchase babies and pass them off as their own. One woman from Scotland, for example, appeared in Glasgow Sheriff Criminal Court in April 1893. She had been married for four years but had no children – something which was the cause of tension between her and her husband. Believing herself to have fallen pregnant, she informed her husband of this. Upon realising her mistake, she continued to allow him to believe she was expecting a baby and made arrangements to procure an infant instead. The child she intended to purchase was already registered, but she registered him again as her own. She subsequently confessed to her husband, who then reported her, and she was imprisoned for twenty days for falsely registering the child as her legitimate daughter.[60] Another similar case ended up in court in 1864. In Gedney vs Smith, Miss Harriet Gedney (a minor at the time of the trial) attempted to obtain a legal declaration of her paternity, following allegations that her mother had purchased her from a woman at York lying-in hospital and attempted to pass her off as her own and her husband's child – the motivation being her inability to conceive and her wish to be better treated by her husband (from whom, incidentally, she had contracted venereal disease). The jury ultimately found against the plaintiff, accepting that the child was not the product of the marriage. There are striking similarities with Collins's earlier novel, and indeed one newspaper report noted the resemblance between the case and a 'modern sensational novel'.[61]

There is, inevitably, a class dimension in many of the cases such as these. As Collins depicts in *The Dead Secret*, the financial security of the middle and upper classes meant they were able to afford to both purchase a child and provide for their upbringing. By contrast, the precarious position of many working-class women in nineteenth-century Britain – and particularly unmarried mothers, who for much of the period had no legal recourse to financial support from the fathers of their children – left them in a vulnerable position. The offer of money may have provided some motivation to such women to relinquish their children, but there can be no doubt that many did so in the hope that these arrangements would benefit their offspring and provide them with a better life than they could otherwise give them – and it may well have been the case that survival rates for infants fostered into other families were higher than for those who ended up in the various orphanages and children's homes that were in operation.[62] Various social commentators went as far as to advocate for such exchanges. Dr William Farr argued that orphaned children would be better cared for by wives without children, rather than left dependent on the workhouse system. Writing in support of Farr's proposal, an article in *The Lancet* in 1866 declared that such a scheme 'may do good to some children who are dying for want of care, and to some ladies who are not getting the full enjoyment of life for want of something to care for'.[63] Whilst it was evidently easier for upper- and middle-class women to afford the costs associated with adoption, nevertheless, childless women from the poorer classes did occasionally benefit from informal adoption. In one case, a childless woman married thirteen years, who had suffered seven miscarriages, adopted an orphan boy, and described him as 'the sunshine of my life'.[64]

In 1895, the social reformer W. T. Stead, best known for his exposure of child prostitution in late Victorian England, used his paper *The Review of Reviews* to establish a 'Baby Exchange'; effectively an adoption agency which aimed to match those in want of a child with those wishing to give up a child. The paper included correspondence from prospective adopters, which reveals the pain experienced by those desiring a family but unable to have children. One woman wrote: 'We have no children and are never likely to have, and are bitterly disappointed. [...] All I want is a little baby I can bring up and love as my own.'[65] Whilst the scheme provided an opportunity for motherless wives, the letters of those volunteering children for adoption depict what a difficult and painful decision this was for so many. One woman in this position wrote: 'It would be a great favour if any kind person did take my little one, as I am unable to keep it as I should like to. I am anxious to get my little girl a home.'[66] The case of another woman who wrote to offer her child for adoption illustrates the difficulties working women faced in providing for themselves and their children, as well as the challenges encountered by mothers working in domestic service – a job which often entailed looking after the children of others, but made it difficult for women to care for their own children. For single mothers in particular (whether unmarried, separated, or widowed), these challenges proved even more difficult, as one woman's letter shows:

> I have been anxious to place my child into a good home for ever since her birth, as her father died before her birth, and it is very hard on myself, which I have had to take a housekeeper's situation, which is very hard for me to keep both of us. I have been obliged to place my child out to nurse since her birth.[67]

Stead's scheme, and others like it, offered a potential solution for mothers who found themselves in situations such as these, as well as for those experiencing infertility. Adoption by another family might have been preferable to placing children out with potentially unscrupulous nurses or baby farmers, but it could also mean a permanent separation between mother and child, a grief-inducing breaking of the maternal bond. In practical terms, adoption could not and did not provide the solution for all impoverished women struggling to care for their children. For many women with large families there was little they could do besides manage as best they could.

Excessive Fertility

Average family size did begin to decrease in the later decades of the nineteenth century, but many women throughout the period experienced a large number of pregnancies and births. Big families were often associated with the poorer classes, and in part, this reflects the fact that family size amongst this socio-economic group declined more slowly than amongst other classes from the 1870s onwards, but it is also indicative of prevailing, often negative stereotypes, via which the poor were repeatedly represented as lacking control and responsibility. Following the marriage of her granddaughter, Alice Stanley, to Major Reynard Fox, Maria Josepha Lady Stanley wrote to her daughter-in-law upon the news of Alice's first pregnancy declaring: 'as they are poor, cubs will come thick & fast',[68] which indeed they did: her first pregnancy ended in a stillbirth, but nine more children followed (born in just over ten years between 1855 and 1866). During her tenth pregnancy in September 1866, Alice's mother wrote to her father: 'I have heard that Alice is again in the usual state, it was no surprise.'[69] Large families were common amongst all classes of society, and many women for a period of several years, sometimes extending to decades, experienced pregnancy as 'the usual state': Lady Stanley was one of nine children, and Alice one of ten. The Dickenses and the Darwins both raised large families, as well as Queen Victoria (whose nine children went on to produce forty-two grandchildren), and in the late eighteenth and early nineteenth century, despite the succession crisis that ensued following Princess Charlotte's death, Prince William – later William IV – had ten illegitimate children with the actress Dorothea Jordan.

Unlike the poorer classes, amongst whom large families were also fairly commonplace, the wealthier middle and upper classes rarely faced accusations of a lack of control as a consequence of their numerous children. *Maternity: Letters from Working Women* provides statistics on 348 of the respondents to the call for letters detailing maternal experiences. Between them, these women (in the late nineteenth and early twentieth centuries) experienced 218 miscarriages, 81 stillbirths, and 1,396 live births: a total of 1,695 pregnancies – thus averaging 4.8 pregnancies per respondent. This is still somewhat lower than earlier in the nineteenth century, and points to the fact that women of all classes appear to have been employing means to reduce the number of births by this time. At this point, there was increasing debate around the subject of contraception, but the primary reasons behind the fertility decline appear to have been the postponement of marriage and, within relationships, the employment of abstinence or withdrawal, rather than other forms of contraception.[70] The use of drugs to induce abortion may also have played a role.[71] Opposition to, and lack of knowledge about contraception, meant that many women were unable to prevent or space out their numerous pregnancies. One mother of a large family subsequently recalled: 'I had nine. No way of stopping them. If there had been, I would have done.'[72] She was herself one of fourteen – the last of these born when her mother was 45. Writing in the early twentieth century, one campaigner for increased birth control cites the case of one mother 'who for twenty years was either carrying or nursing a babe', and who asked 'Do you think […] that if I had known how to prevent it I would have had fifteen children?'[73] Similar ignorance is indicated by one of the contributors to *Maternity* following the birth of her third child:

> I said to a friend one day, 'If only I could feel that this was my last, I would be quite happy'. 'Well,' she said, 'why don't you make it your last?' and she gave me advice. As a result of this knowledge, I had no more babies for four and a half years.[74]

The nature of the advice given is unclear, but the account indicates that information about contraception was shared between at least some working-class women. However, another contributor expresses concern at the idea of deliberately preventing pregnancy. A mother of seven children, she writes: 'I submitted as a duty, knowing there is much unfaithfulness on the part of the husband where families are limited.'[75] It is evident from some of the accounts that marital rape – though not legally defined as such at the time – was a common experience for some women, and that they had no opportunity to limit their family size, as the experience of one mother of seven children illustrates:

> I was quite unprepared for marriage and what was expected of me. [...] I found [my husband] had not a bit of control over his passions, and expected me to do what he had been in the habit of paying women to do. [...] I do wish there could be some limit to the time when a woman is expected to have a child. I often think women are really worse off than beasts [...] Practically within a few days of the birth, and as soon as the birth is over, she is tortured again. If the woman does not feel well she must not say so, as a man has such a lot of ways of punishing a woman if she does not give in to him.[76]

Large numbers of pregnancies and births could impact significantly on women's health and well-being. Poverty often exacerbated the suffering of mothers with large numbers of children, but wealthier women were not exempt from the problems which could result from numerous pregnancies – often closely spaced. On the experience of her mother, Emma Darwin (wife of Charles), whose last child was born when she was 48, Henrietta Darwin wrote: 'My mother had ten children and suffered much from ill health and discomforts during those years.'[77] Years earlier, Charles Darwin had written to a university friend, congratulating him on the birth of his tenth child, but adding, 'please to observe, when I have a 10th, send only condolences to me'.[78] Catherine Dickens's mental and physical health also suffered as a result of her ten children and two miscarriages – and the cervical cancer from which she died may have been a consequence of excessive childbearing. In January 1850, when Catherine was in the early stages of pregnancy with her ninth child, a friend of her husband's wrote to him to urge caution in relation to childbearing: 'There can never be too many Dickenses in the world; but these *overbearings* exhaust the parent tree, and those who cannot hope to repose in the shade of the saplings, must shrink from the risk of its decay.'[79] In 1841, Maude Adeane, daughter of Sir John Stanley and one of eleven children herself, at that time a mother of nine (she would go on to have three more), appeared 'almost worn out', according to her sister-in-law, Lady Stanley, who wondered if 'a different husband would have made her a different woman', but concluded 'perhaps not if she had had as many children'.[80] An acquaintance of the Stanleys, Margaret Hamilton, a mother of seven, also seems to have suffered as a consequence of her large family. Henrietta Stanley wrote, in 1843, that Margaret was 'only able to do the necessary work of life. If she is spared having any more children she will get strong in time but […] she perfectly dreads another pregnancy.'[81] This 'dread', experienced by many women, speaks to the lack of control over reproduction, which often could not be prevented even to protect women's health. Our contemporary moment – in Britain at least – speaks largely to the progress that has been made in terms of women's right to choose if and when to have children, but elsewhere there are signs of regression, and women in many US states may well now identify with this feeling of dread that Margaret, and many other nineteenth-century women, experienced.[82] The language here speaks to the genuine fear that some women lived with at the prospect of falling pregnant – knowing that there was little they could do to prevent it.

Financial struggles were inevitably as much of a concern as their own health for mothers of large families amongst the poorer classes of society. Without any form of social support, some mothers were forced to work all through their pregnancies and go back to work shortly after giving birth. Many women returned to work – often in arduous jobs which involved long hours and physical labour – only a matter of days after giving birth. One report cited a case in which 'a woman left her work at 6 p.m., was confined in the evening, and presented herself again at work next morning'.[83] It was not until 1891 that legislation was introduced in an attempt to prevent women from returning to work for four weeks after childbirth, and as this was an enforced leave of absence with no financial compensation, it was hardly an ideal solution. Even after this there is evidence of women trying to circumvent this legislation by concealing the date of their confinement – which was certainly motivated by financial concerns. Despite the poor conditions in which many working mothers lived and worked, there seems to be little indication that this impacted on their fertility. One medical man, commenting on the position of factory workers in Manchester in the 1830s, suggested that 'the married operatives of this town are generally prolific'.[84] Several of the respondents in *Maternity: Letters from Working Women* testify to the difficulties faced in raising a large family whilst in a precarious financial position. One woman, a mother to eight children, recalls her struggles after an accident prevented her husband from working: 'I worked and starved myself to make sick-pay [...] go as far as possible. I got so weak, and fainted several times after heavy days at the machine.'[85] Another mother of eleven states that she was 'obliged to work before [she] was able' following her confinements, in order to feed her large family.[86] Friedrich Engels, in *The Condition of the Working Class in England in 1844* (1845), observes that following childbirth, many women return to the factory 'after eight, and even after three to four days, to resume full work. [...] Naturally, fear of being discharged, dread of starvation, drives her to the factory in spite of her weakness, in defiance of her pain.'[87] A lack of state support for mothers, combined with the challenges faced in limiting family size, exerted significant pressure on the poorest in society, with potential long-term consequences for both mothers and children.

Whilst state support for families was extremely limited, mothers who gave birth to triplets, from around the mid-nineteenth century onwards, might receive something known as the 'Queen's Bounty' – a donation from Queen Victoria to assist with the costs of raising three (or more) infants. However, this was not a formal benefit to which families were entitled. As one commentator noted, 'the Queen sometimes gives a donation to the mother of three children, but there is no such thing as the

"Queen's Bounty". It is merely a charitable donation granted to assist the poor and indigent in the unforeseen demands caused by additions to their families.'[88] Nonetheless, families did apply for and were, in several cases reported by the newspapers, granted the 'Queen's Bounty', and it must have been particularly welcome to those couples who already had a large number of children. One woman from Bradford received money from the Queen following the birth of triplets – three sons – in September 1888. She was already the mother of a large family, and a widow following her husband's death two months prior to their birth.[89] Another woman, near Cardigan in Wales, was awarded the Queen's Bounty following the birth of quadruplets, all of whom – against the odds – survived birth. Their arrival followed the earlier birth of their twin siblings, along with six other siblings. In 1889, a woman referred to only as a 'female tramp' gave birth to triplets in the workhouse at Bishop Stortford in Hertfordshire, although it is unclear whether, as a workhouse inmate, she qualified for the Queen's Bounty.[90] Another case of triplets born in a workhouse – in North Shields in 1892 – suggests not: a newspaper report of the fortnightly meeting of the Board of Guardians shortly afterwards implies workhouse inmates did not qualify for any such support:

> Mr J. Eskdale intimated that there had been a triple birth in the Workhouse, and asked if it was the intention of the Board to apply for the usual three guineas (Laughter.) – The Chairman replied that [...] he hardly thought under the circumstances that the application would be admissible.[91]

The laughter reported here speaks to the contempt in which workhouse inmates were often held. In fact, two of the babies subsequently died, therefore the claim would have been inadmissible regardless of the mother's residency in the workhouse. The number of families who benefited from the Queen's Bounty was extremely small. One study estimated that the proportion of triplets to single pregnancies in England was 1 to 4,473 – and all three had to survive in order for the mother to qualify for the payment. Many mothers of triplets or more were refused the allowance because one of the children had not survived. In one example, the mother of triplets who lost one of the infants shortly after birth, received the following reply to her application:

the request [...] cannot be complied with. Her Majesty's donation of £3 is only granted where the three children survive. In this instance only two children survived; the third, although born alive, did not live long enough, which fact precluded the applicant receiving her Majesty's bounty under this interesting circumstance.[92]

The financial pressures faced by mothers of large families were considerable, and in addition to rendering it essential that some women worked during and immediately after pregnancy, for those simply unable to cope with the ensuing poverty, it might also lead to the workhouse. For some mothers, more drastic action seems to have been taken. Several cases of infanticide appear to have been motivated by financial pressures and the need to reduce outgoings and increase income. In one case, a woman named Mrs Griffiths, who had borne twelve children, was accused of murdering several of her offspring through poisoning. One of the newspaper reports discussing the case notes that 'Some of the deceased were in burial clubs' – implying that the murders had taken place in order to claim the money for the disposal of the infants' bodies.[93]

Even without the financial pressures under which the poorer classes of society so often existed, excessive fertility was often a source of frustration and sometimes misery for those more comfortably off, as the experience of Queen Victoria illustrates, whilst it also at times posed a serious threat to the health of the mother. Henrietta Stanley (later Lady Eddisbury then Baroness Stanley of Alderley) and her politician husband, Edward (Baron) Stanley were parents to a large number of children.[94] Having nine living children, when she once again found herself pregnant in autumn 1847, both her and her husband were greatly distressed by the prospect of a tenth child. Edward Stanley described the situation as 'most grievous',[95] whilst Henrietta referred to her 'horror'[96] at the expectation of yet another child. In fact, this pregnancy did not proceed, Henrietta having taken it upon herself to try and ensure it would not,[97] but it was not to be her last. In December 1848, she once again suspected herself to be pregnant, in a letter to her husband revealing she feared an 'unpleasant cause' for her symptoms. She gave birth in July 1849, at the age of 41, having had her first child over twenty years previously. One of her friends wrote to her on the occasion of the child's birth, declaring: 'I cannot fancy you with a new baby of yr. own when one is beginning to think of you in the character of a grandmother.'[98] Henrietta's experience was not an unusual one, though. For women who married young and experienced no fertility issues, childbearing could easily stretch over twenty years or more, and there was often little they could do about it. Whilst for some women, then, pregnancy proved elusive, others spent their twenties and thirties (and in some cases much of their forties) almost constantly pregnant – sometimes with significant consequences for their physical and mental health, as well as finances. Pregnancy, then as now, could be physically and psychologically draining, a time of joy or a period of fear and trepidation – whether wanted or unwanted, first or tenth.

2

Negotiating Pregnancy

Be still, sweet babe, no harm shall reach thee,
Nor hurt thy yet unfinished form;
Thy mother's frame shall safely guard thee
From this bleak, this beating storm.
Isabella Kelly[1]

* * *

Germ of new life, whose powers expanding slow
For many a moon their full perfection wait,—
Haste, precious pledge of happy love, to go
Auspicious borne through life's mysterious gate.
Anna Laetitia Barbauld[2]

Not long after her wedding to future Prime Minister William Gladstone, in 1839, Catherine Gladstone fell pregnant. On hearing this news, her sister, Lady Lyttelton, wrote to Catherine, her delight evident: 'I am longing to tell every one that a sapphire eyed babby is on its way with a white soft skin & dark hair, how I shall love it.'[3] Catherine, daughter of a baronet, respectably married, and residing in a castle in north Wales, enjoyed the privileges these facts afforded to her, and which would, in turn, benefit her eight children. Lady Lyttelton's delight, then, at the prospect of a new baby is understandable. A few years later, in 1852, Ellen Johnston, a factory worker from Lanarkshire in Scotland, fell pregnant whilst still in her teens and unmarried. For poor, unmarried women in nineteenth-century Britain, the realisation that a baby was on the way was often, by contrast, devastating, but, unlike many others in her situation, Ellen Johnston looked forward to the arrival of her child: 'I did not [...] feel inclined to die when I could no longer conceal what the world falsely calls a woman's shame. No, on the other hand, I never loved life more dearly and longed for the hour when I would have something to love me.'[4] Despite their vastly different circumstances, pregnancy was a time of joyful anticipation for both these women.

The language of these two accounts speaks to the differing experiences of Catherine Gladstone and Ellen Johnston: Lady Lyttelton 'long[s] to tell every one' the news of her sister's pregnancy, whilst Ellen works to 'conceal' her condition. Concealment, though, is difficult: the pregnant body becomes insistently visible as the pregnancy progresses, often inviting comment and sometimes uninvited touches. Late pregnancy in particular is an overwhelming presence – not least for the mother herself, constantly reminded, through the baby's movements or the common discomforts of the third trimester, of the approaching birth. Today, the visible pregnant body is often celebrated; the growing 'baby bumps' of public figures, particularly royalty, are scrutinised and celebrated by the media, and celebrities willingly pose with their visibly pregnant bodies on display. Nonetheless, still there are occasions when pregnancy's insistent presence is a source of discomfort, as I am reminded when, eight months pregnant, I visit a friend whose latest round of IVF has once again failed. In the nineteenth century, outside of immediate family, it was more common to conceal rather than celebrate pregnancy, and this is reflected in art and fiction from the period, in which the pregnant body is notable by its absence.[5] A portrait of Princess Charlotte painted whilst she was pregnant in summer 1817 contains no suggestion of her condition (see figure 2). The various paintings and photographs of Queen Victoria provide no evidence of her numerous pregnancies (see figure 1). The Victorian novel, whose plot so often hinges on the details of birth, and which frequently perpetuates the idea of motherhood as the conclusion of women's stories, typically omits both the pregnant body and scenes of childbirth. Tropes of Victorian popular fiction – marriage plots, the fallen woman narrative, the inheritance plot – depend on women's reproduction, yet the maternal body is rendered almost invisible. Works including Elizabeth Gaskell's *Ruth* (1853), George Eliot's *Adam Bede* (1859), and Thomas Hardy's *Tess of the d'Urbervilles* (1891) explore the consequences of unmarried motherhood, but draw a veil over the pregnant body even as they detail the heroine's 'fall'. Charlotte Brontë's novel *Jane Eyre* (1847) concludes in typical nine-teenth-century fashion: with the heroine's transition into motherhood. As with most Victorian fiction, though, there is no explicit reference to pregnancy or childbirth; the experience of these is deemed insignificant – or unsuitable – and therefore obscured from the reader. By contrast, some medical literature offered graphic portrayals of the pregnant body, though often in the form of a disembodied torso – a symbolic indication of the disjuncture between medical constructions of pregnancy and women's lived experiences. One notable exception to this detached and corporeal medical construction of pregnancy is found in a work entitled *Obstetric Tables*, by a surgeon-accoucheur named George Spratt, published in 1833. Here are included several images of the developing pregnant body, which focus on the whole of the female form. Each depicts the same woman in an identical position: she stands side-on, head covered with a bonnet and lowered demurely, a faint flush on her cheeks. A cape is worn around her neck, hanging down to her thighs, but her breasts and belly are clearly visible, both depicted growing gradually larger (see figure 3). They are extraordinary portraits, and there is something disturbingly voyeuristic about them, particularly as the intended audience is medical men, but they are amongst very few images from this period detailing the pregnant woman, rather than a partial representation of the pregnant body, which, beyond medical literature, is heavily obscured.[6]

In reality, of course, the heavily pregnant body could not be obscured, no matter the demands of delicate nineteenth-century sensibilities. Both Princess Charlotte and the Duchess of Kent (mother of Queen Victoria) were reportedly 'very big' with child towards the end of their pregnan-cies.[7] In May 1840, after attending a ball at the palace where she saw the Queen, Lady Charlotte Guest commented in her diary, 'There is now no doubt of her being likely in due time to give an heir to the throne.' Presumably it was the Queen's expanding figure (and perhaps the fact that she 'danced little') which led to this conclusion.[8] Furthermore, there is a stark contrast between representations of pregnancy (or the lack thereof) in public discourses, and women's reference to both their own and others' pregnancies in private writing: diaries and letters. Such writings speak to the continuities between women's experience of pregnancy in the nineteenth century through to the present day. Charlotte Brontë's own account of her (short) experience of pregnancy in the weeks before she died, in which she urges her friend not to speculate, whilst evidently wondering herself, is undoubtedly a familiar one: 'Don't conjecture [...] for it is too soon yet – though I certainly never before felt as I have done lately.'[9] The nervous anticipation which accompanies pregnancy – then and now – is also evident in Emma Darwin's diaries, in which she records some details of her pregnancies. During her first pregnancy in August 1839, she writes: 'Half way now I think from symptoms'. Heavily pregnant with her second child in early 1841, she notes the weeks of her pregnancy: '38' on 21 February. Around three months pregnant with her first child, in her marking off of each week of pregnancy in her diary, we find a parallel with today's smartphone pregnancy apps, which enable expectant mothers to track their progress towards the birth of their child. Kate, Lady Amberley, records eagerly escorting her mother 'to look at baby clothes',[10] and a few weeks later, reflects on the 'happy prospect before us', writing, 'I am most happy thankful and hopeful for the future.'[11] However, the hopeful anticipation of pregnancy was frequently also accompanied by anxiety and physical discomfort. Maternal mortality was high enough for all women to be aware of the potential dangers of childbirth, and high-profile cases such as that of Princess Charlotte in 1817 were attestation that social status and wealth would not protect against these. Then, as now, whilst some women enjoyed pregnancy, for others it was a time of extreme discomfort and ill health. Regardless of the different ways women experienced pregnancy in the nineteenth century, it was, inevitably, a significant life experience – whether enjoyable or uncomfortable, wanted or unwanted – belying its erasure in nineteenth-century art and fiction, and indeed in subsequent historical accounts of the period.

The terminology around pregnancy in the nineteenth century speaks to the reluctance to acknowledge the pregnant body and its meanings. The term 'pregnant' is used in advice and medical literature, and also appears in newspaper reports, but it is rarely found in novels of the period, and even in life writing such as diaries and letters, there sometimes appears a reluctance to include explicit references to pregnancy. Instead, it is frequently alluded to in euphemistic terms, such as via references to women's 'interesting condition' or the French term '*enceinte*'. Other terms (some of which date back centuries further) include 'in the family way' and 'with child'. Writing in 1803, Eugenia Wynne described her pregnancy with the phrase 'in the encreasing way'.[12] In a letter to her mother, Queen Victoria, in 1864, Victoria, Princess Royal writes, 'I have hopes again'.[13] Elsewhere, pregnancy is constructed as illness, with expectant women described as 'unwell'. In one diary written in the mid-nineteenth century, a wife's pregnancy is hinted at via references to her general health: she is variously described as 'quite well', 'so well', 'very tired', and 'unwell', and also experiences several fits of 'hysterics'.[14] It is only via reference to the child's birth that the diary can be understood to be referring to pregnancy in these moments. Emma Darwin similarly refers to her pregnancies in terms of general health in her journals. In March 1842, a series of entries point obliquely to the early months of her third pregnancy: 'began to be languid and unwell'; 'I began to be a little better'; 'very bad again in the evenings'; 'I very bad'. In September that year, the day before the birth of her daughter Mary, she wrote: 'Very feverish and violent headache'.[15] The language of illness as allusion to pregnancy is also echoed in her husband Charles Darwin's letters. Responding to an invitation during one of Emma's pregnancies, he declined – 'Mrs. Darwin not being well enough to go out at present'.[16] To another correspondent around two months before the birth of their first child, he wrote, somewhat enigmatically: 'Emma is only moderately well & I fear what you said is true "she won't be better till she is worse"'.[17] A few days later, he wrote to his sister, Caroline Wedgewood: 'The poor thing [Emma] has been but poorly every other or third day since we came back, which has been a great disappointment to me: But she is, I hope essentially going on well & undeniably growing.'[18] This allusion to the increasingly visible pregnant body contrasts with the veiled terms in which pregnancy is described. Emma, mother to ten children, spent many years pregnant, and frequently experienced discomfort as a consequence. In 1842, before the birth of their third child, Charles disclosed in a letter that 'Emma [...] is uncomfortable enough all day long & seldom leaves the house,—this being her usual state before her babies come into the world.'[19] The dating of the letter means Emma was only some three months pregnant at this stage, suggesting she experienced many months of discomfort during pregnancy.

The language of illness around pregnancy was undoubtedly in part a reflection of the sickness many women endured during this time, particularly in the early months of pregnancy, evidenced by the experiences of Charlotte Brontë, Emma Darwin, and many others. In 1816, Elizabeth Shaw, wife of salesman John Shaw, who spent much time away from home, wrote to her husband whilst pregnant in anticipation of the months ahead: 'I am looking forward to nothing but sickness in your absence – you will miss it all.'[20] In another letter, she writes: 'I scarcely ever am 5 minutes without being sick and that does make me very low sometimes'.[21] Lady Lyttelton, early in her first pregnancy, wrote to her sister Catherine Gladstone reporting that she was 'very bad after eating, no breath whatever, & tight & rather fainty feeling'.[22] Catherine was also pregnant with her first child: 'How do you bear your sickness?' her sister enquired, 'You never did endure nausea! Do you look ill?'.[23] In her book *The Way They Should Go: Hints to Young Parents* (1896), Jane Ellen Panton (daughter of the painter, William Powell Frith and mother of five children) offered a frank assessment of pregnancy, describing it as 'a time of misery', and lamenting the extent to which women were obliged to keep it concealed: 'it is,' she wrote, 'nonetheless wretched because it has to be borne in absolute silence, and because to the miserable discomfort, we have to add secrecy, and have to conceal everything and appear as usual, when we really only long to creep away in silence and die.'[24] Not all women experienced pregnancy in such negative terms: some were lucky, and appear to have escaped sickness and ill health entirely during pregnancy. Pregnant with her daughter, Alicia Mary, in 1853, Catherine Temple Pears wrote to her sister, 'I am very well, and as strong and active as I can well expect to be',[25] although in subsequent letters she complains of headaches, faintness, indigestion, and toothache. 'This can't be helped,' she wrote of her various symptoms, 'But it is disagreeable and at times distressing.'[26] Kate Russell, the Viscountess Amberley, wrote in a letter in the early weeks of her first pregnancy: 'My health is flourishing, feeling quite vigorous no fainting etc.'[27] Around the same time, she recorded in her journal her happiness at her pregnancy: 'I felt as if great changes had come over me in the great blessing I have now & the promise of still more happiness in the future.'[28] Several years later and some four months pregnant with her son Bertrand Russell in December 1871, she wrote to her mother: 'I am to be confined in May. I am so well I shd. not know it except for certain physiological facts, I have never had 2 minutes discomfort of any sort or kind.'[29]

The veiled allusions to pregnancy which are found throughout nineteenth-century writing (both private and public) represent a reluctance to speak openly about women's bodies, about sex and its consequences, and about pregnancy and childbirth. This undoubtedly contributed to women's ignorance around these issues. Thomas Hardy reflects on this in his novel *Tess of the D'Urbervilles*, in which the eponymous heroine returns home, unmarried and pregnant, and reprimands her mother for keeping her in ignorance: 'Why didn't you tell me there was danger in men-folk? Why didn't you warn me?'[30] Tess's ignorance of sex and its consequences was not merely a fiction: whilst some women were undoubtedly well informed prior to having children themselves, multiple accounts of nineteenth-century women's own experiences testify to ignorance on this subject. Mrs P. Marrin puts it bluntly in her autobiographical account of late-Victorian childhood: 'Sex was a well-kept secret. Any visitor or neighbour who got anywhere near the subject in conversation was silenced by sign language by my mother.'[31] In *Maternity: Letters from Working Women*, the words of one respondent echo those of Hardy's heroine: 'When I had to have my first baby, I knew absolutely nothing, not even how they were born. I had many a time thought how cruel (not wilfully, perhaps) my mother was not to tell me all about the subject when I left home.'[32] One woman recalled feeling very unwell in the months following her wedding, but had no idea she was pregnant. Her sister's only response and counsel to the question of her ill health was: 'well you're married'.[33] Another notes that 'Although during pregnancy I realised I was to become a mother, I had never been taught what I should do or should not do during that time.'[34] In the late nineteenth century, *The Wife's Handbook* lamented the ignorance of newly married women, and suggested mothers had a responsibility to enlighten their daughters: 'Mothers should instruct their daughters entering upon the marriage state in all matters relating to the generative functions. But how seldom they do so, and how often are a young woman's health and happiness blighted through this foolish neglect!'[35] This sentiment is echoed by one of the correspondents to the Women's Co-operative Guild, who laments her own ignorance during pregnancy and labour, and resolves to enlighten her daughters:

I can truthfully say I was ignorant of anything concerning married life or motherhood when I was married. In fact, when the midwife came to me when I was in such pain, I had not the slightest idea where or how the child would come into the world. And another thing, I was not even told what to expect when I was leaving girlhood – I mean the monthly courses. I often wonder I got along as well as I have. I will say here that I do not intend my daughters to be so innocent of natural courses. I feel it is unkind of parents to leave girls to find these things out. It causes unnecessary suffering.[36]

Jane Panton also made a plea for providing women with clear information about pregnancy and what to expect:

[L]et us know that the intense and ghastly depression and fearful sickness [of pregnancy] are nothing more than a passing phase, and that the time will come when neither will distress us, we can look forward again, and not feel absolutely certain that we are quite different to anyone else, and that these symptoms mean some secret and deadly ailment, which can only end fatally at the very earliest opportunity.[37]

By keeping women in ignorance of the details of pregnancy and childbirth out of a misplaced sense of decorum, society risked causing undue anxiety and worry to expectant mothers – and the testimonies of those mothers who began their maternal journey ignorant of the physical aspects of pregnancy and childbirth testify to this. Queen Victoria, by contrast, evidently saw the benefits of keeping her daughters in ignorance over the realities of childbearing, believing that providing them with too much information might deter them from having children. This was clearly in her mind when she wrote to her eldest daughter the Princess Royal (who was married with children at this point) ahead of the marriage of her second daughter, Princess Alice:

Let me caution you to say as little as you can on these subjects before Alice (who has already heard much more than you ever did) for she has the greatest horror of having children, and would rather have none [...] so I am very anxious she should know as little about the inevitable miseries as possible[.][38]

This suggests notions of decorum and delicacy might not have been the only reason for keeping women in ignorance of the details of pregnancy and childbirth.

Advice literature, aimed predominantly at middle-class wives and mothers, frequently did allude in more explicit terms to the pregnant body, but even in these writings there is a clear aversion to explicitly referencing the functions of the female body. One work explaining the early signs of pregnancy notes that 'ceasing to be unwell is the first and most important sign'. This is an almost indecipherable veiled reference to the cessation of menstruation during pregnancy.[39] Given that implicit allusions to pregnancy in fiction and life writing often take the form of references to women *as* 'unwell', there is some room for confusion here. I spent some time pondering the implications of this statement when I first encountered it, trying to reconcile it with my own experience of nausea and exhaustion in early pregnancy, during which time I felt decidedly unwell, before realising its meaning. Despite this reticence, many advice books did provide detailed information on the physical changes women could expect to experience during pregnancy, including morning sickness, changes to the breasts, faintness, and 'quickening' – the first movements of the child felt by the mother (not to be confused, as one advice book points out, with flatulence).[40] 'Quickening' was often taken as a sure sign of a pregnancy – by which point a woman might be four or five months into her pregnancy. Kate, Lady Amberley, pregnant with twins in October 1867, recorded the moment in her diary: 'I quickened today'.[41] The common symptoms of pregnancy might also contribute to determining if a woman was pregnant, before the advent of reliable tests in the latter half of the twentieth century.[42] Whilst many of the symptoms described in these works are familiar to mothers today, others appear less so. *Advice to a Wife* suggests 'emaciation' as one of the early signs of pregnancy: 'the face, especially the nose, pinched and pointed; features altered; a pretty woman becoming, for a time, plain' – before resuming her 'pristine comeliness' as the pregnancy progresses.[43] *The Wife's Handbook* includes 'dribbling of the saliva from the mouth' and toothache as possible signs of pregnancy – but notes that extraction of teeth during pregnancy should be avoided, as it may cause miscarriage; instead, a 'solution of cocaine' is advised to help to manage the pain.[44] Chavasse also hints at other possible signs by which a medical man might determine pregnancy with some certainty but which, he suggests 'would be quite out of place to describe in a popular work of this kind'.[45] He is probably referring here to changes in the colouration of the vagina – mentioned in multiple nineteenth-century medical books as a sign of pregnancy. This information, though, is not deemed appropriate for sharing with the woman reader, presumably out of a sense of delicacy, and despite the fact it concerns her body.

Discourses such as these, then, to some extent work to reinforce women's ignorance about their own bodies, even as they purport to inform. By contrast, *The Wife's Handbook*, published later in the century and aimed at 'the wives of working men', does include 'a violet hue of the vaginal passage' as one of the possible symptoms of pregnancy, and even provides advice on how women can ascertain if this is the case for themselves, although it also refers to 'other signs which can only be detected by a skilful doctor'.[46] The cessation of menstruation was frequently deemed the most reliable sign, but *The Wife's Handbook* warns that in newly married women, this might be a 'consequence of the excitement produced in the whole system by the first sexual embraces'.[47]

Despite the uncertainty regarding the signs of pregnancy, and the lack of any conclusive evidence in the form of a reliable pregnancy test, the readers of advice literature could nonetheless attain a fairly accurate idea of the expected date of birth by referring to the tables for determining the 'expected time of confinement' which appeared in several works.[48] Introducing the table in *The Young Wife's Own Book*, the author suggests the reader consult it in order to establish 'when your troubles will be over'[49] – the language here reinforcing the notion of pregnancy as a period of discomfort and ill health (and in addition underestimating the challenges of the postnatal period and early infant care).

Despite the ambiguity of much literature on pregnancy, many advice books aimed at married women contain rigorous guidance on how expectant mothers should conduct themselves during this time. Reflecting wider cultural discourses, much of this advice seems to serve a wider ideological purpose in encouraging women to behave in a certain way, by placing the responsibility for the unborn child squarely on their shoulders. Advice covered almost every aspect of a woman's life, including dress (no tight clothing), diet (plain food, no alcohol), exercise (regular, not too strenuous), washing, sleep, and the treatment of the various ailments of pregnancy. Dire warnings often accompanied this advice: idleness and indolence could result in a 'lingering and painful labour' and bring 'misery, anguish, and suffering in its train'.[50] However, walks that are too long might cause 'flooding' (haemorrhaging) or 'miscarriage',[51] and 'riding, dancing, and out-door games requiring much exertion, must be entirely abstained from'.[52] Sea-bathing might also cause premature labour or miscarriage.[53] A tepid bath is recommended – but a 'shower-bath', by contrast, 'gives too great a shock, and might induce miscarriage'.[54] A lack of fresh air will cause a woman's blood to 'become impure'.[55] 'Light puddings' are deemed acceptable, but 'Rich pastry is highly objectionable'.[56] Many works were particularly outspoken on the subject of women's dress. Throughout the Victorian period, corsets were commonly worn, including pregnancy corsets, with adjustable lacing (so the latter were not necessarily overly restrictive for the pregnant body). The wearing of tightly fastened garments during pregnancy was widely seen as posing a risk to the developing child. One work warns that 'Tight lacing is injurious both to the mother and to the child, and frequently causes the former to miscarry', whilst in some cases damaging the nipples to the extent that women are unable to breastfeed.[57] Another cautions that tight clothing: 'is often the cause of miscarriages, of weak and ill-formed children, of false positions of the child in the womb, and consequently difficult and dangerous labour, of abscess of the breasts from compression of the nipple, rendering sucking impossible, of flatulency, and numerous other minor troubles'.[58]

The Wife's Handbook is similarly stringent in its condemnation of tight clothing, but recommends the 'Knitted Corset Company, Nottingham' for garments which provide 'support without pressure'.[59] In light of these unwelcome (though not very likely) possibilities, the question arises of why women might continue to wear tightly fastened under-garments during pregnancy. One work, perhaps unwittingly, suggests a possible reason behind this, by advising the reader that 'No attempt at concealing your condition by tight-lacing, or even tight-fitting dresses, should under any consideration whatever be made.'[60] Whilst construct-ing motherhood as women's destiny, nineteenth-century culture also worked to obscure the pregnant body. The assertion here suggests some women absorbed these messages and were uncomfortable enough with their own expanding figures to attempt to conceal them from the public gaze. The warnings regarding the potential dangers of tight lacing might also have led to some women to attempt to deal with unwanted pregnancies by the wearing of such garments.[61]

Advice to pregnant women during the nineteenth century, then, was a combination of guidance which is still promoted today, and the pseudoscientific – and sometimes bizarre (although, in this respect it might be seen to parallel some of the more questionable advice the internet has to offer to today's mothers). The idea of 'maternal impressions' falls firmly into this latter category. The theory, which dates back thousands of years, posits that distressing sights or experiences during pregnancy can impact on the formation of the child. Congenital abnormalities as well as mental disorders were often believed to be the result of these 'impressions'. Although some were sceptical, others were firm believers in this idea. An article published in *The British Medical Journal* in 1875 cited several cases in which women's distressing experiences during pregnancy appeared to have affected the unborn child. These include a woman startled by a mouse whose child was born with a birthmark in the shape of a mouse. In a similar case, a woman startled by a rat allegedly gave birth to a child with a rat-shaped birthmark. Unfortunately, the same woman was subsequently startled by a dog in her next pregnancy, with predictable results. In another of the cases cited, a woman startled by a toad gave birth to 'a child resembling a toad, which died in a few moments'.[62] In *London Labour and the London Poor* (1851), Henry Mayhew cites a case 'within [his] own knowledge, where the sight of a man without legs or arms had such an effect upon a lady in the family way that her child was born in all respect the very counterpart of the object that alarmed her'.[63] In April 1853, the 'Weekly Return of Births and Deaths in London' included the case of the 6-week-old daughter of a builder in Islington, who 'died of "atrophy from imperfect development"'. Mr Watts, the registrar, adds that 'The mother was frightened six weeks previously to her confinement by a fox, which flew at her, being attracted by the smell of some butcher's meat which she was carrying on her arm.'[64] The implication clearly is that the event impacted the child's development, ultimately leading to her premature death.

Women, too, often subscribed to this theory, even, in some cases, in the face of evidence to the contrary and scepticism from medical practitioners. One doctor recalled the case of a woman who:

assured me recently that the deaf-mutism and idiocy of her son were due to the circumstance that a dumb man had begged from her, and frightened her during her pregnancy. She was incredulous when I expressed my opinion that they might more reasonably be ascribed to the facts that her child was stillborn after a labour of forty-eight hours' duration, was not brought to life for ten minutes, and suffered from convulsions for three weeks.[65]

The most famous example of this alleged theory in practice was undoubtedly the case of Joseph Merrick – better known as the 'Elephant Man' – whose physical deformities were believed to have been caused by his mother's unexpected encounter with an elephant whilst pregnant with him, as Merrick himself detailed in his short autobiographical pamphlet, published in 1884:

The deformity which I am now exhibiting was caused by my mother being frightened by an Elephant; my mother was going along the street when a procession of Animals were passing by, there was a terrible crush of people to see them, and unfortunately she was pushed under the Elephant's feet, which frightened her very much; this occurring during a time of pregnancy was the cause of my deformity.[66]

Although the theory of maternal impressions is evidently outlandish and without scientific basis, it nonetheless served an ideological purpose in helping to promote the idea that women, particularly whilst pregnant, were safest when confined to the home, thus reinforcing the notion that women's roles and lives should be primarily lived out within the domestic space of the home and the family. Furthermore, whilst the notion of a woman witnessing a beggar with no arms and legs and subsequently giving birth to a child with no arms and legs is patently ridiculous in terms of any possible causation, the notion of a more general link between distressing experiences and the health of the baby appears more plausible – and indeed is exhibited in the refrain which pregnant women today frequently encounter when stressed or upset: 'it's not good for the baby'. In some nineteenth-century advice and medical literature we find a more nuanced message, which avoids the idea of external circumstances having a direct and visible effect on the baby's physical form, but nonetheless encourages particular types of behaviour from pregnant women. *The Wife's Handbook* states that 'During pregnancy a woman should avoid, as far as possible, everything of a disagreeable nature, especially unpleasant sights. She should keep her mind free from all harass and care. This is important if she wishes to bear a healthy child.'[67] Obstetrician Robert Lee was sceptical of the theory of maternal impressions in terms of a direct link between physical malformation and women's experiences in pregnancy, arguing that 'such a relationship as popularly imagined is most improbable'. He does, though, consider the possibility that 'mental disturbances' can 'produce an influence on the foetus *in utero*', and suggests that 'a maternal impression may affect, not the bodily, but the intellectual condition of a child'. This view, he suggests, is one to which mothers themselves adhere: 'The instances of mental abnormality have been numerous which have come under my notice. Such cases of imbecility or deficiency of intellect in the child are almost always attributed by the mother to mental disturbance previous to its birth.' Consequently, he concludes that 'emotional disturbances during pregnancy' can have a detrimental effect upon the unborn child.[68] This message was reinforced by stories which appeared in the press of women miscarrying or going into premature labour following receipt of shocking news: in one such account, a mother of six, Mrs Hopper, delivered a premature baby upon hearing the news of her husband's death in a mine near Durham.[69] Ultimately, such discourses worked to justify the careful policing of women's behaviour during pregnancy. There is a question mark over the extent to which women in the nineteenth century adhered to the advice provided by the plethora of guides designed for the young wife, but there can be little doubt that women – then as now – found themselves facing extensive social and cultural pressures as they attempted to negotiate their pregnancies and journeys towards motherhood. Women's maternal experiences, therefore, were undeniably affected by these pressures, as well as by the physical and emotional side of pregnancy.

* * *

Convention today dictates that most women in Britain don't publicly announce their pregnancy until the end of the first trimester, as this period carries the highest risk of miscarriage. As Charlotte Brontë's tentative letter makes clear, establishing the existence of a pregnancy was not straightforward in the nineteenth century, and even amongst friends and family, the news of a pregnancy might not be revealed for several months. Writing to his wife in 1819, John Shaw checked whether or not it was permissible for him to reveal the news of the baby due to arrive shortly: 'I suppose I may be allowed to tell the folks at Rochdale and Colne that we are promised an increase in the family ere it be long.'[70] In spite of the apprehensiveness that sometimes accompanied pregnancy and the prospect of childbirth, announcements to friends and family were often met with great joy. Catherine Temple Pears (wife of Steuart Adolphus Pears, assistant master at Harrow), already a mother herself, wrote to express her delight at the news of her sister's pregnancy in April 1856 – and to offer advice:

I […] write just to tell you how rejoiced I am at your happy prospect. You must be glad indeed, as I was. I well remember how proud and important I felt, how very valuable I felt myself! […] There is joy and sorrow before you, they must be mixed up together in all that relates to one's children. Now as I can't come I shall deluge you with letters of advice, and you can take it or not, as you like. As to sickness, that is a very troublesome matter, but it wears off, and I believe is rarely troublesome after the first three months. I found great relief from having something to eat before I got up in the morning, a cup of tea and a little bit of bread or biscuit. When I had this, I was not sick that morning. I was never troubled with it except with the first child. I feel so pleased about you, dear Alicia.

She continued, echoing many of the advice books aimed at pregnant women:

You would never be fanciful, but when you feel much disinclined for a walk, or any exertion you should follow your own feelings, and not long walks, indeed dear, they are bad. If you want to know anything that I can tell you I shall be so glad to answer you.[71]

Her letters indicate that whilst pregnancy was often presented only in veiled terms in advice literature and other public discourses, amongst those women who experienced it, it was commonly discussed, and experiences shared.

Royal pregnancies in particular attracted considerable public attention. Queen Victoria was not exempt from the pressures that many of her subjects faced during pregnancy, despite her position as monarch, and found herself having to relinquish some of her duties to her husband during her many pregnancies and confinements. She evidently found pregnancy trying. Recalling her childbearing years sometime later, she wrote to her eldest daughter, Victoria Princess Royal, then recently married herself:

aches – and sufferings and miseries and plagues […] I had 9 times for eight months to bear with those above-named enemies and I own it tried me sorely; one feels so pinned down – one's wings clipped – in fact, at the best (and few were or are better than I was) only half oneself – particularly the first and second time.[72]

Albert was not always sympathetic to her suffering. During her last pregnancy, in 1856, he accused her of being selfishly preoccupied with her physical condition:

I, like everyone else in the house make the most ample allowance for your state […] We cannot, unhappily, bear your bodily sufferings for you – you must struggle with them alone – the moral ones are probably caused by them, but if you were rather less occupied with yourself and your feelings and took more interest in the outside world, you would find that the greatest help of all.[73]

Victoria was adamant, though, that men could not possibly understand the trials experienced by women during pregnancy and childbirth. Writing after the birth of her first child, she declared: 'men never think, at least seldom think, what a hard task it is for us women to go through this very often'.[74] She echoed this sentiment almost twenty years later, writing to her daughter, Vicky, ahead of the birth of her second grandchild: 'Oh! If those selfish men – who are the causes of all one's misery, only knew what their poor slaves go through! What suffering – what humiliation to the delicate feelings of a poor woman, above all a young one – especially with those nasty doctors.'[75]

Neither did Victoria expect her daughters to enjoy pregnancy. In spring 1858, rumours began to circulate suggesting both Victoria and Vicky were pregnant (Vicky, having married young, was still only 17 at this point, whilst Victoria was not yet 40, and had given birth to her youngest child only a year earlier). The Queen was distressed by the reports. She wrote to her daughter stating: 'It is most odious but they have spread a report that you and I are both in what I call an unhappy condition! It is odious [...] Really too bad. [...] [A]ll who love you hope you will be spared this trial for a year yet.'[76] 'If I had had a year of happy enjoyment with dear Papa,' she continued in her letter to Vicky, 'how thankful I should have been! But [...] I was in for it at once – and furious I was.'[77] Within a few weeks of receiving this letter, Vicky did fall pregnant with her first child. On hearing this, her mother wrote declaring the 'horrid news [...] upset us dreadfully'. She predicted, however (incorrectly), that 'it will all end in nothing'.[78] Vicky, though, asserted that she felt deep pride at the prospect of 'giving life to an immortal soul'. Her mother's response was more prosaic: 'I think much more of our being like a cow or a dog at such moments; when our poor nature become so very animal and unecstatic.'[79] Nonetheless, she urged her daughter to be cautious during her pregnancy – echoing advice books in declaring 'any noise or even suspicion of fright, might be very hurtful for you now'.[80] In 1864, the Princess Royal wrote to her mother informing her of her fourth pregnancy. The Queen was again distressed by the news, and seemed to take it as something of a personal slight:

> I cannot tell you how grieved and how surprised I am at the news conveyed in your letter [...] I thought you both knew how highly important the doctors [...] thought it that you should have two years complete rest before these – for you – particularly trying events again began [...] I will say no more except that I pray God fervently to protect you and the child! I little needed this additional anxiety in my present sorrow and worry![81]

Victoria's reaction was perhaps partly borne out of maternal anxiety. Vicky, though, was evidently somewhat hurt. She responded to her mother a few days later: 'I am sorry that the news I gave you should distress you as to most it is not a cause of sorrow but of gratitude. I have had a good rest, [and] my health is strong and good.'[82]

Despite the injunctions to rest – particularly in the latter stages of pregnancy – offered by multiple advice books, many women remained active throughout their pregnancies. This suggests a contrast between the construction of pregnancy in medical and advice literature, and the lived experience of many nineteenth-century women. Lady Charlotte Guest, who bore ten children between 1834 and 1847, travelled with her husband even when heavily pregnant, recording in her diary, 'I determined that I would [...] run all the risks of dangers and fatigue rather than part from him again. I always feel it my duty to be with him.'[83] Her comments suggest a distinction between wifely and maternal duties – and a privileging of the former in this case. Writing before the birth of their first child, Charles Darwin notes that he and Emma are 'living a life of extreme quietness' and have 'given up all parties', suggesting she was mindful of the advice proffered to pregnant women.[84] Shortly after her wedding to the painter George Howard in 1864, Rosalind Stanley fell pregnant. Her father wrote to her mother about her 'condition', declaring: 'I shall say she must be shut up if she is not careful of herself.'[85] When Victoria, Princess Royal, found herself expecting her first child, she was forbidden by doctors to travel.[86] Her mother, however, throughout much of her pregnancies, continued with both her royal duties and private excursions. Some four months pregnant with her first child in June 1840, Queen Victoria was subject to an assassination attempt when driving in an open carriage with Prince Albert, just outside the gates of Buckingham Palace. Despite the circumstances and her condition, the couple continued their drive. A month before the birth of her youngest child, Princess Beatrice, Victoria's journals record her taking walks, driving out, attending theatrical performances, and receiving visitors (including politicians and foreign ambassadors), as well as her preoccupation with matters of state, including the Anglo-Persian war then underway, and the general election of that year. On Sunday, 15 March 1857, Victoria attended church, where, she records in her diary, a shorter service took place, in consideration of her condition, as she could 'no longer bear the fatigue of a long service'.[87] Nine days before Beatrice's birth, she continued busy, but was growing frustrated: 'getting impatient, as I am certainly going beyond my time!' she wrote in her journal.[88] She suffered with a troublesome cough, and found herself 'feeling very weary and wretched', but even the day beforehand she was able to take a walk in the grounds.[89]

The Viscountess Amberley was frustrated by the repeated injunctions to rest that were pressed upon her during her first pregnancy. These included a letter from her father-in-law, former Prime Minster Earl Russell, to her husband, who wrote to congratulate his son, whilst also sounding a note of caution: 'I write a line to wish you joy of Kate's well doing. But she must be cautious as she is a foolish child, & you are little better.'[90] Kate evidently was somewhat offended by this, and in a subsequent letter, he offered his apologies, whilst suggesting the advice was not entirely unjustified: 'I must beg your pardon for calling you a "foolish child" as you have been so very prudent, but really skating seems in some degree to justify me.'[91] Kate did not heed his advice, recording in her diary the same day: 'skated for ½ an hour, none the worse!'.[92] A few weeks later, however, she attended a ball and appeared to be following at least some of the advice typically levelled at pregnant women: 'I did not dance at all – I did not wish it nor did A[mberley].'[93] A subsequent journal entry several weeks later, though, records her riding a pony.[94] Her father-in-law and others remained concerned over her behaviour. In June 1865, in the final trimester of her pregnancy, Earl Russell again wrote to his son to express his concerns – and those of other members of the family: 'Lady Stanley, Mama & I in the character of [Dickens's] Mrs Gamp think that Kate ought not to be allowed to go to Leeds. She might be surprised like the Prs. of Wales.' (Princess Alexandra had recently given birth to her first son two months earlier than expected.)[95] A few days later, he wrote again: 'I take for granted that Kate will consult with people, & take wise advice before she determines to go to Leeds.'[96] The advice not to travel was echoed by Kate's doctor, but she went nonetheless – with no obvious ill consequences. Her frustration at the unasked-for advice with which she was constantly bombarded during this first pregnancy led her to conceal her condition from almost everyone until late into her second pregnancy. During this time she travelled to America, where she fared reasonably well, despite feeling tired, faint, and ill at times.[97] She returned home in January, and recorded her family's reaction in her journal: 'They were all very much surprised to see my condition none of them knowing I was in a family way but Mama whom I had told before I started but she had kept my secret perfectly.'[98] She adopted a similar course during her third pregnancy in 1871, writing to her mother, 'I don't wish it to go beyond you and Maude […] that I am to be confined in May.' Her mother wrote back in agreement: 'It is much better to keep those things to oneself and then people do not advise one to take care.'[99] The onslaught of well-meaning advice is a familiar experience for expectant mothers today; in this respect, the pressures women face during pregnancy have changed little, and many women will identify with Lady Amberley's desire to minimise these intrusions.

Although much advice literature encouraged women to rest during pregnancy and constructed the pregnant body as an 'ill' body, such advice held little relevance for poorer women, many of whom had to work throughout their pregnancies in order to support themselves and their families – either undertaking paid labour, or the hard domestic labour involved in looking after family and home. Indeed, some poorer women were forced into both these occupations throughout their many pregnancies. One woman who attended the General Lying-in Hospital in London in 1884 reported a sore stomach, and her case notes suggest the cause of this was 'perhaps from leaning against washtub' throughout her pregnancy. She continued her work at the washtub even after her waters broke, only attending the hospital several days later.[100] The correspondents whose letters appear in *Maternity: Letters From Working Women* provide numerous examples of the hard work some women had little choice but to undertake during pregnancy. One woman describes dropping a heavy washing-tub whilst pregnant – an accident which she believed caused her to lose her baby.[101] Another, who had taken up factory work to provide clothes for her eldest son, who had won a scholarship, was forced to stop working due to sickness caused by pregnancy. Despite paying into a 'Sick Loan' scheme, she was unable to claim any benefit as her illness was pregnancy related and therefore not covered by the scheme; pregnancy, it seems, was only treated as an illness when convenient.[102] In some cases, a husband's lack of work meant women had to undertake paid work whilst pregnant – as one correspondent describes:

I am the mother of three children. When the youngest was coming my husband was out of employment, so I had to go out to work myself, standing all day washing and ironing. This caused me much suffering from varicose veins, also caused the child to wedge in some way, which nearly cost both our lives. The doctor said it was the standing and the weight of the child. I have not been able to carry a child the full time since then.[103]

The frequency of pregnancies for many women also meant they were often caring for very young children throughout their pregnancies, allowing them limited opportunities to rest. One woman describes struggling through her sixth pregnancy with five other children to care for – the eldest only ten. During the final months of the pregnancy, the two youngest children contracted measles, and she had to nurse them. The 'strain' she was under impacted her own health, and she was ill for weeks – but within eighteen months she found herself pregnant again. In total, she experienced thirteen pregnancies over a twenty-year period (two of which ended in miscarriage).[104] Another describes suffering with pain in her side during her third and fourth pregnancies: 'I attribute this pain to having to carry one child about so much whilst in a state of pregnancy with another, and not being able to employ anyone to assist me in the more laborious duties, such as washing, scrubbing, etc., to give me the necessary rest which my condition demanded.'[105] For working-class women, often struggling to survive on their husbands' low wages, low income and families to feed sometimes meant choosing between feeding their children or themselves, and many women suffered from malnutrition during pregnancy. One woman describes how she 'nearly lost [her] life through want of nourishment' while pregnant with her first child – during which time her husband was out of work. The child's health also became affected, and they died after only a few months: 'No one but mothers who have gone through the ordeal of pregnancy half-starved, to finally bring a child into the world to live a living death for nine months, can understand what it means,' she wrote.[106] Another notes that 'during the carrying of all my children, except the first, I have had insufficient food and too much work'.[107] Many women endured the trials of hard work and poverty whilst experiencing severe nausea and sickness during their pregnancies. One woman who went through seven pregnancies (two ending in miscarriage and two in stillbirths) described feeling constantly sick during these times: 'troubled with nausea and vomiting, which kept me very weak'.[108] Others describe a range of symptoms and ailments which they had no choice but to endure, including cramps, constipation, jaundice, and toothache. *The Wife's Handbook*, aimed at poorer women, advises the reader not to 'neglect her household duties on account of pregnancy', but perhaps somewhat unrealistically in light of the pressures these women faced, advises against the 'Lifting of weights or pushing about of heavy things', and encourages pregnant women to take 'a couple of hours' rest' during the day, as well as 'eight or nine hours' rest' each night.[109]

Middle- and upper-class mothers did not face the same challenges as working-class women in terms of work – either paid or domestic. Most had at least some help from servants, and fewer women amongst these demographics worked at all. Those that did typically did not carry out the type of hard labour associated with factory work or domestic service. Nonetheless, there were examples of working mothers amongst every class of nineteenth-century society, many of whom worked throughout their pregnancies. Many women writers raised a family whilst also producing numerous novels: these included Elizabeth Gaskell, mother of seven, including a stillborn daughter and two sons who died in early infancy; Mary Elizabeth Braddon, mother of six and stepmother to several more; and Florence Marryat, mother of eight. Another example of the working mother in Victorian England was Fanny Eaton. Born in Jamaica as Fanny Entwhistle, she travelled to England in the 1840s, where she married James Eaton, with whom she subsequently had ten children. Between 1859 and 1867 she worked as an artists' model for members of the Pre-Raphaelite Brotherhood, including Dante Gabriel Rossetti and John Everett Millais. In a painting by Simeon Solemon, entitled *The Mother of Moses* (1860) (see figure 4), she is featured holding a baby – possibly her newborn son.

Queen Victoria occupied an exceptional position as a 'working mother'. Three days before the birth of her sixth child, Princess Louise, in March 1848, she complained in her journal of being 'overwhelmed [...] by an immense number of business letters'.[110] Victoria, however, had advisors, servants, and her husband on whom she could rely to carry out many duties both professional and domestic. For those struggling to make ends meet, who could not afford either medical care or domestic help, and who frequently had large families to raise and sometimes had to go out to work themselves during their pregnancies, expecting a baby was often far from a joyful experience – particularly for those who experienced multiple pregnancies with little choice in the matter. Pregnancy for many women was accompanied by fear: about how a large family could be supported, but also for the life of both mother and baby – particularly when access to healthcare was limited by financial constraints. This fear could in itself impact significantly on women's experience of pregnancy, as one woman recalled, reflecting on her experience in the late nineteenth century:

The first feeling of a young mother (to be) [...] is one of fear for herself when she finds out her condition. As time goes on she will probably lose this fear in the feeling she is to have something all her very own, but in some instances the dread grows, and in a sense fills her whole being. This must of necessity weaken her bodily and mentally, and, of course, makes her time of trial harder to bear.[111]

Anxiety about finances was frequently a concern during pregnancy, as Hannah Mitchell recalled: 'When I realised that I was to become a mother, fresh problems presented themselves, and I cannot say that the prospect gave me any pleasure at first. Living on our small income was hard enough for two.' She continued:

I foresaw that the coming of a baby would mean giving up my own work, for a few months anyhow. At first I felt desperate, and wept many bitter tears, but by and by, as I recovered from the nausea of the first few weeks, I began to feel more hopeful. I remembered my sister-in-law who now had four children, and still only eighteen shillings a week to keep them on.[112]

The physical demands of pregnancy – and, for many women work and domestic duties – were thus also often accompanied by significant mental and emotional pressures borne out of the anxieties associated with pregnancy and the coming birth.

Whilst married women living in comfortable situations might experience pregnancy as a hopeful time, for unmarried women who found themselves pregnant, the experience could be very different. The shame associated with pregnancy outside of marriage meant some women concealed their pregnancies, took steps to induce abortions, or even took their own lives. In 1881, a 26-year-old woman, Hannah Moorhouse, drowned herself and her three illegitimate children. Pregnant for a fourth time, she had been told by her father that she must leave his house.[113] In February 1886, a 20-year-old domestic servant named Frances Jackson, apparently pregnant, took her own life believing the father of her child had abandoned her.[114] In a similar case in 1896, a lady's maid, believing herself to be pregnant by her soldier lover, killed herself. The subsequent post-mortem, however, showed that she was not pregnant, but had a tumour.[115] In summer 1898, a farmer's daughter, Ethel May Boon, aged 23, also ended her own life. A post-mortem revealed she was pregnant, and the inquest jury reached a verdict of 'suicide whilst temporarily insane, brought about by mental anguish during pregnancy and while unmarried'. The headline of one of the newspaper reports of this case reads 'A Farmer's Daughter's Disgrace and Death' – reinforcing the idea of the shame associated with unmarried pregnancy.[116] For these women, and for many others, death was deemed preferable to the disgrace of bearing an illegitimate child.[117] Women who found themselves pregnant outside of marriage risked abandonment by their families and the father of the child (if he could not be persuaded to marry the woman), as well as dismissal from their jobs. Young women working in domestic service could find themselves in a particularly vulnerable position and were sometimes subject to sexual harassment from both fellow servants and members of the family for whom they worked. In 1861, Lord Stanley wrote to his wife of a rumour then in circulation: 'They say Ld Raynham is gone crazy & is to marry a housemaid who persuaded him he had got her with child & he thinks in honour he must marry her.'[118] In fact, Lord Raynham went on to marry Lady Anne Duff, a daughter of the Earl of Fife, in 1865. There may have been no truth in the rumour, or the housemaid may, like many other women in her position, have been abandoned by the father of her unborn child. Stanley's words, though, are revealing: the idea of a member of the aristocracy marrying a housemaid simply because he had impregnated her is deemed 'crazy'. Evidently, the expectation was that the housemaid should be left to fend for herself.

It was not only women from the poorer classes of society who found themselves in this position, however. In September 1839, various newspapers reported on the case of a young girl, aged only 16 or 17, who had become pregnant by a medical man at an expensive boarding school where she was being educated. The newspaper reports the case as 'seduction', but it is possible that this was, in fact, rape. When her condition was discovered, her mother refused to allow her back into the house, or to help her even when she faced complete destitution. When she attempted to return to the house, the police became involved and she was charged and forced to appear in the magistrates' court, where her mother again refused to take any responsibility for her pregnant daughter. The fate of the girl is unknown, although the magistrate speculated she would soon become 'chargeable to the parish' – in other words, it seems likely she would end up in the workhouse.[119] In another case the following year, a young woman, pregnant and presumed to be unmarried, attempted suicide by taking laudanum. The newspapers reported on her 'respectable' appearance: 'From the appearance of her dress, which consisted of a black silk cloak and gown (nearly new), a red scarf, and straw bonnet, and from the softness of her hands, there is no doubt that she is very respectably connected.'[120] This focus on the girl's appearance and social status remains a disturbing feature in cases of sexual assault today, in which victims' dress and behaviour is frequently subject to intense scrutiny.

Unmarried women who found themselves pregnant were often left with few options other than the workhouse. The discovery of such a pregnancy frequently led to women's abandonment by their families and to the loss of their professional positions – particularly those in domestic service, whose 'respectability' was closely bound up with that of their employers, few of whom would countenance the continued employment of an unmarried, pregnant woman in their home. Local parishes, which were required to assist those residents who found themselves in the workhouse, were also less than enthusiastic in their support of such women. Parishes were responsible for those born within their boundaries, so any children born within the workhouse were viewed as a particular burden. Consequently, parishes would try and ensure those women who were not born there did not give birth there and could apply for removal orders to have people taken away to the parish of their birth – even heavily pregnant women. One case illustrating this occurred in 1848, when a pregnant woman named Elizabeth Barnes was forced to seek assistance from the workhouse. The parish in which she was resident sought her removal to the parish of her birth to which she should rightfully be charged, but the receiving parish opposed her transferral on the grounds that pregnancy was a form of sickness, therefore rendering her irremovable. The court, however, decided that pregnancy should not be treated as illness. The case illustrates the reluctance with which workhouses received pregnant women. This is also evident in a report from 1836, which argued that 'advantage has been taken of the workhouse by pregnant women, both married and single'. It cites the case of a woman who had appealed to be allowed to enter the workhouse some months before she was due to give birth. Her request was refused, and she was advised she was not eligible to enter until 'her time should draw near'. The author of the report comments that 'if encouragement be given to [pregnant women], the workhouse will be turned into a lying-in hospital'.[121]

The harsh conditions of the workhouse were intended to deter all but the most impoverished from seeking help there. In 1839, the Poor Law Commissioners condemned the practice, carried out by some workhouses, of compelling 'single women, mothers of children or pregnant [...] to wear a dress of a peculiar colour as a mark of disgrace'.[122] At the workhouse in Eton, for example, according to a report which appeared in the newspapers in the same year, the Board of Guardians passed a resolution stating: 'all single women received there in a state of pregnancy, or after delivery, whether it be their first lapse, or whether they be old traders in bastardy, shall be stigmatised by a kind of felon's dress'.[123] Similarly, at another workhouse, both single pregnant women and sex workers were required to wear a yellow dress – essentially as a marker of their disgrace.[124] The Commissioners concluded, however, that 'The sole object of the workhouse is to give relief to the destitute poor' and that it 'is not intended to serve any penal or remuneratory purpose', therefore 'Any attempt to inflict disgrace or punishment on the mother of a bastard should be avoided.'[125] Despite the instructions of the Commissioners, though, the practice of openly condemning single pregnant women appears to have continued in a number of workhouses. In 1842, the Commissioners issued further guidance on the administration of the New Poor Law, which included advising that pregnant women (along with nursing mothers, the sick, infirm, and elderly) should not be subject to either confinement or an alteration in diet, unless first approved by the medical officer.[126]

In part, the attempts to punish single pregnant women in the workhouse were intended to act as a deterrent to try and discourage women from repeatedly entering the workhouse when pregnant. There were cases of women spending much of their lives in the workhouse: entering whilst pregnant and returning in this condition multiple times. At Bedminster Workhouse in the 1880s, one resident, 30-year-old Jane Tanner, had four children in the workhouse, whilst another, Mary Weare gave birth six times there. Their cases were brought to the attention of the Local Government Board Inspector because they were suspected of becoming pregnant whilst resident in the workhouse – something the system was designed to prevent, by separating the sexes onto different wards.[127] A similar case was investigated at Blaby Workhouse in 1896, where a woman named Elizabeth Gee appears to have twice become pregnant whilst resident there. As part of this inquiry, a nurse at the workhouse testified to the fact that two other women had previously become pregnant whilst in its environs.[128] The fact of women becoming pregnant whilst in the workhouse raised the possibility of exploitative and abusive relations between staff and residents, although in this case it was determined that the women fell pregnant whilst on visits outside of the workhouse.

The possibility of women becoming pregnant whilst in the workhouse as a consequence of what was termed 'immoral relations' with staff – but which in reality is likely to have been sexual abuse – is suggested by several other cases reported in the nineteenth-century press. At St Luke's Workhouse in Chelsea in 1863, the Senior Relieving Officer, a Mr Roger, was accused of fathering the child of a pauper woman.[129] A few years later, in 1869, the master of Prescott Workhouse was accused by a female inmate of 'gross immorality': 'She accused the master of having had intercourse with her on several occasions, in consequence of which she became pregnant, and ultimately miscarried.'[130] In 1883, the master of Toxteth Union Workhouse, one Mr Cartwright, was accused of 'certain charges of immorality' by the husband of a woman then pregnant and resident in the workhouse. She gave evidence in support of the charges, but ultimately it was her reputation that was called into question.[131] It is clear from these reports that whilst many women arrived at the workhouse pregnant, others became pregnant – in circumstances which were often shrouded in obscurity – whilst resident at these institutions. For these women, already enduring extreme poverty, pregnancy must have been an intensely distressing time. Workhouses were far from comfortable places to reside, with considerable social stigma attached, whilst residents generally had little hope for their future prospects. This, combined with pregnancy – in some cases resulting from rape – must have exerted an unimaginable toll.

For the wealthier classes, even those who did not welcome pregnancy, the experiences of those women who found themselves in the workhouse and in danger of sexual assault from those who were supposed to be supporting them must have been inconceivable – so far removed were they from their own comfortable lives. Nonetheless, women from Queen Victoria to the inmates of Britain's many workhouses frequently experienced pregnancy as a time of discomfort, ill health and anxiety, though often accompanied by excitement and joy at the prospect of motherhood. For many women, anxiety increased as the period of confinement drew near. Those living in comfortable circumstances might be able to prepare for the birth by hiring monthly nurses, appointing doctors and accoucheurs, and preparing the birthing room, but no woman could be certain what the birth itself would involve, and what the outcome might be in terms of both her own and her baby's health – and even life. For women of all classes, childbirth was approached with a degree of apprehension. The anonymous writer of *The Mother's Thorough Resource Book* observes this trend, noting that during pregnancy, 'women are apt to become a prey to inquietude and restlessness of mind. The approaching confinement afflicts them with an indescribable terror, and they experience a heavy foreboding and deep despondency, as though some calamity were about to happen.'[132] Infant and maternal mortality rates no doubt heightened anxieties in the later stages of pregnancy, but nonetheless, the combination of apprehension and nervous, joyful anticipation is something familiar to mothers past and present as they await the onset of labour.

3

Confinement and Delivery

When I enfold thee in my arms, sweet Babe,
My heart will scarcely breathe lest it should wake
The sleeping wings of its new-nestling bliss.
When thou art born, my Child, all will be well[.]
Gerald Massey[1]

On 14 April 1857, Queen Victoria gave birth to her ninth and last child, Princess Beatrice, at Buckingham Palace. In the days leading up to the birth, the weather had been bad and the Queen plagued with a 'troublesome cough', which left her feeling quite unwell at times, but nonetheless she had managed several walks in the grounds, including visiting her horses in the stables. She was also in a state of some anxiety regarding the health of her aunt, the Duchess of Gloucester – the last surviving child of George III – who died shortly after Beatrice's birth. By this time, Victoria was well used to the discomforts of late pregnancy, but she was also almost 38 years old, and already mother to a large family, so perhaps wearier with this pregnancy than with previous ones. As with her earlier deliveries, she recorded some of the details of the birth of the baby in her diary: 'She came into the world at 2 o'clock on the 14th, having caused me a very long wearisome time. I was amply rewarded, & forgot all I had gone through, when I heard dearest Albert say "it is a very fine child, & a girl!" & it was as inexpressible joy to me.'[2]

As with the birth of Prince Leopold four years previously, Victoria was administered chloroform during her labour and delivery, providing some relief from the pain. However, as Dr John Snow, one of the medical men attending the birth observed in his case notes, the delivery was not entirely straightforward:

> The labour occurred about a fortnight later than was expected. It commenced about 2 A.M. [...] when the medical men were sent for. The labour was lingering [...] At 11 o'clock I began to administer chloroform. [...] Her majesty expressed great relief from the vapor. [...] [T]he royal patient made an effort which expelled the head, a little chloroform being given just as the head passed. There was an interval of several minutes before the child was entirely born: it, however, cried in the meantime. [...] The Queen's recovery was very favourable.[3]

If this image of Victoria, with the baby partially delivered, is not one we would typically associate with her, the birth nonetheless reflects her privileged position. The Queen's labour was eased by the use of chloroform, and she was supported in the birthing room by her husband, as well as Snow and her attending physician, Dr Charles Locock. Her monthly nurse (a figure often employed by middle- and upper-class women to provide support before, during, and after childbirth), Mrs Lilly, who had been with her for every delivery, was also there, and her surroundings were – at least relatively speaking, compared to other birthing rooms of the time – clean and sanitary. The positive outcome for both mother and child might be deemed at least partly due to the circumstances in which Victoria gave birth. Following the birth, Mrs Lilly continued to attend to her and the baby, in addition to an assistant monthly nurse. As with her previous babies, the job of breastfeeding the child was carried out by a wet nurse. Shortly after the birth, Dr Locock was rewarded with a baronetcy. Writing in her diary two weeks after her delivery, Victoria describes the newborn Princess: 'a pretty, plump, flourishing child, [...] with fine large blue eyes, marked nose, pretty little mouth & very fine skin'.[4]

Whilst Queen Victoria was giving birth to Princess Beatrice, some 200 miles from Buckingham Palace another woman was also heavily pregnant and nearing her delivery date. On the evening of Thursday, 23 April 1857, an 18-year-old woman arrived at Bradford Workhouse in the early stages of labour seeking the limited medical assistance that was available. The woman gave her name as Ann Brooks, and a false address. Her real address was reportedly 'a house of ill-fame', and it is possible that she was a sex worker.[5] She remained at the workhouse overnight and the following morning was examined by the rather Dickensian-sounding Mrs Bull, the nurse in the lying-in ward. Apparently observing no symptoms of impending labour, Mrs Bull reported the case to the workhouse master, who subsequently discharged Ann Brooks. After walking a short distance from the workhouse, she collapsed in the street, where she gave birth alone to a premature and stillborn child before medical assistance could be summoned. Her case was reported in the local papers, and there was some outrage at her treatment. *The Leeds Times* demanded to know 'why a woman – no matter what her character may be – was turned ruthlessly adrift upon the report of an incompetent woman[?]'.[6] The Board of Guardians at the workhouse subsequently investigated events, but concluded that no fault lay with the workhouse staff, who had acted partly on their previous experience of 'false representations made in similar cases of application by pregnant women at the house'.[7] In such cases, the workhouse alleged women claimed to be in labour in order to gain admission, when in fact the birth did not occur for some time afterwards. Yet the workhouse was hardly a desirable environment – many were crowded, unsanitary, and with no trained medical assistants in residence – and only desperation can have led women to give birth to their children there. It is possible that Ann Brooks's child would have died regardless of her treatment at the hands of workhouse staff, but nonetheless her case is indicative of the tragedy which frequently attended women giving birth in the workhouse.

Another particularly tragic case of this – which echoes the experience of Ann Brooks – occurred in August 1866, when a 16-year-old girl named Mary Walker arrived at the Union Workhouse in Nottingham, requesting admittance as she was in labour. She had previously stayed at the workhouse on several occasions, often in the so-called 'Lock' ward, which was reserved for those suffering from venereal disease (suggesting she may also have been a sex worker). The matron and nurse believed she was not in labour and would not be delivered that day, so refused her request. Shortly afterwards she gave birth to a stillborn child in the street, surrounded by 'a crowd of people'[8] – the normally largely private act of childbirth here turned into a public spectacle. The subsequent inquest determined that the child had been dead some days, so the workhouse was not held accountable, but her experience demonstrates the harsh treatment often meted out to those attempting to gain admittance to the lying-in wards of Britain's workhouses.

The differing experiences of childbirth for women from various social classes was also highlighted in press reports following the birth of the first child of the Prince and Princess of Wales (see figure 5). On 8 January 1864, Alexandra, Princess of Wales, joined a skating party at Virginia Water near Windsor, where she was 'pushed in a sledge on the ice'.[9] She was some seven months pregnant. Returning to Frogmore House in Windsor, she unexpectedly went into premature labour. Dr Browne, a local surgeon-apothecary, was quickly summoned, but the labour was rapid and he arrived only twenty minutes before the baby was born. With no nurse present, the Princess's Lady of the Bedchamber, Lady Macclesfield, stepped in (her own experience as a mother of fourteen – later seventeen – no doubt aiding her). The celebrated medical men who had been due to attend the birth of the second in line to the throne – Dr Sieveking, Dr Farr, and Dr Locock – arrived long after the event had concluded. The royal baby's arrival inevitably provoked much anxiety: premature infants inevitably suffered a higher mortality rate. The new Prince was small: despite one newspaper erroneously reporting he weighed 9lb, in fact he was less than 4lb. Fortunately, the daily reports issued by the palace reported that the infant Prince was 'perfectly well', as did Queen Victoria, writing to her eldest daughter in Prussia: 'The dear little baby is kept in cotton-wool and has to be kept warm but is quite healthy and very thriving.'[10] His appearance two months before he was expected led his aunt and grandmother to speculate on the reasons for this: 'I hope the event was not premature but if not she must have made a great mistake in her reckoning,' wrote the Princess Royal.[11] It seems there was no mistake, however, and the baby had indeed made an early appearance – possibly, the Queen speculated, the result of 'general weakness, and perhaps not lying down quite enough'.[12] The Princess Royal's response echoes the sentiments of popular advice literature for expectant women: 'Do you not think that dear Alix did a little too much? She stood and walked for ever, and with her long back and long waist one ought to rest doubly; she did not seem to feel fatigue or to know what pain was when moving about.'[13] The press and public, reassured that the baby appeared healthy, were delighted with the news of a new heir to the throne,[14] and made much of the circumstances of his birth. 'That the first-born of the son of England,' wrote one newspaper:

> should have been ushered into the world by a surgeon apothecary, and have found not one article of even the most needful apparel ready to receive him – so that had it not been for the experience of the Countess of Macclesfield, [...] the poor little Prince would have found himself in as ill provided a case as the child of the poorest Berkshire day labourer – was indeed a combination of circumstances defying the possibility of anticipation.[15]

Other papers echoed this sentiment, with one noting that 'a prospective king of England was as ill provided for at his birth as the son of the poorest peasant'.[16] In reality, of course, the birth of the Prince was hardly comparable to that of the offspring of 'the poorest peasant'. Although luck certainly played a role in his survival following his premature arrival, the trappings of wealth and the privileges these bestowed undoubtedly improved his chances. The additional challenges faced by premature babies born to families who were struggling against poverty is illustrated by the experience of Victoria Rosina Barker, the wife of a stonemason, who lost two premature children. In the case of the death of the second, a daughter, an inquest was held due to a suspicion that the infant had starved to death. The mother testified that she had, at various points, sought medical advice, that she had given the child the breast (as well as a patented baby food and a little gin), but that it had not thrived. She noted that her husband was a weak man, and often out of work. The jury, however, concluded that 'The child was too weak to take sufficient nourishment to sustain life.' It appears, then, that the premature birth of the child, rather than the poverty in which her family existed, was the cause of her death. In returning their verdict – 'Death from Natural Causes' – the jury noted that Mrs Barker appeared to be 'a thorough good mother and carried out her duties to the best of her abilities'.[17] There was, inevitably, a significant divide between the care (nourishment, medical attention) she could offer her prematurely born children, and that afforded to the son of the Prince and Princess of Wales. Victorian class distinctions were nowhere more evident than in the birthing room.

* * *

Women in nineteenth-century Britain gave birth at home, in hospitals, workhouses, and asylums – sometimes on the streets. During childbirth, they might be accompanied by a doctor, nurse, midwife, by a friend or family member. In some cases – particularly those involving concealed pregnancies – they gave birth alone. In the later stages of pregnancy, women were encouraged to rest, but for many poorer women, the demands of both the workplace and home and family meant this was impossible. Many births were straightforward, but maternal and infant mortality, stillbirth, medical (including instrumental) interventions, a lack of effective pain relief (certainly in the early decades of the period, and for many women who could not afford decent medical care, beyond that), and women's lack of knowledge and understanding of childbirth meant it was also an event that had significant potential to be experienced as traumatic.[18] There was, then, nothing approaching a universal experience of childbirth: every mother experienced childbirth differently; each individual birth was unique. Social status played a role in how women experienced birth – in terms of access to medical care and maternal health, for example – but it was far from the only factor. In some respects, a positive outcome was as much as a matter of luck as anything else. Women's experiences in the birthing room are, like pregnancy itself, largely absent from public discourses, but they are revealed in medical case notes, in diaries and letters, and in the records of public institutions such as lying-in hospitals and workhouses.

The language of illness which pervades allusions to pregnancy in nineteenth-century writing is also in evidence in the often-veiled references to childbirth. The onset of labour is frequently described as 'illness' – not only in public discourses but in private writing as well. Ahead of the birth of one of Catherine Gladstone's eight children, her sister Lady Lyttelton wrote to her, stating: 'You are not likely to feel ill for a fortnight to come but still depend upon it, the baby is on its way.'[19] Agnes Cowper's reference to her own birth in 1874 in her autobiography, published in 1948, is indicative of a wider trend: 'During the morning [...] my mother was taken ill and at noon a small, healthy babe was ushered into the world.'[20] Fiction too was frequently silent on the subject of childbirth – at least in Britain. French writer Émile Zola's novel *La Joie de Vivre* (1883) contains an unusually lengthy and graphic description of childbirth, which at one point includes the image of a baby's arm protruding from the mother's vagina. Zola's original work emphasises the corporeal aspects of the birthing process, the messy reality of childbirth, as an English translation from 2018 reveals: 'She lay there, uncovered up to her breasts, belly open to the air and legs spread wide, without even a quiver, exposing the full spectacle of her bloody, gaping maternity.' The doctor's manipulation of the child in order to extract it is also detailed, before it finally emerges: 'There was a spurt of excrement, and with a final spasm the child slid out, in a shower of blood and foul waters.'[21] In an 1886 English translation of the book, entitled *How Jolly Life Is*, much of this description was censored. Although references to pregnancy and labour are more explicit than is typically found in the Victorian novel, all of the graphic details are removed and the birth itself reported in a manner which ultimately works to obscure it: 'After a long and agonizing period of suspense, a baby was born.'[22] The stark differences between the French and English versions of this scene exemplify the reluctance to make explicit references to childbirth in nineteenth-century British culture, not only art and fiction but also in advice literature to new mothers. Whilst pregnancy is occasionally referenced in Victorian fiction (though typically in veiled terms), labour and childbirth are almost entirely absent. *Tess of the D'Urbervilles* is representative of this trend: despite the fact that the birth of the heroine's child is central to the plot, her pregnancy is obscured – hinted at only in the references to her listlessness, depression, and self-imposed confinement to the house. These vague allusions are followed by a scene in which Tess's sister brings her the baby to nurse as she works in the fields; the birth itself is entirely effaced in the narrative. In dozens of other nineteenth-century novels, babies appear with no reference to pregnancy or childbirth, often as a 'reward' for the heroine at the end of the narrative. In Elizabeth Gaskell's *Mary Barton* (1848), we do hear Mrs Barton's cries of agony before her husband departs for the doctor (by the time they return, she is dead), and in Mrs Henry Wood's *Lord Oakburn's Daughters* (1864) we also witness the early stages of labour, but these works are the exception in terms of their portrayals of the physical aspects of maternity, and even so they avoid any explicit reference to birth itself. There is, then, a clear disjuncture between literary representations of childbirth, and women's lived experience of it.

Advice literature frequently offered reassuring words to the heavily expectant mother. *Advice to a Wife*, for example, includes some concluding remarks on pregnancy intended to calm the nervous mother-to-be:

[E]verything being in readiness for the coming event [...] all the patient has now to do is to keep up her spirits, and to look forward with confidence and hope to that auspicious moment which has been long expected, and which is now about arriving, when she will be made a mother! And which event – the birth of her child [...] – she will realise as the happiest period of her existence: she will then be amply repaid for all her cares, all her anxiety, and all her anguish[.][23]

Advice books were at pains to assure readers of the safety of childbirth. *The Wife's Handbook* declares: 'Let [the birthing mother] trust the doctor, and all will be well.'[24] *Advice to a Wife* warns against the hiring of 'a foolish ridiculous nurse' who might 'tell of any horrible case which she might have had', suggesting – entirely inaccurately – that such cases do not exist 'except in [the nurse's] imagination'.[25] For some women, these words no doubt held true, but birth was a risky business for both mother and child, and for many women the experience proved traumatic. The spectre of both maternal and infant mortality haunted the birthing room in nineteenth-century Britain, but there were also additional risks of injury to mother and child, as well as the possibility of a lengthy and painful labour with limited pain relief. To attempt to prepare women for childbirth by denying there was any risk attached to it was a dangerous strategy and, in some cases, will have contributed to women experiencing the event as traumatic. Awareness of the risks to the lives of mother and child was a source of very real anxiety for women and their families, evident in the language used in diaries and letters following successful deliveries. After the birth of her second child, Queen Victoria records her gratitude to God for having 'preserved me so mercifully through so many dangers & trials',[26] and after the birth of Princess Alice in April 1843, she writes that she and Albert 'felt so grateful to God for again so mercifully protecting me this time'.[27] In 1846, following the birth of Princess Helena, she expresses 'my humble & most fervent thanks for my safety', writing 'I was so happy & thankful all was safely over.'[28] Victoria continued to express her thankfulness in her journal following all her deliveries, writing after the birth of her youngest child, Princess Beatrice, of her 'gratitude towards an All Merciful Father in Heaven who has preserved me, & restored me almost completely to health & strength'.[29] The entries are indicative of an acknowledgement that one successful delivery did not necessarily guarantee another, and that social status could not entirely protect one from the potential dangers of childbirth. Queen Victoria would have been particularly aware of the risks: her ascension to the throne – indeed, her very existence – was a direct result of the death in childbirth of Princess Charlotte and her son.

* * *

A wealth of advice literature offered detailed information on preparations for childbirth for those who could afford such arrangements, including the hiring of attendants, recommendations on who should and should not attend, equipment needed, what to wear, and guidance on the birthing room itself. The latter should be 'large', 'airy and well-ventilated', whilst it was suggested that a 'four-post mahogany bedstead is the most convenient for a confinement'.[30] The mother should be dressed in a 'clean night gown', with 'a short bed-gown' worn over it, a 'flannel-petticoat', and a 'dressing gown'.[31] Slightly bizarrely, *The Wife's Handbook* suggests 'shoes and stockings' may be kept on.[32] The bed should be covered to protect it, and the temperature of the birthing room carefully monitored and adjusted as necessary. Attendants at the birth should comprise 'One lady friend', the doctor, and the monthly nurse.[33] Extreme care should be exercised in the selection of these attendants, and there is a wealth of advice relating to this. Amongst that offered by Chavasse is the suggestion that a 'fat dumpling of a nurse should be avoided'. 'Some nurses,' he goes on to note, 'are as fat as butter.'[34] Typically, advice literature suggests that any woman attending the birth should be a mother herself, as 'A single woman cannot so well enter into the feelings of a lying-in patient.'[35] The subtext of this is that women who have not experienced childbirth may have little understanding of what to expect. However, the mothers of birthing women were often advised against attending the birth of their grandchild: 'of all persons she is the most unsuitable, as, from her maternal anxiety, she tends rather to depress than to cheer her daughter'.[36] Queen Victoria did, however, attend the birth of her daughter Princess Alice's eldest daughter (also named Victoria) in April 1863. She gives an account of it in her journal, which to some extent endorses the idea that the mothers of birthing women were prone to maternal anxiety on such occasions: 'I stood close to the bed, stroking darling Alice's shoulder & feeling terribly agitated, but I was able to control myself completely, thank God!'[37] It was generally not recommended that husbands attend the births of their children. *Advice to a Wife* poses the question, 'Should the husband be present during the labour?' and responds, 'Certainly not; but as soon as the labour is over, and all the soiled clothes have been put out of the way, let him instantly see his wife for a few minutes, to whisper in her ear words of affection, of gratitude, and consolation.'[38] The reference to the removal of 'soiled clothes' implies the husband should absent himself from the birthing room as a matter of decorum. Husbands, then, according to this discourse, should be kept away from the messy reality of the birthing room, admitted only once the evidence of this has been cleared away. It is evident from some accounts, though, that husbands *did* attend the births of their children. Queen Victoria's descriptions of the births of her children in her journals make clear that Albert was close at hand. Following the birth of their first child, Victoria Princess Royal, she wrote in her diary: 'Dearest Albert hardly left me at all, & was the greatest support & comfort.'[39] And after the birth of her first son (later Edward VII) less than a year later, she wrote: 'I don't know what I should have done, but for the great comfort & support my beloved Albert was to me, during the whole time.'[40] That Albert was not just a passive bystander at the births of his children is suggested by Victoria's journal entry following the birth of their fifth child, Princess Helena, in May 1846: 'My beloved one was always at my side, holding my hands or arms, fanning & comforting me.'[41] He continued to support Victoria through the births of all her children, announcing the sex of Princess Beatrice upon her arrival in April 1857. Victoria again notes her gratitude in her journal, observing 'My beloved one's love and devotion, & the way he helped in so many little ways, was unbounded.'[42] In contrast to the advice offered by Chavasse and others, then, for Victoria, 'Albert's untiring, love, tenderness & care' proved her 'greatest support' during the trials of childbirth.[43] It is clear from other accounts that husbands were frequently in attendance, or at least close by. John Russell, the Viscount Amberley, records the doctor's announcement on the birth of his first child that the baby was a boy, suggesting his presence in the birthing room,[44] whilst Robert Lee includes several case studies in which husbands are consulted about the treatment of their wives during labour and delivery.[45]

Despite these detailed instructions relating to the preparation of the birthing room and those attending the birthing mother, many advice books of the period shied away from providing any explicit details of childbirth. Whilst including a wealth of advice on preparations for childbirth and its intended audience, early editions of *Advice to a Wife* efface childbirth itself. Although Chavasse elaborates on the commencement of labour, as well as recommendations on preparing for childbirth, explicit references to birth itself are notably absent. Section I, on Pregnancy, concludes with a subsection entitled 'Preparations for Labour'. This includes some discussion of the onset of labour, and advice on the appropriate time to call the medical man. The reader is advised (somewhat optimistically) that a first labour may last six hours, and the section concludes with a caution against administering too much brandy to the labouring woman and an instruction to:

> Cheer the patient, by telling her of the comparative safety of confinements, and by assuring her that, in the generality of instances, it is a natural process, and that all she has to do is to keep up her spirits, and to adhere strictly to the rules of her medical adviser, and she will do well.[46]

This section on Labour makes no allusion to the delivery, and the section following focuses on Lactation, so childbirth and its immediate after-effects are entirely obscured. Any woman ignorant of the manner in which children are born would gain little knowledge of this from this book.

The Mother's Thorough Resource Book (1860) is similarly obtuse in its allusions to childbirth. On the onset of labour, it suggests that 'certain symptoms generally indicate its approach', without elaborating on what those symptoms might be.[47] Unlike the early editions of Chavasse's work, it does include a chapter on Childbirth, but nonetheless manages to avoid any specific mention of what actually occurs. It advises the mother to obey 'the injunctions of the medical man' and says little about the birth itself. A subsection entitled 'Delivery' begins: 'When the delivery is effected, the patient may place herself composedly upon her back.'[48] Whilst the extensive market for advice literature for mothers-to-be perpetuated the idea that women were in need of guidance on pregnancy and motherhood, the silences around the female body and its functions meant they paradoxically failed to provide women with useful knowledge on the actual process of childbirth. It is impossible to know the extent to which such information was communicated privately between women, but certainly it is clear that there were women who entered the birthing room with little or no understanding of the physical aspects of childbirth they were about to experience – and the advice literature available would do nothing to alleviate this lack of knowledge.

Some later advice books for wives do provide more detail on both labour and childbirth – including later editions of Chavasse's work. The tenth edition, published in 1873, contains information about the various stages of labour, including the appearance of the 'show' (the mucus plug, the appearance of which is an indication of the start of labour) and instructions on when to 'bear down'.[49] It also recommends, if a woman 'be in great pain' letting her 'cry out', which raises the question of whether some women were encouraged to keep silent during childbirth. Lionel A. Weatherly's *The Young Wife's Own Book*, published in 1883, provides advice on the stages of labour, the best position for the mother, and what to do should the child be born without a medical attendant present.[50] H. Arthur Allbutt's *The Wife's Handbook* (1885) is particularly detailed in its advice on birth itself, and thus attempts to address the gap in poorer women's knowledge of sex and reproduction (although it is explicitly addressed to married rather than single women).[51] Allbutt provides comprehensive information on the 'signs, stages, and treatment of labour', as well as on the delivery, explaining in detail the process via which babies are born:

In the first stage the mouth of the womb expands so as to allow the baby's head to pass into the vaginal passage; this stage comes to an end with the bursting of the bag of waters in which the baby floats in the womb. In the second stage the child is forced along the passage till it is driven forth at the outer opening of the generative organs. In the third stage the after-birth is born.

These works indicate a distinct shift, then, in the latter decades of the nineteenth century, during which time more detailed information on labour and childbirth was made available to women – or at least those able to access the range of advice literature available. Allbutt notes that 'ignorance causes [...] terror' in first-time mothers, and his work is in part an attempt to address this ignorance.[52]

One contributor to *Maternity: Letters From Working Women*, whose first child was born at the very end of the nineteenth century, highlights her own ignorance in this respect:

> I had a stepmother who had had no children of her own, so I was not able to get any knowledge from her; and even if she had known anything I don't suppose she would have dreamt of telling me about these things which were supposed to exist, but must not be talked about. About a month before the baby was born I remember asking my aunt where the baby would come from. She was astounded, and did not make me much wiser.[53]

Another contributor describes how her ignorance extended through the labour itself: 'When my baby was born I had been in my labour for thirty-six hours, and did not know what was the matter with me.'[54] Recalling her experience in the early twentieth century, Maggie Fryett, born in 1891, married at 17 and eventually the mother of nine children, expounds on the state of her ignorance prior to giving birth to her first child:

> When I got married I didn't know where a baby come from even. My Mum told me nothing. I know my first baby, I was down at my mother's on a Friday night. She were reading the paper. I felt a pain [...] And she say 'That ain't half as bad as you're going to have' [...] Later on she say [...] 'You're going to have your baby. You know that, don't you?' 'I don't know,' I say. 'I were that innocent, I were.' I say 'Where the baby come from then? Does it come out from the navel? Have I got to be cut down here?' I thought they were going to have to split me. She say, 'No, it comes from where it went in.' And when my husband come, I say 'You get out of here. I don't want you near me.'[55]

Whilst middle- and upper-class women might have had greater access to advice literature for young wives, this did not necessarily serve to enlighten them. A parallel with Maggie Fryett's ignorance is found in Elma Napier's memoirs of her early life, in which she suggests that her mother (an American heiress who married Sir William Gordon-Cumming) had also assumed the baby would emerge from the navel – like Fryett – right up until the time of the birth: 'Till the day I was born [she] thought that I would come out of her navel, nearly dying of shame when she realized that every footman in the house had known otherwise.'[56] Such ignorance, even during labour itself, would have rendered childbirth a traumatic experience for some women in nineteenth-century Britain. Certainly, many women had little knowledge of the extent of the pain of childbirth prior to their first delivery. This is suggested by a letter from Lady Lyttelton to her sister, Catherine Gladstone, following the birth of her first child in 1840: 'It was much worse than I expected & I did not feel the last pains at all natural & I shall be much awed at the next time.'[57] Today, excessive pain in childbirth is one of the risk factors associated with the development of symptoms of postnatal PTSD.[58] In the nineteenth century, this would have been exacerbated by women's lack of knowledge about what to expect in childbirth.

For women who did not deliver children alive, childbirth was undoubtedly immensely more traumatic. One case which highlights this is detailed by Robert Lee in his *Lectures on the Theory and Practice of Midwifery* (1844). He attended a 30-year-old woman from Manchester (a former factory worker) in labour with her fourth child in January 1830. Despite having 'given birth to three children at the full period, without assistance', her pelvis had become so distorted as a consequence of *mollities ossium*, or *osteomalacia* (a disease characterised by a softening of the bones) during her fourth pregnancy that successful delivery was no longer possible. She was thus delivered via craniotomy – and even that proved difficult, such was the extent of the distortion. In July 1832, she was again in labour, and once more a craniotomy was carried out in order to deliver the child. Further pregnancies followed: in June 1833, whilst she was three months pregnant, Lee attended her and induced miscarriage by breaking the waters. In February 1835, he induced premature labour at the beginning of the seventh month of her pregnancy, and she delivered a stillborn child. A further attempt to induce premature labour in January 1836 failed, and the patient continued almost to full term, at which point a craniotomy was again performed over a period of several hours. This time, the patient did not recover, and died the following day. The post-mortem showed severe damage to the uterus – likely caused by the instruments used to perform the operation (see figure 8).[59] Despite the evidence from her fourth labour that it would be almost impossible for her to deliver a live child, she went on to experience four more pregnancies. We can only speculate on her exact circumstances, as her identity is unknown, but it would seem safe to assume that, as a married woman with no access to reliable contraception, she had little choice in the matter.

Although her child survived, Hannah Mitchell's experience of childbirth (in 1896) was also exceptionally difficult, as she detailed in her autobiography:

> I hoped for a good night's rest, but I scarcely had retired before my labour began. My baby was not born until the following evening, after twenty-four hours of intense suffering [...] [M]y strength was gone, and I could do no more to help myself, so my baby was brought into the world with instruments, and without an anaesthetic.
>
> This operation was sheer barbarism and ought to be regarded as 'wilful cruelty' and dealt with accordingly.[60]

As a consequence of her experience, Mitchell resolved 'to bring no more babies into the world'.[61]

Whilst some women experienced unimaginably difficult births, leaving them childless and with little prospect of future motherhood, others enjoyed far more positive experiences. Harriet Wynne, writing of her sister Betsey's experience of childbirth in September 1805, noted that 'She really had an uncommon good time' and Betsey's own account attests to this: 'I did not feel quite well this morning [...] I could not sit down at table finding myself worse. I sent for [the accoucheur] and was safely delivered at twenty minutes after nine in the evening of a nice little girl.'[62] Lady Charlotte Guest 'suffered about as little as was possible' during the birth of her eldest child in summer 1834, as she recorded in her diary (writing some three weeks after the event): 'I had written home, and had got half through a long letter at twelve o'clock, when I was taken ill. At two my dear child was born. I was soon pretty well.' She records, as well, the touching first meeting between her husband and daughter:

No one had told him of the little one till he reached the top of the stairs, when Mamma met him and told him that he had a little girl. He was quite overcome when he entered my room immediately after, and he kissed me and our dear infant. It was a very happy meeting.[63]

The birth of her fourth child, in January 1838 (only three and half years after the arrival of her first baby) was similarly straightforward – 'almost without pain', as she noted in her journal. She returned to work, translating the *Mabinogion* from Welsh to English, only five days later.[64] Just before the birth of her fifth child in March 1839, she worked on her translation for up to twelve hours a day. Her good fortune in the birthing room continued; on this occasion, she gave birth to a son before the arrival of the doctor:

I was all day quite well but woke about 3 o'clock the next morning [...] in a little pain. And within half an hour had the pleasure of giving birth to my fifth child and third boy, with less suffering than I believed possible. Even with less pain and in a shorter time than with dear little Merthyr [her fourth child] last year.

Two days later, she resumed work – correcting proofs for her book.[65] Alice Fox Pitt Rivers (née Stanley) also experienced very short labours, as her mother noted following the birth of her second child in September 1856, announcing 'Alice's safe confinement of a boy in a shorter time than the last even which only took 61 minutes'.[66]

Despite abominating the experience of being pregnant, the births of Queen Victoria's nine children also appear to have been relatively straightforward. She described her 'last five confinements' as 'being as quiet and comfortable as possible'.[67] Her first labour, in November 1840, lasted some sixteen hours, and was evidently painful, but ultimately uncomplicated, as she recorded in her journal afterwards:

Just before the early hours of the morning of the 21rst. I felt very uncomfortable & with difficulty aroused Albert from his sleep, who after a while, got Clark sent for. He came at ½ p. 2, Albert bringing him into the Bedroom. Clark said he would go to Lucock [*sic*]. Tried to get to sleep again, but by 4, I got very bad and both the Doctors arrived. My beloved Albert was so dear & kind. Lucock said the Baby was on the way

& everything was all right. We both expressed joy that the event was at hand, & I did not feel at all nervous. After a good many hours suffering, a perfect little child was born at 2 in the afternoon[.][68]

Victoria details the births of all her children in her diaries in a similar fashion, suggesting a desire to narrate the maternal experience. Though she encountered no significant problems during her nine deliveries, she does note down the extreme pain she experienced in the case of most of her births: 'my sufferings were really very severe,' she wrote, following the birth of her first son, and she recorded her 'severe suffering' again following the birth of Prince Alfred in August 1844, though it was mitigated by his arrival: 'An immense, healthy boy, was born, the joy over which, made me at once forget all I had gone through.'[69] In April 1848, following the birth of Princess Louise, she wrote: 'I shall never forget all I suffered.'[70] Her journal entry here, though, makes only brief reference to the birth, and is more concerned with the tumultuous political events in Europe, signifying her unique position as mother and monarch: for Victoria, the personal and political were often closely bound up with one another. In her first diary entry following the birth of Prince Leopold, in April 1853, she briefly describes the birth before going on to express anxiety about the Budget.[71] During the births of her two youngest children, Victoria's suffering was relieved by the use of chloroform, which she described as 'soothing, quieting & delightful beyond measure'.[72]

Lady Henrietta Stanley also seems to have fared well during the births of her many children. Following the arrival of her tenth child in 1843, her mother-in-law wrote to a friend: 'I think Henrietta expects she has a patent for producing children without trouble or delay – if she is not *quite* satisfied with this performance, which seems to me to have been quick enough in all reason.'[73] Two decades later, Henrietta's daughter, Lady Kate Amberley, despite expressing a fear of losing her own life during the birth of her first child, experienced a straightforward – and relatively brief (especially for a first labour) – delivery, though painful. Her son was born, weighing 9lbs, after less than three hours of labour. The details are recorded in her diary by her husband:

Kate felt a little uncomfortable in the morning, but perfectly well all day […] Waking at 4 a.m. I was informed by Kate that she was in pain.

It was slight, and she tried to prevent me leaving her. However, after a brief struggle, I got up and told her mother, who, finding there was no doubt, at once sent for [Dr] Merriman. The pains rapidly increased, & by 5 became terrible. From that time until delivery they never ceased. Merriman arrived at 6.30 & at 6.50 I heard him say 'It's a boy,' & heard its sweet little cry. [...] [Kate] was quite well all day but much exhausted.[74]

However, she was not so lucky with her second birth, going into premature labour with twins in March 1868. Dr Priestly[75] was sent for, but could not be found, so she was attended by 'Miss Garrett': Elizabeth Garrett Anderson – the first woman to qualify as a doctor in Britain. Both babies were breech ('foot presentations').[76] They were born within fifteen minutes of each other, but the second twin (the smaller of the two) was stillborn. The surviving baby, a daughter, in contrast with Kate's first child, weighed only 5½lbs at birth.[77] Kate's third and final labour occurred four years later, in 1872, when she gave birth to her youngest son, Bertrand Russell. As with her first experience of childbirth, the child was large (8lb 11½oz) and the labour quick but painful. The account of events again comes from her husband's entries in her diary:

> [The doctor] arrived at 5.30, & immediately after he sat down the water broke. Almost at once the head was born, & I heard baby's first scream. [...] He was born at 5.45. The pains were awful. [The doctor] remarked that not one child in 30 was as big & fat.[78]

The size of the baby suggests it may have been overdue. Due to the increased risks associated with extended pregnancies, women going up to two weeks beyond their due date in Britain today are typically induced, a process which can lead to a more painful, shorter and more intense labour, as I discovered during the birth of my second child. Induction – often accomplished via the breaking of the waters – was not uncommon in nineteenth-century Britain, but was typically used in cases where there was a perceived need to deliver the child early, such as in cases of women suffering from deformity of the pelvis where complications in delivering the child were expected. Women were not, though, generally induced when their pregnancies extended beyond the expected time. In June 1841, Lady Stanley wrote to her daughter-in-law Henrietta of a case of extended pregnancy in a neighbour, Mrs Leycester, who appears to have 'gone 6 weeks beyond her time'. Eventually, she was 'taken ill in the night & delivered of a fine girl' in a delivery that was by no means easy, the doctor concluding that 'being a month older than she should be the skull was too hard to give way'. Consequently, Mrs Leycester seems to have 'suffered severely'.[79]

A previous history of successful and straightforward childbirth was, of course, no guarantee for future deliveries, as Lady Amberley's experience indicates. Mary Wollstonecraft (see figure 7) gave birth to her first child, Fanny Imlay, in May 1794, in a labour which appears to have been straightforward, as she wrote to a friend a few days later: 'nothing could be more natural or easy than my labour [...] My nurse has been twenty years in this employment, and she tells me, she never knew a woman so well.'[80] The following day, she was able to leave her bed. Three years later, however, she lost her life shortly after the birth of her second daughter, Mary Godwin (later Mary Shelley). The births of the first six of Catherine Dickens's children appear to have been relatively straightforward, but the seventh proved difficult due to complications probably arising from a breech presentation. Although both mother and baby survived, the birth was evidently fraught with risk – to both mother and child. Dickens, in some distress, sent for Charles Locock, attendant at the births of Queen Victoria's children. Afterwards, Dickens reported that 'Kate suffered terribly' and that he had been 'horribly alarmed'.[81]

As well as the physical risks associated with childbirth, the process could also be emotionally traumatic, particularly for single women, or those in unhappy relationships. One fairly extreme example of this is the experience of Lady (Anne Isabella) Byron, who gave birth to her daughter Augusta Ada (later Ada Lovelace – considered the first ever computer programmer) in December 1815. Lady Byron had married the previous January, but it was not a happy union. Her husband, the poet Lord Byron (who had previously fathered a child with a maid, and possibly another with his half-sister) was heavily in debt, drank, was rumoured to be unfaithful to his wife, and was, at times, verbally and physically abusive. His behaviour became so extreme that his wife began to suspect he was insane.[82] During her labour, he threw furniture and bottles around in the room directly beneath the birthing room. Following the birth of the child, he enquired if it had been born dead. Shortly afterwards, he falsely informed his wife that her mother had died, and some three weeks later told her she must leave. She did – taking the child with her.[83] They were never reconciled.

All four of Byron's (legitimate and illegitimate) children were girls – the fourth born to Claire Clairmont (sister of Mary Shelley) in 1817. This may have been a source of frustration to him at a time when greater value was typically placed on sons – particularly amongst the aristocracy, for whom the inheritance of titles, wealth, and property was at stake. Indeed, Byron may not have allowed (or rather instructed) Lady Byron to leave with their baby had she produced a boy. The sex of a child could not be determined until a woman was delivered (this technology did not emerge until the 1970s), although theories abounded as to what factors determined the sex, and how the baby's sex might be ascertained prior to birth. *Advice to a Wife* supported the idea that sex is determined by the time of the month at which the child is conceived: 'conception in the first half of the time between menstrual periods produces female offspring, and male in the latter'.[84] Queen Victoria, pregnant with her first child, wrote to her Uncle Leopold: 'If all one's plagues are rewarded only by a nasty girl, I shall drown it, I think.'[85] She did indeed give birth to a girl: Victoria, Princess Royal, and wrote in her diary of her disappointment: 'alas! a girl & not a boy, as we both had so hoped & wished for. We were, I am afraid, sadly disappointed.'[86] Her response to the birth of her first son the following year is markedly different. She writes in her diary: 'at 12 m. to 11, I gave birth to a fine large boy. Oh! how happy, how grateful did I feel to that Almighty Providence.'[87] The wider public also shared this preference for male heirs to the throne: after the birth of her third son, Prince Arthur, in 1850, Victoria noted in her diary: 'People seem delighted at the birth of our 3rd son, — as much pleased as if it were the 1rst, — I am sure I am, & Mama also.'[88] On the birth of her ninth child though (a girl), having produced four male heirs already, Victoria confessed to having 'much wished for' another daughter.[89] In 1858 (having married four years previously), Marie Henriette of Austria, wife of Queen Victoria's cousin Leopold II of Belgium, gave birth to the couple's first child, a daughter. On hearing the news, Victoria, Princess Royal, recently married herself, wrote to her mother: 'I am indeed delighted that poor Marie's troubles and trials are safely over,' but she added, 'What a disappointment that it is a little girl!'[90] In fact, further 'troubles and trials' awaited Marie.

Her second child was a boy, named Leopold, but he died at the age of 9, leaving the couple with two daughters. When a fourth pregnancy – a final attempt to secure a male heir following young Leopold's death – ended in the birth of another daughter, the marriage broke down. On another occasion, upon hearing news of the birth of a third daughter to Marianne, Princess of Anhalt, and wife of Prince Frederick (Fritz) Charles of Prussia, Queen Victoria wrote to her daughter: 'poor Marianne how very unfortunate to have a third girl and how angry Fritz Carl will be [...] What will they call this poor unwelcome thing?'[91] When Victoria's second daughter, Princess Alice, gave birth to a girl in April 1863, Victoria noted in surprise: 'Neither [Alice nor her husband Louis] seem to regret its being a daughter.'[92] Following the birth of Lord and Lady Amberley's first child, a son, in 1865, Lord Russell, father of Lord Amberley and soon to be prime minister, wrote to congratulate his son: 'It is very gratifying that it should be a boy.'[93] When Consuelo Vanderbilt married the ninth Duke of Marlborough in 1895, she was told by her husband's grandmother, the Dowager Duchess of Marlborough: 'Your first duty is to have a child and it must be a son.' She then proceeded to ask, 'Are you in the family way?'[94] The new Duchess duly obliged, producing two sons (and disinheriting heir presumptive, Winston Churchill, in the process). When her second son was born in 1898, only a year after the first, her mother-in-law praised the Duchess, as she 'lay in [her] bed, exhausted but content', commenting that 'American women seem to have boys more easily than we do.'[95] Once the inheritance of titles, estates, and wealth had been secured through the appearance of at least two boys ('an heir and a spare'), however, daughters might be considered more welcome than sons. Henrietta Stanley gave birth to the ninth of her surviving children, Kate (later the Viscountess Amberley) in 1842, having previously delivered four sons and four daughters. Her mother-in-law wrote to her husband, Edward, Lord Stanley on the occasion, declaring: 'Your news was most welcome on every account – a girl is better than a boy as you have plenty of the latter & there is less trouble and expence [*sic*] in setting the former forward in the world, let alone their being often greater comforts to parents.'[96] Lord Stanley later exhibited some preference for boys, writing on the news of his daughter Blanche's delivery of her fourth child and third girl in November 1859, 'I suppose a little boy would have been more acceptable.'[97] He expressed similar sentiments following his daughter

Rosalind's delivery of a girl in July 1865: 'Very glad to hear of the safe arrival of a granddaughter even though it is not a grandson.'[98] Elma Napier, writing of her birth in 1892 in her later memoir, laments the fact that she was not a boy:

> I have made many blunders in the course of my life, but the first and the worst was that of being born a girl. Three brothers followed me in quick succession, but I have never quite lived down the humiliation of not being the heir. Mother had a bad confinement; and when she learnt what kind of a child I was she knew that she would have to do the whole thing over again.[99]

The desire for sons was not exclusive to the upper classes. Agnes Cowper, the daughter of a ship's captain and his wife, born in Liverpool in 1874, writes in her autobiography of a conversation with her mother regarding her own birth: 'My mother has since told me how extremely disappointed she felt when told that her second baby was a daughter.'[100]

However, whether producing girls or boys, members of the wealthier classes typically gave birth in the comfort of their own homes, often attended by the best medical professionals money could buy, as well as a bevy of servants. Whilst this did not, of course, guarantee a positive outcome for mother or child, it was a markedly different experience from that of women belonging to the poorer classes of society, who frequently had to contend with poverty and all the potential consequences of this on their confinements. The experience of the newly married Mrs Layton in the early 1880s was fairly typical in this respect. With her husband out of work, she 'wonder[ed] how [her] confinement was to be paid for'. Shortly before her baby arrived, he did find work as a railway carriage cleaner, providing some financial relief. Nonetheless, her experience of childbirth was undoubtedly affected by a lack of resources: whilst aristocratic women had easy access to medical practitioners and (by the mid-nineteenth century) effective pain relief, the same was not true of the working classes. Mrs Layton 'had rather a bad time' as she 'had to be delivered with forceps and had nothing to lull the pain, so had to feel all that was going on'.[101]

Those who gave birth in Britain's many workhouses (sometimes attended only by fellow workhouse inmates) typically had very limited access to any form of pain relief, or indeed to much sympathy from those who attended them – particularly if they were unmarried. There was significant anxiety around the number of single women giving birth in Britain's workhouses, with estimates from the early 1860s suggesting these totalled between 7,000 and 8,000 a year.[102] Newspaper stories often reinforced the notion that those born in the workhouse were destined to a life of poverty – and possibly of crime and immorality. This is suggested by the case of John Ketley, who in 1889 was charged by police after attacking the porter in Braintree workhouse where he was then residing. Newspaper reports noted that Ketley 'was born in the workhouse' and 'spent most of his life in prison or the workhouse'.[103] Although such stories speak to Victorian anxieties around crime, they also demonstrate the inadequacies of the workhouse system, which was not designed to offer any real opportunity for self-improvement: inevitably, those who entered the workhouse – or who were born there – were often trapped in a vicious cycle of poverty and want. Even for 'respectable' married women caught up in this cycle, escape from the workhouse (all too often temporary) frequently presented its own challenges. One 28-year-old woman, married to an abusive husband, gave birth to her fifth and sixth infants in the workhouse. Having managed to escape the institution, she lived 'in a deplorable cottage' and could not afford to clothe her youngest children. Two weeks before she was confined with her seventh child, her husband 'was fighting [her] as if she was another man', and '[t]he very night the baby was born the midwife had to send for a policeman, the husband was carrying on in such a dreadful manner.'[104] For women in situations such as these, there was little hope of escape from either the poverty in which they existed or the abusive marriages in which they found themselves trapped.

Whilst giving birth in Britain's many workhouses was often a far from positive experience, for some women, even the workhouse appeared out of reach, and multiple newspaper reports tell of women giving birth in the streets or other public places. In some instances, this was no doubt in order to conceal the birth, as suggested by multiple reports of abandoned and murdered newborn babies. In other cases, women were turned away from the workhouse – often because it was assumed that their confinement was some time off. In one tragic case, in Dewsbury in West Yorkshire, in April 1857 (the same week that Queen Victoria gave birth to Princess Beatrice at Buckingham Palace) a woman named Hannah Halstead ('an unfortunate outcast') had recently been released from Wakefield House of Correction, where she had been imprisoned for the crime of begging. She was heavily pregnant and when labour commenced (presumably with nowhere else to go) she took shelter in a privy (an outside toilet) attached to a house in Daw Green – a hamlet in the parish of Dewsbury, only a few miles from the prison in Wakefield. Here, in these inauspicious surroundings, Hannah Halstead gave birth to her baby, who, on delivery, fell into the 'night soil' (the human excrement contained in the privy). The child died shortly afterwards. Its body was taken to the Union Workhouse in Dewsbury, where a post-mortem determined that exposure and haemorrhage from the umbilical cord had contributed to the child's death. The coroner's verdict was recorded as 'died from pneumonia'.[105]

These cases illustrate the precarious position of those women without access to the trappings and privileges of wealth and status, and the cost they frequently paid in terms of the lives of their babies. All too often in nineteenth-century Britain, birth and death were close bedfellows, and even if the infant survived, its arrival might still herald the death of the mother. Women such as Hannah Halstead were at greater risk of harm as a consequence of their poverty, but money, wealth, and 'respectability' could not protect women entirely from the potential dangers of childbirth. Hygiene, medical practices, maternal health, and poverty were all significant factors, but luck also played a key role. The inequities of nineteenth-century society, though, meant poor women in many respects faced an increased risk. Tens of thousands of women lost their lives during or shortly after delivery; some were publicly mourned but there were countless others whose identities and experiences have been entirely lost to history.

4

A Dangerous Business:
Maternal Mortality

I shall not long enfold thee thus – not long, but well
The everlasting arms, my Babe! will never let thee go.
Caroline Bowles[1]

Claremont House in Surrey today houses a school, but in 1816, it was presented as a wedding gift by George IV to his daughter and heir, Princess
Charlotte and her husband Prince Leopold, who moved into the property
in August that year. The young couple did not enjoy the property for
long, though. In autumn 1817, Charlotte and Leopold were in their home
awaiting the birth of their first child, who, if all went well, would one
day become monarch. The baby was expected around 19 October, but by
early November had still not arrived. On 3 November, signs of the baby's
imminent arrival finally materialised. Following a gruelling labour, and
some two weeks after her due date, Princess Charlotte gave birth to a stillborn baby boy, after a labour lasting some fifty hours. She was attended by
Sir Richard Croft, previously physician to her grandfather, King George
III. Although it was clear the baby was in a difficult position, Sir Richard
declined to use forceps, and instead allowed the birth to progress naturally.
Caesarean section was not considered due to the high risk it posed to the
life of the mother. Croft's decision not to intervene and its implications
were later the subject of much debate, and a driving factor in his suicide a
few months subsequent to this scene. Although the child's birth had been

much anticipated, and his loss was felt by many, Princess Charlotte was young and healthy, and in the first few hours following the birth of her dead son, there seemed every prospect of recovery and future pregnancies. A circular issued at ten o'clock on the evening of 5 November, and printed in *The Times* the following day, reported the death of Princess Charlotte's baby but added that 'Her Royal Highness is doing extremely well.'[2] However, just after midnight on 6 November, her condition suddenly deteriorated – probably due to internal haemorrhaging. She woke with crippling stomach pains, and Sir Richard found her vomiting and bleeding. She died in the early hours of the morning and, a few days later, was buried with her infant son. She was just 21 years old at the time of her death, which plunged a nation into mourning and a monarchy into crisis.

In December 1888, in Stockport, Cheshire, a young, unmarried woman, heavily pregnant, was discovered lying on the floor of a derelict shop. Her name was Sarah Isabella Pitcher, and she was just 22 years old – the daughter of a paint-maker from Manchester. She had previously worked as a domestic servant, but had been forced to relinquish her position following the discovery of her pregnancy. The exact circumstances which led to her pregnancy are not known, but female servants were at risk of sexual abuse from other members of the household. Whether or not her pregnancy resulted from a consensual relationship, finding herself jobless, homeless, and pregnant, it was almost inevitable that she would end up at the workhouse, though she appears to have tried to avoid this eventuality. In the six weeks following her dismissal, she was forced into 'a most precarious existence', in a world with an unforgiving attitude towards pregnancy outside of marriage.[3] Following her discovery in the shop, she was taken to Stockport Workhouse, where, like Princess Charlotte seven decades previously, she gave birth to a stillborn child. Conditions in the workhouse were particularly difficult at this time: a few years later, in 1894, a commission found that the women's ward was 'dangerously overcrowded', and that 'the patients required more nursing and hospital treatment than the nurses were able to give them'.[4] Some of the wards on the female hospital block were described as 'no better than barns'.[5] Shortly after the birth, Sarah was gripped by convulsions – possibly a consequence of pre-eclampsia (a condition of pregnancy characterised by high blood pressure, which, if left untreated, can cause seizures and prove fatal) – and died. She was buried in the Southern Cemetery in Manchester on 15 December 1888.

✳ ✳ ✳

The causes of the deaths of these two women, resulting directly from complications during childbirth, are preventable or treatable today. Had they been living in the twenty-first century, it is likely that they, and their children, would have survived. Childbirth in the nineteenth century, though, was a risky business, and maternal mortality affected women from every class of society – as indicated by the wildly different social statuses of these women. Nevertheless, they were relatively unlucky: the maternal mortality rate in Britain during this period was approximately 5 per 1,000 births, or 0.5 per cent, remaining relatively stable throughout the century despite fluctuations in differing environments and circumstances. This compares unfavourably with today's rates of approximately seven deaths in 100,000 births, or 0.007 per cent, but, nonetheless, most women in nineteenth-century Britain could expect to survive childbirth. Despite this, Princess Charlotte and Sarah Pitcher are representative of thousands of other women who died as a direct result of pregnancy or childbirth in this period and whose deaths are largely forgotten. The exact number of women who died over the course of the century is difficult to estimate, as causes of deaths were not always accurately recorded – particularly prior to the introduction of civil registration in 1837. Even after this, the cause of death as it appeared on death certificates did not always indicate if a woman was pregnant or had recently given birth, and in cases where women had died as a consequence of illegal abortions, the cause of death might be deliberately obscured. The 1877 *Annual Report of the Registrar-General* suggests that in the thirty years between 1847 and 1876 alone, over 100,000 women in England died in childbirth,[6] pointing to the fact that over the course of the nineteenth century, hundreds of thousands of women lost their lives as a consequence of complications during pregnancy and childbirth. Many of these women died in extreme pain, leaving husbands widowers and children motherless. Doctors could do little to prevent haemorrhaging, or to arrest the development of infection; indeed, a lack of understanding of hygiene practices meant doctors were sometimes responsible for spreading infection. Despite some improvements in medical care and understanding across the period, pregnancy and childbirth remained fraught with risk to the life of the mother. Behind the statistics lie a multitude of human tragedies: of suffering, grief, lives cut short, and maternal bonds broken. These figures represent the stories of thousands of women who died to become mothers in nineteenth-century Britain.

The women whose deaths are detailed here spanned the social spectrum: from the very wealthiest to the poorest and most destitute. Those in this latter category often found themselves – like Sarah Pitcher – giving birth in the workhouse, and this could be fraught with particular danger. Charles Dickens's *Oliver Twist* (1838) begins with the birth of the eponymous protagonist in the workhouse, closely followed by the death of his mother: 'The patient [...] stretched out her hand towards the child. The surgeon deposited it in her arms. She imprinted her cold white lips passionately on its forehead; passed her hands over her face; gazed wildly round; shuddered; fell back – and died.'[7] The death of Oliver's mother reflects the experiences of many nineteenth-century mothers – poor, and often unmarried – whose lives ended in similarly tragic circumstances. It leaves Oliver alone and unprotected and paves the way for the story that follows. Her fate mirrors that of many other women throughout the period who died in Britain's workhouses during or shortly after childbirth. The grief that the deaths of women like Sarah Pitcher occasioned is largely undocumented, but for women whose lives are more closely detailed in the archives, we can gain a sense of the loss that was felt. Princess Charlotte's death was received as a national tragedy, giving rise to a public expression of grief comparable to that which followed the death of another Princess of Wales 180 years later. On the day after Princess Charlotte's death, *The Times* reported that 'The regret of the public throughout the metropolis was proportionate to the magnitude of this double disaster. It is but little to say, that we never recollect so strong and general an expression and indication of sorrow.'[8] Dozens of newspaper, artistic, and literary tributes followed, including a poem by the popular poet Anna Laetitia Barbauld, which encapsulated the nation's grief – as well as the indiscriminate nature of maternal mortality:

> Yes – Britain mourns; as with electric touch
> For youth, for love, for happiness destroyed,
> Her universal population melts
> In grief spontaneous, and hard hearts are moved,
> And rough unpolished natures learn to feel

For those they envied levelled in the dust
By fate's impartial stroke[.][9]

A monument depicting Charlotte's ascension to heaven was erected in St George's Chapel, Windsor, funded by private subscription (see figure 6). Yet her death was also, for her husband, father, and mother, a more personal tragedy. Charlotte's father, the Prince Regent, was overwhelmed with grief, and her mother fainted on hearing the news. The first reports in *The Times* described her husband, Prince Leopold, as 'distracted and inconsolable'.[10] Some two weeks after her death, his physician and advisor, Baron Stockmar, wrote to a friend describing Leopold's grief: '[Y]ou can picture the state in which he is. He is too good, too resolute, too devout to give himself over to despair, though life seems already to have lost all value for him, and he is convinced that no feeling of happiness can ever again enter his heart.' Over forty years later, Stockmar confirmed the lasting impact of Charlotte's death on Leopold, writing that 'He has never recovered the feeling of happiness which had blessed his short married life.'[11]

The grief experienced by Charlotte's loved ones on her death mirrors that of thousands of other families in nineteenth-century Britain. In 1893, a woman named Lily Clarke 'gave birth to a stillborn baby and died herself in less than twenty-four hours'. Years later, her sister, Alice Maude Chase, wrote down her recollections of that time: 'Our grief was unspeakable. […] [M]y mother's moans and wails nearly broke our hearts and life seemed to stand still suddenly.'[12] This 'unspeakable grief' affected millions over the course of the century. It is well documented in the case of the royal family, but the losses of ordinary people, grieving for mothers, daughters, wives and sisters who died in childbirth, are for the most part unrecorded.

In *Northanger Abbey*, published in the same year Princess Charlotte lost her life, Jane Austen offers an ironic commentary on the depiction of maternal mortality in the popular novel via the introduction of her heroine, Catherine Morland: 'Her mother […] had three sons before Catherine was born; and instead of dying in bringing the latter into the world, as anybody might expect, she still lived on, – lived to have six children more, to see them growing up around her, and to enjoy excellent health herself.'[13] Austen was right to identify maternal mortality as a popular fictional trope, and it was one to which authors continued to revert throughout the period.[14] However, whilst it may have represented a convenient means of dispensing with unwanted fictional mothers, such representations were in some respects reflective of a disturbing reality. Whilst the maternal mortality rate indicates that women survived the vast majority of births, a birth rate of an average of five children per mother meant the individual risk for women was somewhat higher than this.[15] For women bearing five children, the mortality rate can be broadly calculated at 2.5 per cent across her childbearing years, with individual factors – such as maternity care, birth settings, previous birth experiences, and medical conditions – playing a significant role. This increased individual lifetime risk meant that consequently, as one textbook on midwifery noted, there was widespread familiarity with maternal death, and thus with the dangers of childbirth:

> There is scarcely an individual who has not to lament the loss of some dear relative or connexion in childbed. Many a husband is now weeping over the yet scarcely cold corpse of a dear wife, who has fallen a blooming victim to what ought to have been the joyful consequence of her hymeneal vows; and many a mother is lamenting the untimely fate of her daughter, who was consoling herself with the fond hopes of experiencing, when the pains were forgotten, the pleasures of being a mother[.][16]

Despite significant improvements in maternal mortality rates compared with the preceding centuries,[17] there remained a widely recognised association between childbirth and death. The risks involved in childbirth evidently played on the minds of some women during the final weeks and days of pregnancy, which were often a time of hopeful anticipation, but also of anxiety – particularly for first-time mothers, nervous at the prospect of giving birth. In 1819, Kate Courtauld wrote to her sister, in anticipation of and apprehension about the conclusion of her pregnancy: 'It may be I shall see you no more here – none of you any more. I cannot with complacency fix plans for a distant period – when I may perhaps have no concern with all that is done under the sun.'[18] In 1858, shortly before the birth of her first grandchild, Queen Victoria wrote to her pregnant daughter to try and reassure her about the impending birth: 'Don't dread the denouement; there is no need of it; and don't talk to ladies about it, as they will only alarm you.'[19] In fact, it was a difficult birth, and at one point there were fears for the life of both mother and baby;

both survived, but the baby, later Wilhelm II of Germany, was left with a permanent injury to his arm. Writing in 1865, a few days before the birth of her first child, Kate, Lady Amberley reflected on the possibility of her own death: 'If I should die I should like him [her husband] to have [the baby] much with him & make a great companion of it.'[20] Hannah Mitchell, in the late nineteenth century, 'feared the ordeal' but 'tried to keep my fears to myself, remembering that other women got over it, not once only, but many times'.[21] In Queen Victoria's case, anxieties about the possible outcome of her first pregnancy extended far beyond the monarch herself, and became an issue which occupied parliament, the press, and the wider public. Her death in childbirth, and the child's survival, would leave a considerable power vacuum until the child came of age. In July 1840, just under four months before Victoria delivered her first child, parliament passed the Regency Act, which granted Albert the power of Regent in the event of Victoria's death until their oldest child came of age. There was much debate and some opposition to the Bill, alluded to by Lady Charlotte Guest in her diary:

> It is true Prince Albert is very young, not yet of age, that he is a stranger, speaking our language but imperfectly, and knowing nothing of our habits and customs, and that the power he would have, in the event of so melancholy an event as our dear Queen's death, would be very great.[22]

In the event, of course, Victoria survived the birth, and the eight that followed, and was predeceased by Albert. The widespread anxiety over this issue, though, represents the more personal maternal experience of nineteenth-century women played out on the public stage: whilst most women had to contend with their own mortality in the later stages of pregnancy, in Victoria's case, it was the future of the monarchy at stake.

The popular perception of the risks of childbirth is also illustrated by the practice of 'churching', which was common throughout the period. This involved a brief ceremony of thanksgiving for the survival of the mother following childbirth.[23] In a pamphlet on the churching of women, first published in the 1820s and reissued several times in the decades that followed, the Reverend Edward Berens addresses birthing women directly: 'you doubtless, as your time drew near, often addressed your prayers to heaven for preservation and support. You now rejoice [...]

that your prayers were heard.'[24] He implores his reader: 'As your life has been preserved to you, as you are continued in the land of the living, *walk therein before the lord*.'[25] In another work on the subject, *The Mother's Public Thanksgiving* (1860), the anonymous author declares, 'All persons must agree that it is a most excellent custom for mothers to return their thanks to God after their safe deliverance.'[26] The implication, clearly, is that survival of childbirth was by no means guaranteed. The multiple depictions of maternal mortality in nineteenth-century fiction, then, are not altogether unrealistic in their portrayals of the dangers of childbirth. They are, however, frequently employed primarily to forward the plot and are often highly sentimentalised. Such representations are not intended to offer a *realistic* portrayal of the maternal experience, or necessarily to highlight the dangers of childbirth. They rarely address the question of how or why these women were dying; mothers' physical experiences and the specific details of their deaths are obscured. Memoirs, published for the reading public in general, are often as circumspect about the details of maternal mortality as the novel. James Sherman's memoir of scientist, abolitionist, and Quaker, William Allen, published in 1851, provides this brief account of the death of Allen's wife, Mary, shortly after the birth of their first child (a girl also named Mary): 'On 6 September, 1797, she gave birth to a daughter; and on the 11th, four days only after her accouchement, her spirit was summoned to put on immortality.'[27] Tragically, in 1823, Allen's daughter Mary, whose mother lost her life giving birth to her, also died shortly after the birth of her child. The cause of death in her case, according to Allen's diary, was a 'severe bilious attack'.[28] This vague description is suggestive of puerperal fever, sometimes known as childbed fever, an infection which could set in within a few days of childbirth, frequently leading to sepsis and death.

The two most prevalent causes of maternal mortality in the nineteenth century were puerperal fever and haemorrhaging.[29] One work estimated that puerperal fever caused seven out of eight deaths in childbirth.[30] The Registrar-General's report gives a lower estimate for the years 1872–6, but nonetheless suggests over half of maternal deaths resulted from puerperal fever.[31] Symptoms often began with slight chills and a rapid pulse a few hours or days after birth, frequently followed by abdominal pain, mental distress, and rapid deterioration, leading all too often to death. There was no effective treatment, and recovery once infection had set in was more or less a matter of luck. Feminist writer and novelist Mary Wollstonecraft was one of many thousands of victims of puerperal fever. Mary's early life might be described as precariously middle class. Her grandfather was a successful businessman, but her father, a somewhat less successful farmer, squandered much of his inheritance. She was, though, particularly well educated for a woman at this time. She was 38 when she died shortly after the birth of her second child – a daughter also named Mary (later Mary Shelley) – in September 1797.[32] Wollstonecraft's first child, Fanny Imlay, was born three years previously. This earlier birth was straightforward, but the birth of her second child was more complicated. Although the baby was delivered, and appeared healthy, the placenta was retained. Dr Louis Poignand, the attending physician, was tasked with removing it in order to try to prevent continued bleeding and infection: Mary had already suffered several fainting fits consequent on loss of blood. This was rendered more difficult by the fact that the placenta appeared to have broken up. It was an invasive, lengthy, and painful procedure, and, with a lack of understanding about the spread of germs, carried a high risk of infection. Initially, the procedure appeared to be a success, and Mary recovered sufficiently to rest and nurse her baby. But a few days later, she began to exhibit signs of infection. Her doctor deemed it unwise for her to continue nursing the baby, and instead puppies were brought in 'to draw off the milk'.[33] Her condition quickly deteriorated, and despite efforts to save her, on the morning of Sunday, 10 September, she died, leaving her husband a widower and her two young daughters motherless. A friend, present at the birth and subsequent death, wrote afterwards that 'Every skilful effort that medical knowledge of the highest class could make, was exerted to save her.'[34] Ironically, those efforts may well have contributed to her death, by introducing or compounding the infection that subsequently killed her. Her death had a profound effect on her husband and children. Her husband, writer and philosopher William Godwin, describes with poignancy the hope and despair that alternately gripped him in the days and hours leading up to her death in his memoir of his wife published the following year:

> I [...] fought to suppress every idea of hope. The greatest anguish I have any conception of, consists in that crushing of a new-born hope which I had already two or three times experienced. If Mary recovered, it was

well, and I should see it time enough. But it was too mighty a thought to bear to be trifled with.[35]

Following her death, he wrote in the agony of grief to a friend: 'I have not the least expectation that I can now ever know happiness again.'[36] Some eighteen years subsequent to this, the daughter whose birth had ultimately led to her mother's death began to face her own maternal trials. Mary Shelley suffered a miscarriage which nearly cost her her life, and although she survived the births of her own four children, only one would live beyond the age of 3. The subtext of maternal loss is central to the backdrop of her iconic gothic novel, *Frankenstein* (1818). For this family, as for so many others of the time, motherhood and death were closely intertwined.

Mrs (Isabella) Beeton, best known as the author of the *Book of Household Management* (1861), was another well-known victim of puerperal fever. She died shortly after the birth of her fourth child in February 1865. Whilst there were various contributory factors to the onset of puerperal fever, including premature breaking of waters, protracted labour, and placenta retention, undoubtedly a major cause was the medical attendants themselves. Doctors and midwives were often unknowingly responsible for introducing and spreading infection as a consequence of a lack of basic hygiene practices, such as hand washing and the cleaning of medical equipment. This is in part proved by the fact that maternal mortality rates tended to be higher in lying-in hospitals than for women giving birth at home. In the hospital setting, germs could easily be transferred from patient to patient via the doctors. Maternal death rates varied in different hospitals at different periods: one report in 1867 put the death rate at the Queen Charlotte Lying-in Hospital in London between 1857 and 1863 as high as 40 per 1,000 births, and suggested (though did not fully explain) that a key reason for the high mortality rate here was the number of *single* women the hospital treated. By contrast, the number of maternal deaths for the British Lying-in Hospital between 1849 and 1861 averaged seven in 1,000 – only marginally higher than the national maternal mortality rate for the period. On the whole, though, giving birth in a lying-in hospital was riskier than delivering at home.

From surviving case notes, much insight can be gained into the often-traumatic experiences of women who died at the various lying-in hospitals across the country. One particularly tragic case is that of Mary Stephenson, who died aged 31 in February 1824 at Newcastle Lying-in Hospital after giving birth to her fourth child. The hospital, established in 1760 (the first outside London), catered specifically to poor married women. Mary was first admitted to the hospital in October 1822, during the labour of her third child. She suffered from a distorted pelvis – possibly a birth defect, or perhaps the result of rickets. This meant she struggled to deliver her children. Her first baby, born around 1813, was delivered via craniotomy. Her second child, a daughter, was born prematurely at seven months in July 1820. This child survived the birth, although for how long is unclear. Her third labour in 1822 also ended in a craniotomy, after an attempt to deliver using forceps, which lasted two hours, failed. So when she was admitted to the hospital at full term with her fourth child in 1824, she had already experienced significant trauma, losing two of her three babies in a particularly horrific manner. The distortion of the pelvis made it unlikely this fourth child would survive, and doctors anticipated a similar outcome. For a short time, though, it seemed luck was on her side. The baby – another girl – was small, enabling delivery despite Mary's problems with her pelvis, and she showed encouraging 'marks of vitality' after her arrival.[37] The placenta was also delivered and initially it appeared Mary would make 'a favourable recovery'.[38] However, two days after the delivery, she began to experience shivering, accompanied by pain in the abdomen: the first worrying signs of puerperal fever. Her condition deteriorated rapidly, and she died on 13 February 1824 at 2 a.m. Having finally successfully delivered a child at full term, Mary did not live to raise her daughter. She was buried in the nearby St John's churchyard the day after her death.

It is unclear whether the infection from which Mary Stephenson died was transmitted to her via the doctors. For much of the period, in contrast to the modern emphasis on the importance of good hygiene in medical care, there was a reluctance amongst medical practitioners to recognise the role of their own practices in cases of puerperal fever. Writing to Dr Robert Lee in a letter subsequently published in the *London Medical Gazette* in 1832, Dr William Campbell stated, inaccurately: 'I am [...] impressed with the belief that, unless the practitioner has been engaged in the dissection of the bodies of those who have fallen victims, the disease cannot be conveyed by him, from females labouring under it, to others recently delivered.'[39] He did concede, however, that puerperal fever might be spread by doctors attending women in labour after carrying out post-mortems, and describes his own dangerous hygiene practices which led him to this conclusion. These include attending several deliveries wearing clothes in which he had earlier carried material removed during a post-mortem examination of a woman who had died from puerperal fever: a number of these patients subsequently succumbed to the same fate. Similarly, he failed to wash his hands sufficiently or change his clothes after assisting at a post-mortem of another woman who died from puerperal fever before attending two other patients, both of whom died from the same cause. Consequent to these events, he shifted his practice and stopped performing post-mortems prior to attending women in child-birth. By the 1870s, there was wider recognition that puerperal fever could be spread by doctors and midwives. In 1875, midwife Elizabeth Marsden was convicted of the manslaughter of two women after ignoring a surgeon's warning not to attend any births for a period of time in consequence of several of her patients contracting puerperal fever. Three more women in her care subsequently died.[40] A similar case was brought against another midwife, Elizabeth Sarah Berry, in 1891, following the death from puerperal fever of three of her patients, but in this instance, there was no conviction.[41]

In cases where complications arose, the maternal death rate was inevitably much higher. Dr Robert Lee's *Three Hundred Consultations in Midwifery* (1864) provides some – often graphic – insight into the experiences of women encountering difficulties in labour and childbirth. In around one-sixth of the cases detailed, the mother's life was lost, whilst the survival rate for the babies in these cases was even lower, with only around half surviving the birth and one-third of the cases terminating in craniotomies. This high mortality rate for both mothers and babies in these cases is not illustrative of wider outcomes, or even of Lee's own practice as an obstetrician, as he specifically details only difficult cases, which inevitably involved a higher mortality rate. He expresses reservations about the use of both forceps and chloroform in his work, and he is evidently a firm believer in the necessity of craniotomies 'if the condition of the mother is such as to render delivery absolutely necessary'.[42] It was due to the high mortality risks to mothers that Caesarean sections were rarely performed in nineteenth-century Britain and most medical men were in agreement that it was right to preserve the life of the mother over that of the child. Caesareans were, however, more common in continental Europe, particularly in Catholic countries, where religious doctrines outlawed inflicting harm on the unborn child, and thus effectively prohibited the performance of destructive operations such as craniotomies. The debates over whether to privilege the life of the mother or that of the unborn child anticipate some of the recent debates over abortion, and in several US states today, following recent developments there, legislation works to protect the foetus no matter the circumstances of the pregnancy or the risks to the mother. In his earlier work, *Clinical Midwifery* (1842), Lee notes that out of twenty-seven recorded cases of Caesarean sections, 'in twenty-five of them it was fatal to the mother'.[43] Despite Lee's emphasis on saving the life of the mother, even at the expense of the child, his work nonetheless demonstrates the significant number of women who died during or shortly after childbirth whilst in his care. These case studies are particularly helpful for the insight they provide into many of these women's final hours, and stand in stark contrast to the romanticised, sanitised deaths in childbirth that mark the nineteenth-century novel.

First labours frequently carried additional risk for the mother, and consequently for the baby too. Problems which might result in a difficult labour and delivery, such as the distorted pelvis of Mary Stephenson, were likely to go undetected until the labour itself. First labours also tend to last longer, and protracted labours carry increased risk of infection, particularly once the waters have broken. Today, precautions are taken to manage the risks involved in such cases: after my waters broke during my second labour, but contractions failed to start, I was prescribed antibiotics to reduce the risk of infection. In the nineteenth century, there was also a risk of what medical men frequently termed 'exhaustion' – literally a draining away of strength which might be attributed to a wide variety of causes but appeared to be exacerbated by long labours. This increased the likelihood of medical intervention, in the form of forceps or craniotomy, and the associated risks (medical instruments, like the hands of medical professionals, carried a risk of infection). Lee details several cases of first labours terminating in the death of the mother in his work, including that of a 22-year-old unidentified woman who suffered a 'severe' first labour, but who eventually gave birth to a living child. Shortly afterwards, though, she began to experience loss of consciousness, and subsequently died. A post-mortem carried out on her body pointed to the cause of death as the rupturing of 'the longitudinal sinus of the brain' (brain haemorrhage).[44] Another case of a woman who died following her first labour suggests the difficulties in treating conditions that were not properly understood in the nineteenth century, as well as the likelihood that medical treatments and interventions themselves contributed to maternal mortality. The woman's symptoms, which included headache, abdominal pain, swelling of the legs, and convulsions, suggest she was probably suffering from pre-eclampsia. Today, most cases of pre-eclampsia cause no problems and improve soon after the baby is delivered. But limited awareness and understanding of the condition in nineteenth-century Britain meant it posed a very real risk to expectant women who developed these symptoms. In this case, doctors attempted to treat the woman by taking 14floz of blood from her temples: bloodletting as a form of treatment for a wide range of disorders remained common practice throughout the century. Although it is possible this may have reduced her high blood pressure, it was also potentially dangerous given that further blood loss was likely during childbirth. Following several fits, the patient lost consciousness, and was subsequently delivered, via forceps, of a stillborn baby. She died shortly afterwards. As in this case, many of the women who died during their first labour were young. However, Lee includes the case of one patient whose first child was born at the age of 40. Pregnancies in older women carry increased risks – including of stillbirth, as occurred here. As with the previous case, the mother experienced convulsions, again perhaps indicating pre-eclampsia (also more common in older mothers). She died shortly after the delivery of her dead child. Despite the fits, the doctor treating her concluded that the cause of death was likely 'exhaustion', having noted that 'During pregnancy, there had been a very excited state of the brain and disturbed sleep.'[45] As with the previous case, the treatments proffered here – beef tea, arrowroot, brandy, ammonia, and an opiate – were likely ineffectual and some potentially dangerous.

Whilst there were increased risks associated with first labours, a large number of births carried other risks, such as a higher chance of uterine rupture and postpartum haemorrhaging. Women who gave birth multiple times were more likely to experience pregnancies close together, and to give birth later in life, both of which also carried additional risk to the mother. To this day, older mothers continue to face a greater risk of pre-eclampsia and complications during delivery, whilst the NHS advises that women should leave a gap of at least twelve to eighteen months between pregnancies, in part to reduce the maternal mortality risk.[46] Lee's case studies include several mothers of multiple children who died during childbirth, and in some of these cases it is likely the risk of mortality was increased by the patient's history of multiple births. One patient for whom this would appear to be the case is described as the 'mother of a large family'. A seemingly straightforward labour concluded with the rupturing of the uterus, and the patient 'died before the child was wholly extracted'.[47] It seems likely in this case that the uterus was at greater risk of rupturing as a consequence of the number of prior births. Another of Lee's patients – a mother of fifteen children – died following severe haemorrhaging, the risk of which may again have been raised due to the number of previous births experienced. There is a grim irony in the fact that for these women, successful childbearing may ultimately have contributed to their deaths in childbirth. This may have been the case for Catherine Dickens, who bore ten children, but died of cervical cancer in 1879 at the age of 64; the risk of this disease increases with multiple deliveries, and thus her maternal history may well have been a factor in the development of the disease which killed her.[48]

Although pregnancy was, on the whole, less risky than childbirth itself, complications during this time could also terminate in the death of the mother – particularly as effective treatments for dangerous conditions in the nineteenth century were relatively limited. One such condition which, left untreated, could have severe consequences is *hyperemesis gravidarum*, characterised by severe vomiting in pregnancy. This can be extremely debilitating and can cause severe dehydration, although it can be treated today with anti-sickness drugs and intravenous fluids. Public awareness of this was raised in the twenty-first century after Catherine, then Duchess of Cambridge, received treatment for it during her three pregnancies, but in the nineteenth century, successfully replacing lost fluids was a more difficult task. In early 1855, Charlotte Brontë began to display symptoms of *hyperemesis gravidarum*: she was 38, and had married the previous year, having wed relatively late in life at a time when women tended to marry in their early- to mid-twenties. She experienced severe nausea and vomiting and it seems certain she was newly pregnant. In January 1855, she wrote to her friend Ellen Nussey, describing what appear to be some of the early signs of pregnancy: 'My health has been really very good [...] till about ten days ago, when the stomach seemed quite suddenly to lose its tone – indigestion and continual faint sickness have been my portion ever since.'[49] These symptoms left her feeling 'much reduced and very weak' – malnourished and dehydrated. Her long-time servant, Martha, 'tried to cheer her with the thought of the baby that was coming',[50] but the sickness was far beyond that normally experienced in pregnancy, and severely debilitating. At the end of January, a doctor was consulted and suggested 'that her illness would be of some duration, but that there was no immediate danger',[51] but a month later she continued to suffer severely, and her vomit was now mixed with blood. A brief improvement, bringing some hope of recovery, was succeeded by further deterioration. She was around four months pregnant when, on the morning of Saturday, 31 March 1855, the church bells in Haworth – the small Yorkshire village where she lived – rang out to announce her death. She was the last of the six Brontë siblings to die, and was survived by her father, the Reverend Patrick Brontë, and husband, Arthur Bell Nicholls. Her biographer, Elizabeth Gaskell, records some of the final words she spoke to her husband, signifying the destruction of her maternal and marital hopes: 'Oh! [...] I am not going to die, am I? He will not separate us, we have been so happy.'[52] Charlotte had achieved considerable literary success with the hugely popular *Jane Eyre* (1847) and was beginning to write her fifth novel. She had managed to escape the diseases so prevalent in the nineteenth century that had claimed the lives of her five siblings (typhus and tuberculosis), but, ultimately, she was unable to escape the dangers that accompanied pregnancy and childbirth. Robert Lee's case studies also include details of several women who died during pregnancy, prior to reaching full term. Unlike the case of Charlotte Brontë, little is known about their lives and identities, but we do gain some insight into their final moments. They include a 22-year-old woman, who, like Brontë, was recently married and experiencing symptoms of morning sickness. She was between three and four months pregnant when she began to experience severe pains in the abdomen. Several examinations were carried out, and various drugs administered, but she died on 23 June 1850. An examination of her body indicated her death had been caused by complications relating to the distension of the bladder. In other cases detailed by Lee, death followed miscarriage or resulted from haemorrhaging in the early to mid-stages of pregnancy.

It is evident from Lee's case studies that many of the women he treated experienced extreme physical and emotional suffering. In some cases, the hours leading up to their deaths were clearly traumatic in the extreme. In one case, labour lasted forty-eight hours, with the doctor spending five hours 'in violent dragging' in order to deliver the child.[53] The infection from which the patient died may well have been caused by the doctor himself, or from the instruments used. Another woman spent some four days in labour before doctors attempted a forceps delivery, but this was unsuccessful, despite the 'considerable traction used'.[54] Eventually, a craniotomy was performed, but even then it proved difficult to deliver the baby, which was essentially destroyed in the process. Lee notes that 'Two hours of violent efforts were spent in delivering this child, and the mother died soon after.'[55] In another case, a patient suffering with a distorted pelvis experienced a long labour. As in the previous case, Lee resorted to craniotomy in order to extract the baby, and again the infant was destroyed in the attempt. This was a lengthy process, and after several hours the patient was allowed to rest and an opiate given. A subsequent attempt to deliver the remainder of the child failed, and the patient died only partially delivered. These were violent and traumatic deaths. It is difficult to imagine the distress experienced by these women, and the emotional devastation they must have felt at the destruction of their infants. The physical pain must also have been extreme: there is no indication that any form of anaesthetic was given in the first two cases, and it was only administered several hours after the process of extraction commenced in the latter case. Lee's work is concerned with the facts of the case, but in one or two instances he does refer to the resulting grief following the deaths of women in childbirth. Detailing the death of one patient from uterine haemorrhage, he notes 'the distressing scene usually witnessed in such melancholy cases rapidly followed',[56] and in another instance he refers to the 'great grief' of the patient's relatives in the aftermath of her death.[57] Reading through Lee's case notes today, these allusions offer a brief insight into the grief resulting from the deaths of women during childbirth, but it is telling that he rarely – and only ever briefly – touches on the emotional devastation such deliveries and their fatal outcomes must have caused.

Works such as Lee's case studies of midwifery allow us glimpses of the often-traumatic experiences of women who died as a consequence of childbirth in nineteenth-century Britain. Further insights can be found in coroners' inquests of such deaths, which were frequently reported in the newspapers. Whilst most of Lee's cases appear to be middle-class women, these reports at times provide snapshots of the experiences of women at the other end of the social scale, often without any medical support. One such case is that of 28-year-old Eliza Bollends – an unmarried servant whose death was reported in the *Nottinghamshire Guardian* in 1865. Ellen Killburn, Eliza's roommate and fellow servant, woke early one morning and discovered Eliza 'had been delivered of a child'. Eliza confessed that the father of the child was 'a young man at Deeping, Lincolnshire', and expressed a wish to die. Without any medical consultation, she was permitted to leave the house, at her own request – although the mistresses of the house, the Misses Cheetham, 'sent word that they would sooner have her removed if it was safe': an unmarried servant giving birth to a baby was clearly a source of scandal for a respectable household. A few days later, a surgeon was called to examine Eliza and discovered her 'in a state of collapse'. She died shortly afterwards, 'from exhaustion, consequent loss of blood, the exertions of removing, and exposure to cold'.[58] The neglect she experienced is indicative of the contempt in which poor, unmarried mothers were held by many in nineteenth-century Britain: whilst medical and advice literature urged married women to undergo a period of 'confinement' before and after childbirth, Eliza was quickly removed, and did not have access to medical advice until it was too late. The fact of Eliza being an unmarried mother is significant: evidence suggests the maternal mortality rate was significantly higher amongst unmarried women – partly because they were less likely to seek or receive medical support, and more likely to attempt to conceal a pregnancy, as in Eliza Bollends's case.[59] This is also shown in the case of the death of Eliza Lowe, an unmarried woman who left her uncle's house in Derby and took up lodgings in Nottingham in December 1873. Just over a fortnight later, she was discovered dead in her bed alongside the body of a newborn child. The inquest into her death recorded a verdict of 'grievous neglect'.[60] As with Eliza Bollends, it seems likely there was a reluctance or inability to seek medical (or any other) assistance due to her unmarried condition.

Of course, medical intervention may not have saved these women's lives, and, as signified here, carried its own risks. Nonetheless, there was, generally speaking, a widespread faith in the ability and authority of medical practitioners. At times, though, as in the case of the death of Princess Charlotte, they did face criticism. One such instance, which highlights the plight of pregnant women in the days before the NHS, when medical advice was frequently dependent on payment of doctor's fees, is the case of Elizabeth Lane, who died in 1860. The 36-year-old wife of a dairyman and greengrocer, and mother of five surviving children, she fell ill whilst pregnant and appears to have gone into premature labour. Her husband, John Lane, attempted to fetch assistance, but was refused by two medical men – seemingly due to a previous failure to pay the necessary fees. By the time a medical man willing to attend was found, Elizabeth had died, shortly after giving birth to a stillborn son. A coroner's inquest concluded that she had died 'from exhaustion, consequent on premature labour'. The jury criticised the doctors' refusal to attend the case and noted their moral – if not legal – obligation. The attending doctor suggested that her life may have been saved 'if a medical man had been present' and if 'instead of being in an upright position', she had been lying down, thus enabling 'a more rapid return of blood to the heart, which would have been more favourable to her'.[61] Medical knowledge, as suggested here, was certainly fallible in the nineteenth century, but this case illustrates an awareness at the time of the inequalities and injustices which prevented those less fortunate from accessing healthcare, and the potentially devastating effects of this.

In other cases, it was midwives who faced accusations of neglect or incompetence. A coroner's report into the death of Mary Ann Newey, the 36-year-old wife of a bricklayer in Birmingham, in summer 1864, mentions local speculation that the midwife had been at fault, but subsequently refutes this, with the jury concluding that 'the deceased was herself alone to blame in preventing medical aid being called in' – pointing to an increasing reluctance for women to give birth without medical assistance.[62] In 1874, the *Manchester Courier* reported on a case of 'Shocking Neglect by a Midwife', relating to the death of Mrs Louisa Fisher, who died from puerperal fever shortly after giving birth. The parish surgeon reported that he had been called to seven cases which the midwife, Mary Woodhead, had attended, and in six of these the women had died from puerperal fever. Woodhead had ignored pleas for her to stop practising for a short period in the wake of these deaths, but of course she may not have been able to support herself and her family if she did not work. Criticism of the midwife is also evident in the report of the inquest into the death of Ellen Matson in 1878. In a surprisingly graphic account, the report details the midwife's failure to identify 'laceration of the parts' following childbirth. The wound subsequently became infected, and the doctor performing the post-mortem concluded that death had resulted from peritonitis caused by the laceration. The midwife was accused of incompetence, although the jury refused to officially state her negligence, as this would, according to the judge, have resulted in a charge of manslaughter. Such cases were not unique to midwives: Lee's case studies include several instances in which women were physically damaged – sometimes fatally – through medical intervention by doctors. In another case in 1878, in which a 31-year-old woman, Priscilla Mitchell, died from haemorrhaging shortly after giving birth to twins, an inquest severely criticised the attending midwife for her refusal to seek medical assistance for the mother. In his testimony, surgeon Frank Taylor suggested that 'If a properly qualified medical man had been called in the deceased's life in all probability might have been saved.'[63] However, as Lee's work indicates, cases of difficult parturition requiring medical intervention carried increased risk of maternal mortality, and even qualified medical men were limited in what they could do to prevent haemorrhaging and infection. Doctors, too, were sometimes subject to similar charges and accusations. These did not always relate to neglect or poor practice during childbirth, but in some cases to the performance of illegal abortions – potentially dangerous procedures for the women involved even when carried out by qualified medical professionals.

It might be expected that maternal mortality rates for women giving birth in workhouses would be far higher than average, and indeed in certain workhouses this was the case. But surprisingly, a report on maternal mortality in workhouses across London for 1865 suggests a rate at just under 0.6 per cent, although there are some discrepancies in the figures, with Islington workhouse showing a maternal mortality rate of over 5 per cent for the year – far above the average. The report also indicates that 2,728 births occurred in London's workhouses that year, whilst a later report reveals almost 12,000 women gave birth in London's workhouses between 1861 and 1865, with an average maternal mortality rate of around 0.8 per cent. There is a correlation between the amount of space in the lying-in wards and mortality rates, with those with the least space having higher death rates. Significantly, maternal mortality rates for workhouses do not appear to be impacted by the relatively high number of single women attending the workhouse – perceived as at greater risk of maternal mortality in nineteenth-century assessments of outcomes in the Princess Charlotte Lying-in Hospital. At Marylebone Workhouse during this period, around 75 per cent of the women who gave birth were single, and over half were first-time mothers.[64] As these statistics demonstrate, however, to some extent at least, childbirth was a social leveller: no woman was exempt from its associated risks, and the victims of maternal mortality ranged from royalty to the most destitute of women. The cases detailed here represent a small snapshot of the experiences of some of those women who lost their lives. In the final years of the century, as Queen Victoria's reign drew to a close, women continued to die as a consequence of pregnancy and childbirth. Changes in obstetric practice led to some improvements, but there was no significant reduction in maternal mortality rates until the 1930s.[65] One of the last of the many thousands of victims of maternal mortality in nineteenth-century Britain was Alice Maud Kingstone, who was aged just 19. In December 1899, she was taken to Queen Charlotte's hospital in London (named after Princess Charlotte's grandmother), suffering with labour pains. For reasons that are unclear, she was refused admission. She was then taken to the infirmary, where she gave birth to a premature baby, and died shortly afterwards. The inquest that followed Alice Kingstone's death concluded that it was the result of blood poisoning following an illegal operation – a phrase generally used to refer to abortions. These procedures were yet another cause of maternal mortality at the time, but they were also one of very few avenues available for desperate women for whom motherhood was not a viable option – alternatives to which also included abandonment and infanticide.

1. *The Royal Family* by Franz Xaver Winterhalter (1846). The painting depicts Queen Victoria, Prince Albert, and five of their children. Queen Victoria would go on to give birth to a further four. The family sat for the portrait in between Victoria's many pregnancies. There do not appear to be any images – paintings or photographs – showing the Queen visibly pregnant. (Royal Collection Trust / © His Majesty King Charles III 2023)

2. *Princess Charlotte of Wales* by George Dawe (1817). Charlotte sat for the portrait whilst pregnant, but no sign of the pregnancy is depicted. (© National Portrait Gallery, London)

3. One of several images of the developing pregnant body, taken from *Obstetric Tables: comprising graphic illustrations, with descriptions and practical remarks* by George Spratt (1835). (Wellcome Collection)

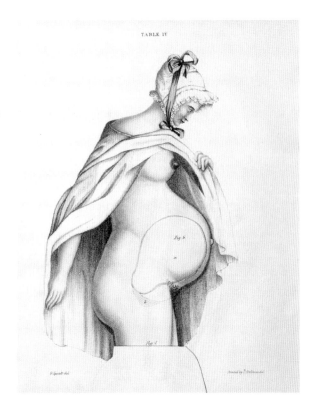

TABLE IV

4. *The Mother of Moses* by Simeon Solomon (1860). Solomon used Fanny Eaton as the model for this painting. Eaton was the mother of ten children born between 1858 and 1879; it is thought that the baby in the painting may be her own child. (© Delaware Art Museum / Bequest of Robert Louis Isaacson / Bridgeman Images)

5. Princess Alexandra (wife of Edward, Prince of Wales, later Edward VII) with eldest son Albert Victor, born two months premature in January 1864.

6. Monument commemorating Princess Charlotte Augusta of Wales in St George's Chapel in Windsor. Etching by T. Fairland after a sculpture by M.C. Wyatt, 1826. (Wellcome Collection)

7. *Mary Wollstonecraft* by John Opie (1797). Wollstonecraft was pregnant when she sat for this portrait. (© National Portrait Gallery, London)

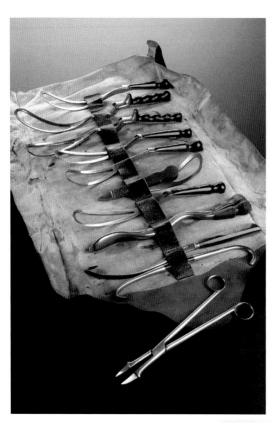

8. Victorian obstetrical instrument set. Instruments depicted include forceps, a vectis (for maneuvering the head out), and destructive instruments used in cases where it was not deemed possible to deliver the child alive. (Wellcome Collection, Science Museum, London, Attribution 4.0 International (CC BY 4.0))

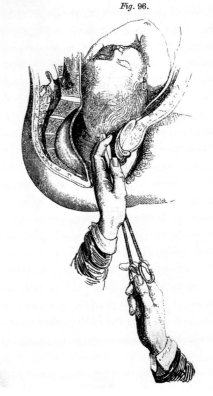

Fig. 96.

9. From Fleetwood Churchill, *On the Theory and Practice of Midwifery* (1855). Image showing the use of the perforator to perform a craniotomy. Destructive operations were performed throughout the period in some cases where delivery proved difficult, and were preferred to caesarean sections due to the lower maternal mortality rate. (Wellcome Collection)

10. Fred Barnard, Sarah Gamp (1872), from Charles Dickens's *Martin Chuzzlewit*. Mrs Gamp came to epitomize the figure of the dissolute and negligent midwife. (Scanned image and text by Philip V. Allingham, The Victorian Web)

11. Memorial to Princess Elizabeth Georgiana Adelaide of Clarence (10 December 1820–4 March 1821). (Photo by James Calford published in *Popular Royalty*, 2nd issue, by Arthur H. Beaven, 1904 (S. Low, Marston and Co., London))

12. The Young Mother by Charles Cope (1845). Cope's painting captures the figure of the often-idealised nursing mother. (© Victoria and Albert Museum, London)

5

Unwanted Pregnancies: Abortion, Abandonment, and Infanticide

[T]he little baby was born, when I didn't expect it; and the thought came into my mind that I might get rid of it, and go home again. [...] I thought I should get rid of all my misery, and go back home, and never let 'em know why I ran away.

George Eliot[1]

In 1896, a woman named Mrs Mary Eliza Sprackland was convicted of 'using a certain instrument with intent to procure the miscarriage' of one Mrs Mackiey, the wife of a shipwright with three children. Further details of Mrs Mackiey's life are unknown, so we can only speculate as to her reasons for desiring an abortion. Shipbuilders were reasonably well paid – certainly better off than factory workers and domestic servants, as this was a form of skilled labour. Nonetheless, it may have been the case that money was tight, that her marriage was unhappy, that she had previously experienced difficult births, or that she simply did not want any more children. Today, most women in the UK take a decision on whether to have children, and how many to have. Mrs Mackiey, like many other women in nineteenth-century Britain, may not have had any choice in becoming pregnant. Whatever her situation may have been, she did indeed miscarry (at a cost of 5 shillings – approximately £20 in today's money). She was one of a number of women who consulted Mary Sprackland with a view to terminating their pregnancies: with 'more than ten other instances [...] known of similar malpractices by the prisoner', Sprackland was convicted and sentenced to five years' penal servitude.[2]

Two years later, in June 1898, Dr William Maunsell Collins, aged 48, appeared at the Old Bailey charged with the murder of Mrs Emily Edith Uzielli, upon whom he had performed an illegal operation with a view to inducing an abortion. The wife of a stockbroker, Mrs Uzielli was mother to two children, aged 8 and 9, and did not wish to proceed with this pregnancy. As with Mrs Mackiey, nothing further is known about her reasons for this. One newspaper report on the case noted that Mrs Uzielli 'went out a good deal into society, and received much company at home'. There is an implied criticism here, reflecting wider discourses around motherhood at this time – a suggestion that Mrs Uzielli prioritised her social life over and above her role as mother. However, her husband testified to his wife's fondness for children, and strong attachment to her own. She visited Dr Collins on 14 March, when she was around seven to eight weeks pregnant. She was 'very anxious not to have a child', and had already attempted to terminate the pregnancy by taking purgatives. These attempts had failed, and she consequently paid Dr Collins 30 guineas (around £2,000 today) for his services. She had told her husband about the pregnancy, but did not tell him of her visit to Dr Collins, suggesting the decision to end the pregnancy was hers alone. Following the operation, Mrs Uzielli had developed peritonitis and subsequently died. A post-mortem examination revealed the cause of death to be 'a wound on the uterus, caused by some blunt or pointed instrument'. Collins was found guilty of manslaughter, recommended to mercy, and sentenced to seven years penal servitude.[3]

Both Mrs Sprackland and Dr Collins made their money from unwanted pregnancies, which were common enough to turn a decent profit for those wishing to capitalise on them. There are notable similarities between these two cases: both Sprackland and Collins were operating in the late Victorian period, and both were charged in relation to procedures carried out on married women, neither of whom had large families. There are also significant differences, reflected in the respective fees Sprackland and Collins charged for their services. Whilst Sprackland was clearly catering to a poorer clientele, Collins's patients included those in much more comfortable circumstances. As demon-strated by the experience of many mothers of large families, both rich and poor, pregnancy was not always a matter of choice but a conse-quence of women's limited control over their reproductive rights due to lack of access to reliable contraception (and knowledge of this) and the fact that sexual abuse and violence were relatively common occurrences (including within marriage).[4] Then as now, some women simply did not want children; then as now, the reasons for wanting to terminate a preg-nancy were both varied and personal – although then as now (at least in some countries), the law intervened to make it a matter of wider con-cern, and to restrict women's choices. For poorer women, large families represented an often-unsustainable financial burden. For many, multiple pregnancies were physically and emotionally draining – sometimes dam-aging. For unmarried women in particular, pregnancy risked reputation, and was potentially catastrophic in terms of both work and marriage prospects. Furthermore, those women who found themselves pregnant outside of marriage had little legal recourse to financial support from the fathers of their children: following the Poor Law Amendment Act of 1834, it was determined that 'A bastard will be what Providence appears to have ordained that it should be, a burthen on its mother.'[5] Later leg-islation granted women the right to apply for an affiliation order to try and secure support from the father of the child, but evidence had to be provided, and in the time before DNA testing could positively identify the father of a child, it was next to impossible to force unwilling fathers to pay for their illegitimate offspring.

Options for women were few. Abortion was illegal, though nonethe-less practised, either by abortionists charging women for their services, or by women themselves, who employed various techniques with a view to deliberately ending their pregnancies prematurely. Many women simply endured the consequences of unwanted pregnancy – whether physical, emotional, financial, or reputational. For the middle and upper classes, large families might be unwelcome but were often, at least, manageable. Queen Victoria resented her many pregnancies, but ultimately accepted her large family. For some women, the resent-ment they felt in relation to their experience of multiple (and often unwanted) pregnancies evidently impacted their relationships with their children. Hannah Mitchell detailed her own mother's bitterness towards her six children in her autobiography: 'My mother's temper [...] grew worse with the advent of each child. [...] [She] had bitterly resented my coming into the world, but the birth of [the] last two [babies] seemed to be more than she could endure and our home became more unhappy than ever.'[6] In cases of pregnancy outside of marriage, to acknowledge the child was to risk significant reputational damage, and so many such pregnancies (and births) were concealed. This may have been the case for Queen Victoria's daughter, Princess Louise, rumoured to have given birth to an illegitimate child in 1867, supposedly subsequently given up for adoption to the son of the Queen's obstetrician, Sir Charles Locock, and his wife. Adoption thus served as one way of dealing with unwanted babies, although formal, legal adoption as it exists today was not possible prior to 1926. Private adoption – as was rumoured to have occurred in the case of Princess Louise – might be arranged or babies might be relinquished to Foundling Hospitals, such as the one established in London in 1739, or children's homes. Some babies in nineteenth-century Britain were simply abandoned by mothers who for a variety of reasons could not support them. In some cases, this was clearly a matter of deep regret for the mothers: tokens were often left with babies at the Foundling Hospital in London, in the hope that at some point in the future mothers might be reunited with their children. Other mothers took more drastic action, leaving their infants with unscrupulous 'baby farmers', knowing that death was a strong possibility – as a consequence of neglect, or the opiates or alcohol administered to keep the babies quiet. In some cases, babies were deliberately murdered. These acts speak to the desperation of women unable to endure motherhood, for whatever reason, but equally with little right to control over their own bodies, and therefore unable to avoid unwanted pregnancies. There was a stigma associated with unwanted pregnancy, and abortion, concealing a birth, abandonment, and infanticide all carried a risk of criminal charges. Consequently, there are few accounts from women themselves of their experience of unwanted pregnancies in the form of diaries and letters. However, some of their voices can be heard in court testimonies, and their stories are found in newspaper reports, coroners' inquest reports, and medical literature.

Abortion

Several pieces of legislation were passed in nineteenth-century Britain criminalising abortion and making it punishable with varying degrees of severity. In 1803, deliberately inducing miscarriage after 'quickening' became punishable by death, whilst abortion prior to quickening could be punished by transportation for up to fourteen years. These laws applied to any woman attempting to terminate her own pregnancy, and to anyone assisting her in this process. The Offences Against the Person Act of 1837 abolished the death penalty for abortion, and also removed the distinction of 'quickening', but the deliberate termination of a pregnancy remained punishable by life imprisonment. Abortion was not legalised in Britain until 1968,[7] although following the passage of the 1929 Infant Life (Preservation) Act, abortions carried out to preserve the life of the mother were not deemed an offence.[8] In fact, these latter operations – in the form of embryotomies and craniotomies – were routinely performed by medical men throughout the nineteenth century but were typically not viewed as illegal abortions. In many of these cases, the unborn child was already dead, but these operations were also performed on live infants – an ethical issue which prompted much debate amongst the medical community.[9] Whilst the morality of such operations was called into question, the legality of them was not. In certain circumstances, then, medical men were effectively able to carry out late-term (in some cases, full-term) abortions, despite the laws criminalising such procedures.

There was, inevitably, some opposition to the performance of destructive operations, and, in some cases, this echoed arguments made against abortion. In a letter to *The Lancet* in 1842, one correspondent objected strongly to Dr Robert Lee's earlier admission that he had attended over 100 births terminating in the performance of a craniotomy: 'Can this be correct? [...] [S]uch a wholesale slaughter of innocents – outheroding Herod.'[10] Opposition to the destruction of infants at full term is unsurprising, but there was also outspoken opposition from many against the deliberate termination of pregnancy at any stage – although some sympathised with the idea that women aborting pregnancies in the first few months should not be punished. Chavasse in *Advice to a Wife*, though, refers to the practice in the early stages of pregnancy of 'using means to promote abortion' as a 'heinous and damnable sin [...]: it is as much murder as though the child were at his full time, or as though he were butchered when he was actually born!' He continues, 'An attempt [...] to procure abortion is a crime of the deepest dye, viz., a heinous murder!' The consequences for the woman were also likely to be dire, according to this account: 'it may either cause her immediate death, or it may so grievously injure her constitution that she might never recover from the shock. If these fearful consequences ensue, she ought not to be pitied; she richly deserves them all.' A medical man himself, Chavasse goes on to suggest that the medical profession is entirely opposed to the inducement of abortions, and that those 'unqualified villains who practise the damnable art' should be transported or hung.[11] Another commentator against abortion argued in the *Daily News* in 1854 that:

> It is no valid argument to maintain [...] that a child born before the seventh month has a slender chance of living, and that therefore no woman ought to be punished for destroying her infant before that period. [...] It is the prevalence of this monstrous and murderous idea which prompts so many to have recourse to procuring miscarriages and abortions, as they fancy that it is not committing murder to effect this before the period of quickening.[12]

The language of abortion in the press parallels that of anti-abortion campaigners today almost exactly. One work, published in 1837 declared: 'The foetus is a living being from the moment of conception, and consequently its destruction is murder.'[13]

Despite the strict laws criminalising abortion and vocal public opposition to the practice, however, many women in nineteenth-century Britain underwent illegal abortions: procuring drugs to induce termination of pregnancy; undergoing illegal operations – often performed by unqualified practitioners, but sometimes by qualified members of the medical profession; or engaging in behaviour which it was believed and hoped might induce miscarriage. That abortion was widely practised despite its criminal status supports more recent analysis showing that criminalising abortion does not significantly impact its occurrence.[14] These were often the acts of desperate women; they could be dangerous procedures, as revealed by coroners' reports from the period, which detail the deaths of many women. Estimating the occurrence of illegal abortions and the number of deaths resulting from them is next to impossible, but newspapers report with some frequency on inquests and criminal charges resulting from such cases, suggesting they were not uncommon. It is worth noting that the stories of abortion which found their way into the newspapers almost always ended in tragedy – in the death of the woman. Successful abortions did not make the papers: they were secretive procedures and are thus inevitably largely absent from the historical archive. Consequently, stories of women losing their lives in illegal operations perhaps result in a perception of nineteenth-century abortions as more dangerous than they were; it is safe to assume that there were far more successful procedures, in which the pregnancy was terminated and the woman survived, than unsuccessful. This is suggested by occasional passing allusions to abortion in women's life writing, as well as by the practice of abortionists: a high death rate would have quickly put them out of business or led to their arrest. The cases in which women did lose their lives as a result of attempts to abort pregnancies speak to a fact which remains in evidence today: whilst criminalising abortion does not prevent women from seeking terminations, it does increase maternal mortality.[15]

The availability of material on the subject of abortion in the nineteenth century means our understanding of it must be gleaned largely from those cases in which the patient lost her life, and such cases do reveal important details about the practices of abortion at the time, as well as about the women who underwent such procedures. In 1889, Dr Frederick Moon, who had practised medicine for some forty years, was charged with the murder of Eleanor Tebbutt 'by means of an unlawful operation',[16] although subsequently found not guilty. As with the patients involved in the Collins and Sprackland cases, Eleanor Tebbutt was married – the wife of a stonemason. She died ten days after receiving treatment from Dr Moon, which he claimed was to treat haemorrhaging and a tumour. The judge, addressing the jury at the conclusion of the trial, suggested that the procedure carried out was appropriate in light of the patient's state of health (the alleged bleeding and tumour), hence his acquittal. Significantly, the Old Bailey records of this case provide only very limited information, as 'details of the evidence' were deemed 'unfit for publication'.[17] One of the recorded single women whose difficult situation led her to seek an abortion was Harriet Letchford, aged 27 from Gillingham, who died after undergoing an illegal operation in 1891. On her deathbed, Harriet confessed that an unidentified woman had performed the procedure, and that she 'was prematurely delivered and burnt the child's body'. She also, significantly, stated that 'such operations [...] were frequent at Gillingham'.[18] Eliza Uttley's death, in 1871, resulted from an abortion apparently performed by the alleged father of the baby, William Collinson, a chemist and druggist, who was charged with her murder, though subsequently acquitted. In October 1896, Dr Timothy Jones and his assistant Henry Richards were charged with the murder of Lily Maud Challenger in Swansea after performing 'an illegal operation'.[19] Jones was subsequently found guilty of manslaughter and Richards as an accessory to manslaughter. In passing sentence, the judge noted that Jones was 'probably induced to take the course taken from compassion for a youth'[20] – indicating the desperation and limited options available for women who found themselves pregnant outside marriage, but also the sympathetic stance of at least some doctors and judges towards this issue. Later the same year, in Stoke Devonport, Dr Edward Alfred Cormack was charged with murder following the death of Jessie Mary Oliver, a single woman aged 23. A post-mortem examination revealed she had died from peritonitis after the premature delivery of a child. Those cases involving medical men point to the fallacy of Chavasse's assertion that the medical profession as a whole was opposed to abortion.

Women did not necessarily require assistance from others in terminating pregnancy – particularly during early pregnancy. Somewhat ironically, in light of the silences around subjects such as contraception and childbirth in advice literature for women, information on actions which might induce miscarriage was readily available in advice books for pregnant women, albeit in the form of instructions on what *not* to do when pregnant. *Advice to a Wife* provides a long list of frequent causes of miscarriage, which includes horse riding, overexertion, falls, dancing, constipation, and taking purgatives or calomel.[21] Though much of this advice was evidently inaccurate, nonetheless at least some of these actions might put a pregnancy at risk, and there is evidence to suggest that women wishing to terminate their pregnancies deliberately engaged in some of these behaviours. In 1806, Eugenia Wynne wrote in her diary of her pity for a 'Mrs Manners', who appears to have been in an abusive marriage: 'She talks cooly of riding hard to procure a miscarriage, and this because [her husband] hates children and beats her for having some.'[22] Wynne's account, like the case of Mrs Uzielli, points to the fact that it was not only women of the poorer classes, or those who found themselves pregnant outside of marriage, who were employing abortion as means of controlling reproduction: amongst every class of society, women on occasion took steps to prevent the continuation of pregnancy.

Nineteenth-century newspapers and journals contain dozens of adverts for various medical solutions aimed at women, and the euphemistic language employed in such adverts often implies they might be used to terminate a pregnancy – as well as for multiple other ailments. One example from the late nineteenth century appeared in some editions of Allbutt's *The Wife's Handbook*. As a rare example of an advice book for women which provides information on contraceptive methods to its readers, it is perhaps unsurprising that such an advert, for a product called 'Nature's Blood Former', should be included here. Amongst a long list of ailments it promises to cure, including breathlessness, palpitations, headaches, and indigestion, is 'Irregularity': in other words, irregular menstruation. The description of the symptoms which may accompany this irregularity are synonymous with those of early pregnancy: 'This Irregularity is accompanied by a distressing feeling of weakness, and the sufferer is always tired, even when rising in the morning.'[23] The implication, then, is that the product might be used to induce early miscarriage. Such evasive language, hinting at the possibility of pregnancy, is common in adverts for similar products, implying they may be used as abortifacients. Adverts for 'Juniper's Essence of Pennyroyal and Essence of Peppermint', for example, suggest that 'these preparations' can 'administer relief in obstructions'.[24] Pennyroyal was a well-known abortifacient, and the 'obstruction' alluded to here can be interpreted as an unwanted pregnancy. Neither the reliability nor the safety of many of the products sold to aid women's 'ailments' – in other words, as abortifacients – was certain. Some undoubtedly produced the desired affect with no serious side effects for the mother, others failed to induce abortion, and many were potentially harmful. In 1846, an inquest was held on the body of a young woman, Mary Ann Johnson, a 20-year-old servant, who died shortly after giving birth to a stillborn child following an attempted abortion using what appeared to be 'a very powerful essence of pennyroyal'.[25] The inquest concluded that the substance was not poisonous, and that the death may have been caused by other pregnancy-related issues, although the timing seems to suggest the attempted abortion may have played a role. One newspaper reporting the case noted that this was 'the same as taken by the lower classes to procure abortion'.[26] It may have had some effect, although in large doses, pennyroyal could also prove toxic to the patient.

Evidently, some women did, at times, attempt to terminate their own pregnancies or sought assistance from medical practitioners or those practising as abortionists. In many cases, the pregnancies were concealed from all but themselves, but on occasion, abortions were sought with the assistance (or even at the insistence) of the men responsible. Several such cases ended up in the courts in the nineteenth century, including, in 1843, that of William Haynes, who was tried for the murder of his wife. She died after he gave her sulphate of potash in an attempt to terminate her pregnancy. A witness at the trial claimed he had told her his wife 'was in the family way, and he gave it her to destroy [...] the infant'. Following his wife's death, Haynes told the surgeon who attended he had given her the substance to induce miscarriage having read about it in 'a book which he bought in the Strand', and that he was motivated by the fact that 'he had such a dislike to children' (there is no indication as to whether his wife felt the same, or to what extent she was pressured by her husband into taking the substance). The post-mortem, however, revealed that his wife was not pregnant at the time of her death. Haynes was found not guilty of her murder.[27]

A few years earlier, in 1834, William Childs, aged 23, was:

indicted for that he [...] feloniously, wilfully, and maliciously did administer, to Mary Jane Wolfe, a large quantity of a certain drug, call[ed] savin, with intent thereby to cause and procure her miscarriage; she, at the time of administering and taking the said drug, being with child, but not quick with child.

The reference to the fact that Wolfe was not 'quickening' when the drugs were administered reflects the fact that this was considered a lesser crime in law at this time than if an abortion had been attempted after quickening. Childs's case is of interest for the testimony provided by Mary Jane

Wolfe, who was 17 at the time she became pregnant, providing a relatively rare insight into abortion in the nineteenth century from the perspective of the pregnant woman:

> My father and mother keep the Chaise and Horses at Hammersmith –
> the prisoner was in their employ as ostler – I formed an intimacy with
> him in April, 1833 – I had connexion with him in a particular way in
> April last year, and continued to be intimate in that way until June – I
> had connexion with him after June – I had reason to suppose I was
> pregnant about the 26th of June – I mentioned my being so to him a day
> or two before that – I was about six weeks advanced in pregnancy then
> – between six weeks and two months – on the 26th of June, he told me
> I must take some medicine to cause miscarriage – I told him I would not
> take it – he persuaded me, and said I had better; for if my parents found
> it out, they would turn me out of house and home, and then I should
> have no place to go to – he gave me a powder [...] – I took some of
> it, but finding it a bitter and disagreeable taste, I was afraid to take the
> whole – [...] [I]n the course of a short time afterwards I was taken very
> ill [...] I am sure I did miscarry[.][28]

Elsewhere in her testimony, Wolfe accused Childs of rape, kidnap, and attempting to force her into marriage. However, cross-examination focused on whether Wolfe had been intimate with any other man, evidence that the problems that still frequently beset rape trials, in which women's sexual behaviour appears sometimes to be deemed of greater relevance than the violent and predatory behaviour of the accused, have a long history in Britain. Although Childs was found guilty of the charge of procuring an abortion, the sentence was respited, so he did not suffer any punishment. There do not appear to be any records of other charges brought against him in relation to the accusations of rape and kidnap made by Wolfe. The case highlights the fact that many young women in nineteenth-century Britain were vulnerable to sexual exploitation and abuse, and indeed that they were sometimes pressured into obtaining abortions against their will. Charges and convictions for rape in twenty-first-century Britain remain notoriously low. Two hundred years ago, the situation was even worse, and women had few options if they found themselves pregnant as a consequence of sexual abuse. An unmarried woman's reputation was liable to suffer regardless of the circumstances of her pregnancy, as Thomas Hardy highlighted towards the end of the century in his novel *Tess of the D'Urbervilles*. It was inevitable, then, that many women in such circumstances sought to end their pregnancies, or to relinquish themselves of the responsibility of their newborn children – either by abandoning them or, in some tragic cases, murdering them.

Evidence that means of terminating pregnancies were sometimes employed by the aristocratic classes can be found in the case of Henrietta Maria Stanley, wife of politician Edward Stanley, the second Baron Stanley of Alderley. The couple had some ten children[29] – the second youngest, Rosalind, was born in 1845. When Henrietta again found herself pregnant in autumn 1847, both she and her husband were upset at the prospect of another child. Writing to his wife on 9 November, Edward Stanley expressed his displeasure – and appeared to hold his wife entirely accountable for the pregnancy:

> This your last misfortune is indeed most grievous & puts all others in the shade. What can you have been doing to account for so juvenile a proceeding[?] [...] I only hope it is not the beginning of another flock for what to do with them I am sure I know not. I am afraid however it is too late to mend & you must make the best of it tho' bad is best.

Henrietta, however, proved it was not 'too late to mend'. Writing to her husband on the same day, she informed him that the pregnancy had ended: 'A hot bath, a tremendous walk & a great dose have succeeded but it is a warning.' Her actions clearly had the desired effect, and though she confessed she felt 'not too well', it is evident there were no significant detrimental consequences for her health. Her husband's response expressed both concern and relief at her actions: 'I hope you are not going to do yourself any harm by your violent proceedings, for though it would be a great bore it is not worth while playing tricks to escape its consequences. If however you are none the worse the great result is all the better.' Both Henrietta Stanley and her husband appear to have viewed the matter from a practical perspective, which speaks to a distinction between the public discourses around abortion and private attitudes towards unwanted pregnancies. In her response to her husband, Henrietta wrote: 'I was sure you would feel the same horror I did at an increase of family but I am reassured for the future by the efficacy of the means' – indicating a willingness to employ similar tactics should further unwanted pregnancies arise in the future.[30] Indeed, she seems to have subsequently considered resorting to similar recourse: in December 1848, she wrote to her husband informing him that she had 'felt very low for some time'. She continued, 'I much fear there is a very unpleasant cause for my malaise, & tho' I conclude it will come to an untimely end the remedy is a bad one.'[31] Her words here suggest another possible attempt to induce abortion for an unwanted pregnancy, but if she did attempt such measures in this instance they were unsuccessful, and she gave birth to another daughter in July 1849.[32] Though there are few documented accounts of abortion such as this amongst the upper classes of society, Henrietta Stanley's experience suggests that women were both familiar with actions which might result in the termination of a pregnancy, and that at least some women employed them when necessary as a means of controlling their fertility. Alternatively, as many of the cases here demonstrate, women visited medical practitioners for the performance of operations designed to induce miscarriage. An article which appeared in the *To-Day* journal in December 1895 supports this assumption, stating that 'such operations are as common as can be among the well-to-do classes'. It continues, 'Performed by skilful physicians, no danger is incurred by the operation, which is done every day; but the fee is large and the matter is very prettily disguised.'[33]

Easily available herbs and medicines, such as pennyroyal and savin, were sometimes used in attempts to induce miscarriage. Knowledge about their purpose was certainly shared amongst women, and was no doubt invaluable to some – particularly women with large families who struggled to make ends meet. In her Introduction to *Maternity: Letters From Working Women*, Margaret Llewellyn Davies highlighted and criticised the widespread use of (unspecified) drugs to induce abortion amongst poorer women:

> Opinions may differ as to the good or evil of the general limitation of families, but there can only be agreement upon the evil which results from the use of drugs to procure abortion. There are many facts which go to prove that the habit of taking such drugs has spread to an alarm-ing extent in many places among working women. [...] The practice is ruinous to the health of women, is more often than not useless for

procuring the object desired, and probably accounts for the fact that many children are weakly and diseased from birth. But [...] [w]here maternity is only followed by an addition to the daily life of suffering, want, overwork, and poverty, people will continue to adopt even the most dangerous, uncertain, and disastrous methods of avoiding it.[34]

That such methods were employed with some frequency is also suggested by some of the letters themselves. One correspondent, who worked long hours throughout her pregnancy, was unable to afford enough food to eat, and who ultimately lost her child shortly after its birth, echoed Davies's sentiments: 'Can we wonder that so many women take drugs, hoping to get rid of the expected child, when they know so little regarding their own bodies, and have to work so hard to keep or help to keep the children they have already got?'[35] Another contributor, who also experienced severe poverty during pregnancy, admitted to attempting to end unwanted pregnancies, and her letter speaks to the desperation of women who found themselves pregnant but unable to afford another mouth to feed:

no one who has not been placed in a similar position can realise how horrible it is to be so placed. I have resorted to drugs, trying to prevent or bring about a slip. I believe I and others have caused bad health to ourselves and our children. But what has one to do?[36]

Poverty was inevitably a key factor in such decisions, as revealed in the case of one of the other contributors: 'I confess without shame that when well-meaning friends said: "You cannot afford another baby; take this drug," I took their strong concoctions to purge me of the little life that might be mine.' In this case, however, the attempt to terminate the pregnancy 'failed [...] and the third baby came'.[37] Another woman confessed to considering an abortion during a difficult pregnancy, again whilst experiencing severe poverty which impacted both her physical and mental health: 'I nearly lost hope and faith in everyone. I felt that even the baby could not make up for the terrible strain I had undergone, and at that time I could fully enter into the feelings of those women who take drugs to prevent birth.'[38] One woman who experienced severe physical effects following pregnancy wrote in the third person about abortion and its potential effects – but her understanding of these difficulties indicates that she is reflecting on her own experience, perhaps unwilling to admit she had resorted to such actions due to the widespread opposition to abortion and potential legal implications:

The [pregnant] mother wonders what she has to live for; if there is another baby coming she hopes it will be dead when it is born. The result is she begins to take drugs. I need hardly tell you the pain and suffering she goes through if the baby survives, or the shock it is to the mother when she is told there is something wrong with the baby. She feels she is to blame if she has done this without her husband knowing, and she is living in dread of him. All this tells on the woman physically and mentally; can you wonder at women turning to drink?[39]

The potential danger to the child in cases of unsuccessful abortions was highlighted in an article reported in *The Medical Gazette* in 1870. A woman, identified only as 'Mrs J. T. S.', believed herself to be in the early stages of pregnancy, and, not wanting another child so soon after her last, 'took several things either to bring on the catamenia, or induce miscarriage' (the phrasing here suggesting a blurring of lines between a late period and early miscarriage or abortion). Evidently, this was unsuccessful, and she subsequently gave birth 'to a puny child [...] which lived ten days'.[40] There may have been no causal link between the substances taken to induce abortion and the infant's death, but the possibility of an association no doubt impacted the mother's mental health. Another respondent to the Women's Co-operative Guild described three cases within her knowledge of women who died after taking drugs in attempts to terminate their pregnancies, and a fourth case in which a mother of seven succeeded in ending her pregnancy. Questioned about it, the latter responded: 'I will not have any more by him, and I should not have cared if I had died.'[41] In 1899, a midwife named Jane White was charged with murder after the death of a woman following an 'illegal operation'. During her trial, another woman – a widow – testified to having written a letter to White which was used as evidence that the defendant was working as an abortionist and was read out in court. The letter is indicative of the demand for abortions, and suggests successful procedures were not necessarily experienced as traumatic: 'I am glad to tell you my trouble is over. It happened on Sunday. I was very bad. I got up yesterday for the first time. I am very grateful to you.'[42] These accounts show that many women were both aware of the options that were available to bring about abortions, and that some of them employed these methods. For many, abortions provided a solution to an untenable situation, as the letter to White suggests: this was a service for which women were often deeply grateful. There were many reasons why women might wish to terminate a pregnancy in nineteenth-century Britain, but whatever the reason women felt unable to continue with their pregnancies, such services, though sometimes fraught with risk, presented women with a route through which they could potentially regain control of their bodies and their reproductive lives. In other cases, when the pregnancy had progressed, some women employed other means to escape from difficult situations – including child abandonment and infanticide.

Abandonment

The abandonment of babies in nineteenth-century Britain was not an uncommon occurrence, and enough of a concern that it found its way into the Victorian novel. In George Eliot's *Adam Bede* (1859), Hetty Sorrell gives birth in secret to a baby which she immediately abandons. The baby dies and she is charged with its murder. In George Moore's *Esther Waters* (1894), the eponymous heroine leaves her baby with a baby farmer so she can work as a wet nurse, not realising the danger in which she is placing the child. She manages to rescue it before it succumbs to neglect – the fate of her two predecessors' babies. Moore's heroine leaves her baby in good faith, and because she has limited opportunities for securing income, but there were concerns that some women were abandoning their infants with unscrupulous baby farmers, hoping they wouldn't survive, as a means of disposing of their unwanted children. For some mothers, though, the abandonment of their children was an act of love, rather than neglect: in desperate situations themselves, they evidently believed they were acting in the best interest of the child, hoping that by leaving them, they were giving them the chance of a better life.

The desire to conceal the birth of a child was undoubtedly behind the abandonment of many infants in the nineteenth century. If they were lucky, abandoned babies survived, but inevitably often they did not. In one case in 1880, two newborn infants were found within a few streets of each other in Leeds. The children were taken to the workhouse, but both subsequently died. The conclusion reached was that the children must have been twins. One press report on the case commented on the strange fact that 'these births should have taken place in broad daylight on a Saturday, in or near to public thoroughfares, without attracting immediate attention'.[43] The identity of the mother and the exact circumstances which led to the decision to abandon her children were undiscovered. We might speculate that it is likely – at a time when formal adoption was not an option, and with little state support in the form of benefits or social services, not to mention the stigma attached to unmarried motherhood – that she felt she had little choice in terms of her actions. Many such cases occurred throughout the nineteenth century, and the identity of the mother often remained unknown. However, this was not always the case, and a number of women did appear in court charged with unlawfully abandoning their infants. One of these women was 25-year-old Mary Doyle, who was 'indicted for unlawfully deserting her child, with intent to burden the inhabitants of the parish of St Martin-in-the-Fields' in September 1847. Another woman, Mary M'Grath, aged 40, was charged with aiding and abetting Doyle. One evening in August, Doyle and M'Grath arrived at the home of Mary Wharton, who had been nursing Doyle's 8-month-old baby. Doyle had struggled to pay Wharton, and she and M'Grath took the child away, claiming Doyle was going to send the child to the country to a person who would bring it up as their own. Shortly afterwards, a woman and her husband discovered the child abandoned nearby. The husband pursued and caught Doyle and M'Grath, and the child was taken by a policeman to the workhouse. In her defence, Doyle pleaded poverty: she had been confined in the workhouse, but they had refused to take her child. She had also tried to leave the child at the Foundling Hospital, but was refused there as well. She could not afford to pay the nurse, and so in desperation abandoned the child. Both Doyle and M'Grath were found guilty, but were recommended to mercy and their sentences respited. The case illustrates the barriers that were in place for poor mothers, and the limitations of state and philanthropic support, which was insufficient (and sometimes unwilling) to cater to the number of mothers and infants in need of care.

Single mothers facing financial hardship in some cases would have had little choice but to abandon their infants – particularly when they acted as a barrier to them keeping or obtaining work, or were the source of tension with the mother's own family. In such circumstances, the only other option may have been the workhouse. Financial hardship for these women was frequently compounded by fathers' refusals to support their illegitimate children, or indeed even acknowledge them. In one case from 1896, a young woman named Mary Boardman attempted to secure the support of her child's father by leaving the child with him, but was subsequently charged with child abandonment. She had previously worked as a servant on a farm owned by the father, Thomas Hewitt, and having left some months previously, returned with the baby saying 'it was for him to keep'. She then 'threw it down in the hay and ran out of the field'. Hewitt denied he was the child's father, 'or that anything improper had taken place between them'. Boardman, however, claimed that Hewitt had previously proposed to her, and then 'took advantage of her' – a term which suggests she was raped. When questioned by police, Boardman told them 'she did not wish to do the child any harm; she left it with its father'. The court accepted that she did not mean to harm the child, and the case was dismissed. Hewitt was served with an affiliation order, but whether or not he subsequently supported the child is unclear.[44] Boardman's case is not untypical and illustrates the vulnerable position of women working in domestic service, as well as the inequities around responsibility for illegitimate children at this time, the burden of which fell almost exclusively on the mother.

The prospects for most abandoned babies were poor, but those abandoned at the various institutions which cared for orphaned or poor children at least stood a better chance than those left in the streets. The most famous of those institutions was undoubtedly London's Foundling Hospital, which was established in 1739 and was in operation throughout the nineteenth century and beyond, taking in thousands of unwanted infants. Institutions such as this were philanthropic endeavours, private charitable efforts intended to address the social evils of child abandonment and infanticide. However, they were not universally welcomed. In the early nineteenth century, a proposal for a foundling hospital in Edinburgh met with strong opposition. The Board of Trustees for a proposed new lunatic asylum in Edinburgh wrote a letter strongly objecting to the proposals for a foundling hospital, arguing that such institutions were 'pernicious to society' and did nothing to reduce the incidences of 'the unnatural crime of child murder', and that 'the number of infants who die in foundling hospitals is great beyond belief'. Furthermore, they suggested, foundling hospitals 'afford too ready a way for indifferent and unfeeling parents, to get rid of their offspring'. They continued: 'A well-regulated state should never permit such institutions, and instead of giving opportunity, and even encouragement to parents to throw away their children, will inflict severe and exemplary punishment on an unnatural mother, convicted of having exposed an infant.'[45] Their deeply flawed arguments seemingly prevailed: the proposed foundling hospital in Edinburgh never materialised; the new lunatic asylum opened its doors in 1813.

In the nineteenth century, the London Foundling Hospital changed its admissions policy so as to cater exclusively for illegitimate children. High demand for places meant that the application policy was strict:

> The mother of the child must make application to the hospital before it is a year old; [...] The committee which considers her case and questions her personally, must be satisfied of the previous good character and present necessity of the mother; that the father of the child has deserted it and the mother, and also that the reception of the child will, in all probability, be the means of rehabilitating her.[46]

Such institutions, therefore, were not merely concerned with providing for children in need but also sought to pass moral judgement on the figure of the mother (not unlike the lying-in hospitals for 'respectable' married women). The entry procedures here speak to the strict moral standards to which women were held in nineteenth-century Britain. Significantly, the foundlings are alleged to have come 'almost without exception from domestic servants', and the girls, upon leaving the hospital, mostly entered domestic service.[47] As noted elsewhere, the position of young, female domestic servants was often one of particular vulnerability, and the origins and destinations of the foundlings suggests that some at least may have found themselves trapped in a damaging cycle with little recourse to other options.

Although London's Foundling Hospital and other similar institutions took in thousands of children, they often did not have the resources to cater to the high demand, and thus many babies were turned away, leaving those mothers unable to afford to raise a child with few options. This and similar institutions provided a means through which women could abandon their infants in the knowledge that they would at least be cared for in a respectable institution. The workhouse represented another possible option, and mothers who did not wish to enter themselves might simply abandon their infants outside. One such particularly moving incident occurred in 1895, when an infant was found abandoned outside the workhouse in Bermondsey. The infant, a boy, was evidently well cared for, and was left with a bonnet, two shawls and a feeding bottle, along with a note which explained the mother's motivation:

> I cannot maintain my darling baby, having other children dependent upon me [...] I am heart-broken to take him from my breast this bitter cold day, but it is for his sake, and may God forgive me. [...] When I am able to pay up what he has cost you I will claim him. God grant it will not be long. Though I think I am doing it for my darling's sake I think I shall go mad.

The note was signed 'A Broken-Hearted Mother'.[48] Later the same day, however, the mother returned to the workhouse to give herself up. She was subsequently charged with 'deserting her infant child'. Even though motivated by poverty and acting in what she believed to be the best interests of the child, the mother's behaviour was deemed criminal. In light of the fact that such behaviour, even when carried out with good intentions, was construed as either immoral or indeed criminal, perhaps it is unsurprising that some women took much more drastic action to rid themselves of unwanted infants – abandoning them in places they were unlikely to be found in time to survive, or even murdering them.

Infanticide

The abandonment of newborn babies frequently led to their deaths, but in such cases, infanticide was often difficult to prove. A charge of murder could only be upheld if there was sufficient proof that the child was born alive, and in many cases this was difficult, if not impossible, to ascertain. In cases where proof of the child being born alive was not available, a mother might be charged with the lesser crime of concealment of birth, as detailed in the Offences Against the Person Act of 1861:

> If any Woman shall be delivered of a Child, every Person who shall, by any secret Disposition of the dead Body of the said Child, whether such Child died before, at, or after its Birth, endeavour to conceal the Birth thereof, shall be guilty of a Misdemeanor, and being convicted thereof shall be liable, at the Discretion of the Court, to be imprisoned for any Term not exceeding Two Years, with or without Hard Labour: Provided that if any Person tried for the Murder of any Child shall be acquitted thereof, it shall be lawful for the Jury by whose Verdict such Person shall be acquitted to find, in case it shall so appear in Evidence, that the Child had recently been born, and that such Person did, by some secret Disposition of the dead Body of such Child, endeavour to conceal the Birth thereof, and thereupon the Court may pass such Sentence as if such Person had been convicted upon an Indictment for the Concealment of the Birth.[49]

In cases of the discovery of deceased newborn infants, coroners' inquests and criminal trials often focused on the question of whether or not the child had been born alive. One such inquest involved Elizabeth Learmouth, a servant, and her infant son, whose body was discovered in a chimney in November 1843. The tragic details of the case were reported in the newspapers, including testimony from Emily Gibbs, a housemaid working in the same establishment:

> The witness [...] heard a dropping down the chimney, and observed the rain was falling; to which Learmouth observed, 'Yes it is, but it will not be much.' Gibbs got a duster, and on wiping the grate found it was blood. She then put her hand up the chimney to ascertain what it was, and having first pulled down a bag of shavings, found a bundle on the top of it covered with blood, which, upon being taken down stairs, was found to contain the body of a child. Witness went up to Learmouth, and told her what had been discovered, when she said, 'Oh, don't let

any one know it, it is my child.' Upon being informed that Mrs Reeve was aware of it, she exclaimed 'Oh, put it away; no one will find it.' She subsequently said it was born about two on Tuesday afternoon, but no one in the house ever supposed she was pregnant.

The jury concluded that the child had died during childbirth, as a consequence of strangulation caused by the umbilical cord, and so Elizabeth Learmouth was found guilty of the less serious crime of concealing the birth.[50]

In a similar case, there was deemed to be enough evidence to bring a charge of murder against the mother. Following the discovery of a newborn baby in a box in a house in Falmouth in 1868, the mother of the child, 27-year-old Jane George, an assistant in a draper's shop, was charged with wilful murder. She claimed to have miscarried a child at six months, but doctors disputed this, declaring that the infant was born at full term. The trial focused in detail on the question of whether or not the child had been born alive, with the prosecution alleging it had, and that its death was the result of 'external violence', whilst the defence refuted these claims. The judge in the case was of the opinion that the prosecution evidence was not sufficient to prove the child had been born alive, and further that there was no evidence that the violence on the child's body had not been caused during the delivery. This decision was partly based on the verdict from an 1832 case, Rex vs. Ann Poulton, which established that a child must be *wholly* born alive in order for it to be considered to have 'a separate existence from its mother'. Ann Poulton had been charged with the murder of her illegitimate daughter, but with insufficient evidence to show the child was born wholly alive, she was found guilty of concealment of the birth rather than wilful murder. The judge advised the jury that it was 'not sufficient that the child respires in the progress of birth' – and this then became case law.[51] Evidence that the child had breathed, based on the state of the lungs, did not necessarily prove that it had been wholly alive, as death may have occurred *during* delivery. In the case of Jane George, the judge thus directed the jury to discharge the accused. She was subsequently charged with concealing the birth but was ultimately acquitted of this charge as well, on the basis that the evidence suggested she had not made significant efforts to conceal the body of her child.[52] At the end of the trial, the judge in the case made a statement:

to impress upon all young women who might find themselves in the unfortunate condition of the prisoner, the duty of not only not concealing their position, but of making their friends acquainted with it, in order that they might receive proper medical and other assistance, and the disgrace of such an occurrence as that which was before them be prevented.[53]

Such urgings, however, failed to take account of the stigma associated with pregnancy outside of marriage.

In another case, a 36-year-old woman named Martha Barrett appeared in the Old Bailey charged with the wilful murder of a newborn infant in 1829, after the burnt bones of the child were found in garden pots at her home. Barrett, described in newspaper reports as 'an ill-looking, emaciated woman',[54] admitted to having given birth to a child but claimed it was born dead. The state of the bones made this impossible to disprove, and, as in many other cases, she was found guilty only of concealing the birth. She was imprisoned for eighteen months. What is revealing in the court testimony in this case is the account of a conversation that took place between the local beadle, who discovered the bones, and the accused. The beadle asked her 'how she could be guilty of so enormous a crime', to which she responded 'in order that no one should have a knowledge of it'. She also stated that no one, including the father of the child, 'had any knowledge of her being in the family way'.[55] Like many other women in Britain at the time, Martha Barrett concealed her pregnancy and gave birth alone, clearly terrified of the potential consequences if her pregnancy was discovered. Her case, along with dozens of others, suggests that shame, or fear of being revealed as an unmarried mother, was a major factor in women's attempts to deal with unwanted pregnancies through concealment of the birth or infanticide.

Other cases offered no prospect of conviction due to the identity of the mother remaining unknown, whilst again the difficult question of whether or not a child had been born alive made any conclusion as to whether or not the child had been murdered impossible to reach. In one such case, the body of a newborn infant was discovered by two young men near Huddersfield, buried in a wooden box. The inquest was unable to establish either the cause of death or whether the child had been born alive, and the coroner recorded a verdict of 'Found dead, without any marks of violence; but whether born alive, or what was the cause of death, there was not sufficient evidence to show.'[56] In cases such as these, the identity of the mother often remained unknown, and we can only speculate on her situation and experience, though many were undoubtedly young, unmarried women, in a number of cases working as domestic servants and unable to risk losing their positions.

Pregnancy outside of marriage was potentially damaging for any woman, but for women in the higher classes, access to financial resources may have helped: women such as Princess Louise might be able to pay to hush up unwanted pregnancies and arrange unofficial adoptions, but these options were unavailable to poorer women; for many, pregnancy outside of marriage posed a very real risk of destitution.

Court records indicate that illegitimacy was most often the motivating factor in cases of infanticide, and that in many cases, it was the mother who was accused of killing her child. Many of these women were young, poor, and desperate, and the occurrence of such cases was all too common. In April 1817, for example, three women appeared at the Surrey assizes charged with the murder of their illegitimate children. These included a woman named only as 'Amelia', described as 'a negro woman', accused of murdering her newborn child in Newington, Surrey. A newspaper report on the case refers to Amelia as a 'servant', but given that she was born into the family she worked for in the West Indies, it seems likely that she was a slave. Initially accused of concealing the birth of her child before killing it, she was eventually acquitted of the crime.[57] In February 1829, Harriet Farrell appeared in court charged with 'the wilful murder of her bastard child'. She was just 17, and had been working as a domestic servant in the employ of a trunk maker and his wife for a few months, when the body of a newborn child was discovered in the privy. Her employer had previously accused her of being 'in the family way', but she had denied it. Again, there was no conclusive evidence that the child had been born alive, so she was found guilty of concealment of a birth.[58] In 1846, the body of a newborn male child was discovered in the privy at Bermondsey Workhouse. An investigation revealed it was the illegitimate child of one of the inmates, Bridget McCarthy, who was suspected of the baby's murder. The surgeon who examined the child 'was of the opinion that the child was born alive but had only partially breathed', but with insufficient evidence that the child was alive at birth and subsequently killed, the inquest recorded a verdict of 'Found dead'.[59]

Whilst newspapers reported, often sensationally, on cases such as these, questions remain over the exact events which led these women into these tragic circumstances. Whether or not these cases were in fact infanticide, what is clear is that these women, and others like them, gave birth alone and unsupported, often in terrible circumstances. Some of them were no doubt ignorant of the potential consequences of sexual relationships, and may not have realised they were pregnant, whilst the vulnerable position that many of them occupied means in some cases, the pregnancy was no doubt a consequence of rape. It is notable that very few of the newspaper reports on cases such as these mention the figure of the father, who is typically entirely absent from the tragedies of these women's lives. The concealment of pregnancy and childbirth prevented these women from accessing any kind of maternity care – sometimes with tragic consequences for mother and child. Access to maternity care, though, did not necessarily guarantee a positive outcome for mother and child: in the days before the NHS, levels of care were in part determined by wealth and social status, and the care provided to pregnant women in nineteenth-century Britain was uneven.

6

Midwifery, Maternity Care, and Lying-in Hospitals

Everybody must be born, and every woman, at least in this kingdom, is attended at the birth of her child by somebody, skilful or unskilful.

Florence Nightingale[1]

In February 1852, Martha Elizabeth Stone, 29 years old and wife of John Stone, was admitted to the Adelaide Lying-in Hospital in London with labour pains. She was the patient of Dr William Yell, secretary and surgeon to the hospital, who had provided her with an admission order, but who did not attend the delivery, despite having suggested that 'her's [*sic*] would be a bad case', and despite the fact that he was seemingly at that time the only doctor attached to the hospital. Instead, she was attended by Mrs Charlotte Neale, who was employed as a nurse at the hospital, but who, by her own admission, 'did not understand anatomy'. Nonetheless, she 'acted as midwife in the absence of medical attendance'. When the labour did not progress, Mrs Neale sent for a local surgeon, Mr Thomas Stillman, who spent ten minutes with the patient before leaving her once again in the care of the nurse. Early the following morning, with Martha Stone's condition deteriorating, Mrs Neale sent again for Mr Stillman, but he did not arrive until sent for a further two times. At 11.30 a.m., Mrs Stone was delivered of a stillborn child, and that evening she also died, having suffered a ruptured uterus. In returning the verdict on Martha Stone's death ('exhaustion caused from internal rupture'), the jury at the coroner's court noted that 'they cannot separate without expressing a very decided opinion that [...] the Adelaide Lying-in Hospital [...] is not entitled to the pecuniary contributions of the public'. Although, as the coroner noted, uterine rupture 'might have taken place under the greatest care' with similar results, careful medical attention would have, he concluded, 'lessened the chances of a rupture'.[2]

The same month that Martha Stone and her child died, another woman also lost her life shortly after giving birth to a stillborn child. Mrs Seale, aged just 23, was attended at her home in Knightsbridge, London by several medical men, including the eminent Dr John Snow, who also attended Queen Victoria during her last two confinements. As in the case of Martha Stone, progress was slow. Mrs Seale was given chloroform to manage the pain, which rendered her unconscious for the 'last two hours preceding delivery'. The child, when it eventually arrived, had died, and 'was small and ill-nourished'. Mrs Seale claimed she felt the baby's movements shortly before labour commenced, but Snow implies the baby had died sometime before. A few weeks later, Mrs Seale also lost her life, although the cause of her death is unclear.[3]

These two cases are illustrative of both the variations in maternity care in nineteenth-century Britain – in particular, between those of means and those without – and its limitations. The Adelaide Lying-in Charity provided for poor married women, and for the most part assisted women in childbirth in their own homes. It was only those who were 'totally destitute' who were admitted to the hospital to give birth ('after [...] due investigation of their cases').[4] We can assume, therefore, that Martha Stone's circumstances were particularly difficult. In contrast, Mrs Seale's Knightsbridge address and her attendance by several respectable doctors point to a more affluent lifestyle. Whilst there is clear evidence of neglect in the case of Martha Stone, it is evident that Mrs Seale, on the other hand, received careful medical attention from experts in the field of obstetrics. The similar outcomes in these cases, therefore, illustrate in part the limitations of maternity care and medical knowledge at the time.

In the intervening two centuries or so, standards of maternity care in Britain have improved dramatically – a consequence of developing medical knowledge, legislation around maternity rights, and increased state support (especially the foundation of the NHS) – although there are still worrying variations in this respect, as recent reports into levels of care at Shrewsbury and Telford NHS Trust reveal.[5] Despite such tragic cases, however, both maternal and infant mortality rates have fallen significantly, largely due to developments in the care provided to pregnant and birthing women. My daughter made a somewhat dramatic entrance into the world; her arrival involved an entire team of NHS medical professionals, including midwives, nurses, obstetricians, surgeons, anaesthetists, and paediatricians – in stark contrast to the experience of Martha Stone. The vast majority of women in Britain today are assisted in childbirth by medical professionals, and most give birth safely in hospitals.[6] In nineteenth-century Britain, most women gave birth at home, with a smaller number delivering in lying-in hospitals, workhouses, or elsewhere. Some women (contrary to Florence Nightingale's assertion, above, and as indicated by the experience of those women charged with concealing births) laboured and delivered alone, others with only family or friends present. Women who gave birth in the workhouse were often attended by the matron, and sometimes by visiting physicians or obstetricians. Elsewhere, women might be attended by midwives, with a range of experience and qualifications. Women of means could pay for the best possible care, in the form of highly experienced and well-known obstetricians, along with monthly nurses and other attendants. Wealth was no guarantee of decent maternity care, though, as the deaths of Mrs Seale and her child illustrate. Many women experienced straightforward births and required very little in the form of medical treatment. Other births were more complicated, leading to sometimes dangerous and devastating interventions by medical attendants. The backdrop to women's diverse experiences of maternity care in nineteenth-century Britain was the significant reforms which took place in this field across the course of the period.

In Britain today, birth is often associated with choice; pregnant women are encouraged to write birth plans, to consider where and how they would like to deliver, and what pain relief and other interventions they might want or require. Or course, birth does not always go as planned. Through both my second and third pregnancies I hoped for a water birth in a midwife-led birthing centre but ended up in hospital on both occasions – with an induction and an emergency Caesarean instead. In nineteenth-century Britain, women were able to exercise very little choice. Pain relief options were limited (although increased as the century progressed, particularly with the introduction of chloroform into the birthing room from the mid-nineteenth century onwards), medical care was almost entirely dependent on financial means – and to some extent 'moral character' – and any complications arising during labour could easily prove fatal for mother and/or child. Medical interventions such as turning,[7] forceps, and embryotomies risked long-lasting physical and emotional damage. Women's consent to perform such interventions was not always sought, and in some cases, birthing women were left unaware of the various treatments administered. Despite these risks, many women's experiences of childbirth were, nonetheless, largely positive, with successful outcomes for both mother and child – especially in those cases involving minimum medical intervention. Advances in maternity care over the course of the century laid the groundwork for the maternity services in place today. Amongst the most significant reforms were the recognition of the importance of hygiene in the birthing room, the increased use of pain relief (specifically chloroform), and the medicalisation of childbirth – including the professionalisation of midwifery. These developments were not without controversy, but did pave the way for a reduction in both maternal and infant mortality, and a better understanding of the experience of the birthing mother.

Midwives and Midwifery

Up until the second half of the eighteenth century, midwifery in Britain was largely female dominated. Women were typically accompanied in childbirth by other women (the term midwife literally means 'with woman') – a practice dating back to ancient times. The reasons behind the use of female midwives were various: childbirth was historically perceived as separate to the concerns of the medical profession (in some respects a social rather than a medical event, which did not, therefore, require the presence of medical men), and historically, women who were mothers themselves were deemed well placed to care for both birthing mothers and their infants. Although medical men had a long history of attending births in which complications arose, questions of propriety were sometimes raised in relation to the attendance of men during childbirth. When Mary Wollstonecraft gave birth to her youngest daughter (Mary Shelley) in 1797, she was attended by a female midwife, Mrs Blenkensop, and her doctor commented on 'the propriety of employing females in the capacity of midwives'[8] – though whether because they were able to bring direct experience of childbirth to bear, or because it was deemed more appropriate for intimate examinations of the female body is unclear. Zola's *Joie de Vivre* (1884), translated into English as *How Jolly Life Is!* in 1886, articulates the potential discomfort the birthing mother might feel in the hands of a male medical attendant in the character Louise's response to the suggestion that a medical man be brought in in case of complications during childbirth: 'Why did they go on torturing her in this way? They knew very well that the thought of being delivered by a man had always been intolerable to her. She was possessed by a feeling of morbid shame.'[9] Ironically, though, it was also a sense of 'propriety' which was at least partially responsible for preventing women from receiving adequate medical training for much of the nineteenth century. Anatomy in particular was deemed an unsuitable topic of study for women by many. An article published in *The Glasgow Herald* in 1862 expressed outrage at the possibility – especially at the idea of women studying alongside men: 'That young men and young women should be set to study anatomy and midwifery, and such things, *together*, is utterly revolting; and we cannot understand how any woman could desire it.'[10] One article in favour of allowing women to become physicians, published in *Macmillan's Magazine* in 1868, drew attention to one of the most frequent objections to this idea: 'It is sometimes said that the study of anatomy and physiology would tend to injure or destroy the fine instinct of purity which characterises most women.' It goes on to suggest, though, that this will prove 'groundless'.[11] In fact, debates around the propriety of women studying anatomy may have been a smokescreen for male opposition to women applying to join the medical register.[12] Furthermore, it is clear that some midwives did access various forms of training, including informal apprenticeships with doctors and practising midwives.[13] Conversely, whilst concerns were raised about the propriety of providing women with a medical education, there was also some anxiety around the figure of the unqualified midwife, who was frequently called in to attend poorer women unable to afford to pay (male) doctors. Whilst some doctors objected to these women practising, others recognised the need for competent (if not qualified) midwives in order to meet the growing demand of an increasing population. The credentials of women practising as midwives were typically based on experience – including their own personal experiences of childbirth – and reputation, rather than formal education, but this did not necessarily detract from their capabilities. In her autobiography, Hannah Mitchell, born in 1872, gives an intriguing picture of her grandmother, whom she describes as 'midwife and general help to all the farmers' wives', which harks back to earlier stereotypes:

> In earlier times I think she would have been burned as a witch. Although she possessed great skill in the use of herbs and the care of the sick, at times her manner was so forbidding and her temper so uncertain, she might well have been suspected of dealings with the evil one.[14]

In fact, the perception of a historical association between witchcraft and midwifery has been called into question, and may have been part of a wider campaign by the male medical establishment in the eighteenth century to discredit female midwives as their own practices began to encroach into this area.[15] Mitchell's allusion here speaks to a long history of problematic stereotypes associated with the figure of the midwife which prevailed into the nineteenth century – in particular, the notion of the drunk and/or incompetent midwife. There is no suggestion that Mitchell's grandmother ever received any formal training, and her 'qualifications' as a midwife may well have been based primarily on her own experience as the mother of nine children. This, though, was frequently deemed a necessary and indeed relevant part of midwives' training – an extension of the notion that only women who were mothers themselves ought to be present in the birthing room.[16] Mitchell notes that her grandmother was '"uncertificated" and mostly unpaid', but that there was 'nothing of [Dickens's] Sairey Gamp' about her.[17] Her statement points to the fact that negative stereotypes about female midwives were prevalent enough to require refutation. Nineteenth-century midwives, then, faced criticism for their lack of qualifications and medical knowledge but were simultaneously, for much of the period, denied access to these things, whilst childbirth had long been deemed 'women's business', rather than the realm of the medical man. The medical establishment and the popular press were largely responsible for the perpetuation of these negative stereotypes,

which were rooted partly in a form of gatekeeping but also in class prejudice. Nonetheless, most practising midwives were both experienced and
competent. Newspaper reports tend to focus on cases where something
has gone amiss and records of practising midwives are few, but those that
have survived suggest many had undergone some form of training (albeit
sometimes informal), acted with competence and compassion, and were
responsible for thousands of successful deliveries.[18]

By the early nineteenth century, however, the involvement of medical
men in childbirth was becoming increasingly common. The attendance
of male midwives, or accoucheurs, began to emerge in the seventeenth
century, but it was the late eighteenth century before the practice of
employing medical men, rather than female midwives, became commonplace, and it was well into the nineteenth century before obstetrics
became an essential part of the curriculum for trainee doctors. In 1825,
a group of medical men formed the Obstetrics Society, in an attempt to
try and regulate the profession. This was succeeded by the Obstetrical
Society of London in 1858. As the male-dominated medical profession
took an increased interest in childbirth and maternity care, the figure of
the female midwife – often with no formal training, particularly prior
to reforms in the latter decades of the nineteenth century – became the
subject of increased scrutiny and criticism from some quarters. Anxieties
around this figure were heightened by numerous newspaper reports of
criminal or neglectful behaviour by unqualified and seemingly unscrupulous midwives, as well as by fictional depictions of careless – sometimes
drunken – midwives and nurses, epitomised by Charles Dickens's Sarah
Gamp in *Martin Chuzzlewit* (as Mitchell's comment suggests), who attends
'a lying-in or a laying-out with equal zest and relish' and whose society
'it was difficult to enjoy […] without becoming conscious of a smell of
spirits'.[19] Such depictions, though, including reports of midwives facing
criminal charges, contributed to the demonisation of this figure, and to
a negative and skewed impression of the abilities of the female midwife.
Some midwives did face trial on criminal charges, but so too did multiple
medical men, and there is little beyond anecdotal evidence to suggest that
birthing women suffered any more at the hands of negligent midwives
than they did under the care of male doctors.

There were, over the course of the nineteenth century, numerous
cases of charges laid against medical men, who, despite their

qualifications, on occasion proved to be neglectful or incompetent, in some cases causing the death of the child and/or the mother or leaving women with significant lasting damage following childbirth. Despite this, members of the medical profession were often far more critical of women practising as midwives. Such criticisms coincide with the moves by some in the medical profession to include midwifery under its remit from the eighteenth century onwards, although others, including the Royal Colleges, initially opposed this (it was this resistance by the colleges which in part delayed the passing of the Midwives Act until 1902). Writing in 1748 in *An Essay Upon Nursing*, William Cadogan argued that 'the Preservation of Children should become the Care of Men of Sense because this business has been too long fatally left to the Management of Women'.[20] By the mid-nineteenth century, many figures within the medical profession were demanding that women in childbirth be assisted by qualified medical practitioners. Edward William Murphy, Professor of Midwifery at University College London, was one of those calling for change, as illustrated in his lecture which appeared in the *Association Medical Journal* in 1853:

> The history of midwifery [...] proves that the public are gradually becoming more and more alive to the importance of education amongst those who profess to practise it. Formerly, the universal rule was to separate the practice of midwifery altogether from the medical profession. Medical education was not thought [...] essential for security [...] The charge of parturient woman was therefore committed exclusively to the midwife. However, her incompetency to meet all the difficulties and accidents that presented themselves soon became manifest [...] In process of time, [...] the public found out the truth, that the midwives knew little or nothing, and that it was essential for their security that the person in whom they confided should be educated.[21]

By this point, as Murphy goes on to note, change was already underway, with those of means frequently electing to employ a medical man over a midwife. Midwives therefore were frequently employed by the poorer classes, sometimes as part of the provision offered by the various lying-in hospitals and charities, but also in the role of assistants to medical men. Murphy argued that 'Midwives are now but rarely met with, except amongst the lowest classes; and even here, I know by experience, they are received with reluctance. The poor certainly employ them; but "'tis not their will, their poverty consents".'[22] Murphy's objections, given his position as a Professor of Midwifery, are likely linked to the medical profession's wider gatekeeping which sought, certainly in some quarters, to limit women's ability to practise any form of medicine, but this type of discourse reinforced negative stereotypes, and was bolstered by the numerous cases reported in the press involving seemingly incompetent, unqualified, neglectful, and sometimes drunken midwives – on occasion with tragic consequences. In November 1860, an inquest examined the death of 20-year-old Ann Wilks, who was living as a housekeeper in her uncle's house and was unmarried. During her confinement, she was attended by a midwife named Hannah Rogers. Following the birth of a baby boy, the midwife attempted to remove the placenta, but employed such force that severe damage was caused to the internal organs, and Miss Wilks died shortly afterwards. The inquest noted that such force 'would not be resorted to by a professional man' – although Robert Lee's published case studies include several incidents in which medical men applied excessive force, sometimes inflicting significant damage. One witness at the inquest suggested that the midwife was drunk. Hannah Rogers provided no testimony beyond suggesting that she had acted as a midwife in 'a hundred cases'. The jury at the inquest returned a verdict of manslaughter.[23]

In 1866, an inquiry was held into the deaths of a 27-year-old woman, Jane Matthews, and her newborn son. Mrs Matthews was attended at the birth of her sixth child by two midwives, Mrs Carter and Mrs Jones. The midwives left their patient one and a half hours after the birth of the child, despite Jane Matthews's pleas for them to stay. Around two hours later, she died. A subsequent post-mortem revealed the cause of death to be haemorrhaging. The child also died – though whether before or after birth is unclear. The doctor who testified at the inquest declared that Mrs Matthews 'had died from sheer neglect', arguing that 'No properly qualified midwife would have left her for two hours unattended' – though again there are accounts of similar neglect by medical men throughout the period. The two midwives also gave evidence at the inquest. Frances Carter's testimony demonstrates her lack of formal training, but this was not unusual given the restrictions on female education at the time:

I am a midwife. I have no diploma, and I have gone through no course
of instruction. I have never attended any lectures. I can read a little,
but I can't write. My husband [...] writes out the certificates of death
for me when people's children die. I arranged to attend the deceased
for 6s. I found that the deceased was getting very low, and I gave her
a powder. I do not know what the powder contained. [...] I do not
know the cause of the woman's death. I issue cards, and give them
about to working people, and I have a board with the word 'midwife'
upon it up over my door.[24]

Mrs Jones, who had delivered the baby, claimed she was certified, but that
she had lost the certificate in a fire some years previously. This was the
second time she had been called on to appear at a coroner's court following the death of one of her patients. In this case, the coroner concluded
that 'the ignorant stupidity of the midwives had caused the deceased to
lose her life'.[25] Ultimately, though, if accusations of 'ignorant stupidity'
held true for some midwives, that was at least partly a consequence of the
difficulty they had in accessing an adequate education – something for
which patriarchal society at the time was largely responsible. It was cases
such as these which increased the pressure on lawmakers to regulate the
profession of midwifery, though it would take many years to achieve this.

In other cases, criminal charges were brought against midwives. In
1883, a 63-year-old midwife, Martha Schofield, from Sheffield, was
accused of having 'unlawfully and maliciously inflicted grievous bodily
harm' upon two women and a child. Schofield had consulted a doctor
after sores appeared on her hand, and it was discovered she was suffering
from what newspaper reports described as 'a loathsome disease of a highly
contagious character' – in other words, syphilis. Schofield claimed to
have contracted this from one of her patients. She was told by the doctor
not to attend women in childbirth whilst suffering from the disease, but
continued to do so, infecting several of her patients who subsequently
infected their husbands and children. Schofield pleaded not guilty to
the charges and was committed for trial.[26] There she was found guilty
and sentenced to twelve months' imprisonment with hard labour.[27] The
details of Schofield's case are somewhat unusual, but warnings to doctors
and midwives to avoid practising after contact with certain diseases and
infections (particularly puerperal fever) were not that unusual. In 1896,

another midwife, Elizabeth Hughes, was charged with manslaughter over the death of 23-year-old Elizabeth Wistow, after attending her despite having attended another patient who died of puerperal fever and being instructed not to practise for three weeks.[28] She was subsequently found not guilty and acquitted – the case deemed to be one of misadventure rather than criminal negligence. Again, it is worth acknowledging the various forces at work in relation to these cases: Hughes's and Schofield's actions may have been irresponsible in the extreme, but in a country in which there was no sick pay and no welfare state, people frequently had to work regardless of circumstances in order to survive. Ignorance due to lack of education may also have played a role here, and the midwives may not have realised the consequences of their actions, as information about the spread of disease was part of the medical knowledge largely inaccessible to midwives.

In 1883, a midwife by the name of Harriet Vinson was charged with manslaughter following the death of 32-year-old Emma Elliot shortly after the birth of her sixth child. Vinson was said to have 'neglected her patient while under the influence of drink'.[29] Giving evidence at the trial, Emma Elliot's husband told the court he had heard of Vinson 'as a midwife who had attended a large number of confinements successfully' – indicative of the extent to which maternity care, amongst some social classes at least, was dependent on word of mouth. It is also, though, testament to Vinson's capability as a midwife, and it was inevitably the case that midwives attending hundreds of births a year would lose some patients, given the maternal mortality rates at the time. Nonetheless, the details of this case are disturbing. According to one eyewitness report, Vinson consumed the best part of a bottle of gin during the birth, pulled the afterbirth away in pieces, and made no efforts to stop the subsequent bleeding. Vinson was found guilty and sentenced to eight months' hard labour.[30]

As elsewhere, the quality of care provided by midwives attending workhouses varied significantly. In 1836, a coroner's inquest examined the death of a newborn child, in relation to its treatment by Mrs Charlotte Bright, head midwife at Marylebone Workhouse, who was accused of causing the death of a newborn child through 'unskilful treatment and mismanagement'. Bright 'declared her belief that when the child was born it had been dead thirty-six hours', but this claim was disputed by a surgeon who had examined the body and declared that the child was 'perfectly healthy' but that 'it had sustained great injury in the neck, the vertebrae being dislocated; the bones of the head also appeared to have been compressed in the birth'. The surgeon concluded that the child was 'alive in the birth' and that his death was caused by 'the injudicious treatment of the midwife' who appeared to have used 'more force [...] than was necessary'. He declared: 'There can be no doubt that the neck was dislocated by the unskilful treatment at the birth, and the discolouration of the throat was produced by the pressure of the midwife's hands in prematurely accelerating the delivery.' The jury agreed and concluded that the child 'met its death by the injudicious management of the midwife'.[31] This 'injudicious management' is a reflection of the difficult position of midwives in the prevailing patriarchal society, where women were also largely denied the benefits of a good education.

These cases are indeed often harrowing, yet not without interest, but they nonetheless contribute to a wider cultural misrepresentation of the figure of the midwife in nineteenth-century Britain. This is obviously not to say that some women did not experience poor care at the hands of midwives, but inevitably, negligent and incompetent midwives are overrepresented in newspapers and coroners' reports: good outcomes were, of course, outside the remit of both the press and the coroner. The testimony of working women discussing their experiences of maternity care is also somewhat subjective in this respect, with midwives rarely mentioned except in a negative context, though many working-class women were delivered by them. Many of the women whose experiences of childbirth in the late nineteenth and early twentieth centuries are detailed in *Maternity: Letters From Working Women* were attended only by midwives, with varying experiences. One mother of six alludes to the fact that she was never attended by a doctor, only by 'an old midwife', and on one occasion by no one at all, when the child arrived before the midwife could be summoned.[32] All her labours seem to have been relatively short and the births straightforward, suggesting the competency of the midwife, but other women were not as fortunate. Another contributor describes how she too was attended only by a midwife but accuses her of neglecting the baby following the birth: 'the midwife having lodgers to attend to, left him unwashed for an hour after birth. She never troubled to get his lungs inflated, and he was two days without crying.' This account speaks to the impact of poverty not only on birthing women, who were limited in terms of the maternity care they could afford, but also the midwives who attended them and who typically earned very little: in this case, the midwife's income was clearly supplemented by renting out rooms. The contributor comments on this in her account: 'When we are poor, [...] we cannot say what must be done; we have to suffer and keep quiet.' However, it is worth noting that the accusations she levels at the midwife here do not necessarily tally with modern understandings of poor maternity care: it may have been a need to attend her lodgers that led the midwife not to wash the child, but the World Health Organisation today advises that babies are not washed for twenty-four hours after birth – as the vernix (the natural film which covers the baby) protects the skin from breakdown after birth.[33] The mother recalls how the child was 'always weakly', did not walk for a long time, and suffered from fits – attributing this to the poor care he received at birth.[34] However, the reference to the midwife neglecting to 'get his lungs inflated' suggests the baby may not have breathed initially at birth, and this, rather than the midwife's actions – or indeed the poverty in which the family existed, which would have increased the risk of malnutrition and diseases such as rickets – may have been responsible for the child's 'weakly' state. In another case, a doctor refused to attend a woman in labour and so she was attended by a midwife instead. The child subsequently died during the birth, but given infant mortality rates, the care received may have had nothing to do with the infant's death. The doctor, on being informed of this development, 'said he was very glad, as he wanted his rest'. In a subsequent pregnancy, the mother sent for the doctor, but 'he was drinking, and sent another midwife'.[35] In both these cases, it is the doctor who appears negligent. Some correspondents do reference the figure of the drunken midwife – although this at times appears to be conjecture and rumour. One woman recalls that during her second pregnancy, 'I heard that the midwife I had the first time had started drinking, so I was afraid to have her.'[36] In another account, the correspondent employed a qualified midwife without realising she was 'addicted to drink'.[37] Another suggests that it was common knowledge that many nurses and midwives drank.[38] This statement does not, of course, provide any evidence that midwives were particularly prone to drink, but rather suggests the circulation of the negative stereotypes associated with midwives amongst the general population. Several newspaper reports of negligent midwives also suggest they may have been drunk whilst practising, including some cases in which the mother subsequently died.[39] In 1836, Poor Law Commissioners for Halstead Union Workhouse in Essex dismissed a drunken midwife, along with the master of the workhouse, who had allegedly refused to provide adequate medical care for female inmates during their confinements.[40] Again, these reports reinforce a negative view of midwives, but the cases they detail are exceptional, and should not detract from the important role midwives played in the maternal lives of women in nineteenth-century Britain.

The accounts from poorer women, however, suggest they may have absorbed some of these messages regarding the capabilities of midwives rather than medical men, and what they do indicate is that many of them exercised very little control over the care they were able to access during pregnancy and childbirth. Prior to the introduction of the New Poor Law in 1834, those in need could appeal directly to local overseers for support when they found themselves struggling. A record of such appeals is found in pauper letters from this period, and these frequently mention the need for money to obtain nursing care for women during or after their confinements. These letters reveal the difficulties the poor frequently faced in securing any kind of assistance for birthing women. In one case from 1825, a Samuel White wrote to request help for his wife and family:

> I have six Children two of them in arms, my wife in Confinement and a Nurse in the house, besides – which I have had three Children bad with the Measles and the youngest but one is left in such a weak state as to be not likely to walk alone this six Months if ever.[41]

In 1829, a man named David Rivenall wrote to beg assistance for his wife, recently confined with twins and now 'in a dangerous state'.[42] In another example from 1833, a man named John Smoothy wrote to appeal for money to help with the care of his daughter-in-law, who 'have been Confind nerly five weeks and she had a very bad brast and is fost to keep a woman in the house all the time for she cannot situ up but avary little at a time and she cannot maintain the cous' [*sic*].[43] These letters highlight the plight of the poor in the early decades of the nineteenth century, forced to resort to a form of begging in order to try and obtain any kind of maternity or other healthcare. Obtaining the services of a midwife who was responsible, knowledgeable, and experienced was frequently a matter of luck. In some cases, the women attending childbirth were not midwives, let alone qualified. Writing of her youth, Mrs P. Marrin, born in 1890, noted, 'There were no trained midwives, and any woman who knew how came into deliver the baby in the absence of the doctor.'[44] One woman recalls how she 'happened to get a woman who did not know her work'. Consequently, she claims, she developed childbed fever and was 'seriously ill for three weeks'.[45] In a number of cases, midwives refused to call in a doctor, often with detrimental consequences to both mother and child.[46] Such accounts testify to the huge benefits brought about not only by the reforms in midwifery and maternity care, but particularly by the increase of state support for poor mothers, and later following the establishment of the NHS in 1948. By the early twentieth century, the situation was beginning to improve, at least in terms of the training and registration of midwives,[47] but there was still much to be done, as one contributor to the Women's Co-operative Guild notes:

What is really wanted is a supply of real good midwives who could be got for a month to see to all requirements for the patient and the home while the woman has a fair chance of recovering. It is the system of midwives attending too many cases at the same time that is responsible for a lot of the trouble, as the woman gets neglected and are forced to get about before they are fit.[48]

The idea of the neglectful midwife is also referenced in a case from the late nineteenth century, detailed in *Maternity*. At between three and four months into her pregnancy, the woman experienced a miscarriage, and was attended by a midwife, who did not realise the mother was carrying twins and had only miscarried one of the foetuses. A few months later, she went into premature labour, unaware that she was still pregnant. The child 'was weak and did not move much' and died at 9 months old. The mother in her account to the Women's Co-operative Guild laments the lack of proper care she received: 'If I had been able to have a qualified midwife when I had the miscarriage, we should have known there was another child, and if I could have been medically treated, all that suffering could have been prevented, and I might have had a strong child.'[49] However, detecting the existence of multiple foetuses prior to the development of ultrasounds was not straightforward, and even in late pregnancy and childbirth this was not always apparent until the babies appeared, so there is little to suggest the attending midwife was at fault, or that the attendance of a medical man would have resulted in a different outcome. In December 1840, an accoucheur was called to attend Mrs Doud, the wife of a merchant tailor, in Clifden in Galway. She was delivered of twin boys. The next morning, though, the accoucheur was once again summoned, and Mrs Doud gave birth to a third baby – a girl – to the accoucheur's 'great surprise'.[50] The limitations of medical knowledge and technology in the mid-nineteenth century meant it was not always possible to detect issues which would be easily identified today, and it was not necessarily the case that medical attendants were negligent in their treatment of patients.

The negative attention paid to cases involving unqualified and incompetent midwives in the press increased the pressure on the government to regulate the profession, and as the century progressed women were gradually able to access some training, as well as obtain certificates of midwifery, although full regulation did not occur until the early twentieth century. Institutions such as the Nightingale Training School at St Thomas's Hospital in London and the Ladies' Medical College, also in London, offered some training in midwifery for women from the 1860s onwards. Attempts by women to register for the midwifery examination at the Royal College of Surgeons in 1875 (which, if successful and the examination passed, would have enabled them to be included on the Medical Register) prompted the resignation of the examiners, including celebrated obstetrician Arthur Farre (who had attended various royals during childbirth), in protest. It was not until the 1876 Medical Act that women were enabled to be licensed as doctors. The General Lying-In Hospital in Lambeth, London trained midwives from 1879 onwards. The Trained Midwives Registration Society (later the Midwives Institute) was established in 1881, with the aim of 'rais[ing] the efficiency and improv[ing] the status of midwives and to petition parliament for their recognition',[51] although many women practising as midwives received some form of informal training prior to this. Campaigns to regulate midwifery intensified towards the end of the century, with eight Bills introduced in parliament between 1889 and 1900 – none of which were successful. In 1897, the Association for Promoting Compulsory Registration of Midwives published a letter in several newspapers in support of the latest Bill:

The object of the Bill is to ensure that women who assume the name of midwife shall have some knowledge to fit them for their work. This would protect thousands of mothers and children from the terrible suffering so often caused by the casual and ignorant persons who now are free to assume the name – suffering well-known to those whose work takes them among the poor, but of which the public only gets a glimpse when some flagrantly bad case (often in a Coroner's Court) attracts the attention of the Press. [...] We believe that the improvement and supervision of midwives working among the poor would prevent some of the most pitiful tragedies that desolate their homes.[52]

In 1902, the Midwives Act for England and Wales was passed, formally regulating midwifery. It required midwives to be certified and introduced a penalty for those practising without the necessary qualifications. An exception was made, though, for 'bona fide' midwives – those with a long history of good practice: a recognition of their important contribution (in contradistinction to the negative image of unqualified midwives perpetuated by the press and by some medical men). The Act laid the groundwork for the improvements in maternity care that we see today.

Despite the anxieties around and stereotypes of female midwives in some quarters in the nineteenth century, many, indeed perhaps most, were experienced, highly skilled, and provided high levels of care for their patients, regardless of a lack of professional qualifications. The cases which made the papers were undoubtedly rare, and it is worth noting that the almost total absence of most of these women from the historical record might be taken as indicative of good practice; it was the rare exceptions of bad practice which made the papers. The census, along with trade directories from the latter half of the nineteenth century, lists thousands of midwives practising in the towns and cities of Britain, and most of these women do not appear elsewhere on the historical record. They provided an invaluable service for women throughout the period – particularly, though not exclusively for poorer women, who could not afford doctor's fees. Indeed, in the earlier decades of the nineteenth century, it was common for midwives to be present even at the births of the wealthier classes, albeit often alongside a medical man. One midwife – a German woman named Marian Theodore Charlotte Heidenreich von Siebold – attended the births, in 1819, of both the future Queen Victoria and, three months later, Victoria's future husband, Prince Albert. However, unlike the unqualified midwives who frequently attended births in Britain, Madame Siebold was a qualified obstetrician, having taken her exams in Germany in 1814.[53] Despite her royal connections, she went on to establish an institution providing maternity care for poor women in 1845.[54] On the whole, though, the 'good' midwife does not figure much in the historical records: often from poor backgrounds themselves, midwives leave little in the way of autobiographical writing. Mothers, writing of their experience of midwives, rarely mention them in any detail unless in a negative context: in multiple writings they appear only as unnamed midwives attending women during birth. Occasionally, their voices can be heard – in court testimonies, for example, in cases where they have been called forward as witnesses. In 1881, in one such case, a midwife named Mary Anne Morley testified in the trial of a 21-year-old woman, Sarah Norman, who was charged with 'the wilful murder of her female child'.[55] Mary attended Sarah during the delivery of her daughter, and her testimony reveals some of the care she provided:

> I am a midwife; I went to see the prisoner on 9th December, to attend her; she gave birth to a child at 11.30 that night; it was a fine, full-grown female child—I attended her from the 9th to the 14th December daily, and Mrs. Charwood, her mother-in-law, undertook the charge of the baby from the 14th—no doctor attended the prisoner—she was in excellent health and very good spirits.

Despite the tragic outcome of this case (Sarah killed her child whilst suffering from puerperal mania), Morley's account suggests the maternity care the patient received was not at fault.

Midwives played a role not only in attending those who could not afford to pay a doctor, but also in supporting medical men in their practice. In his autobiography, published in 1892, Hamlet Nicholson,[56] the son of a shoemaker and a midwife, provides some information about his mother's profession. Sarah Nicholson (née Law) was born in the 1770s and was mother to a large family. As Nicholson's account makes clear, her maternal experience was central to her work as a midwife in Rochdale, whilst her competence meant she was often called upon by the local doctor:

My mother, having had a large family, was, on account of her experience, soon brought into requisition as midwife; and she ultimately became known as such, all over the town. Indeed, so successful did she become, that she was entrusted frequently by the principal doctor, Dr. Wood, with cases of well-to-do ladies when he could not attend, or, being in attendance, might be hurriedly called away.

As a midwife, Sarah Nicholson attended both rich and poor, and Nicholson notes that 'in the cases of very poor women she would not make a charge for attending on them during their confinement, there being at that time no "Ladies' Charity" in the town'.[57]

A detailed account from a practising midwife's perspective is found in the autobiography of a Mrs Layton, entitled 'Memories of Seventy Years', which was included in the Women's Co-operative Guild's publication, *Life As We Have Known It*, first published in 1931. Mrs Layton, born in 1855, worked as maternity nurse and subsequently a midwife, although she did not receive formal hospital training. Her first experience of childbirth was assisting 'an old woman who called herself a midwife' during her sister's labour. Her recollections of the experience provide some insight into the practice of midwifery in the mid-Victorian period:

When I remember the methods adopted to carry out childbirth and the puerperal period in those days, it seems wonderful to me that so many mothers lived to bring a large family into the world. In some instances the poor unfortunate patient was not allowed to have her face and hands washed for days. [...] Then, after the trying ordeal they had gone through, they were not allowed to go to sleep for some hours.[58]

She was subsequently recommended to attend a woman during her confinement when a nurse could not be found, and from then worked as a maternity nurse. She was advised by doctors 'to go in for midwifery', but could not, for many years, afford either the fees or the time required for training, so 'had to content [herself] with being a maternity nurse', whilst hoping she 'should ultimately become a midwife'. From the doctors with whom she worked, Mrs Layton obtained significant midwifery knowledge – both theoretical and practical, including on delivery using forceps. She also attended 'several post-mortems with a doctor', including one particularly moving case 'of a young girl who was pregnant and had poisoned herself'. The doctor opening the womb, she recalls how she saw 'the dear little baby lying so snugly in its mother'. Such experiences proved both 'interesting and instructive', and eventually she began to attend cases without a doctor – 'sometimes as many as a hundred cases in a year'. Although recognised within her community as a midwife, she still had not undertaken any formal training. Eventually she saved the money to do so, but then failed the exam. The Midwives Act of 1902 prevented women such as Mrs Layton, without formal training and qualifications, from practising as midwives, but some provision was made for experienced, competent midwives. Women who could prove they had been practising for more than a year, were of good character, and competent, could apply for the status of 'bona fide' midwife and thus be formally registered as practitioners.[59] Whilst recognising the valuable contribution made by unqualified midwives, the Act also attempted to protect women from unscrupulous and neglectful midwives, noting that any midwife 'guilty of any disgraceful conduct in her practice [...] shall be liable to have her name erased from the roll'.[60] Mrs Layton 'was recommended for a certificate as a bona fide midwife', which she duly received. She subsequently became involved in the Co-operative Guild's campaign for better maternity provision for working women.[61]

Some midwives, as well as some doctors, also worked as abortionists. In 1892, midwife Jane Inglis was found guilty of causing the death of Margaret Ann Young, a domestic servant, through the performance of an 'illegal operation'.[62] A few years later, Jane Talbot was charged with causing the death through an illegal operation of one of her patients – a single woman named Ellen Eliza Robotham. She was sentenced to death but recommended to mercy.[63] Around the same time, Jane White, described as a 'bona fide midwife' – presumably one of the long-experienced midwives with a good reputation who would subsequently qualify for official status under the 1902 Midwives Act – was charged with the murder of one of her patients following an 'illegal operation' in 1899. Witnesses at White's trial gave evidence suggesting she had also worked as an abortionist for some years, providing drugs intended to terminate pregnancy.[64] The role of these women as both midwives and abortionists speaks to the demand for 'illegal operations', and perhaps also to the resourcefulness of those women: for poorer women working as midwives, wages were low, and income often had to be supplemented in other ways. Furthermore, at a time when women struggled to exercise control over their reproduction, these women were providing a vital service within their communities.

Lying-In Hospitals

Whilst many women were attended by midwives in their own homes, others gave birth in Britain's various lying-in hospitals. The state throughout this period provided little in the way of medical support, so women were largely dependent on their own means or upon charity. Charitable support came in the form of Lying-in Hospitals and Societies, which operated throughout Britain, providing care for poor women who could not afford to pay for maternity services themselves. Amongst the earliest of these institutions was the British Lying-in Hospital (established 1749), the City of London Lying-in Hospital (established 1750), and the General Lying-in Hospital (established 1752) – all based in London. Similar institutions were founded elsewhere around this time: in Newcastle in 1760, and in Edinburgh in the early 1790s, amongst other places. All of these institutions were essentially hospitals which women could attend to give birth with some medical assistance. Also in operation were lying-in charities, which assisted women giving birth at home, through the supply of provisions, and in some cases medical attendants, to assist in childbirth and afterwards. The Lying-in Charity in Colchester, Essex was established in 1796 and remains in operation in the twenty-first century. Today the charity provides grants of up to £250 to expectant and new mothers for the purchase of essential items for young babies. Grants are means tested and available for residents of Colchester who are either pregnant or have a baby under 6 months old. When the charity was first established, however, like other institutions and societies of its kind, eligibility also depended on marital status.

The vast majority of these charitable endeavours throughout the eighteenth and nineteenth centuries were intended only for *married* women. Women who fell pregnant outside of marriage were typically not seen as deserving of charity and would therefore need to rely on their own resources or the workhouse. When it was first established, the British Lying-in Hospital was named the Lying-in Hospital for Married Women; and the stated aim of the Newcastle Lying-in Hospital was to provide for 'poor married women'. Similarly, the City of London Lying-in Hospital was designed to assist 'poor pregnant married women'. The latter began to admit some single women in the late Victorian period, but the rules were not formally relaxed on this issue until 1912. Furthermore, such charitable institutions did not merely rely on women's assurances that they were married: patients typically had to be recommended by the charities' patrons and subscribers, and were often asked to provide documentary evidence in the form of a marriage certificate. The requirements of the Newcastle hospital were fairly typical in this respect:

> Every woman desiring admittance into the hospital must produce a certificate of her marriage, including the time and place of marriage, and state the settlement of her husband, and how such settlement was obtained: and to those facts she and her husband must jointly swear.[65]

In addition to proof of marriage, lying-in charities often required proof of moral character. The Newcastle hospital operating procedures stated: 'No woman can be admitted labouring under any contagious distemper, or not having a fixed residence, except her husband be a soldier or sailor.'[66] Such language speaks to nineteenth-century attitudes towards the 'deserving' and 'undeserving' poor: only those women deemed 'respectable' were considered worthy of charitable assistance during childbirth. This is further reflected in a pamphlet addressed to potential benefactors of the City of London Lying-in Hospital, published in 1823, which provided a stirring overview of the type of women the charity aided, positioning the charity's aims in relation to ideas of national pride and patriotism:

> Those for whom this Establishment [...] claims pre-eminence are the wives of industrious mechanics, who have brought the arts of England to their present splendour, refinement, and perfection: they are also the wives and widows of soldiers and of seamen, whose personal vigour and in-born native courage have added unsullied glory to our gracious Monarch's crown, solid union to his people, and unrivalled honour to

themselves; and whose valour has saved and defended their country in war, and extended its commerce in peace; also of men who have been visited with misfortune, and have sunk from prosperous stations – who have pined in sickness, and have been lost in poverty.[67]

The Gateshead Lying-in Charity, whose object was 'the Relief of Poor Married Women at their own houses, during their confinement', like other similar organisations required inquiries to be made into a woman's character before the aid of the charity could be given. Subscribers to the charity were given tickets, which were then distributed to married women as needed. On receipt of a ticket, a pregnant woman took it to the 'Lady Visitors' who worked for the charity, and who would then inquire into the woman's character: 'if on inquiry she be found an improper person the Lady is then empowered to detain the Ticket, and a fresh blank is to be given to the Subscriber'.[68] For charities such as these, then, maternity care was dependent on society's perceptions of women's behaviour and morals. These attitudes – particularly the prejudice directed towards the figure of the unmarried mother – remained influential through much of the twentieth century. As late as the 1970s, whilst unmarried mothers were not denied maternity care, many were forced to give up their babies for adoption. Enquiries into this practice are still ongoing today.[69]

As charitable organisations, lying-in hospitals were obviously reliant on donations (perhaps one reason for the careful policing of recipients of the benefits they offered, in line with wider public attitudes towards the single mother). At times, as with other institutions such as London's Foundling Hospital, donations fell short whilst demand outstripped what the charities could offer. This is reflected in an advert for donations for the British Lying-in Hospital in 1865 which cited a deficiency of £254 over the past year, and advised that there were sixty poor women currently awaiting admission.[70] Some women who might otherwise have been eligible for care in one of these lying-in institutions might, then, have to give birth either at home, with whatever medical attendants they could afford, or, for those in dire poverty, and in particular for single women, in the workhouse. The limited options available for unmarried mothers is reflected in the fact that this demographic continued to constitute a significant proportion of the women who gave birth in workhouses in nineteenth-century Britain.[71] Whilst some workhouses employed a matron or midwife (though not necessarily qualified) to assist birthing women, others relied on female inmates to attend their fellow paupers during and after childbirth. Social reformer and Poor Law Guardian Louisa Twining (of the family who owned the Twinings tea company) described one such situation in one of the many workhouses she visited:

> The Lying-in Ward, which, until a short time before I went, was only a General Ward, without even Screens, had an old inmate in it who we discovered to have an ulcerated leg and cancer of the breast; yet she did nearly everything for the women and babies, and often delivered them too.[72]

For those women who were able to gain entry to lying-in hospitals, standards of maternity care might generally be expected to be better than what was often provided by the numerous unqualified and untrained midwives typically brought in by the poor to attend home births, or indeed the maternity care available in most of Britain's workhouses. Indeed, in complicated cases in lying-in hospitals, patients might be attended by one of the obstetricians who typically catered to the wealthier classes of society. Charles Locock, for example, who delivered Queen Victoria's children, was the physician to the General Lying-in Hospital in Westminster, whilst other leading obstetricians, including Robert Lee and Gustavus Murray, also attended women in various lying-in institutions. Lee records several of the cases he attended in London's lying-in hospitals in his work *Three Hundred Consultations in Midwifery* – where he was primarily brought in to attend cases where complications had arisen. Delivery in a lying-in hospital did not, of course, guarantee decent levels of maternity care, or a positive outcome, as the cases of Martha Stone, who died at London's Adelaide Lying-in Hospital, and Mary Stephenson, who died in Newcastle Lying-in Hospital in 1824, illustrate. It is worth noting, though, that the medical notes in the latter case point to the fact that the patient did not follow earlier medical advice to allow doctors to induce premature labour at the end of the seventh month in order to enable her to deliver a live child. Although she avoided a stillbirth and delivered a daughter, the prolongation of the labour as a consequence of the deformity of the pelvis may well have led to the infection from which she subsequently died.[73]

Another risk faced by women giving birth in lying-in wards in hospitals or workhouses was the possibility of the spread of infection, and in particular puerperal fever. With limited understanding around the spread of disease for much of the period, outbreaks remained relatively common and were a cause for alarm and anxiety. Recognition that midwives and doctors could spread the disease led to advice that anyone dealing with a case of puerperal fever should not attend another woman during childbirth for a period of several weeks, although, as the multiple inquests into the deaths of women in childbed show, this advice was not always followed. Beyond this, the difficulties involved in preventing the spread of the disease presented a particular challenge within lying-in hospitals and wards. Such were the rates of disease in some of these institutions that Florence Nightingale, writing on the issue, suggested that:

> Unless [...] it can be clearly shown that these enormous death-rates can be abated, or that they are altogether inevitable, does not the whole evidence with regard to special lying-in hospitals lead but to one conclusion – viz., that they should be closed? Is there any conceivable amount of privation which would warrant such a step as bringing together a constant number of puerperal women into the same room, in buildings constructed and managed on the principles embodied in existing lying-in institutions?[74]

The advantages that such institutions appeared to offer to women from the poorer classes of society were thus to some extent undermined by the potential dangers they posed to maternal health. By the end of the century, however, the increased use of good hygiene practices and antiseptics in lying-in hospitals had significantly reduced mortality rates in these settings and so, conversely, they began to appear safer than other birthing locales.[75] This significant shift in practices around maternity care foregrounds the move to predominantly hospital births later in the twentieth century. With an emphasis on good hygiene and good medical practice more generally, hospitals gradually came to be viewed as the safest location for birthing women, providing them with access to a range of medical professionals and equipment if needed, effectively centralising maternity care. By the 1970s, there was general agreement on the advantages of hospital births, with one government report from 1971 recommending all women should deliver in hospital, rather than at home.[76]

Obstetrics: Interventions and Pain Relief

Whilst birthing attendants and locations were partly dependent on class and status, so too were the types and standard of obstetrics care women received. As the field became increasingly the domain of the medical man, so too did many of the interventions and procedures that often accompanied childbirth, in particular, the use of instruments and the administration of pain relief. In these various settings, and attended by variously qualified medical attendants, women might experience straight-forward or more complicated births. Any vaginal intervention – whether by a hand or an instrument – posed a risk of infection, whilst the use of instruments, particularly forceps, could cause significant physical damage to both mother and child. Women were not necessarily fully informed of the procedures carried out by medical staff in the birthing room, or of the possible risks attached to these interventions. In some instances, as confirmed by the debates around puerperal fever, for example, the medi-cal profession also remained ignorant of some of the risks involved in certain procedures. Today, interventions during childbirth are performed when the baby is in distress or the mother is struggling to deliver, and thus remain associated with increased risk. Midwife-led birthing centres and home births are only recommended for uncomplicated cases, and one measure of this is whether or not interventions – in the form of induced labour, the use of forceps or the ventouse, or the performance of episi-otomy or Caesarean section – are required. Significantly, interventions during childbirth are today identified as a risk factor for the development of symptoms of postnatal post-traumatic stress disorder (PTSD). Now, these interventions tend to be managed in consultation with patients, and take place in conjunction with pain management, but for women in the nineteenth century, there was frequently no consultation, and no option of pain relief.

The most common interventions employed during this period in cases of complicated labour included turning, the use of forceps to try and enable delivery (still commonly used today), and the employment of destructive instruments to perform craniotomies in cases where delivery was otherwise considered impossible. Caesarean sections were rarely per-formed due to the high maternal mortality rate: one work on obstetric operations published in 1880 suggested a maternal mortality rate of 85 per cent, based on seventy-seven cases in which Caesarean was performed in Britain.[77] There was significant debate within the medical community over whether or not women should be consulted or even informed about the performance of the various procedures sometimes employed during childbirth. One French work on midwifery, by M. Chailly, translated into English, advocated concealing from the birthing mother the nature of interventions – particularly in cases of instrumental delivery:

> Almost all writers [on obstetrics] recommend a rule which I do not think it is wise always to observe. They suggest that, before applying the instrument, it should be shown to the patient[.] [...] I think it is much more likely to alarm the patient than to tranquilize her, unless her mind should be unusually firm. The sight of the instrument alone terrifies most women[.]

Consequently, he suggests, the best course of action is to 'keep the patient in ignorance of what you are about to do, assure her that the hand alone will suffice, [and] conceal the instrument from her sight'.[78] He also proposes that the operation of 'turning' the child should be concealed from the patient: 'she should be told that only a slight change is to be effected', and 'the accoucheur should never delay the operation [...] because he has not obtained the consent of the patient.' 'Indeed,' he continues, he 'should not even ask consent, for it only alarms the patient and frequently causes her to object.'[79] An explanation of the risks attached to certain procedures in the process of obtaining consent can indeed be alarming (I have a vague memory of signing a consent form which detailed, amongst other things, risk of death, prior to my daughter's delivery by Caesarean section). Ultimately, though, the performance of invasive and often painful procedures without the patient's knowledge or consent risks potential long-term mental and emotional (as well as physical) consequences, whilst medical ethics today require patients to be fully informed of the procedures to be carried out.

Not all obstetricians agreed with Chailly's approach to patient consent. The translator of his work into English, an American Professor of Midwifery named Gunning S. Bedford, included a note in his edition disputing Chailly's conclusions on this point: 'On the contrary, I think [the patient] should not only be informed of [the operation], and her assent obtained, but she should likewise know that her child will incur more or less hazard in consequence of the operation.'[80] An article in the *British and Foreign Medical Review* agreed with Bedford's approach:

> Chailly [...] would perform the operation of turning without the consent of the patient, and would 'carefully conceal from her the true nature of it' [...] Dr. Bedford's advice is surely more judicious: that the necessity of interference should be impressed upon the patient's mind; and secondly, that what we are about to do should be frankly communicated to her.[81]

Robert Lee also argued that the patient – or at least those close to her – should be kept informed of proceedings. He suggested that in cases of a forceps delivery, patients should be made aware of what is happening, if possible:

> [I]t is right, before proceeding to apply the blades, to state to the husband and relations, and even to the patient herself, if she is in a condition to comprehend, the reason why you have resolved to trust no longer to the efforts of nature, and even to explain to her what you are going to do.[82]

Lee's statement suggests that whilst the woman's consent was deemed desirable, it was not considered essential, and there can be no doubt that women were sometimes subject to significant interventions by medical practitioners during childbirth without either comprehending or consenting to these. Lee's work includes details of a case in which he was called in to treat a patient 'extensively lacerated with forceps' during labour. The practitioner in this case, according to Lee, 'unadvisedly employed the forceps without a consultation, and before the husband and her relative were convinced of the necessity of interference'.[83] This raises questions about the role of the husband in providing consent for interventions during childbirth in the nineteenth century. In another case cited by Lee, which ultimately resulted in the death of both mother and child, the husband asked doctors not to perform the recommended craniotomy.[84] Another of Lee's consultations resulted in the death of the mother, undelivered of her child, after the husband refused to grant consent for the premature induction of labour.[85] However, case studies from Lee and others suggest that the mother's consent was generally sought in cases where the induction of premature labour was recommended. This recommendation was often made where delivery at full term was anticipated to be problematic – due, for example, to distortion of the pelvis caused by rickets – and likely to result in the death of the infant. Evidently, though, patients did not always consent, as in the case of Mary Stephenson at Newcastle Lying-in Hospital, who was advised to deliver prematurely, but chose not to follow this advice.

The use of instruments during childbirth was relatively common in nineteenth-century Britain: both forceps and destructive instruments used to perform craniotomies. Such interventions could be painful, particularly prior to the regular use of pain relief such as chloroform in childbirth and could also have long-lasting physical and emotional effects. Whilst in some cases the use of instruments was likely the best course of action, in other cases they appear to have been employed somewhat injudiciously. Robert Lee details a case in which he attended a woman who had not been in labour two hours before her inexperienced medical attendant saw fit to employ the forceps. He used 'great force' in his attempts to deliver the child but was unsuccessful. The child was born without assistance a few hours later.[86] The mother subsequently developed symptoms of puerperal peritonitis. Maternity 'care' such as this put the lives of mothers at risk, and instrumental deliveries cost the lives of many mothers and infants over the course of the nineteenth century. For many, they would also have involved almost unendurable levels of pain. Prior to the introduction of chloroform into the birthing room in the late 1840s, women might be administered alcohol or opium (although some practitioners cautioned against the use of these substances). Whilst such approaches may appear outdated, not very many years ago, attending a prenatal group, I and the rest of the expectant mothers were advised to consider a glass of wine in the early stages of labour to help us relax (not NHS recommended), whilst upon arrival in the hospital during my first labour, I was immediately given a co-codamol – a painkiller containing codeine, a type of opiate. There are multiple options available to ease the pain of women in labour today, including gas and air, various pain medications, and anaesthetic in the form of epidurals. Some women choose to deliver without any pain relief, but it is, for the most part, a choice in the UK today, and unlike for many in the nineteenth century, women are not forced to endure unbearable pain.

From the 1840s, ether and subsequently chloroform came to be widely used, the latter following experiments by Scottish doctor James Simpson. The first woman to be administered chloroform in childbirth was Jane Carstairs, the wife of another Scottish doctor, in November 1847. It rapidly became popular, though it was not entirely safe: an overdose could mean death. In January 1848, a teenage girl named Hannah Greener died after receiving chloroform during a procedure to remove a toenail, raising concerns about its safety. John Snow, who would go on to administer the drug to Queen Victoria, developed a method for delivering chloroform in carefully measured doses, to avoid the possibility of overdose.[87] Despite these scientific advances, there were strong objections to the use of pain relief in childbirth in some quarters, partly on religious grounds: the biblical proclamation in Genesis – 'in sorrow shalt thou bring forth children' – was repeatedly cited as evidence against the use of anaesthetics during childbirth. Some obstetricians also objected to its use on medical grounds. In one case of difficult labour described by Lee, in which the infant had already died and delivery had to be achieved using destructive instruments, he states: 'I would not allow chloroform to be given to make her insensible [...] because consciousness is a safeguard to patients in all the operations of midwifery.'[88] Simpson and many other medical men held no truck with such objections, however: 'pain is useless to the pained', Simpson declared,[89] and undoubtedly plenty of birthing women would have agreed.

For many women of the time, including Queen Victoria, chloroform transformed their experience of childbirth. Writing in the 1830s, before the introduction into the birthing room of substances such as ether and chloroform, British actress Fanny Kemble reflected on the pain women experienced during childbirth, and the religious objections to the use of pain relief:

> I cannot believe that women were intended to suffer as much as they do, and be as helpless as they are, in child-bearing. In spite of the third chapter of Genesis, I cannot believe that all the agony and debility attendant upon the entrance of a new creature into life was ordained.[90]

Chloroform works by depressing the nervous system, but – unlike modern epidurals – it affects the consciousness as well as the nerves, causing unconsciousness (and ultimately death) if too much is given. Despite the risks from chloroform, and the controversy surrounding its use, there can be no doubt it provided valuable relief – particularly during difficult labours. In 1848, Darwin wrote of his intention to administer chloroform to Emma during the birth of their sixth child: 'My poor dear wife will be employed in July in bringing into the world, under the influence of Chloriform [*sic*], a sixth little [Darwin].'[91] On 23 July 1863, Princess Marie of Baden gave birth to her first child, Princess Alberta, at Osborne House on the Isle of Wight. Amongst those in attendance at the birth were the celebrated obstetrician Arthur Farre and Queen Victoria. Unfortunately, it was not a straightforward delivery, as the Queen described in a letter to her eldest daughter: 'darling Marie is safe with her magnificent baby but it was an awful labour – 48 hours in pain and 18 in constant labour!' With little progress being made, Farre advised that Marie would need to be delivered with instruments. He 'put her completely under chloroform and she was like as if she slept'. The baby was then delivered 'without her knowing or feeling any thing, and [she] only woke when she heard the child cry and immediately said she wished to have a prayer read to her for she was so thankful.'[92] Other women refused chloroform so as to be cognisant of the baby's arrival. In November 1852, Lady Blanche Airlie (formerly Stanley) gave birth to her first child: a 'beautiful large girl'. Despite having 'a very sharp time', she 'was very brave & wd. not have chloroform so as to hear the first cry'.[93] Chloroform could indeed affect women's awareness, causing drowsiness or even unconsciousness, as the experience of Princess Marie shows, and Queen Victoria's daughter experienced something similar the same year: following the birth of her first child in April 1863, Princess Alice was 'too exhausted & half stupefied by the chloroform to take any notice' of her newborn daughter's cries.[94]

For women who experienced extreme pain during difficult childbirths (a factor today associated with the development of symptoms of postnatal PTSD), the benefits of chloroform undoubtedly outweighed its drawbacks. Its numbing effects, particularly in cases of severe laceration caused by instruments during lengthy extractions of the infant, would have been invaluable. Olive Schreiner was administered chloroform during the birth of her daughter, which undoubtedly spared her the pain inflicted by the instruments used during the delivery: 'I was 2 and a quarter hours unconscious under the chloroform and the instruments tore me [to pieces], but it had to be.'[95] Sixteen hours after delivery, though, her baby unexpectedly died. Whilst chloroform and other drugs might numb the physical pain of childbirth, they could do little to subdue the deep emotional distress experienced by those women who lost their babies: through miscarriage, stillbirth, or early infant death.

Maternal Loss: Miscarriage, Stillbirth, and Infant Death

> DEPARTED Child! I could forget thee once
> Though at my bosom nursed; this woeful gain
> Thy dissolution brings, that in my soul
> Is present and perpetually abides
> A shadow, never, never to be displaced
> By the returning substance, seen or touched,
> Seen by mine eyes, or clasped in my embrace.
> Absence and death how differ they! and how
> Shall I admit that nothing can restore
> What one short sigh so easily removed?
> *William Wordsworth*[1]

In the Royal Vault at St George's Chapel in Windsor Castle are the tombs of more than a dozen monarchs and consorts of Great Britain. As well as Elizabeth II and Prince Philip, these include George VI, Henry VIII and his third wife Jane Seymour, and the beheaded Charles I. Also interred is the coffin of Princess Elizabeth Georgiana Adelaide of Clarence, the infant daughter of the Duke and Duchess of Clarence – who would later be crowned King William IV and Queen Adelaide. A short distance away in the royal residence of Frogmore House is a statue of the Princess. It depicts a baby sleeping on a child's chaise longue, a foot poking out from under the covers, knees slightly raised, and one hand resting on her chest (see figure 11).

The monument was commissioned by her grieving parents following her death at the age of just 12 weeks on 4 March 1821. Upon her birth, Elizabeth Georgiana stood second in line to the throne after her father, and ahead of her then 1-year-old cousin Victoria, who was to become Queen. Born six weeks premature, Elizabeth Georgiana was not expected to live long, and was baptised on the day of her birth in anticipation of her surviving only a few hours or days. However, prior to her death, she had appeared reasonably healthy, despite her premature arrival; newspaper reports leading up to her death suggest she was 'extremely well'.[2] Reporting her demise, the *Morning Chronicle* noted that 'Notwithstanding the premature birth of her Royal Highness, she continued to enjoy good health, and gained strength so rapidly, that not only her illustrious parents, but also her Physicians and Attendants, entertained the most flattering hopes that she would survive, and that the period of danger was almost over.'[3] Early infancy in nineteenth-century Britain, though, was especially precarious: around one in five children did not survive their first year.[4] After a promising start, the young Princess suddenly developed fever and convulsions, and died shortly afterwards.[5] The Duchess was with her daughter at the time of her death, and some of the newspaper reports detailed her reaction – a public intrusion on a very private grief as a consequence of the implications of the young Princess's death for the monarchy's future: 'Her feelings at the moment [of Elizabeth's death] cannot be described. The Duke conducted the Duchess to her room, where, through his soothing attention, after some time, she recovered some degree of tranquillity, and then returned to gaze on the lifeless body of her lovely babe.'[6] Less than two years before Elizabeth's birth, the Duchess of Clarence had given birth to another daughter, Princess Charlotte Augusta Louisa. Like her younger sister, she was born several weeks premature. Princess Charlotte died only a few hours after her birth, on 27 March 1819. Six months later, on 5 September 1819, Adelaide suffered a miscarriage. Following the death of Princess Elizabeth Georgiana, the Duchess again fell pregnant, this time with twin boys, but they were stillborn on 8 April 1822. No more children were born of the marriage, although there were rumours of further unannounced pregnancies and miscarriages. William's ten illegitimate children by actress Dorothea Jordan could not inherit the throne and, following his death, it was Victoria who succeeded him.

The deaths of royal infants inevitably elicited public expressions of grief, but this sense of loss was no less acute for those mothers at the opposite end of the social scale, whose circumstances often rendered their children more susceptible to an early death. In the late 1840s, Henry Mayhew, as correspondent for the *Morning Chronicle*, gathered information for the paper's supplementary series on 'Labour and the Poor in the Metropolitan, Rural, and Manufacturing Districts of England and Wales'. Amongst the multiple testimonies he collected from working people was that of a woman named only as Susan in London, who had been left a widow with two young children, whilst pregnant with another. She attempted to make her living through needlework (so-called 'slop-work', on cheap clothing), but struggled to earn enough money, and her income was disrupted as a consequence of her confinement. After struggling for several weeks, with a sickly baby and having pawned the sheets off the bed, she was eventually unable to pay the rent, and was forced into the workhouse, where she was separated from her children:

> I felt it a hard trial to have my children taken from my bosom: we had never been parted before, and I can't help remembering what were my feelings then as a mother who had always loved her children […] A mother's feelings are better felt than described, and then, oh, my God! what I felt no tongue can tell!

Shortly after this, her baby contracted measles:

> I knew it was very bad and asked leave to go and see him. The mistress [of the workhouse] was very kind and gave me leave. I found my child very bad, and the infant in my arms seemed declining every day. My feelings then were such as I can't tell you.

She applied for relief to be settled on her 'out of doors' – in other words, outside of the workhouse – and this was granted, but by that time one of her children had died, and after leaving the workhouse, her second son also died. She then lived with a man with whom she again fell pregnant – this time with twins, one of whom only lived a short time. Facing rent arrears once more, she was turned out into the streets, again pregnant, with her surviving twin and little girl. At the time she provided her testimony to Mayhew, she had married and was earning money 'charing and washing', whilst her daughter supplemented the family income through slop-work.[7]

✳ ✳ ✳

Both Susan and Adelaide, Duchess of Clarence, suffered multiple maternal losses. Testimonies of both these grieving mothers appeared in the newspapers (in the case of Susan, part of a move in the mid- to late nineteenth century towards attempting to document the lives of the poor), and they are representative of thousands of other mothers whose experiences of grief and loss have not been recorded. These multiple losses – through miscarriage, stillbirth, and/or early infant death – were far from unique: many women suffered various combinations of such losses throughout their childbearing years. In 1843, *The Lancet* carried an article detailing the case of a 34-year-old woman, named only as 'Mrs F', who had been married nine years and experienced eight pregnancies, all but one ending in miscarriage, stillbirth, or infant death.[8] A similar article in 1874 detailed the case of a woman who experienced six stillbirths, some delivered via craniotomy, prior to the birth of a son who lived three years, followed by a further stillbirth.[9] Mary Shelley, whose own mother Mary Wollstonecraft died from puerperal fever shortly after she was born, lost three of her four children in infancy, and experienced a difficult miscarriage which almost ended her own life. Novelist Elizabeth Gaskell gave birth to a stillborn daughter, and later lost two boys in early infancy. Isabella Beeton experienced several miscarriages and lost two children in infancy: one at eight months and one at three years. Pre-Raphaelite model and artist Lizzie Siddal gave birth to a stillborn daughter in May 1861, and then took her own life whilst pregnant again a few months later. A factor in her suicide may have been the postpartum depression from which she suffered following the birth of her stillborn daughter. In the late nineteenth century, the writer and campaigner Olive Schreiner experienced multiple miscarriages, and her only child, a daughter, died within a few hours of her birth. Out of 348 respondents to the Women's Co-operative Guild's call for letters detailing maternal experiences, the total number of miscarriages experienced was 218, and the number of stillbirths 83, giving a combined rate of 21.5 per 100 live births. One hundred and forty-eight respondents experienced miscarriage or stillbirth – and twenty-two of these experienced both. Forty-one respondents experienced multiple miscarriages, and fourteen multiple stillbirths. Out of 1,396 live births documented, 122 infants died within the first year of life (a mortality rate of 8.7 per cent) – thirty-eight of those within one month of birth. Eighty-six out of the 348 mothers lost children within the first year of life.[10] The high incidence of miscarriage, stillbirth, and infant loss did not necessarily detract from its emotional impact, although at a time when women wielded limited control over their bodies and fertility, loss was not inevitably experienced in negative terms.

The line between miscarriage and stillbirth is not necessarily clear cut. Today the NHS defines miscarriage as 'the loss of a pregnancy during the first 23 weeks'.[11] Stillbirth, according to the NHS, occurs when 'a baby is born dead after 24 completed weeks of pregnancy'.[12] The key difference between the two is linked to viability: an infant is extremely unlikely to survive if born before twenty-four weeks (in most circumstances, abortions must be performed before twenty-four weeks in Britain for this reason).[13] In the nineteenth century, the distinction between the two was also often based on viability, with medical literature variously referring to the sixth or seventh month of pregnancy as the latest point at which women might experience a miscarriage, with later losses deemed stillbirths. However, some literature does reference miscarriage in the eighth month – though often referred to as 'abortion' as the word was used interchangeably with miscarriage and did not carry the exclusive connotation of a deliberate termination of pregnancy as it does today. In *Advice to a Wife*, for instance, the author informs the reader that 'If a *premature expulsion of the child* occur[s] before the end of the seventh month, it is called either a *miscarriage* or an *abortion*; if between the seventh month and before the *full* period of nine months – *a premature labour*.'[14]

Miscarriage

Today in Britain, an estimated one in four pregnancies end in miscarriage. Most miscarriages occur within the first three months of pregnancy, and in cases of early miscarriage, the person miscarrying may not even realise they are pregnant. These very early losses, up to five weeks of pregnancy, are sometimes referred to as 'chemical pregnancies'. In the nineteenth century, many of these losses would have gone undetected, occurring before pregnancy was confirmed or even suspected. Today, these pregnancies and losses are more easily detectable due to early pregnancy testing. A blue line, faint but distinct, raises hope, but the next day there is bleeding, and the line is fading, and then it is gone. If I had waited another twenty-four hours to test, we never would have known: a barely visible loss. We are lucky: it is our only loss, and came between my second and third successful pregnancies. For others, this is as far as it gets. Miscarriage follows miscarriage. Twelve-week scans confirm silent miscarriages: no bleeding, and no other symptoms to suggest the pregnancy has failed, but there is no heartbeat. The end of the first trimester, a successful scan, offers hope: a milestone that indicates the pregnancy is progressing as it should, and the period in which most miscarriages occur has passed. But between 1 and 2 per cent of pregnancies end in miscarriage in the second trimester, and around 1 per cent of pregnant women in the UK today suffer recurrent miscarriages (defined as three or more).[15] Silence has long surrounded the subject of miscarriage – particularly early miscarriage, which often requires no medical intervention and frequently occurs before pregnancy is announced. In November 2020, the Duchess of Sussex revealed that her second pregnancy had ended in miscarriage. Writing about the experience, she said, 'Losing a child means carrying an almost unbearable grief, experienced by many but talked about by few. [...] [D]espite the staggering commonality of this pain, the conversation remains taboo, riddled with (unwarranted) shame, and perpetuating a cycle of solitary mourning.'[16] Other public figures, including MPs, have also spoken openly about their experiences of miscarriage in an attempt to break down the taboos and silences around this subject, and to campaign for greater rights for those who experience pregnancy loss.[17] In the nineteenth century, when there was an even greater reluctance to talk openly about women's bodies, women often had little choice but to suffer in silence.

Medical advancements in maternity care have dramatically reduced maternal and early infant mortality, as well as the number of stillbirths, but the miscarriage rate remains high, and there is only limited understanding of its causes, although early miscarriage is believed to be caused predominantly by chromosomal abnormalities. One nineteenth-century source estimated the miscarriage rate at approximately 20 per cent,[18] but early miscarriages were undoubtedly frequently missed prior to the advent of reliable pregnancy testing, so the actual rate is likely to have been higher than this. There is some evidence from the nineteenth century which appears to indicate rates of miscarriage varied within different demographics. One article, which appeared in *The Transactions of the Edinburgh Obstetrical Society*, points to a miscarriage rate of one in seven amongst the poorer classes, and one in four amongst women over 40.[19] As nineteenth-century advice literature for pregnant women, as well as medical writing, demonstrates, a woman's actions and behaviour were frequently seen as significant factors in miscarriage risk. Chavasse in *Advice to a Wife* warns young wives not to 'establish the habit' of miscarrying – as if this lay solely within their control. He further reinforces the notion of fault in relation to miscarriage by declaring that 'the majority of miscarriages may be prevented.' Whilst there is widespread understanding today that miscarriage is not the fault of the mother, it is typical for mothers to examine their own behaviour and to experience feelings of guilt following pregnancy loss. The language which is still used around miscarriage is not helpful here: the phrase 'she lost the baby' seems to imply blame and suggest that this might have been prevented, highlighting uncomfortable parallels with the nineteenth-century context. Chavasse subsequently lists 'the most common causes' of miscarriage, which include:

> long walks; riding on horseback; or over rough roads in a carriage; a long railway journey; over-exerti[o]n [...] and sitting up late at night; too frequent sexual intercourse [...] large parties, [...] violent emotions of the mind; [...] sudden shocks; [...] obstinate constipation [...] fashionable amusements; dancing; late hours; [...] indeed, anything and everything that injuriously affects either the mind or the body.[20]

Although most of these behaviours are no longer recognised as posing an increased risk of miscarriage, the NHS does urge caution in relation to horse riding, due to the risk of falling. George Eliot's *Middlemarch* (1871) illustrates this risk in its depiction of Rosamond Vincy, who disobeys her doctor-husband and continues to ride whilst pregnant. She subsequently suffers the consequences of her rash behaviour after the horse takes fright, 'caus[ing] a worse fright to Rosamond, leading finally to the loss of her baby'. Rosamond, though, refuses to accept that the incident caused the miscarriage, arguing that 'the ride had made no difference, and that if she had stayed at home the same symptoms would have come on and would have ended in the same way'.[21] As well as encouraging women to avoid these potentially dangerous risks, *Advice to a Wife* includes a long list of actions and behaviours alleged to help to ward off miscarriage, including early hours, resting, a 'light and nourishing' diet, 'gentle walking', 'a trip to the coast' (but no sailing or bathing) and the eschewing of 'all fashionable society and every exciting amusement'.[22] Elsewhere, one medical writer argues that 'maternal ignorance is the cause of many miscarriages'.[23] The same article, though, suggests that the administration of mercury to syphilitic mothers may help prevent miscarriage. Mercury can be harmful to unborn babies (today, the NHS recommends that pregnant women limit tuna consumption as it contains higher levels of mercury than other fish), and has been associated with miscarriage, so evidently medical as well as maternal ignorance had the potential to impact women's experience of pregnancy loss in nineteenth-century Britain. There can be no doubt that some women absorbed some of these messages regarding the causes of miscarriages. Emmeline Way (formerly Stanley) suffered from multiple miscarriages. Writing on the occasion of her latest loss to her sister-in-law Henrietta Stanley, Emmeline's mother, Lady Maria Stanley, attributes blame to her daughter:

> I am sorry for Emmy but she is so imprudent I am not surprised & perhaps it may be all the better for her if she has no more [...] Emmy must go through much privation & self denial I am sure to hatch another – & she would enjoy her liberty if she once made up her mind to expect nothing. She brought this on herself by walking about the hay field in that very hot weather.[24]

Multiple miscarriages were not uncommon amongst women who bore children, as well as those who did not. Lady Henrietta Drummond, wife of banker and politician Henry Drummond, had five living children, but also allegedly suffered twenty miscarriages.[25] Lady Blanche Kay-Shuttleworth, wife of MP Lord Ughtred Kay-Shuttleworth, apparently endured around twelve miscarriages, as well as six successful pregnancies.[26] One contributor to *Maternity: Letters From Working Women*, had four children and ten miscarriages: 'three before the first child, each of them between three and four months. No cause but weakness, and, I'm afraid, ignorance and neglect.'[27] Another had five children, as well as five miscarriages. As with the previous contributor, she speculates on the cause of her losses:

> I had my first three children before I was twenty-four [...] Then I had three miscarriages in the next eight years. I had two more children later, in one and a half years. Since then, [...] I have had a misplaced womb, and have had two more miscarriages since, one being of twins five months, and one three months. I believe it was having children too fast that weakened my inside and brought on miscarriages.[28]

Another woman (mother to five children), who experienced three miscarriages, speculates: 'I think what caused my miscarriages was with having children so quickly, and having to work rather hard at the same time.'[29] Evidence suggests that pregnancies close together may pose some risk to infant and maternal health, although this appears to be linked to premature labour and stillbirth rather than miscarriage.[30] However, certain types of work – particularly heavy physical work involving lifting or bending – may well have impacted women's pregnancies and increased the risk of miscarriage. Whilst middle- and upper-class mothers were urged to rest during pregnancy, this often was not a possibility for women from the poorer classes. Speculation from mothers themselves as to the causes of miscarriage in some instances echoes the problematic discourses around miscarriage found in nineteenth-century advice literature, as the testimony of one working-class mother reflecting on her three miscarriages shows:

> I have had several miscarriages – one caused through carelessness in jumping up to take some clothes off the line when it commenced to rain, instead of getting a chair to stand on, another through taking some pills which were delivered as samples at the door, and a third through a fright by a cow whilst on holidays.[31]

The stresses of day-to-day life, as well as unexpected noises and events – such as the encounter with a cow described here – are unlikely to affect a pregnancy. However, more significant psychological stress may impact pregnancy, and potentially increase the risk of miscarriage or stillbirth. Catherine Dickens, wife of Charles, experienced at least two miscarriages,[32] along with ten successful pregnancies. The first of her pregnancy losses appears to have been brought on by shock following the unexpected death of her younger sister Mary at the age of just 17 and occurred between the births of her two eldest children, Charles (Charley) and Mary. Charley was only a few months old at the time of Mary Hogarth's death, and the impact on Catherine of her sister's loss and the miscarriage was significant. Her second documented miscarriage occurred in December 1847, only a few months after the birth of her seventh child, Sydney, in April of that year. Travelling with her husband in Scotland, she lost the child during a railway journey, and was ill for some time afterwards.[33]

For some women, then as now, the consequence of multiple miscarriages was involuntary childlessness. One woman details her experience of this in *Maternity: Letters From Working Women*:

> I have not had any children to bring up, but I have had the misfortune to have had eight miscarriages [...] [Y]ou must understand they have not been brought on by neglect or ill use, but by my having a severe attack of influenza in 1891 before I was married, which left me with weakness of the womb.[34]

Charles Dickens's sister, Letitia, suffered recurrent miscarriages, eventually adopting a child with her husband. Olive Schreiner suffered at least three miscarriages after losing her daughter the day after she was born, and also considered adoption. Her grief and sense of loss is palpable in her letters: 'I have had a bad mis-carriage [...]. If I never have another child I mean to adopt two. It's curious how much I want my baby, the one that died. It comes over me in fits as if I could go looking for it everywhere.'[35] The recurrent miscarriages also took a physical toll, as she revealed in a letter to her sister-in-law:

> I had a mishap, the third I've had since my baby's birth [...] The first one I had hardly seemed to make me ill at all. I kept about my work, and was as strong as ever in a week's time. The second one made me pretty weak, but this one seems quite to have prostrated me. It is a month ago now and I feel weaker than I did two days after the birth of my baby.[36]

The term 'mishap', employed here by Schreiner, was a common euphemism for miscarriage. In a letter to her sister, Lady Lyttelton informed her that 'L[ad]y Emma Vesey has had a mishap & is very weak.'[37]

In June 1822, Mary Shelley suffered a traumatic miscarriage. A month or so beforehand, her husband, Percy, had written to Mary's stepmother, Mary Jane Godwin, advising her that his wife was 'about three months advanced in pregnancy', and noting that 'the irritability and languor which accompany this state are always distressing, and sometimes alarming'. A few weeks later, on 16 June, Mary lost the baby, and bled heavily. Shortly afterwards, Shelley wrote to his friend, Leigh Hunt, informing him: 'Poor Mary [...] has been seriously ill, having suffered a most debilitating miscarriage. She is still too unwell to rise from the sofa, and must take great care of herself for some time.' Mary herself resumed her journal on 7 July, writing, 'I am ill most of this time. Ill, and then convalescent.'[38] Unbeknownst to her at this time, this was to be her last pregnancy: as she returned to her journal, her husband was already dead, having drowned whilst sailing off the Italian coast from Livorno to Lerici, and Mary was a widow. On 15 August, Mary wrote to her friend Maria Gisborne, describing the events leading up to her husband's death, including a detailed account of her miscarriage, and of the treatment administered by Shelley to stem the bleeding:

> [O]n the 8th of June (I think it was) I was threatened with a miscarriage, and after a week of great ill health, on Sunday, the 16th, this took place at 8 in the morning. I was so ill that for seven hours I lay near lifeless – kept from fainting by brandy, vinegar, and eau-de-Cologne, etc. At length ice was brought to our solitude; it came before the doctor, so Clare and Jane were afraid of using it, but Shelley overruled them, and by an unsparing application of it I was restored. They all thought, and so did I at one time, that I was about to die[.][39]

The miscarriage followed on from the premature deaths of three of her children (in 1815, 1818, and 1819), leaving her with one surviving child. For Mary Shelley, then, maternity proved both physically and emotionally traumatic, and her grief at the loss of her infants and pregnancy was surely compounded by the sudden loss of her husband less than three weeks later. Shelley's lengthy convalescence following a difficult miscarriage was not an unusual experience. One woman, who experienced three miscarriages, wrote that 'To me the after-effects of the miscarriages have been worse than confinements, for it takes months to get over the weakness.'[40] Like Shelley, Catherine Dickens had to contend with the emotional distress and physical recovery from miscarriage whilst at the same time dealing with intense grief following the death of a loved one – her sister, in May 1837. This combination of physical and emotional trauma was also often a significant factor in the maternal experiences of the many women who experienced stillbirths in nineteenth-century Britain, as the accounts of the Duchess of Clarence and many other women demonstrate.

Stillbirth

Stillbirth occurs in approximately one in every 250 pregnancies in the UK today – a rate of approximately seventeen stillbirths every day. This is higher than many other developed countries,[41] but nonetheless a marked improvement on two centuries ago. Like miscarriage, it is a subject around which there has long been notable silence, though in recent years the conversation has begun to shift, not least as a result of public figures speaking out about their own experiences.[42] Estimating the stillbirth rate in nineteenth-century Britain is difficult, as there was no legal requirement to record stillbirths until the passing of the Births and Deaths Registration Act of 1926 in England and Wales (and not until 1939 in Scotland), despite calls by numerous medical men in the nineteenth century for stillbirths to be registered. In the Annual Report of the Registrar-General for 1877, the stillbirth rate was estimated at 4 per cent – although the uncertainty of this figure is acknowledged.[43] In an article published in 1873, Fred W. Lowndes, assistant surgeon to the Liverpool Ladies' Charity and Lying-in Hospital, examined a range of statistics from multiple sources, and concluded that the stillbirth rate in Britain ranged from 3 to 10 per cent, with an average rate of 4 per cent.[44] Understanding of the causes behind stillbirths today remains somewhat limited, and in some cases no cause of death can be identified, although they are sometimes linked to problems with the placenta and other maternal health issues. There is a slightly higher risk of stillbirth for male babies, though the reasons for this are not fully understood. The differing risk factors for boys and girls were also recognised by the medical profession in the nineteenth century. Lowndes, in his article on stillbirth, speculated that this is 'probably due to the larger size of male children' (and different growth rates in male and female infants are a point of interest for those researching stillbirth today). He also identified another group at increased risk of stillbirth: illegitimate children. This, he noted, is:

> just what we would expect to find when we consider the circumstances
> that generally attend the births of these unfortunates, a secret delivery,
> the absence of many measures which would be adopted in the case of a
> legitimate infant, and if not downright unfair play by wilful omission,
> certainly no regret on the part of those immediately concerned that the
> infant has not survived its birth.[45]

Illegitimacy is not, of course, in itself a risk factor for stillbirth, but Lowndes is probably right to highlight the circumstances attending the births of illegitimate children which potentially increased the risk of stillbirth in nineteenth-century Britain. The most prevalent factor in the occurrence of stillbirths, though, according to Lowndes, is prematurity, and there can be no doubt that there was and is a significant link between premature delivery and both stillbirth and early infant mortality.

In March 1868, Kate Russell, Lady Amberley, gave birth – prematurely – to twin girls. Prematurity was, and remains, a particular risk factor for multiple births, and thus there is an increased risk of stillbirth and early mortality. In the case of Kate Russell, the first of the twins, Rachel Lucretia, was born weighing 5½lbs, and survived, but the second, an unnamed girl, did not. Their mother gives an account of the birth in her diary:

> [T]he second [twin] never breathed but it's [*sic*] heart beat for some time
> and Mama did all in her power to bring it to life and so did Miss Garrett[46]
> but they did not succeed. I saw it one moment in Maude's[47] arms but not
> again as I did not wish it at the time; but ever since I have been very
> sorry I did not see it and so grieved it did not live but at the time I felt
> I had one and did not at all realize I had lost anything. I hear it was

the largest of the two and very dark and like [her husband] Amberley – Lizzie [the wet nurse] dressed it in a nightgown and Mama had it sent down to Alderley[48] unknown to me and buried in dear old Wee's[49] grave. Mama did not tell me until some time after as she waited for me to say something and I never liked to mention the subject. I was very glad that I knew where it was.[50]

Kate Russell's account of the death of one of her twin daughters suggests this loss was experienced as traumatic – indicated by her reluctance to mention her, and the deep grief she felt, despite her initial response. It is evident that the death of her daughter played on her mind following the birth, and that she grieved its loss deeply. Elizabeth Garrett, who attended the Viscountess during the birth, seems to have taken a more stoical – perhaps heartless – view of the matter, as Kate recounted in her diary: 'Miss Garrett, I heard afterwards, shocked [Lady Amberley's family] by not caring enough about the loss of one [twin]; she shocked me by saying she supposed Amberley did not mind as he was so Malthusian. He did mind he told me.'[51] Her thoughts then revert to the lost child ('I heard it looked lovely when laid out'[52]), hinting at the extent of her maternal grief. Lady Amberley may have derived some comfort from her surviving daughter, but she too was destined to die young, succumbing to diphtheria at the age of 6. Her death in summer 1874 followed on from that of her mother, who died of the same disease only a few days earlier, having nursed both Rachel and her son Frank and from them contracted the disease herself.[53] The first few months of life may have been the most precarious, but a lack of protection against communicable diseases rendered everyone potentially vulnerable. Had she been born in Britain today, Rachel Lucretia would have been vaccinated against diphtheria within a few weeks of her birth.

Fifteen years earlier, Lady Amberley's sister, Alice Fox, also suffered a stillbirth, as detailed by her mother in a letter: 'Poor Alice was confined yesterday morg. […] – she is doing well but the child was born dead.' Although she professed to be 'very sorry' for her daughter, Lady Stanley quickly moves on to discuss an amusing letter she has received from her son, and other day-to-day affairs.[54] Stillbirth was a common enough occurrence to be treated by others without much shock or grief, despite its often devastating effect on the mother: several months later, Alice was still 'very very low'.[55] Elizabeth Gaskell's experience also testifies to the long-term impact of stillbirth. In July 1833, Gaskell gave birth to a stillborn daughter – her first child, and the first of three losses she would endure as a mother. Three years later, she wrote a sonnet entitled 'On Visiting the Grave of my Stillborn Little Girl':

> I made a vow within my soul, O child,
> When thou wert laid beside my weary heart,
> With marks of Death on every, tender part,
> That, if in time a living infant smiled,
> Winning my ear with gentle sounds of love
> In sunshine of such joy, I still would save
> A green rest for thy memory, O Dove!
> And oft times visit thy small, nameless grave.
> Thee have I not forgot, my firstborn, thou
> Whose eyes ne'er opened to my wistful gaze,
> Whose suff'rings stamped with pain thy little brow;
> I think of thee in these far happier days,
> And thou, my child, from thy bright heaven see
> How well I keep my faithful vow to thee.

The composition of the poem three years after the loss of her daughter speaks to the long-term grief felt by mothers who lost their children through stillbirth. Gaskell would go on to lose two more children: a baby son in the late 1830s, and another son, Willie, who died from scarlet fever at the age of 9 months in 1845.

Infant Death

Whilst childhood in nineteenth-century Britain was beset by risk, particularly from various diseases against which there was no vaccination and frequently no reliable cure, the first hours, days, and weeks of life were particularly precarious, and many mothers found themselves facing the devastating loss of their infants during this time. Infant mortality (the death of a child within the first twelve months of life) averaged approximately 20 per cent across the period, whilst child mortality (death within the first five years of life) was closer to 30 per cent. In the second half of the nineteenth century, infant mortality averaged 15 per cent but there were significant differences according to location and circumstances: in some urban industrial areas, particularly inner-city slums, infant mortality was especially high, and this was also the case amongst those infants left with so-called 'baby farmers'. Causes of early infant death were multiple, but, as with stillbirth, premature birth was a key factor. *The Annual Report of the Registrar-General* for 1882 suggested 24,066 infants died as a result of premature birth in England that year.[56]

Mary Godwin (prior to her marriage to Percy Shelley) gave birth aged just 17, to her first child, an unnamed daughter, on 22 February 1815, some two months premature. On 23 February, Percy Shelley wrote in Mary's journal: 'the child unexpectedly alive, but still not expected to live'. The next day, they began to hope that their daughter would, against the odds, survive: 'favourable symptoms in the child; we may indulge some hopes'.[57] In the end, though, she lived less than three weeks. On 6 March, Mary wrote to her friend, Thomas Hogg, to inform him of her daughter's death:

[M]y baby is dead— [...] It was perfectly well when I went to bed—I awoke in the night to give it suck it appeared to be sleeping so quietly that I would not awake it. It was dead then, but we did not find that out till morning—from its appearance it evidently died of convulsions— [...] Shelley is afraid of a fever from the milk—for I am no longer a mother now[.][58]

Mary was devastated by her daughter's death. She wrote in her journal:

Stay at home [...] and think of my little dead baby. This is foolish, I suppose; yet, whenever I am left alone to my own thoughts, and do not read to divert them, they always come back to the same point – that I was a mother, and am so no longer.[59]

A few days later she wrote in her diary: 'Dreamt that my little baby came to life again; that it had only been cold, and that we rubbed it before the fire, and it lived. Awake and find no baby. I think about the little thing all day.'[60] She continued to be haunted by dreams of her dead child. It is of note that Mary Godwin constructs her response to her daughter's early death as 'foolish' – indicative, perhaps, of the frequent occurrence of such deaths, and an expectation that mothers would not be unduly affected by them. Perhaps she was also aware that the death of an illegitimate child (Percy Shelley was still married to his first wife, Harriet, at this point), born to a teenage mother was hardly viewed as a great tragedy by wider society at this time. Following the loss of her daughter, Mary was soon pregnant again, and gave birth to a son, William, on 24 January 1816. She married Percy Shelley in December 1816, following the death by suicide of his first wife, Harriet, and in September 1817, Mary had another daughter, named Clara. She found some relief from her grief in the births of her children, but it was not to last: Clara died in September 1818, followed by William in June 1819, leaving her childless once more. At the time of William's death, she was again pregnant, and she gave birth to Percy Florence – her only child to survive infancy – in November 1819. It was in the midst of these years of pregnancies, births, grief, and love, that Mary wrote *Frankenstein*, which, in its representations of dead and absent mothers, and of lost children, seems to reflect Mary's own traumatic experiences of motherhood: daughter to a mother lost in childbirth; mother to lost children.

Mary Shelley's grief is reflected in numerous accounts of children lost in infancy in nineteenth-century Britain. On 31 January 1839, Sophy Marianne Wedgwood, daughter of Caroline and Josiah Wedgwood, died at the age of just 7 weeks. Her death devastated her mother, and for months afterwards she was overcome by grief. Sophy was born on 13 December 1838, and though there was evidently some concern, throughout December and for much of January, promising accounts were sent of her development. On 26 December, Caroline's cousin Emma Wedgwood wrote to her fiancé Charles Darwin (Caroline's brother), reporting that 'the baby was getting stronger & better every way'.[61] On 23 January, however, Emma wrote with less positive news: '[Caroline] seems very anxious still about the little baby & says she was quite shocked on comparing it with another of the same age to see what a poor puny little delicate thing it is. It has been unwell again.'[62] Only a few days after this, on 31 January, Emma wrote in her diary: 'Caroline[']s baby died.'[63] Several months later, Charles Darwin wrote to his second cousin reporting on his sister's progress:

I had a letter yesterday from Caroline, the first I have received for a long time: she appears in much better spirits, & even writes about baby-linen & such points, which shows she can now somewhat master her grief.— I do not believe the deaths of but few babies have caused more bitter grief than hers, & I fear it will be a great draw back to her happiness through life.[64]

Sophy was Caroline's first child. She would go on to have three more – all daughters – although the first of these was not born until 1842. The relative lengthy gap between the births of her first and second child may have been due to her grief at the loss of her daughter. Years later, she was still suffering from the emotional impact of this loss.[65] Shortly before the death of Emma and Charles Darwin's daughter Annie, aged 10, in April 1851, Caroline wrote to her sister-in-law assuring her of her understanding of the pain she was enduring: 'I can indeed with truth say it is impossible to feel more for you than Jos & I do!'[66] Maternal loss, for Caroline and numerous other women in nineteenth-century Britain, was not a passing phase, but often a lifelong source of grief and distress. Annie was the second of the Darwins' ten children to die. In September 1842, Emma gave birth to a daughter, Mary Eleanor, who lived only twenty-three days, dying on 16 October. On 7 October, Charles Darwin had reported that 'Emma & baby are going on fairly well.'[67] A few days later, however, she was dead – the cause of death unclear. Emma wrote of their grief in a letter to her sister-in-law, Fanny Wedgwood, shortly afterwards:

Our sorrow is nothing to what it would have been had she lived longer and suffered more [...] With our two other dear little things you need not fear that our sorrow will last long though it will be long indeed before we either of us forget that poor little face.[68]

Her words suggest some degree of resignation to infant loss: an experience familiar to so many Victorian mothers. And indeed, her and her husband's grief at the loss of Annie, at the age of 10 (when Emma was heavily pregnant with her ninth child), appears much more palpable. Darwin wrote of their 'bitter and cruel loss',[69] and Emma of her struggles to care for her other children in the immediate aftermath of Annie's loss: 'My feeling of longing after our lost treasure makes me feel painfully indifferent to the other children but I shall get right in my feelings to them before long.'[70]

The Darwins' experience was far from unusual: few families with large numbers of children were spared the loss of at least one child before they reached adulthood. Queen Victoria was comparatively lucky in this respect, despite outliving three of her children. Her experience appears to have made her somewhat complacent: writing to her eldest daughter of her granddaughter who was ill, she declared: 'You are only a beginner and will find that babies and little children always are dreadfully pulled down and in a day – and then get up as quickly again, so don't be alarmed.'[71] The Princess Royal was not as fortunate as her mother had been, though, and lost two of her eight children before they reached adulthood. Such losses tended to be even more common amongst the poorer classes, who had to contend with poverty as well as the risks and diseases which had the potential to affect all children. In her memoirs, Alice Maud Chase details the extent of losses in her own family. Her father, Reuben Moody, born in 1827, married Eleanor Bewsey in 1855. They had thirteen children in the space of fifteen years, but 'the first was stillborn and five of the others died in infancy'. Eleanor then died herself at the age of 35, and Reuben Moody subsequently remarried – Alice's mother, Priscilla. She had nine children, but 'her first three baby girls died as babies and nearly broke her heart'. Three of the remaining children from the first marriage subsequently died as well, followed by one of Priscilla's twin boys, who lived only eleven weeks.[72] Of the twenty-two children fathered by Reuben Moody, ten died in childhood.

Henrietta Stanley was mother to a large family, and three of her children appear to have died in infancy. She wrote movingly to her husband, whose work as a politician frequently kept him away from home in London, of the illness and death of their youngest child in August 1849 at less than a month old, apparently from cholera, and her subsequent grief. On Sunday, 12 August, she informed him of her anxieties about the baby girl:

I am so fretted about dear baby […] Yesterday afternoon the little thing was uncomfortable & when the nurse came she could not suck from wind. She has continued poorly all night & today I was quite shocked […] at the change which had taken place in the baby, so thin & its little hands cold & shrivelled.

She continued her letter the following day, and noted that baby is 'no better, pinched & blue' at seven that morning, but shortly after she appeared improved. By midday, though, she was deteriorating again: 'I am more and more anxious,' her mother wrote, 'Poor dear little lamb it looks so worn & piteous.'[73] Revealing that the doctor 'is to decide about her being baptized', she wrote, 'I shall be so wretched to lose her she is such a darling.' Her symptoms and appearance gave little grounds for hope, however: 'She sleeps continuously & when she is roused to take food her eyes look quite dead.'[74] On Monday night, with no significant signs of improvement, Henrietta arranged for the baby to be baptised: she was named Mary Ethelflida. 'I did not care what name,' she wrote to her husband, 'for I fear she will not bear it long here.'[75] Her fears were realised, and the child died shortly afterwards. On 14 August, her mother-in-law wrote to Henrietta in response to the news of the baby's death: 'I did not think a hope remained of recovery & I could only be glad you was [sic] spared a prolonged anxiety.'[76] Perhaps unsurprisingly, Henrietta seems to have taken little comfort from these words, and was deeply affected by the baby's loss. Having been disappointed to find herself pregnant again, she blamed herself for the child's illness, writing shortly before its death, 'I feel it quite a punishment for having said I did not wish for a child.'[77] A few days after her daughter's death, she, like Mary Shelley, appears to have been continually haunted by her loss. She wrote again to her husband: 'My dear little one would have been a month old today – you can have no idea how present she is to my mind, I am surprised at it myself.'[78] Her words recall Mary Shelley's suggestion that her response to the loss of the baby was 'foolish'. The extent of Henrietta's grief surprises her, again implying an expectation that mothers should be prepared, and to some degree hardened, to the possible loss of their children at a time when early infancy was so precarious. The lived maternal experience of loss in nineteenth-century Britain, however, as these accounts demonstrate, does not bear this out, and the intensity of mothers' grief for their lost babies is evident. Nine of Henrietta's children survived infancy, but their survival did not diminish her grief at the deaths of their lost siblings.

The intensity of maternal grief is also evident in the letters of Victoria, Princess Royal, following the death of her son, Prince Sigismund, from meningitis shortly before his second birthday in June 1866:

My little darling, [...] my pride, my joy, my hope is gone – gone where my passionate devotion can not follow, from where my love can not recall him! [...] What I suffer none can know – few know how I loved! It was my own happy secret – the long cry of agony which rises from the inmost depth of my soul reaches Heaven alone.[79]

Queen Victoria, whilst sympathetic, felt her daughter's loss was not comparable to the loss of her husband Prince Albert five years previously: 'Think what is a child in comparison with a husband', she wrote to her daughter.[80] Her attitude suggests a parallel with that of medical practitioners at the time, who typically privileged the mother's life over that of the infant, but her words provided little comfort to her daughter: 'The nature of [my] sorrow none can judge but myself,' she responded.[81] Writer Olive Schreiner's letters following the death of her daughter sixteen hours after her birth similarly show intense grief and loss, as well as a desire to remember her lost child, contrary to those urging her to try and forget. Indeed, it is evident she found some consolation in remembering: 'People say "forget". They don't know that the one joy is that one can never forget: that as long as I live I shall feel that little dead body lying in my breast comforting me.'[82]

Schreiner was also consoled by the photographs she had of her child: 'they are only taken by [her husband's] little hand Kodak, but they are all I have', she wrote to a friend.[83] By this time, photography, in its early years a luxury only available to the wealthier classes, had become more accessible. Whilst most parents could not afford a memorial such as the one erected in memory of Princess Elizabeth of Clarence, they nevertheless frequently kept mementos of their lost children. Clothes and locks of hair were often preserved and treasured, and in the latter decades of the nineteenth century, these mementos often took the form of photographs, sometimes taken after death ('memento mori' pictures). For many, these would be the only photographs of their children, something deemed an unnecessary or unaffordable expense whilst the child lived. One writer details how her grandmother lost a child at the age of 7 following a fall, and that 'her photograph was the only one that Grandma had on her wall'.[84] Catherine Temple Pears wrote in a letter of an acquaintance who had recently lost her son:

Mrs Cunningham is having a picture of her dear little boy taken. The lady who was to take it before he died during his illness, was put off by them because they thought they had better wait till he got to look a little better, then came the last attack, and she never I believe even saw him, certainly never began the picture. After his death, there was a wonderfully beautiful and radiant smile on his sweet little face, and they had a cast taken.[85]

In her account of the suffragette movement, Sylvia Pankhurst recalled the death of her brother Henry Francis (Frank) from diphtheria in 1888: 'Those were awful days; Mother seemed altogether distraught, and as though she could not look at us.' Following his death, 'A lady came and painted two portraits of the little dead boy', but her mother, Emmeline Pankhurst, 'could not bear to see them; she kept them in her bedroom cupboard, out of sight'.[86] Emmeline Pankhurst also kept the memory of her dead child alive by naming a subsequent baby after him – a relatively common practice in the nineteenth century. Heathcliff in Emily Brontë's *Wuthering Heights* is named after a son of the Earnshaws who died in childhood. In the anonymously written short biography of 'Margaret Jane', the author's grandmother – who was born in 1855 in north-east England – references the fact that Margaret Jane named two children after others she'd lost: 'As the two unsurviving infants had been named Edward and Eliza, the two born afterwards inherited their names.'[87] The Pankhurst's later son, born less than a year after his brother's death, was also named Henry Francis, but known as Harry. Sylvia Pankhurst wrote that 'To [Emmeline] Pankhurst, in her pregnancy, he had been "Frank coming again".' Although he lived longer than his brother, he too was destined to die young, losing his life to 'infantile paralysis', as his sister describes it, in 1908. Following his death, Emmeline told her daughter, 'Sylvia, remember, when my time comes, I want to be put with my two boys!'[88]

Catherine Dickens also lost two sons, Walter and Sydney, both of whom died in their twenties, as well as an infant daughter, Dora, in addition to suffering at least two miscarriages. Dora, like so many Victorian infants, lived only a few months. Born in August 1850, she died suddenly after suffering from convulsions on 14 April 1851. At the time of her daughter's death, Catherine was away from home. She had suffered bouts of ill health, including postnatal depression, for many years, and her husband was anxious at the possible effect of the unexpected news of their daughter's sudden death on her health. Consequently, he wrote to Catherine, advising that Dora was very ill, but without revealing the fact that she had already died:

> Little Dora, without being in the least pain, is suddenly stricken ill. She awoke out of a sleep, and was seen in one moment to be very ill. Mind! I will not deceive you. I think her 'very' ill.
> There is nothing in her appearance but perfect rest. You would suppose her quietly asleep. But I am sure she is very ill, and I cannot encourage myself with much hope of her recovery. I do not—and why should I say I do to you, my dear?—I do not think her recovery at all likely.
> I do not like to leave home, I can do no good here, but I think it right to stay. You will not like to be away, I know, and I cannot reconcile it to myself to keep you away. Forster, with his usual affection for us, comes down to bring you this letter and to bring you home, but I cannot close it without putting the strongest entreaty and injunction upon you to come with perfect composure—to remember what I have often told you, that we never can expect to be exempt, as to our many children, from the afflictions of other parents, and that if,—if—when you come, I should even have to say to you, 'Our little baby is dead,' you are to do your duty to the rest, and to shew yourself worthy of the great trust you hold in them.[89]

Maternal grief was part and parcel of the experience of motherhood in nineteenth-century Britain. As Charles Dickens's letter to Catherine makes clear, no parent could expect to be exempt from such losses. Amongst many other families to suffer were William and Catherine Gladstone, parents to eight children, including Catherine Jessy Gladstone, who died at the age of 4 in 1850. Following her death, many letters of sympathy were sent to the Gladstones from friends, family, and acquaintances, amongst them one from Catherine's sister-in-law, Lavinia Glynne. Like many of the other letters received, it offers religious consolation, but also speaks of Lavinia's own maternal loss:

> May God help you my poor dearest thing under this sad sad trial; the first of all our little flock to be taken! except my poor tiny 6 hours boy – oh think of the Everlasting arms where she now rests so peacefully,

all suffering past, all anxious thought for her soul too at an end, & her young spirit happy for all Eternity; you have an Angel child![90]

The reference to Lavinia's '6 hours boy' seems to imply this was a less sig-nificant loss than that suffered by Catherine at the death of Jessy, recalling Emma Darwin's suggestion that her sorrow at Mary Eleanor's death would have been greater had she lived longer. It may be the case that Elizabeth Gaskell also felt the loss of Willie, at nine months, more profoundly than the loss of her unnamed baby boy, although references to the latter in her letters are very few. On Willie's death, though, she wrote, many years later, that he died 'just as he had made himself a place in the hearts of all who knew him'.[91] As with Mary Shelley, the influence of Gaskell's losses is evident in her fiction, which frequently deals with maternal grief. *Mary Barton* (1848), written shortly after Willie's death as a distraction from her grief, opens with the death of a mother and baby in childbirth, and subse-quently depicts the poignant death of young twins from fever. The second twin's death is depicted as a 'hard struggle' as his mother is 'wishing him', as Alice Wilson explains to Mary:

> 'There's none can die in the arms of those who are wishing them sore to stay on earth. The soul o' them as holds them won't let the dying soul go free; so it has a hard struggle for the quiet of death. We mun get him away fra' his mother, or he'll have a hard death, poor lile fellow.'
>
> So without circumlocution she went and offered to take the sinking child. But the mother would not let him go, and looking in Alice's face with brimming and imploring eyes, declared in earnest whispers, that she was not wishing him, that she would fain have him released from his suffering. Alice and Mary stood by with eyes fixed on the poor child, whose struggles seemed to increase, till at last his mother said with a choking voice, 'May happen yo'd better take him, Alice; I believe my heart's wishing him a' this while, for I cannot, no, I cannot bring mysel to let my two childer go in one day; I cannot help longing to keep him, and yet he sha'not suffer longer for me.'[92]

Once the mother releases the child, he dies soon afterwards.

Here, maternal love is depicted as preventing the child from departing this world. Elsewhere, as with much of the discourse around miscarriage, women's actions and behaviour were at times cited as responsible for the deaths of children in early infancy. Amongst the working classes in particular, there were concerns about 'overlaying' – the accidental suffocation of infants whilst sharing a bed with others – and this was frequently deemed the cause of infant deaths whilst bed sharing, although now it is thought likely that sudden infant death syndrome and infant illnesses were responsible for many of these.[93] For many people, of course, there was no option but for the baby to share a bed with parents or other family members. There were, though, also concerns that such occurrences were used to cover up cases of infanticide. One work suggested (undoubtedly exaggerating actual occurrences, whilst simultaneously perpetuating negative stereotypes of working-class mothers), 'this is a very common mode of destroying new-born children; it is easily accomplished, [and] no characteristic signs of left', and noted that 'In some cases it is to be feared that the temptation of the burial-club money is responsible for violent death by smothering.' It goes on to suggest that the use of alcohol amongst the poor was also a contributing factor:

> Many cases of overlaying, no doubt occur from the mother being in an intoxicated condition, when she is less likely to be aware of her dangerous proximity to the child, and when the infant may probably have been previously stupefied with alcohol conveyed to it in the mother's milk.[94]

The risk factors identified here – bed sharing, financial need, and the use of alcohol – speak to both the realities and stereotypes of working-class motherhood, and such constructions risk demonising the impoverished mother. They are also referenced in multiple newspaper reports on the death of infants through overlaying. One typical example of this is the report on an inquest into the death of an 18-month-old child named Lilian Holyland in 1895. The illegitimate daughter of a labourer, she slept in between her parents, both of whom it was suggested were 'addicted to drink'. The description of the bed which the family shared speaks to the extreme poverty in which they lived: 'The bed [...] consisted of old clothes laid on the floor, which was of brick. The room itself was about seven or eight feet square, and totally unfit, in witness's opinion, for habitation.'[95] However, it was not only poorer women whose behaviour was perceived as risking their infants' lives. In January 1845, Queen

Victoria wrote in her diary of the death of the newborn son of her cousin, Princess Augustus, 'who had unfortunately only survived his birth a few minutes!' Though sympathetic, she is also critical of her cousin's behaviour during the latter stages of her pregnancy:

> This is most sad, & grieves & shocks us much. Poor Augusta, this is a dreadful blow for her, but she ought to have remained quietly at home, instead of risking the long journey to England, & paying visits, too near the time of her confinements. This sad event is I fear the result of her imprudence, but it does not make it less hard & distressing for her, — I pity her with all my heart.[96]

'Prudent' behaviour, which frequently meant restricting women's actions and freedoms, was thus deemed a requirement across all classes, and the idealised mother in nineteenth-century Britain was the one who adhered to these patriarchal invocations.

Strict guidance on women's bodies and behaviours also extended to the postnatal period, a time of particular difficulty for mothers grieving the loss of their babies through stillbirth or early infant death. The loss of a child could have a devastating emotional impact, and women who experienced late miscarriages, stillbirths, and early infant death still had to endure childbirth and all its attendant risks. Physically and emotionally traumatic births could have profound and lasting consequences for maternal health, and many women struggled with their mental health in the weeks and months after giving birth. The postnatal period, then, was a time of difficulty for many, variously marked by challenging physical recoveries, anxiety, declining mental health, and grief. For many, though, it was a period of intense love and great joy, as they became acquainted with their new arrival, and at times new motherhood involved a combination of these various emotions, as women adjusted to life after childbirth.

Postnatal Bodies and Minds

Oh! Child and mother, darling! Mother and child!
And who but we? We, darling, paired alone?
Thou hast all thy mother; thou art all my own.
That passion of maternity which sweeps
Tideless 'neath where the heaven of thee hath smiled
Has but one channel, therefore infinite deeps.
Augusta Webster[1]

'Such a dear baby!
And yet I *cannot* be with him, it makes me so nervous.'
Charlotte Perkins Gilman[2]

In September 1840, 29-year-old novelist William Makepeace Thackeray set off by boat to travel from London to Ireland with his wife, Isabella – seven years his junior. The pair had married in 1836, and Isabella had produced three daughters: the youngest, Harriet, had been born just a few months earlier, in May 1840. The couple's middle daughter, Jane, had died aged only 8 months in July 1839. Isabella had been struggling since the birth of Harriet, and the family were travelling to Cork to visit Isabella's mother and sister in the hopes that this would improve Isabella's mental health. Thackeray was convinced she was merely suffering from 'lowness of spirits',[3] but on the voyage over, it became clear Isabella's condition was much more serious than previously thought. Having taken herself to the ship's water closet, Isabella flung herself off the boat into the sea. She was in the water for twenty minutes before she was rescued: she 'was found floating on her back, paddling with her hands, and had never sunk at all'.[4] Further attempts at self-destruction followed, and by the time they arrived in Cork, Isabella appeared 'quite demented'.[5] In the days that followed these attempts on her own life, Thackeray tied a ribbon around her waist, which he wore around him, so that he might wake if she attempted to leave the bed. After a short time, Isabella showed some signs of improvement, and Thackeray declared she made 'wonderful progress towards convalescence'. His belief that 'her recovery [was] near at hand', proved ill-founded, however.[6] Isabella never fully recovered, and spent much of her life in asylums and under the care of nurses. When Thackeray's letters were published in 1945, they included an appendix consisting of a provisional diagnosis for Isabella Thackeray from Dr Stanley Cobb, Psychiatrist in Chief at Massachusetts General Hospital. Cobb concluded that her maternal experiences had significantly impacted her mental health: 'four years of marriage, though happy, brought heavy physical burdens – three pregnancies in quick succession. Added to this were all the adjustments to marriage and the grief over losing a child.' Having reviewed the details of her case, Cobb offered a retrospective diagnosis:

> The diagnosis is schizophrenia, of a type that often begins with depression and ideas of unworthiness a few weeks after childbirth. Some of these patients get well spontaneously in a few months and the diagnosis of a 'post-puerperal depression' is made. Others seem to drift into a permanent state of apathy and live the rest of their lives in an unreal world of fantasy, with gradual mental deterioration. Such was the fate of Mrs. Thackeray.[7]

This approach to diagnosing women's mental illness is, of course, problematic: it implies the (male) medical professional can, without direct examination of or communication with the patient, accurately determine both the diagnosis and the cause – echoing the power dynamics between female patient and male doctor often in evidence in Victorian society. Nonetheless, the details of the case do appear to support the conclusion that Isabella Thackeray, like many other women then and now, suffered a deterioration in her mental health that was directly linked to her experiences of maternity and childbirth.

* * *

For many women in nineteenth-century Britain, the birth of a child was a moment of great joy, and recovery from childbirth swift. Indeed, such was the case for Isabella Thackeray following the birth of her first two children. Three days after the birth of their second daughter, Jane, in July 1838, Thackeray wrote to his mother, informing her that Isabella 'produces children with a remarkable facility' and 'is as happy and as comfortable as any woman can be'.[8] Many women relished the bonding and intense maternal love that followed the birth of a child, and this is reflected in their accounts of their new babies. Letters and diaries refer frequently to babies' development. Betsey Wynne, shortly after the birth of her son Charles in 1800, wrote in her diary: 'My dear little baby grows exceedingly', and later commented on the appearance of his first tooth.[9] Following the birth of her first child, Charley, in 1837, Catherine Dickens wrote to her sister: 'My darling boy grows sweeter and lovelier every day. Although he is my own I must say I never saw a dearer child.'[10] Sisters Lady Lyttelton and Catherine Gladstone wrote constantly to one another of the joy they found in their infants – of first teeth, weight, eating and sleeping habits, smiles and laughter, and how 'dear' they look in a 'little night cap'.[11] 'It is so curious to feel so completely bound up in a person one has known so short a time,' reflected Lady Lyttelton.[12] The letters of Catherine Temple Pears also reference various infant milestones: 'Baby has two teeth and can get herself along the floor', she wrote to her son Henry in 1858.[13] These moments of maternal joy in the days and weeks following childbirth were, for many women, just that – brief moments of light at a time often marked by darkness, and a deterioration in mental health, as the later experience of Isabella Thackeray shows – and indeed Catherine Dickens also suffered periods of postnatal depression. Maternal joy and mental health struggles were not mutually exclusive.

Childbirth could precipitate significant physical- and mental-health problems, whilst new motherhood for some women proved an overwhelming experience. Sent home from hospital following the birth of my first child, my husband struck down with an ill-timed stomach bug, I experienced an anxiety bordering on panic at the prospect of being left in charge of this small, helpless baby. A few weeks later, the health visitor reviewed my responses to the questionnaire given to all new mothers. There were some indicators of postnatal depression, although looking back it seems to me these were simply a consequence of the overwhelming emotions of new motherhood combined with severe sleep deprivation. Five years later, after the birth of my third child, that initial anxiety had receded, but the birth – an emergency Caesarean section – left me barely able to move, reliant on heavy painkillers, and injecting myself with anti-clotting medication for ten days afterwards. Despite these complications, my recovery from the births of all three of my children was rapid, and I was supported by twenty-first-century medicine, a national health service, and maternity laws which entitled me to financial support and an extended period of leave from work. Yet despite these mitigating factors, in many respects the postnatal period frequently felt overwhelming. How much more so, then, for women in nineteenth-century Britain without access to these privileges, and subject to the pressures arising from the prevailing ideologies around motherhood?

In nineteenth-century medical and advice literature, the period imme-diately following childbirth is widely recognised as a precarious time for mothers. Such works frequently construct the postnatal period as poten-tially dangerous for mothers, not only in relation to the events of the birth itself, but also due to widely held perceptions about women's fragile emotional state. As one medical work noted:

> [I]n the period immediately subsequent to childbirth, [...] tranquillity of mind is perhaps more important than at any other; and comparatively slight emotion will often excite dangerous disease: a result at which we must cease to wonder, when the combination of bodily weakness and mental excitement is fairly taken into account.[14]

Such discourses directly link the dangers of childbirth and the postnatal period to women's position as 'the weaker and more emotional sex', thus implicitly associating maternal mortality with this perceived weakness.[15] In the days immediately following childbirth, women were expected to avoid any kind of physical or mental exertion. *Advice to a Wife* is typical in this respect, advising women to keep to their bedchamber for fourteen days before moving to a drawing-room – but only if 'close at hand'. After a period of three weeks, the mother may 'take her meals with the family;

but even then she ought occasionally, during the day, to lie on the sofa, to rest her back'.[16] Tasks such as reading and writing were discouraged in the days immediately following childbirth. Indeed, one advice book suggests that directly after delivery, women should be prohibited even from talking.[17] Many – though not all – women adhered to such advice, as illustrated in part by the breaks in women's diaries following deliveries. There is typically a gap of around two weeks in Queen Victoria's journal following the births of her children, and Lady Amberley's diary was taken up by her husband the day before the birth of her first child, with her resuming writing some three weeks later. In 1850, Lady Stanley wrote to her daughter-in-law Henrietta shortly after her daughter, Emmy, had given birth:

> I only hope Emmy will not be too venturesome[.] Lou Way tells me she tried to *read & write* on the 9th day, but found her eyes would not stand that effort, & Albert [her husband] quickly removed the book & pen – but the mere wish shows how well she felt.[18]

By contrast, Lady Charlotte Guest frequently resumed her translation work very soon after delivering her children. Such behaviour would have been deemed incautious. Lady Blanche Airlie's grandmother, Lady Maria Stanley, wrote urging restraint following the delivery of Blanche's second child in June 1854: 'The better she is now the more careful she shld. be.' She included a cautionary tale of a young woman 'who recovered so well, she was downstairs in a fortnight', but then 'caught cold and died'.[19] Injunctions to rest for some time after childbirth continued well into the twentieth century. When my mother was born in 1949 – a straightforward, uncomplicated home birth – my grandmother was told by the doctor to stay in bed for two weeks. Today, women who experience straightforward deliveries are frequently discharged from hospital within hours.

The strictures around confinement and the constraints placed on women's actions and behaviour immediately following childbirth were often taken seriously and conscientiously followed by many. These women, though, enjoyed the privileges bestowed by wealth and social status, which meant they were not obliged to return either to work or to their domestic duties shortly after birth. Those who gave birth in the workhouse were typically able to rest after giving birth, under the rules governing the lying-in wards at workhouses. Birthing mothers were 'detained in the lying-in ward for one month unless they wish[ed] to leave earlier'.[20] Working women and those raising large families on inadequate incomes, however, often had little choice but to return to work (whether paid or domestic labour) almost immediately after giving birth. In the case of straightforward births, there was, of course, no real need for a woman to stay in bed for up to three weeks. One mother, who was 'very fortunate' and 'enjoyed the best of health' recalled asking the midwife 'what I had to stay in bed for'.[21] For other women, though, an inability to rest and recover following a difficult childbirth could have long-lasting and damaging consequences. Today, the NHS recommends gentle exercise, a healthy diet including plenty of fresh fruit and vegetables, daily washing, and plenty of water in the immediate postnatal period, to help aid recovery from childbirth – to reduce the risk of infection, avoid constipation, and manage the heavy bleeding which typically occurs in this period. For poor women in nineteenth-century Britain, many of these recommendations would have been impossible to follow, and for those returning to work – particularly in factories or as domestic servants – hard labour and long hours could be expected. In the early twentieth century, the Women's Co-operative Guild campaigned for greater maternity rights for working-class women, and many of the correspondents in *Maternity* highlighted the difficult situation in which they found themselves following childbirth. There is an implicit contrast here with those middle- and upper-class women for whom the period of confinement meant total rest in comfortable surroundings. One woman, living away from extended family, 'could not afford to pay someone to look after the house', and so 'got up sooner than [she] should have done', but was taken ill and forced to return to her bed for many weeks.[22] Another, being very poor, was forced to 'get up on the third day' after the birth of her child, as she could not afford to pay anyone to help her.[23] In the late nineteenth century, legislation was introduced in an attempt to provide some protection for working mothers: the 1891 Factory Act prevented organisations from employing a woman within four weeks of her giving birth. For various reasons, this solution was not ideal and it met with some opposition. With no provision for maternity pay, such legislation risked further impoverishing poorer families. It was also difficult to enforce, and whilst preventing paid employment, many women, unable to afford any assistance, were still forced to take up heavy and laborious housework soon after giving birth. Philanthropist and campaigner Lady Goldsmid was amongst those to object to the proposed legislation on the grounds of women's rights, arguing that such 'State interference with adult women' kept them as 'perpetual minors'. She also pointed out that 'the condition of women after childbirth varies in almost every case', and that the legislation did not take account of this. In addition, the financial pressures faced by many working women meant the effects of such legislation could be significant: 'The pressure upon women who have to gain their livelihood is so great in many cases that if the law forbade their returning to their accustomed employment for as long, they would be driven to other work no less and perhaps more onerous.'[24] It was not until the introduction of maternity benefits in 1911 (then a single payment of 30 shillings) that the issue of ensuring poorer women were able to rest and recuperate after childbirth began to be properly addressed.

Postnatal Bodies

Today, physical recovery from childbirth is aided by modern medicine: infection risk is easier to manage with a better understanding of hygiene risks and the wide availability of antibiotics; drugs can help reduce heavy bleeding during childbirth and thus the potential side effects of this afterwards; blood transfusions can be given in cases where a lot of blood has been lost; pain relief medications can make women more comfortable in the postnatal period. As now, many women in the nineteenth century recovered quickly following childbirth and without any significant long-term physical effects. In all cases, though, birth is likely to cause at least some pain and discomfort in the days that follow. *Advice to a Wife* suggests that if 'the parts be very sore', following delivery, bathing them with 'oatmeal gruel' might provide some relief.[25] Even a straightforward birth could be a physically traumatic experience (especially in the context of women's ignorance of childbirth), and, inevitably, risks increased

with more complicated deliveries. Instrumental – and in particular forceps – deliveries posed a particular risk to women's physical health, and
in some cases left them with life-changing injuries. Obstetrician Robert
Lee, who expressed significant concern about the misuse of instruments
to aid delivery in his writing on midwifery, cites several cases in which
birthing women sustained significant injuries during forceps deliveries, in
some cases leaving them with devastating long-term consequences. Lee
himself appears to have been judicious in his use of forceps, and frequently
criticised fellow practitioners who inflicted damage on patients through
their ill-judged and sometimes violent use of these instruments. In *Clinical
Midwifery*, he describes, in graphic detail, the physical damage caused by
forceps in the case of a woman delivered nine weeks previously:

> The perineum, recto-vaginal septum, for about an inch and a half, and
> sphincter ani, were all destroyed, and the power of retaining the con-
> tents of the rectum entirely lost. The case admitted of no relief. This
> wretched state had resulted from laceration and sloughing of the parts,
> from the employment of the forceps in her first labour, and immense
> force exerted to extract the head. The child was dead.[26]

In a similar case, he attended a woman who, two years previously, 'had
been delivered with the forceps in a public institution. The child's head
was grievously injured, and it died in a few hours, and the health of the
mother was not restored for several months.'[27] He also details the case
of a 45-year-old woman, Mrs Crowther, whose nine deliveries were all
complicated, with at least three resulting in stillbirths. During the final,
difficult birth in 1830, Lee performed a craniotomy, but was some two
hours in removing the infant's body. Shortly after the birth, a 'fistulous
communication had been formed between [the vagina] and the bladder'[28]
– a condition which would inevitably have resulted in incontinence. In a
rare glimpse into his patients' lives beyond the delivery room, Lee notes
that 'This unfortunate woman was soon after deserted by her husband,
and has led a life of great indigence and misery ever since.'[29] He records
another similar case of a difficult birth involving forceps resulting in
long-term damage, again leaving the woman incontinent – here as a consequence of the violent application of forceps (again applied by another
practitioner, and not Lee himself):

The blades of the forceps were [...] introduced with great difficulty, and still greater was experienced in getting them to lock. Strong traction was then made for several minutes, and the blades slipped off the head. They were re-introduced, and the efforts to extract renewed, and continued till the instrument again slipped off. This happened several times, but the attempt to deliver with the long forceps was not abandoned till the operator was exhausted with fatigue.[30]

As in the previously cited case, the woman was subsequently 'abandoned by her husband, and was afterwards reduced, in consequence of this misfortune, to the greatest possible misery'.[31] The inclusion of these details in these cases implies a causal link: damage caused during delivery led to incontinence, and subsequently to the women's abandonment by their husbands.

Reflecting on another case from 1851 resulting in extensive damage caused by forceps (again by another practitioner), Lee questioned the value of instrumental delivery:

The last confinement took place four years before; the labour was very protracted and the child was born alive, and the forceps was employed frequently, and great force used in extracting the head. She has never been able to retain her urine since, and has had little or no control over the action of the bowels [...] The perineum has been torn into the rectum; cannot now retain the contents of the rectum thoroughly [...] To estimate properly the value of the forceps in the practice of midwifery, it is necessary that the results of all the cases in which the instrument has been employed should be recorded.[32]

These instances highlight the potential long-lasting physical damage caused by instrumental deliveries – particularly in cases where instruments were applied incautiously by inexperienced practitioners. Such cases typically include details today associated with risk factors for postnatal post-traumatic stress disorder (PTSD): lengthy and painful deliveries; instrumental interventions; long-lasting physical trauma; and, often, infant injury or loss. Lee typically does not record the mental and emotional impact on women, only considering the physical impact of such births on his patients.

Maternity: Letters From Working Women also includes a number of cases of instrumental delivery resulting in long-term health problems. One woman recalls how she was in labour for thirty-six hours, eventually resulting in an instrumental delivery: 'after all that suffering [I] had to be delivered by instruments, and was ruptured too badly to have anything done to help me. I am still suffering from the ill-effects to-day. This is thirty-one years ago. [...] I was unable to sit down for three months.'[33] Another notes, 'I needed chloroform and instruments in each case, and after the birth of my second child, I was a cripple for nearly twelve months.'[34] One woman, recalling the details of the birth of her fifth child, writes, 'I was so injured that for nearly ten years I was an invalid.'[35] Another account of instrumental birth hints at the psychological, as well as physical damage caused. The correspondent writes that the 'forced birth' of her only child 'is too terrible to go through even now after twenty-eight years. Suffice it to say that next morning there was a poor little baby boy with a very large swollen head dreadfully cut, and a young mother dreadfully cut also.'[36] Difficult deliveries such as these women experienced could lead to a range of significant short- and long-term health problems for mothers, including prolapse, incontinence, and uterine rupture. Rupture was also a risk in cases where women experienced multiple and closely spaced pregnancies and births. A gap of less than twelve months between births is associated with an increased risk of premature delivery and other complications, whilst the risk of haemorrhaging, uterine rupture, and, longer term, cervical cancer also increases with multiple pregnancies. Multiple pregnancies impact women's bodies in various ways, some more serious than others.

Nineteenth-century mothers were also not exempt from similar pressures faced by women today to maintain their figures even after childbirth. As well as offering detailed advice on diet, advice literature also often included tips on managing postnatal bodies. In *Advice to a Wife*, Chavasse recommends bandaging the stomach following childbirth: 'It is a great comfort; [...] it induces the belly to return to its original size; and [...] it prevents flooding.' He also sounds a note of warning: 'Those ladies, more especially if they have had large families, who have neglected proper bandaging after their confinements, frequently suffer from enlarged and pendulous bellies, which give them an unwieldy and ungainly appearance.'[37] Abdominal belts designed to address this issue in postnatal women were frequently advertised in various journals – particularly in the latter decades of the period. 'Swanbill Belts', for instance, were recommended for 'young mothers', 'for nothing tends to age a woman so much as the loss of symmetry of figure', but, the advert continues, through the use of these, 'a woman may almost retain her maiden symmetry of figure, even though the mother of a large family'.[38] This suggests striking parallels with the pressures women often face today to lose any additional weight following pregnancy, and 'get back in shape'. Whilst much has changed in the last two centuries, women are still being encouraged to consider the aesthetics of their postnatal bodies.

An inability to rest and the physical consequences of childbirth were not the only risks to women's physical health during the postnatal period. The premature resumption of sexual relations was also a risk factor. Today, healthcare providers emphasise women's choice in discussing when to have sex after childbirth, but in the nineteenth century, the letter of the law meant this was effectively the husband's choice. The author of *Advice to a Wife* advises women against resuming sexual relations in the first month following childbirth: 'No woman should allow her husband to have sexual connection with her until after the end of the first month from her confinement. On this she must strongly insist.'[39] In reality, though, women were entirely dependent on their husbands in this respect. One of the respondents to the Women's Co-operative Guild wrote that 'Some [women] have severe attacks of haemorrhage caused by sexual intercourse soon after birth.'[40] The proximity of many women's pregnancies in nineteenth-century Britain suggests that the resumption of sexual relations soon after birth was commonplace.

Postnatal Minds

Along with the various physical after-effects of childbirth, deteriorating mental health in the postnatal period was also a significant issue for many women. Following childbirth, women may find they suffer from increased anxiety, depression, symptoms of post-traumatic stress disorder, or, more unusually, obsessive compulsive disorder or psychosis. Estimates today suggest that more than 10 per cent of women experience postnatal depression in the year following childbirth, whilst a small number (approximately one in 500 women) experience more severe postpartum psychosis.[41] Today, postnatal mental health receives considerable attention, and forms part of the early checks carried out by medical professionals following childbirth. In the nineteenth century, there was insufficient focus on this area of women's health, although medical discourses reference postpartum nervous disorders, hysteria, and puerperal mania, and these were common diagnoses for women admitted to asylums at the time. Accounts of women's postnatal mental health in medical and advice literature and life writing suggests these disorders were relatively common. Amongst those documented as suffering from postnatal depression were well-known women including Queen Victoria, Catherine Dickens, and the novelist Mary Elizabeth Braddon, as well as Isabella Thackeray. In the short story, *The Yellow Wallpaper*, American author Charlotte Perkins Gilman draws on her own experience of postnatal depression and the treatment to which she was subject in the depiction of the unnamed protagonist, who is taken to a 'colonial mansion' by her doctor-husband to recover from the 'temporary nervous depression' she experiences following the birth of her baby. Her husband prevents her from writing, reading, working, or socialising, as part of the 'rest cure' designed to help her recover. It has, though, quite the opposite effect, and the protagonist descends into madness. In Gilman's story, as well as in her own personal experience, it is the recommended 'cure' for postnatal depression which exacerbates the condition. In Braddon's hugely popular sensation novel, *Lady Audley's Secret* (1862), the eponymous protagonist's alleged madness appears to be associated with motherhood, and inherited from her own mother, who had 'appeared sane up to the hour of [her] birth'.[42] Following the birth of her own child, the (anti-) heroine is abandoned by her husband, becomes 'subject to fits of violence and despair', and resents her baby, who has 'been left a burden upon [her] hands'.[43] Lady Audley ends her days in an asylum, and although the subtext of the narrative raises questions about the diagnosis of madness, her actions – and her mental state – are closely linked to her experiences as wife and mother.

These fictional examples reflect the experiences of many women in nineteenth-century Britain. As now, many new mothers suffered in varying degrees with postnatal anxiety, depression, or psychosis. Anxiety is a common response to new motherhood. Actress Fanny Kemble wrote of her experience of this in 1835, shortly after the birth of her first child:

> I am sorry to find that my physical courage has been very much shaken by my confinement. Whereas formerly I scarcely knew the sensation of fear, I have grown almost cowardly on horseback or in a carriage. I do not think anybody would ever suspect that to be the case, but I know it in my secret soul, and am much disgusted with myself in consequence.[44]

Maternal anxiety, particularly at a time of higher maternal and infant mortality, is inevitable. One of Catherine Gladstone's acquaintances summarised these feelings in a letter following the death of Catherine's sister, Lady Lyttelton, in 1857, which left her large family motherless: 'How one feels one would be torn to pieces oneself thinking of all the evils which might befall one's little ones without a mother's sheltering love.'[45]

For some, though, the birth of a child meant a release from the anxiety of pregnancy and worry about the impending delivery. Queen Victoria evidently felt this way following the births of her children. Writing to her daughter the Princess Royal following the arrival of her first grandchild, she commented: 'Don't you feel such a weight off your mind, such a sense of returning freedom and thankfulness? I always felt that intense happiness on first waking, so different to the mornings of anxious expectation, of dread and anxiety.'[46] The Queen did, though, like many other women, experience some periods of depression following childbirth. Catherine Dickens also appears to have experienced postnatal depression following the births of at least some of her children. After the arrival of her eldest child in January 1837, Catherine initially appeared well, but after a week or so, descended into 'a very low and alarming state'[47] – language which echoes Thackeray's descriptions of Isabella following the birth of their third daughter. As Catherine's biographer Lillian Nayder notes, her sister attributed her mental state to the difficulties she faced in breastfeeding, and indeed recent research has pointed to a link between postnatal depression and struggles to breastfeed.[48] However, Nayder also notes that 'Once Catherine was allowed downstairs four weeks after Charley's birth [...] she quickly recovered', exemplifying how the manner in which women were treated and expected to behave during their confinements could be the cause for deterioration. As with Gilman's protagonist, the physical and mental confinement which accompanied childbirth may have been a factor here. Catherine again suffered with postnatal depression after the birth of her second child, but following subsequent deliveries she resumed activities much more quickly, and this seems to have been beneficial to her.[49]

Queen Victoria experienced several periods of depression following the births of her children. Years later, advising her eldest daughter, Victoria, Princess Royal, on new motherhood, Victoria wrote: 'Occasional lowness and a tendency to cry you must expect. [...] [I]t is what every lady suffers with more or less and what I, during my first two confinements suffered dreadfully with.'[50] Following the birth of Bertie (later Edward VII) in November 1841, she recorded some of these experiences in her journal. On 16 November, five days after his birth, she noted 'I was feeling rather weak and depressed.' Eleven days later, she wrote: 'Have felt rather weak & depressed these last days, but far better today.' By 30 November, though, she was feeling 'rather out of sorts' again, but on 1 December, she noted, 'After a very good night, felt quite myself again, — really, for the 1rst [sic] time.'[51] These allusions suggest Victoria may have been suffering from mild postnatal depression in the days and weeks following the birth of her second child, but in fact the situation was rather more serious than is indicated by her journal. A year later, in December 1842, pregnant with her third child, Victoria wrote to her Uncle Leopold suggesting she had only recently recovered: 'My poor nerves, tho' thank God! nearly quite well now were so battered last time that I suffered a whole year from it.'[52] Even this does not capture the extent of the deterioration in the Queen's mental health following Bertie's birth. She was not simply depressed, but also experienced hallucinations, imagining she saw worms on people's faces, and floating coffins.[53] Dr Robert Ferguson, who attended the births of all of Queen Victoria's children, but also had an interest in psychological disorders, found Victoria weeping, 'overwhelmed with shame at the necessity of confessing her weakness and compelled by the very burden of her mind & her sorrows to seek relief'.[54]

As was typical of the advice proffered to women following childbirth, Victoria was instructed to rest and avoid any physical or mental exertion in the days following the delivery of her children. As with Charlotte Perkins Gilman and Catherine Dickens, this advice may have had a detrimental impact on the Queen's state of mind. Two days after the birth of her third child, Princess Alice, in April 1843, Victoria wrote in her diary: 'It is rather dull lying quite still & doing nothing, particularly in moments when one is alone.'[55] She evidently delighted in company at this time, and was clearly relieved as she was gradually allowed to do more, writing of her 'great relief' at being allowed to sit in an armchair some two weeks after the baby's birth.[56] On her first visit to the garden a few days later, she wrote: 'I felt so happy at being out again. It did me great good.'[57] The end of her confinements came as a relief to Victoria, as she noted in her journal two weeks after the birth of Prince Arthur in May 1850: 'This day, the 15th or the fortnight, I always hail with joy, as it more or less restores me to my liberty, or at least the beginning of it.'[58] In the days immediately following delivery, Queen Victoria was not even permitted to read her letters. That this contributed to low moods is implied by a comment in her journal several days after the birth of Prince Leopold in April 1853: 'Now read all my own letters, I really find, thank God!, that the days go by so quickly & I feel so contented & in such spirits.'[59] Although Victoria did not again experience the extreme symptoms that followed the birth of her eldest son, she nonetheless evidently struggled several more times with symptoms of postnatal depression, including following the birth of her youngest child, Beatrice, in April 1857. It was partly out of concern for her mental health that one of her doctors, Sir James Clarke, advised against any further pregnancies.[60]

Whilst Victoria certainly endured several bouts of postnatal depression, her more extreme symptoms following the birth of Bertie suggest she had experienced some form of postpartum psychosis. Sufferers experience a variety of symptoms, ranging from the relatively mild, if worrying, to the more extreme. These can include hallucinations, delusions, paranoia, and severe depression.[61] In some cases, postpartum psychosis can prove fatal to mother and/or child. In the nineteenth century, a variety of postnatal mental health conditions, including those we might now understand as depression, PTSD, and psychosis, typically fell under the umbrella term of 'puerperal mania' or 'puerperal insanity'. One 1865 definition states that the condition occurs 'during some stage of childbearing [...] either during pregnancy, shortly after parturition, or during nursing'. It notes that the condition 'is one of exhaustion, debility, and prostration; and can be characterised by 'depression, languor, and passiveness' or, conversely, 'by extreme excitement and violence'.[62] Other medical definitions distinguished between insanity of pregnancy, puerperal insanity, and insanity of lactation. Writing in the *Edinburgh Medical Journal* in 1868, Dr James Young defined 'puerperal insanity proper' as 'a state of mania coming on within ten days after delivery', though he noted that other authorities extend this to include a month after delivery. Nineteenth-century writings on the subject identify various risk factors, including a hereditary tendency and an earlier experience of the condition.[63] Some sources also suggest it appeared to be more common in unmarried women.[64] The key factor, of course, in cases of puerperal insanity, was maternity, and medical discourses throughout the period repeatedly highlighted the potentially dangerous impact on women's mental health of pregnancy and childbirth. Sir William Charles Ellis, superintendent of West Riding Pauper Lunatic Asylum, suggested that 'Women who have any predisposition to insanity, seem, both during pregnancy and immediately after delivery, more susceptible of its attacks than at any other periods.'[65] One work on the causes of 'insanity' published in 1818 also points to a direct correlation between women's biological functions and the onset of insanity – suggesting this as an explanation for the apparently higher incidences of insanity amongst women:

> It appears, that of the two sexes, the proportion as to numbers, bears more heavily against the female. This cannot be wondered at, when we take into account the many exciting causes to which females are more particularly exposed: such as those arising from difficult parturition; the sudden retrocession of the milk, immediately on delivery; the irresistible force of sudden terror, – or of severe disappointment, producing grief; or of unexpected fortune, – excessive joy, or surprise. All of these, together with the congestion, which, in sanguineous temperaments may be supposed to take place, at the period when the menses are naturally disposed to depart, will distinctly and conjointly, in habits previously inclined, tend to generate that inordinate action, which constitutes the essence of insanity in its different varieties.[66]

An earlier work suggests problems following childbirth can also lead to the onset of insanity, and cites the insufficient discharge of the lochia following birth as a possible cause:

[I]f we [...] reflect on the violence, and injury, which the womb, and neighbouring parts may have undergone during delivery; [...] and if [...] we add the increased irritability both of the womb, and of the rest of the body, as well from the pains of labour, and those which succeed it, from the dissipation of the nervous power, and diminution of strength [...] we shall not be surprised that a variety of distressing, and alarming disorders, and among the rest that insanity itself, should be the common consequences of too small a discharge of this kind.[67]

These works, on the one hand, recognise the momentous nature of pregnancy and childbirth and its potentially significant effects on both mind and body. They also, though, reinforce prevalent attitudes around gender roles: women are constructed as weaker, and as needing to reserve their strength for the difficulties associated with the maternal role. It was reasoning such as this which was employed to argue against the idea of women taking up an equal role with men in public life.

Asylum and medical records – as well as, in some tragic cases, court records and coroner reports – detail the devastating impact on women suffering from puerperal insanity. Asylum records suggest a significant proportion of female inmates were suffering from conditions associated with pregnancy, childbirth or lactation.[68] Whilst some women suffered with the symptoms of puerperal insanity for only a short period of time, for others the onset of symptoms following childbirth could lead to years of mental ill health, as in the case of Isabella Thackeray. One 57-year-old patient incarcerated in the Hanwell Pauper Lunatic Asylum in Middlesex in the 1830s suffered with mental health problems for over twenty years, having initially developed them 'after she had been confined about a week'. Others improved within a matter of weeks, but further confinements risked the return of symptoms, as Ellis observes: 'Where puerperal insanity has once occurred, whenever pregnancy takes place subsequently, the irritation very frequently reproduces the disease.' He cites the case of one 25-year-old woman, 'H. S.', who, ten days after the birth of her second child in June 1821, 'became insane'. Her husband initially attempted to keep her at home, but eventually she was admitted to the asylum, where she spent around four months. She was discharged, having recovered, but '[s]oon after her next confinement, which took place in about two years, symptoms similar to those which preceded the former attack made their appearance'.[69]

Whilst it is evident that medical knowledge of postpartum mental health was in many respects limited, women who had previously suffered with postpartum depression or psychosis were recognised as being at higher risk of developing these conditions in subsequent pregnancies, and this remains a recognised risk factor for postnatal depression and psychosis today.

Whilst there were some limitations in medical understanding of the causes of deterioration in postnatal mental health, it is likely that some women in nineteenth-century Britain were suffering from what would now be diagnosed as postnatal PTSD. Today, estimates suggest that this condition affects between 2 and 6 per cent of mothers.[70] Risk factors associated with the development of symptoms of postnatal PTSD include 'pain during childbirth and delivery of an ill or stillborn infant[,] [...] hostile and uncaring treatment by medical personnel, patient's feelings of powerlessness, inadequate information given to the patient, patient's lack of consent, and increasing medical intervention'.[71] As accounts of childbirth in the nineteenth century make clear, many women experienced not just one but all of these, albeit they were not necessarily experienced in the same way: the notion of 'powerlessness', for example, would be understood entirely differently in the nineteenth century, when women could expect to have very little agency in the birthing room. Nonetheless, although the context in which women gave birth in nineteenth-century Britain differs significantly from that in which women deliver children today, circumstances such as lengthy and physically damaging forceps deliveries could have led to the development of symptoms now associated with this condition. One case study from the West Riding Lunatic Asylum provides some evidence of this. A 35-year-old woman was admitted to the asylum in January 1869, shortly after giving birth to her sixth child: 'she was melancholic, and had suicidal propensities'. The case notes suggest her last three births had been particularly difficult:

She has had six children during the last twelve years; the first three were unassisted in their births, but for the fourth instruments had to be used; for the fifth the operation of turning had to be performed, and some other means taken to deliver her, but she does not know what, as she was put under chloroform; at the sixth labour she was put under the influence of chloroform, and some very serious operation had to be performed, but she knows nothing as to its nature.[72]

These details are revealing: not only did the patient experience various interventions during childbirth, but she was unaware of exactly what had happened to her – suggesting she did not give consent for the various operations. This account, whilst not directly associating the difficult births with the patient's mental condition, nonetheless is suggestive in light of what we now know about the risk factors for postpartum PTSD.

James Young cites the case of one 29-year-old woman – the mother of four children – named Rosina Walker. She recovered well from her first three pregnancies, showing no signs of puerperal mania, but appeared somewhat depressed during her fourth pregnancy. For the first few days following the birth of her fourth child, in November 1866, she seemed to be recovering well, but then symptoms of depression increased, and she 'occasionally imagined things'. On the seventh day following the birth, her symptoms became more extreme:

> She suddenly jumped out of bed at 11 o'clock […] exclaiming, 'I am dying; I am not getting better.' She immediately became more outrageous, and began to scream and roar […] She had made frequent attempts to get out at the window, and got downstairs several times even while undressed.

When Young arrived, she was 'raving and furious', and refused medicine, believing it to be poison. She continued 'quite maniacal', at one point 'calling the devil to come out from beneath the bed', and was consequently sent to an asylum on 9 November, where, it was recorded, she continued to be 'suicidal and dangerous' and was diagnosed with 'violent puerperal mania'. Her extreme symptoms, including hallucinations and delusions, continued. She died on 19 November, and an autopsy revealed an infection of the uterus, suggesting her maniacal symptoms resulted from a physical cause.[73]

The death of a young woman named Mrs Robson, aged 22, on 2 January 1824, may also not have been a direct result of puerperal mania, although she exhibited symptoms of the disorder in the days before her death. She gave birth to her first child on 17 December 1823 at Newcastle Lying-In Hospital and shortly afterwards showed symptoms of puerperal mania: a 'considerable incoherence of manner and dejection of spirits' as well as an indifference towards her child, including an unwillingness to nurse it. She did not initially display symptoms of any other illness. She was 'sullen and dejected' but this was thought to be due to some 'domestic anxieties'. Initially, she appeared to improve: 'Her spirits were calmed and she was induced both to take food and to nurse her child.' On 5 January, however, 'she had been suddenly attacked with an alarming train of symptoms indicating serious mischief in the head'. She experienced 'great pain in the head' and her 'intellects were confused', with occasional 'wild bursts of delirium'. She was treated by having 12oz of blood drawn, and when this failed to have any effect, leeches were placed on her head in an attempt at further bloodletting. Foreseeably, this proved unsuccessful and she died shortly afterwards. The post-mortem examination showed evidence of bleeding on the brain.[74] These cases point to the blurred line between physical and mental health following childbirth, as well as to the limitations in medical knowledge which could severely impact outcomes.

The deaths of Rosina Walker and Mrs Robson do not appear to have resulted from puerperal mania, which in these cases may have been symptoms of other conditions. In some cases, though, sufferers were driven to take their own lives and, on occasion, that of their baby. Court records detail dozens of cases of infants killed by their own mothers, apparently whilst suffering from puerperal mania. In some of these cases, the mothers were found not guilty on the grounds that they were *non compos mentis* at the time of the killing. These include the case of Elizabeth Hodges, who was tried in January 1838 for the murder of her daughter, Sarah. Elizabeth Hodges gave birth on 4 December 1837. At her trial, the sometimes-midwife who attended her, Mary Ann Harvey, reported that her patient 'did not get through her confinement well—she never was well'. In the weeks following the birth, the midwife reported that Elizabeth 'was frequently in a very melancholy state of mind' and that 'she thought she should make away with herself'. On one visit, the midwife discovered a razor lying open on the table, for which Elizabeth could offer no satisfactory explanation. When Mary removed the razor, Elizabeth is reported to have said 'take it away, for fear I should do any accident or mischief'. However, the midwife reported that despite these symptoms, Elizabeth appeared fond of the child. On 31 December, Mary once again visited Elizabeth at home. She found both her and her husband in a disturbed state, and upon enquiring about the whereabouts of the baby, discovered it had been murdered. She described the scene in her testimony at Elizabeth's trial:

> I ran to Mrs. Hodges, took hold of her hand, and said to her, 'My dear
> girl, what have you done with the child?'—she said, 'It is dead'—she
> did not answer me the first time I spoke to her—I asked her two or three
> times before she gave me any answer—when she did answer, she said,
> 'It is dead'—I said, 'Dead! my dear girl, where?' and asked her what
> she had done with it—she said, 'In the copper'—I flew instantly into
> the other room where the copper was, and there I saw the baby—[…]
> I then took hold of Mrs. Hodges' hand, and asked her how she could
> do such a deed—she gave me no answer, but looked in a most wild,
> distracted state[.]

Following the discovery of the dead child, a surgeon, James Hayes, also attended the house, and was called upon to give evidence at the trial. When he arrived, he discovered the child 'lying on the table, wrapped up in a blanket, dead':

> I went into the room where Mrs. Hodges was, and said to her, 'This
> is a shocking business, Mrs. Hodges: how could you do this; how was
> it?'—she was not at all communicative to me, but at last she said she had
> smothered the child, by placing a pillow over its face—I asked her if the
> child struggled at all—she said it struggled a little—she said she after-
> wards took it into the other room, and put it into the copper, having
> previously put some water into the copper—I asked her what time she
> did it—her answer was, before her husband came to bed—I asked her
> how she could do it—she gave no answer to that.

On examination, the surgeon suggested Elizabeth's state of mind may have been related to the drying up of her milk in the fortnight prior to the baby's death, reporting 'that would very likely have an effect on the head of a person so circumstanced'. Consequently, he suggested, 'she was not at all aware of any thing she did', adding 'It is not unfrequented for women during parturition, and shortly after, to be affected with a mania peculiar to that state—it is called puerperal mania—deficiency of milk, and the milk flowing upwards, would very probably cause such consequences.' In light of the evidence provided, Elizabeth Hodges was subsequently found not guilty, as she was deemed to have been 'insane at the time of commit-ting the offence'.[75]

* * *

As nineteenth-century medical discourses around puerperal insanity make clear, the period of lactation was also seen to pose a risk to the mental health of mothers. This is evident in the case of Elizabeth Hodges, as well in wider discourses on the subject. Sir William Charles Ellis suggested that, 'After delivery, insanity more frequently arises from the brain sympathizing with the uterus, from the stoppage of the lochia, or from its sympathizing with the breasts, from cold, or any other cause interrupting the secretion of the milk.'[76] Ellis cites a number of cases of women who developed insanity following the premature cessation of their milk production.[77] Another work on the subject of the causes of insanity noted that 'There are some instances on record amongst females, who, from the sudden failure of the milk, soon after parturition, have been attacked with violent mania.'[78] In this and other respects, the period of infant feeding could be a fraught time for new mothers. Difficulties in breastfeeding, experienced by women including Catherine Dickens and Lady Amberley, could precipitate periods of depression or low mood. Some women, such as Queen Victoria, found the practice distasteful and preferred to employ wet nurses. Others, including some of Queen Victoria's daughters, found great joy in nursing their own infants. As with every other aspect of motherhood, women faced significant social and cultural pressures during this time, and, like the discourses around motherhood more generally, the feeding of infants was the subject of much debate, with women's own accounts of infant feeding often contrasting starkly with wider cultural discourses around it.

9

Infant Feeding:
Breasts, Bottles, and Wet Nurses

'… blest the Babe,
Nurs'd in his Mother's arms, the Babe who sleeps
Upon his Mother's breast, who, when his soul
Claims manifest kindred with an earthly soul,
Doth gather passion from his Mother's eye!'
William Wordsworth[1]

In August 1869, an inquest was held into the death of 9-month-old Bessie Pay, the illegitimate daughter of a domestic servant named Jane Pay, who had been employed as a wet nurse shortly after the birth of her daughter, and who had left Bessie in the care of a Mrs Mary Waters. The child was seemingly in poor health – suffering from 'atrophy, sickness, and diarrhoea'. The mother reported that her charges, by contrast, were 'fine, healthy children'. It was suggested at the inquest that 'Most probably if the child had not been deprived of its natural food it would have lived.' The coroner concluded that 'This was a typical case, showing that young women having produced children put them out to nurse, and sold their sustenance – that which was sent by nature for their own children's support – to the offspring of others. They allowed their own to die, whilst those they suckled lived.' The verdict of the jury was 'Death from natural causes, accelerated by the deprivation of breast-milk through the mother going out as a wet nurse to another child.'[2]

The case of the death of Bessie Pay speaks to the complexities and social inequities around infant feeding in nineteenth-century Britain. Women such as Jane Pay were often constructed as the epitome of the 'bad' mother: unmarried and neglectful of her own child for the sake of earning money by nourishing someone else's. By contrast, for much of the period, the figure of the nursing mother was closely bound up with the idea of idealised maternity. This is reflected in works of art, such as Charles Cope's *The Young Mother* (1845) (see figure 12), in which the nursing mother gazes adoringly at her infant as she feeds him; in fiction, such as Thackeray's *Vanity Fair* (1847), in which breastfeeding provokes 'intense raptures of motherly love';[3] and throughout advice literature, which typically exalted the figure of the nursing mother, and strongly encouraged mothers to breastfeed: 'As instinct impels the infant to the mother's breast, and has inspired that breast with maternal love, this beautiful link in the chain of nature should never wantonly be snapped asunder.'[4] This, though, was an age of contradictions, and it was also a time in which infant feeding became increasingly commercialised, with a multitude of new products, from baby bottles to various types of formula (as well as the numerous advice books on the subject) made available to the mothers of Britain. Throughout the period, attitudes towards and practices around infant feeding shifted considerably, influenced by current trends, individual choices and constraints, advice literature, medical advice, and (particularly in the latter decades of the nineteenth century) the growing market for infant formula and bottles. Decisions about infant feeding were also at times influenced by financial status, as the case of Bessie Pay illustrates. For much of the century, the use of wet nurses amongst the aristocracy was commonplace. At the opposite end of the socio-economic scale, some working women had little choice but to hand (bottle or spoon) feed, as they were forced to return to work shortly after giving birth. Women working as wet nurses, such as Jane Pay, ironically, were not always able to breastfeed their *own* children, who might be left in the care of family, or careless or unscrupulous child minders, including the baby farmers who became so closely associated with high levels of infant mortality. All of these issues were the subject of significant debate, and in some of the contested discourses around infant feeding, we can locate the origins for the often-heated discussions on the subject today. Such discourses often belie women's lived experiences of breastfeeding, although they also undoubtedly influenced them, as mothers tried to negotiate between social and cultural expectations, practicalities, unexpected challenges, and personal choice.

These negotiations will be familiar to many mothers today. In 2011, after giving birth to my first child, I struggled to breastfeed. The hospital was reluctant to discharge me until the baby had latched, and a seemingly end-less stream of doctors, midwives, nurses, and lactation consultants sought to manoeuvre the baby and me into various positions in an attempt to solve the problem. Despite deciding prior to the birth that I would try to breast-feed but would not put undue pressure on myself, I was overwhelmed with guilt. Eventually, frustrated and exhausted, I discharged myself and took the baby and my accompanying sense of guilt and failure home, where, miraculously – or possibly because the environment was now a lot less pressured – the baby latched (and then obstinately refused to take a bottle for several months). I was, of course, aware of the (sometimes acrimonious) breast-versus-bottle debate, but largely unprepared for the emotional and physical impact of infant feeding: the guilt at my initial failure to breast-feed; the exhaustion at his total dependence on me; the panic (and more guilt) at waking one night to discover I had fallen asleep with the baby still in my bed and he had rolled onto his front and was lying face down on the mattress; the sickness and pain after I developed mastitis (the doctor insist-ing that I feed through the pain); and much later, the sense of loss at feeding my youngest child for the final time. I watched friends struggle with sim-ilar issues, and read message boards in which breast- and bottle-feeding mothers took aim at one another: 'breast is best' versus 'fed is best'. The injunctions to breastfeed, though sometimes given with the best intentions, did not always take account of the difficulties this sometimes presented, and the consequent sense of guilt and failure when things did not go to plan. For some mothers, the weighted issue of infant feeding undoubtedly contributes to deteriorating postnatal mental health. My experiences, and those of other mothers in twenty-first-century Britain, are not dissimilar to those of women in the nineteenth century, who also faced competing pressures around infant feeding. These included the ideologies surrounding motherhood and maternal behaviours, commercial pressures from those marketing infant feeding products, as well as the practical and physical constraints that sometimes limited women's choices around infant feed-ing. Women's experiences of maternal breastfeeding, wet nursing, hand and bottle feeding in nineteenth-century Britain were, like other aspects of maternity, diverse, and there is often a contrast between the messages found in wider social and cultural discourses on the issue, and women's lived experiences.

Maternal Breastfeeding

Nineteenth-century advice and medical literature, with few exceptions, encouraged maternal breastfeeding, often constructing it as a moral, sometimes even a religious duty. Charles Vine's *Mother and Child* (1868) is fairly typical in this respect:

> [I]t is the bounden duty of every woman to nurse her own child; and the mother who, through indolence or carelessness, neglects to perform this duty, incurs a vast amount of responsibility, deprives herself of a sweet privilege, and robs her infant of that nourishment which God designed for its special use and support.[5]

Whilst many commentators stressed the benefits of breastfeeding for the child, particularly when contrasted with the dangers inherent in bottle- or hand feeding, many also stressed the potential advantages for the mother of nursing her own infant. In *Mother and Child*, the author suggests that during the period of lactation, 'the mother [...] acquires a calmness of mind and a serenity and cheerfulness of countenance, heightened no doubt by the pleasing consciousness that she is performing one of the sweetest duties that can devolve upon woman.'[6] Fictional depictions of motherhood further perpetuated the association between breastfeeding and idealised maternity. In Elizabeth Gaskell's *Sylvia's Lovers* (1863), breastfeeding appears to quell the eponymous heroine's more rebellious instincts: 'till she held her baby to her breast, she bitterly wished that she were free from the duties and chains of matrimony. But the touch of its waxen fingers, the hold of its little mouth, made her relax into docility and gentleness.'[7] In William Thackeray's *Vanity Fair* (1848), the recently widowed Amelia Sedley finds comfort from her grief in nursing her child:

It was her life which the baby drank in from her bosom. Of nights, and when alone, she had stealthy and intense raptures of motherly love, such as God's marvellous care has awarded to the female instinct – joys how far higher and lower than reason – blind beautiful devotions which only women's hearts know.[8]

By contrast, the mother who does not breastfeed is often depicted in negative terms in nineteenth-century fiction. An extreme example of this is found in Bram Stoker's *Dracula* (1897), in which the figure of the vampire is associated with a dark parody of the act of breastfeeding. Newly vampirised Lucy Westernra – at the start of the novel seemingly destined for marriage and motherhood – becomes associated not only with the figure of the street walker via her transformation into a vampire, but also with the Victorian archetype of the 'bad' mother. Whilst (married) motherhood and breastfeeding were closely associated with idealised notions of femininity, the vampire Lucy subverts these ideals by feeding *from* the bodies of small children.

Elsewhere, nineteenth-century fiction at times reflected and sometimes interrogated current trends and practices around infant feeding. In Maria Edgeworth's *Belinda* (1801), the character of Lady Delacour alludes to the trend for women of the wealthier classes to nurse their own children, and its influence on her own experience as a mother:

It was the fashion at this time for fine mothers to suckle their own children – so much the worse for the poor brats. – Fine nurses never make fine children. There was a prodigious rout made about the matter; a vast deal of sentiment and sympathy, and compliments and inquiries; but after the novelty was over, I became heartily sick of the business; and at the end of about three months my poor child was sick too – I don't much like to think of it – it died. – If I had put it out to nurse, I should have been thought by my friends an unnatural mother – but I should have saved it's [*sic*] life.[9]

At the other end of the century, George Moore's novel, *Esther Waters* (1894), also contains an idealised vision of the nursing mother – here compared to the Madonna: 'The little lips caught at the nipple, the wee hand pressed the white curve, and in a moment Esther's face took that expression of holy solicitude which Raphael sublimated in the Virgin's downward-gazing eyes.'[10]

Despite these positive representations of maternal breastfeeding in advice literature and fiction, there were certain circumstances in which mothers were advised against nursing their own babies – in particular, when the mother's health was perceived as 'delicate', or when she suffered from a (physical or mental) complaint that might, according to some medical discourses current at the time, be transmitted to the child via the breast milk. One work on the subject advises that 'Every woman whose constitution and health are good, ought to suckle her infant, but everyone who is delicate, affected by chronic disease, or has little breast milk, should avoid it.'[11] Another suggests that 'However anxious some mothers may be to bring up their offspring at the breast, it may be absolutely necessary, both for their own and their child's safety, to forego this privilege' in some circumstances.[12] These include cases in which the mother is consumptive or where there is an 'inherited tendency to this disease', women who are 'nervous and excitable', as 'The influence of the mind upon the milk secretion is very great', and women whose nipples are 'so depressed' as to prevent them from nursing. In relation to this latter point, attention should be paid to the wearing of corsets in pregnancy, which can have a harmful effect on the breasts.[13] Similar advice is still given today, with women discouraged from wearing 'tight restrictive clothes and bras which can restrict milk flow'.[14] The NHS also advises mothers taking certain medications (such as contraceptive pills) or suffering from particular health conditions (including HIV) not to breastfeed. In the nineteenth century, when treatments were not always available to prevent the spread of diseases such as tuberculosis from mother to child, it was evidently sensible to avoid breastfeeding. In other cases, however, such guidance was based on differing understandings and medical conceptions – in particular around the links between mind and body. This was particularly the case in discourses around mental health. Whilst a deterioration in mental health in the postnatal period might, in rare cases, pose a risk to the infant, there was no inherent risk from the breast milk itself, as some writings on the subject suggest. One advice book declares that 'The milk is so soon changed in its character by the emotions of the mind, [such] as fear, anger, or other strong passions, that the effects upon the child are in some cases most disastrous.' Consequently, the author concludes, 'a passionate temper, or great excitability of mind, ought to be regarded as a complete disqualification in a nurse.'[15] This is echoed in other advice books for mothers. In one, published in 1853, the author writes:

[W]here the mother has previously suffered from any mental disease, or now suffers from extreme infirmity of temper, from an irascible temperament, or great nervous debility, or from susceptibility to extreme grief or sorrow, she cannot reckon upon conferring benefits on her children by supporting them with corrupted milk.[16]

Another issues an even starker warning:

When passions of a more intense, or more abiding, character are aroused, their effects will be [...] grave; and several cases are recorded, in which the death of young infants has been immediately consequent either upon violent anger, or upon extreme anxiety and depression, on the part of their nursing mothers, whose milk has been converted into an energetic poison.[17]

There are echoes here of the pseudoscientific theory of 'maternal impressions', which also identified problematic and unfounded associations between mental excitement and the health of the infant. William Carpenter, in *Principles of Human Physiology* (1842), reiterated these claims, suggesting that 'the Mammary secretion may acquire an actual *poisonous* character, under the influence of violent mental excitement.' He cites a case in support of this claim:

A carpenter fell into a quarrel with a soldier billeted in his house, and was set-upon by the latter with his drawn sword. The wife of the carpenter at first trembled from fear and terror, and then suddenly threw herself furiously between the combatants, wrested the sword from the soldier's hand, broke it in pieces, and threw it away. [...] While in this state of strong excitement, the mother took-up her child from the cradle, where it lay playing, and in the most perfect health, never having had a moment's illness; she gave it the breast, and in so doing sealed its fate. In a few minutes the infant left-off sucking, became restless, panted, and sank dead upon its mother's bosom.

He goes on to offer an explanation for these events: 'the milk must have undergone a change which gave it a powerful sedative action upon the susceptible nervous system of the infant.' He cites two other cases in which the mothers dwelt on their fears of losing their infants whilst nursing, only for the babies to die shortly afterwards. Such cases, Carpenter argues, 'should serve as a salutary warning to mothers, not to indulge either in the exciting or in the depressing passions'.[18]

Such discourses reinforce the notion that women's characters and temperaments must adhere to prevalent constructions of idealised femininity: deviation from these was deemed to risk the health of both mother and child. In Braddon's *Lady Audley's Secret*, the anti-heroine, who claims to be suffering from some form of mental illness, refers to this 'madness' as 'the hidden taint that I had sucked in with my mother's milk'.[19] Women also feared passing on common illnesses through breastfeeding – and at a time when childhood illness was more difficult to treat, and infant mortality high, their concerns are understandable. In one case, a mother recalled contracting a 'severe chill': 'It was all on my chest; and having baby on the breast, it drew the cold from me, and with that took ill of catarrh of the stomach, and died at four months.'[20] Whilst women today are encouraged to feed through most mild illnesses, there was potentially a greater risk in the nineteenth century, when treatments for any condition were so much more limited.

Advice on breastfeeding also typically included recommendations on how often to feed and for how long. Many advice books recommended weaning at nine months, and 'feeding on demand' was typically discouraged. Mrs Beeton was one of several advice writers to warn against feeding babies through the night, highlighting the perceived dangers for the mother's health:

[The mother] wakes languid and unrefreshed from her sleep, with febrile symptoms and hectic flushes, caused by her baby vampire, who, while dragging from her, her health and strength, has excited in itself a set of symptoms directly opposite, but fraught with the same injurious consequences – 'functional derangement'.[21]

Allowing babies to share the mother's bed and to feed through the night was also associated with 'overlaying' – the accidental suffocation of the child. Advice books frequently highlighted high infant mortality rates, and the positive impact of maternal breastfeeding versus artificial feeding in relation to this. Some of the risks, though, could not always be mitigated: amongst the poor, women often had little choice but to share their beds with their babies – and often several other family members as well. Poorer women also had limited access to advice literature and might therefore be unaware of the recommended safest practices around infant feeding. Whilst some of the advice offered was questionable, in other respects these works did provide some guidance which would help to keep infants safe and healthy. One woman, a mother of five, whose account of motherhood is detailed in *Maternity: Letters From Working Women*, hints at this in recalling her own experiences: 'I knew very little about feeding children; when they cried, I gave them the breast. If I had known then what I know now, perhaps my children would have been living.'[22] Her account highlights both women's ignorance of maternal matters, and the unreliability of some of the information that was available. Despite claims to the contrary in nineteenth-century advice literature, breastfed babies are highly unlikely to suffer any negative consequences as a result of 'overfeeding'. Women might also receive contradictory advice from medical practitioners. One woman recalls that 'being such a strong child the doctor told me to give it the bottle; but, on the other hand, the nurse persuaded me to keep it to the breast'. She goes on to lament the nurse's advice, which she blames for the subsequent development of 'gathered breasts' (breast abscesses).[23]

The diet of breastfeeding mothers continues to be a much-debated issue: what to eat, what to avoid, when and how much to consume – these questions have occupied breastfeeding mothers and those advising them for centuries. I remember detailed discussions whilst nursing my children on what foods might cause wind or disturb sleep; if a varied diet would avoid picky eating later on; and whether a glass of wine or two was acceptable or not. One theory which continues to hold sway in some quarters today is the idea that stout is good for breastfeeding, as it is believed to increase milk production (this is likely due to the barley, which may increase the production of prolactin, but any positive effect is likely to be counteracted by the alcohol, which has been shown to decrease milk supply).[24] This has long been a belief amongst mothers and some medical advisors. One work from 1885 advised that 'a nursing mother may often find her strength maintained, and her supply of milk increased, by taking a glass of stout at lunch and another at dinner', but cautioned against excess.[25] The belief in the benefits of stout was evidently persistent enough to raise concern amongst some commentators. In 1882, an article in *The Lancet* declared: 'If all nursing mothers were teetotallers, it would be far better for the totality of British babies', but suggested that 'some infants would […] be the worse'.[26] One account evidencing the belief in the benefits of stout for breastfeeding mothers comes from the biography of Margaret Jane, whose sister-in-law apparently 'suckled her youngest child until he was about 4 years old'. During this time, the child's 'father brought in a glass of stout for her often. The family would ask the child what he got after his mother had finished her "glass" when he would smile broadly and reply "a great big titty". It wasn't thought quite nice by Grandma and her family.'[27] Such anecdotes show that some of the beliefs around breastfeeding which persist today can be dated back to the nineteenth century and beyond.

Whilst maternal breastfeeding was, with few exceptions, constructed as an overwhelmingly positive experience (for mothers and babies) in medical and advice literature, as well as in fictional representations, women's actual experiences of breastfeeding in nineteenth-century Britain were inevitably more complex. For some women, breastfeeding was a straightforward and pleasurable experience. Shortly after the birth of her first child, Lady Lyttelton reported, 'babee [*sic*] eats without any trouble, & without giving me hardly any pain'.[28] In 1858, Catherine Temple Pears wrote to her sister of her regret at weaning her daughter:

> I am only just finishing weaning Baby and I never felt before so much annoyed at giving up a little dear. She has been very pleasant to me, so fond and ready to be comforted at any time by pulling my neck or face with one hand and sucking the other little thumb.[29]

For others, the experience was less positive: then as now, breastfeeding could be difficult, uncomfortable, painful, and exhausting – both mentally and physically. Problems with milk flow, inverted nipples, or tongue tie might prevent babies from thriving, leaving women with little choice but to find alternatives to nursing themselves. An inability to breastfeed was sometimes a source of much distress for nineteenth-century mothers, evoking feelings of guilt or failure. Conversely, it was no doubt a cause for relief for others. Some women, such as Queen Victoria, simply did not want to breastfeed – not an unusual choice amongst women from the upper classes, and in part linked to ideas of refinement: Victoria, like many others, felt this was a practice unsuited to gentlewomen. Other mothers were discouraged from breastfeeding by their husbands. This (perhaps surprising) reluctance on the part of some husbands can be attributed, at least in part, to the discourses which discouraged sexual activity during periods of lactation, claiming this would have a detrimental effect on the quality and production of breast milk. One work touching on this subject claimed that 'conjugal intimacy diminishes the secretion of milk, by exciting the womb and determining blood to it'.[30] Mary Wollstonecraft, an advocate of maternal breastfeeding, commented on this in 1792 in *A Vindication of the Rights of Women*: 'There are many husbands so devoid of sense and parental affection that, during the first effervescence of voluptuous fondness, they refuse to let their wives suckle their children.'[31] Almost 100 years later, Olive Schreiner suggested husbands sometimes prefer their children to breastfeed: 'One of my friends told me that her husband liked her to suckle her children long, because then, owing to the absence of the period, which rarely shows itself during suckling, they could more frequently have intercourse.'[32] *The Wife's Handbook* offered slightly confusing advice on this subject: 'During sucking, husband and wife must not embrace too often, otherwise the milk will be spoilt in quality and the wife's health will suffer. On the other hand, sexual connection at this period, in moderation, is beneficial.'[33] Objections to maternal breastfeeding sometimes came from other family members, as one woman's account from the early twentieth century suggests: 'I heard a young mother with her first baby say the other day her husband's mother had told her not to bother with her breasts, it made a young woman look old giving her baby breast.'[34] By contrast, some advice writing suggested breastfeeding was beneficial to women's appearance: 'nursing […] is particularly favourable to beauty', and will 'clear the complexion and brighten the countenance',[35] advised one work.

Whilst medical considerations, advice literature, and personal choice played a role in decisions around infant feeding, in some instances, women were simply unable to breastfeed. Whatever the reasons for this, it could be a cause of distress for mothers who had intended to nurse their own children. This was the experience of Kate Russell, Lady Amberley following the birth of her first child in August 1865, and she was forced to employ a wet nurse, as her husband records in her diary the day after the child's birth: 'Baby would not suck, & had to be fed by Mrs. Potts, whose child is four months old.' The following day, he writes more of his wife's struggle to breastfeed, and his own attempts to alleviate the problem:

Tho' perfectly well K[ate] had much trouble today from baby not sucking. He would not or could not do it. Another baby took a little but K still suffered much pain in her breast. In the evg. [...] I sucked a little thinking it might do good, but I could not get much. Since I had to apply all my sucking power to get any milk it is no wonder the infant found it too hard for him. The milk was not nasty, but much too sweet to be pleasant; like the sweetest of syrup. It seems very badly managed by nature that little babies should not always find it as easy to suck as little puppies; but if this is one of the arrangements that was made in consequence of original sin of course we must not complain of it.

It is evident, however, that both he and Kate were unhappy with the situation. The next day he noted: 'Baby still refuses to suck. K. was not very happy or comfortable [...] I was annoyed at the nursing not being successful.' Despite his mother-in-law's assurances that 'she is sure to nurse with perseverance', the problem continued. There was a glimmer of hope a few days later when he heard the baby 'had taken K's breast' but it was evident Kate was still struggling: 'K. very low and weak; nurses her baby but has not enough to give it.' The following day he wrote: 'K. cannot bear the notion of a wet-nurse & I dislike it nearly as much, but there seems no hope of her nursing now.' However, Kate continued to resist the hiring of a wet nurse, in part, it is clear, because of a belief that mothers should nurse their own children, as suggested by her husband's entry in her diary:

I thought [the baby] looked pale, & am afraid we must get him a wet-nurse if he is to thrive.

[..] Dear K. struggled hard against the wet nurse, but in the evening declared her readiness to give up nursing if the child's health would be better with another woman. A terrible disappointment to her, for we both care very much about ladies nursing, but I doubt not her strong sense of duty will overcome the reluctance to relinquish this harassing attempt to feed her baby when nature does not provide the means of doing so.

This view was supported by the attending medical man, Dr Merriman, and the wet nurse arrived shortly afterwards. Kate, her husband records, 'was of course dreadfully unhappy but bore it very well'.[36] She had more success nursing her subsequent children, breastfeeding both her surviving twin, Rachel, born in March 1868, and her second son, Bertrand, who arrived in May 1872. Of the latter, she wrote in her diary: 'I have plenty of milk and cd nurse him entirely I am sure it agrees with me as I feel so well.'[37]

Catherine Dickens experienced similar problems following the birth of her first child, and found breastfeeding comparably distressing. According to her biographer, Lillian Nayder, this was a factor in her postpartum depression. Charley Dickens was born on 6 January 1837, and shortly afterwards Catherine's sister Mary wrote to their cousin describing recent events:

> After we thought she was getting quite well and strong it was discovered she was not able to nurse her Baby so she was obliged with great reluctance as you may suppose to give him up to a stranger. Poor Kate! it has been a dreadful trial for her [...] It is really dreadful to see her suffer. Every time she sees her Baby she has a fit of crying and keeps constantly saying she is sure he will not care for her now she is not able to nurse him. [...] She has got a very nice Nurse for him but poor Kate looks upon her now with very jealous eyes.[38]

Whilst some women happily relinquished their babies to wet nurses, then, for others, such as Kate Amberley and Catherine Dickens, the failure to breastfeed was a source of much distress. The potential link between Catherine Dickens's failure to nurse and her postpartum depression is given credence by recent research which suggests women who experience problems breastfeeding are more susceptible to the condition.[39]

Lady Amberley and Catherine Dickens occupied relatively privileged positions in Victorian society: both comfortably off, like Queen Victoria they were easily able to afford to hire wet nurses for their infant sons. Women who worked might be prevented from breastfeeding by the demands of their job. With no right to maternity leave or pay, some women had little choice but to return to work shortly after giving birth in order to feed their families. In 1844, an article in *The Spectator* drew attention to this issue: 'The most horrible cruelty [...] is practised [..] upon mothers who give suck to children, and who are dragged from the cradles of their babes to spend the day in the factory, with their breasts boiling over with milk, and their babes crying at home for that nutrient.'[40]

The account of one working-class woman, writing in the early twentieth century, testifies to some of the problems faced by working women in terms of infant feeding:

> I never knew so many bottle-fed babies as there is now. Nearly all the young married women cannot give breast. How is it? Now, I think because they work so hard before, do not get enough rest, therefore have no milk. And, then, some will not begin with their own milk, because they know they have to go out to work.[41]

Conversely, breastfeeding was the cheapest means of feeding infants – possibly one reason why some women, such as Margaret Jane's sister-in-law, breastfed for extended periods. It was not always possible for working-class women to relinquish breastfeeding on doctors' advice, as the experience of Margaret Jane, related by her granddaughter, shows:

> When grandfather was out of work, times were very hard for the family. He was unemployed when Grandma was pregnant on one occasion and as there was only a gap of fourteen months between them eventually, she was still breastfeeding her present baby. She was very poorly and had to visit the doctor – she must have been unwell as doctors' bills were a great burden on honest folk who believed in paying their debts. He told her she must stop the breast feeding at once but she told him she couldn't do so as she had no money to buy milk.[42]

Pressures on working women in particular meant they weren't always able to breastfeed their own children, but might struggle to afford alternatives. Unlike the wealthier upper and middle classes, they were typically unable to pay for the services of a wet nurse, and therefore had to leave their infants with family or poorly paid childminders, where they would be either bottle or spoon fed, sometimes with substances of questionable quality. At least one advice book, though, suggests working-men's wives were particularly adept at breastfeeding, in contrast with the women of the leisured classes: 'Working-men's wives have usually splendid breasts of milk – enough and to spare for their infants; while ladies of fortune, who have nothing but pleasure to do, have not half enough, and even in many cases nothing at all, for their babies!'[43] Although women were strongly encouraged to feed their own infants, discourses such as this posit the working-man's wife as an ideal wet nurse – and many women from the middle and upper classes preferred this option to nursing themselves.

Wet Nursing

Women from wealthier backgrounds could elect to pay another woman to breastfeed their baby for them. For some women, the notion of breastfeeding their own babies was distasteful, and not something to be considered. Queen Victoria epitomised this view, employing wet nurses to feed all of her children – although, ironically, given her frustration at her excessive fertility, breastfeeding her children herself may have assisted in preventing some of her many pregnancies. Frequent breastfeeding could serve as an effective form of contraception, and there is evidence that some women employed it as a means of preventing further pregnancies. Today, this is known as the 'lactational amenorrhoea' method, and research suggests it can be up to 98 per cent effective, particularly in the first six months after childbirth.[44] The author of one work on midwifery noted, 'Many women suckle for fourteen or twenty months to prevent pregnancy, and I have known those who continued a wet nurse for six years for this purpose.'[45] Whilst frequent breastfeeding might help prevent pregnancy, it was not always a reliable method of contraception. One woman recalls the circumstances of her second pregnancy: 'When my baby was five months old I began to turn against my food; was nursing baby at the time, so did not think for one moment I could be pregnant again, but it was so.'[46] Although unsuccessful in preventing pregnancy in this instance, this account, from a working-class woman, is indicative of the fact that lactation was a known form of contraception amongst some women.

Queen Victoria, determined not to breastfeed, hired a series of wet nurses to feed her own children, one of whom was Mary Ann Brough, employed as wet nurse for the Prince of Wales in 1842. For reasons that are not entirely clear, Mary was fired from her position a few months later – one paper reported that the dismissal was due to Brough 'disobeying the physician's orders',[47] another that it was a consequence of her 'fondness for gin'.[48] Twelve years later, Brough killed six of her own children, although she was subsequently found not guilty of murder on the grounds of insanity. Whilst newspaper reports typically refrained from speculating on the potential nefarious influence of Brough's milk on the young Prince, they consistently mention the former relationship between the two in reporting Brough's crimes. In light of the prevalent discourses around wet nursing and breast milk, such references can be implicitly understood to be gesturing towards the question of the significance of this. Yet despite this negative experience and the anxieties it provoked, Queen Victoria continued to oppose the idea of aristocratic women nursing their own infants. When her daughter, Princess Alice, chose to breastfeed, Victoria expressed her distaste for the practice: 'A Child can never be as well nursed by a lady of rank and nervous and refined temperament,' she wrote, 'for the less feeling and the more like an animal the wet-nurse is, the better for the child.'[49] When Alice disregarded her advice, Victoria reputedly named one of the cows in the royal dairy after her.[50]

The notion of the breastfeeding woman as 'animal-like' was not uncommon. In 1841, Lady Stanley wrote to her daughter-in-law, with news of her infant granddaughter. Presumably referring to the wet nurse, she wrote: 'Baby flourishes with her Italian cow.'[51] Alice was not unique amongst aristocratic mothers in choosing to nurse her own children. Henrietta (later Baroness) Stanley nursed her numerous children herself, although not entirely without trouble. Writing to her mother-in-law following the birth of her eighth child, she stated: 'I have now no ailment but pain with nursing which is absurd at my stage of the business.'[52] Following the birth of her youngest child in 1849, however, she found herself unable to breastfeed, and a wet nurse was hired.[53] The practice of hiring wet nurses amongst the upper classes was prevalent enough to attract commentary, and often criticism. One advice book for mothers, published in 1831, condemned the 'multitudes amongst the noble and rich of our land, who, without the shadow of a reason or necessity, commit their infants to the breast of an alien!'[54] Olive Schreiner, in a letter written in 1886, speculated on the reasons for this apparent trend:

> The reason why fashionable women do not suckle their children is because doing so entirely spoils the shape of the breast and nipple. After suckling even one child the breast droops, whereas a woman may have ten children without it affecting her breast if she does not suckle them. It is also supposed (quite falsely I think) to make a woman wrinkle and grey; it also spoils their dresses and they have to be always near their children.[55]

In some cases, such as that of Lady Amberley, or in instances in which the mother died shortly after the birth of her baby, maternal breastfeeding was not possible, and wet nursing posed less risk to the health of the infant than hand or bottle feeding, so was the preferred option for many. In cases where the mother had died, the mother-substitute, in the figure of the wet nurse, was typically perceived as an acceptable, because unavoidable, alternative. Shortly before Margaret Gladstone[56] died from puerperal fever following the birth of her only child in 1870, she took leave of the family and household servants from her death bed. Her mother's diary records her encounter with the wet nurse who was to nurse the motherless child:

> The wetnurse caught her attention by sobbing, and never having seen her or heard of her, [Margaret] looked inquiringly at John [Gladstone – her husband]; he said this is baby's nurse. When she heard this, she tried to raise herself a little and said with deep earnestness in broken accents 'Do the best you can for baby – in God's name.'[57]

The figure of the wet nurse was frequently a source of particular anxiety in nineteenth-century Britain – for a multitude of reasons. Servants generally were liable to provoke anxiety and distrust: they lived with the family, but were not part of the family, and therefore their loyalty could not be guaranteed. They might conceal criminal pasts – or criminal intentions – unbeknownst to their employers, or might play the role of spy, privy as they were to the secrets of private family life. The mid-Victorian sensation novel played on these fears, via its depiction of transgressive servants and the disruption of family life, whilst newspapers frequently contained reports of criminal servants. In light of her proximity to the most vulnerable members of the family, it was especially important that the wet nurse should be both trustworthy and morally upstanding – whether she was brought into the family home or the infant sent out to nurse. Pseudoscientific theories regarding the influence of character traits on the breast milk further contributed to the anxieties around this figure. In addition, there were also concerns about the physical health of the infant if the moral character of the wet nurse was deemed questionable. A woman infected with venereal disease might, according to nineteenth-century medical discourses, transmit the infection to the child.[58] One advice book for mothers notes that this 'most loathsome and horrible of all diseases has been communicated by nurses to sucking infants', and cites the case of one household (both family and servants) who were all 'infected with the venereal disease by a nurse who was admitted into the family, without previous inquiry into her character' (raising some questions about the nature of the household's various relationships with the nurse).[59]

Even when checks were carried out to establish the character of the wet nurse, this was not necessarily a guarantee that the child would be safe in her care. One advice book relates the story of a family 'well known to the writer', whose baby was put out to nurse. Passing the house of the wet nurse one evening, the father of the child heard his baby's cries. Receiving no answer, he entered the house and found a distressing scene:

> The poor babe was found lying on the floor, with its arm broken, and the woman's own child in a heavy sleep on the bed. A phial with laudanum stood on the table, with a sugar basin and spoon, which had evidently been used for the purpose of administering the drug.

The wet nurse was discovered to have been at a public house, having 'given to each of the infants a strong dose of laudanum, which she thought would secure their quietness until her return'.[60]

The administration of laudanum, an opiate, to infants was not uncommon – nor was it necessarily perceived as inappropriate. In 1846, the *London Medical Gazette* reported on a case of a baby who was given two drops of laudanum by his nurse. Although the coroner's jury determined that the laudanum had caused the baby's death, it was deemed 'excusable homicide' as the nurse had acted with 'good intent' having previously 'administered laudanum to children to ease their pains' with no ill effect.[61]

In an earlier case, in 1829, a young infant named Joseph William Denham was left in the care of a wet nurse named Maria Goff whilst his parents travelled on the continent. Whilst under her care, the child was accidentally administered laudanum by the wet nurse's mother, who apparently mistook it for another medicine. The baby died as a consequence.[62] Although there were plenty of cases of mothers administering – deliberately or accidentally – opiates to their infants, discourses around wet nursing repeatedly emphasised the importance of the watchful maternal eye in avoiding such tragedies.

Of course, by necessity, wet nurses must themselves be mothers; many represented themselves as respectable married women looking for work to support their families, but concerns were raised about the possibility that some women were deliberately becoming pregnant (outside of marriage) in order to secure positions as wet nurses, and subsequently abandoning or even murdering their own babies (as the coroner appeared to imply in the case of Jane Pay). Whilst some infants were 'put out' to nurse – meaning they were temporarily sent to live with a wet nurse and her family – particularly amongst the wealthier classes, wet nurses were often brought in to live with the family, and rarely permitted to bring their own children with them. This raised questions about the fate of the wet nurses' own babies; a subject of some public concern, particularly in the latter decades of the century. One newspaper article on the subject noted that:

> When such a nurse is wanted it is always a condition that she shall be 'single' and 'respectable' – two conditions somewhat hard to combine, and by no means conducive to morality. What follows? The unfortunate bastard babe is 'put out' [...] with a baby-farmer. The result is that in nine cases out of ten the child dies.

It goes on to cite the case of a 'lady of title', mother to 'ten children, all of whom were wet nursed', and reveals, 'For those ten children, eleven others perished.'[63] In *Mother and Child*, the author, advising his readers on the hiring of wet nurses, notes that if the wet nurse's 'own child be living it should be ascertained that this be not carelessly thrown aside, but placed under the charge of some careful and conscientious person'. 'It is lamentable to reflect,' he continues, 'in how many instances the child of the wet-nurse is allowed to pine away, not alone from mismanagement, but too often from gross and cruel neglect.'[64] In *Esther Waters*, Moore inter-rogates the practice amongst the wealthier classes of employing poorer women as wet nurses. The eponymous heroine takes a job as a wet nurse following the birth of her own child, whom she is forced to put out to nurse. She subsequently discovers that the babies of two previous wet nurses died, whilst their milk sustained the infant of her employer. She confronts her employer about this practice:

> When you hire a poor girl such as me to give the milk that belongs to another to your child, you think nothing of the poor deserted one. [...] [F]ine folks like you pays the money, and Mrs. Spires and her like gets rid of the poor little things. Change the milk a few times, a little neglect, and the poor servant girl is spared the trouble of bring up her baby and can make a handsome child of the rich woman's little starveling.[65]

She relinquishes her position when her child falls ill and retrieves him just in time. Moore's novel is partly didactic, intent on raising the issue of the fate of the children of wet nurses, and draws attention to some of the moral and ethical concerns around this practice. The work highlights the paradox inherent in the practice of wet nursing. Aristocratic babies grew fat on the milk of these women, whilst, in some cases at least, their own babies suffered. Queen Victoria and Prince Albert, on hiring Mary Brough as a wet nurse for the Prince of Wales, were said to have 'expressed their anxiety that [Brough's baby] should be taken care of' and covered 'the expense of placing it with a wet nurse'.[66] This concern, though, would not have extended to the child of the wet nurse chosen to nurse Mary Brough's child, and so there may well have been distressing consequences to the Queen's decision not to breastfeed her own child.

Even the most sympathetic and understanding of mothers would put her own child's needs over those of the wet nurse's offspring, for this was the service for which they were paying. This tension is evident in a letter written by Henrietta Stanley to her husband, shortly before the death of their youngest child: 'We are sadly plagued with the wet nurse who just now wants to go home but Williams will send for her child tomorrow – we must do anything rather than lose the nurse, the only chance our darling has is having a good nurse.'[67] With her child seriously ill, Henrietta

Stanley's desire to keep the wet nurse by her baby's side, even though this meant delaying contact between the wet nurse and her own child, seems inevitable. There can be no doubt that such situations placed the children of wet nurses at risk. The risk was a concern not only to wet nurses and their employers, but in some instances their husbands as well. When Lady Amberley was forced to hire a wet nurse, after struggling to nurse her son herself, she found herself in need of another only a few days later, as her husband records in her diary: 'Our new wet-nurse was taken away by her husband, who had not been consulted about the arrangement.'[68] There are no further details about the personal circumstances of the wet nurse in question, but this brief diary entry highlights the competing forces to which working women's bodies were subject. Breast milk was an economic resource – a means through which a woman could potentially earn money – but it was also a source of nourishment for her own children. In both these roles, as mother and worker, married women had to consider not only their own personal choices, but those of their husbands as well, who exerted considerable legal control over their wives' bodies and freedoms throughout much of the nineteenth century. In some circumstances, with the employer's consent and support from family, arrangements might be made to ensure regular contact between the nurse and her own child. One woman, Mrs Layton, born in 1855 and one of fourteen children, recalls how her mother worked as a nurse for the local clergyman's wife 'whenever there was a baby born'. On such occasions, she writes, 'We took it in turns to take my mother's baby there [to the parsonage] for her to feed at the breast three or four times a day.'[69] Not all wet nurses were granted such privileges, however, and many women had to make the best arrangements they could.

As on the subject of maternal breastfeeding, advice literature offered detailed guidance on the hiring of wet nurses. Vine's *Mother and Child* is typical in this respect. It argues that 'The Moral Character and Disposition of the nurse are of the utmost importance' as 'She is to be the mother's substitute for many months.' It continues: 'A nurse should be cheerful and obliging in her manner, neat and cleanly in her person, steady and temperate in her habits, – she should be a moral and religious person. Excitability of disposition, inattention to truth, or any other moral defect, are strong objections to her selection.'[70]

She should, Vine goes on to note, be aged between 20 and 30, have delivered her own child very near to the birth of her charge, and be healthy in appearance. Hair colour – whether blonde or brunette – is deemed unimportant, but elsewhere, this is considered significant. In *Children and How to Manage Them in Health and Sickness* (1860), for example, mothers are advised against hiring wet nurses with 'red' or 'intensely black' hair.[71]

Whilst advice literature and newspaper reports, as well as fictional works such as Moore's novel, provide a wealth of information on the subject of wet nursing, further insights can be gleaned from women's letters and diaries. This written record, though, relates predominantly to the experiences of middle- and upper-class women: those likely to hire, rather than work as, wet nurses. First-hand experiences of wet nurses themselves are inevitably largely absent from the historical record. Others speak for them, but we rarely hear them speak for themselves. One exception to this lies in court records, where wet nurses are sometimes called on to testify. However, the figure of the criminal wet nurse is disproportionately present in such records, hence, as with the figure of the criminal midwife, they risk skewing our understanding of the experiences of such women. Criminal cases involving wet nurses contributed to prevailing social and cultural anxieties around this figure, by seemingly reinforcing the potential dangers of allowing a relative stranger into the home to care for a young baby. Nonetheless, they do provide some insight into the lives of women working as wet nurses in nineteenth-century Britain. Amongst the various cases of this kind is that of Hannah Gorman, convicted of theft and sentenced to transportation in July 1807. Gorman was working as a wet nurse in the family of a bootmaker, Richard Willis, when several missing items, including shoes and napkins, were found in her possession. She claimed to have come by some of these by innocent means, and denied knowledge of others, but was found guilty and sentenced to transportation for seven years. Gorman's case speaks to some of those anxieties surrounding the figure of the wet nurse as well as to her potential for disrupting the family home, but it is also suggestive of the relative positions of the family and their servants, the theft of various household items suggesting Gorman may have been attempting to supplement a limited income. This is reinforced by a similar case from November 1836, in which a woman named Eliza Holmes was found guilty of theft, having taken a number of items from the home of her employer, where she worked as a wet nurse. In her defence, Holmes pleaded poverty. One of the constables giving evidence at her trial stated that 'she asked for forgiveness, saying that she had two children'.[72] In spite of the mitigation she offered for the crimes committed, like Gorman she was sentenced to transportation. It is unclear what became of her children.

Despite the harsh sentences, these women were guilty of the relatively minor offence of stealing household items. Across the nineteenth century, however, several women working as wet nurses were tried for the much more serious crime of infanticide – accused of murdering either their charges or their own children. Amongst these was Catherine Michael, who was tried in April 1840 for the murder of her son, George Michael. Catherine Michael had been working as a servant when she was allegedly raped. After having the baby, she sent it to live with a woman named Sarah Stevens whilst she went out to work as a wet nurse in another family. The baby lived with Stevens for nine months, before Michael appeared with a bottle of what she claimed was medicine, and requested that Stevens administer it to the child each evening. Although Stevens claimed not to give the baby any, it appears her young son administered some. The baby fell ill shortly afterwards and died. Subsequent investigations revealed the medicine to be laudanum. In attempting to secure the assistance of a medical man, Michael informed him that 'If I am hanged for it, I could not support the child on my wages.' She was found guilty of the wilful murder of her child, but was 'Strongly recommended to mercy by the Jury, conceiving there were some extenuating circumstances in the case, being seduced and thrown on the world'. Consequently, her sentence was respited.[73]

At a time when opportunities for women in particular were limited, wet-nursing offered the possibility of an income, but, like so many other jobs available to working women, it often paid little, and in addition meant there was little alternative but to arrange for their own children to be hand fed.

Hand Feeding

The alternative to maternal breastfeeding or the employment of a wet nurse was hand or bottle feeding – sometimes referred to as 'artificial feeding'. This was typically more common amongst the poorer classes of society, at least some of whom had to return to work and therefore could not breastfeed themselves and did not have the available income to afford a wet nurse. Higher maternal mortality amongst this socio-economic group may also have been a factor here. This is reflected in Dickens's representations of orphans, including Oliver Twist and Pip (*Great Expectations*), both of whom are raised 'by hand'. Of the options available, this was undoubtedly the riskiest in terms of infant mortality. Feeding equipment that was not properly cleaned, as well as contaminated milk, water, or bread (sometimes mixed with milk to make 'pap'), could easily cause sickness and diarrhoea, which could prove fatal. These risks were recognised in some quarters in the nineteenth century. One work on infant feeding from 1860 points to the benefits of breastfeeding and the potential risks of hand feeding in terms of infant outcomes:

> Feeding a child on breast milk exclusively [...] produces a good development in 63 per cent., medium development in 23 per cent., and bad development in 14 per cent. [...] [A]s opposed to these results, injudicious feeding by hand produces 10 good, 26 medium, and 64 per cent. bad development.[74]

An article which appeared in the *Journal of the Royal Statistical Society* in 1894 included an analysis of 1,000 fatal cases of diarrhoea in infants, and also identified a link with hand feeding: 'Under 3 months of age for every infant fed entirely on the breast dying of diarrhoea, 15 die who receive other food in addition to or instead of breast milk', whilst deaths amongst babies exclusively hand fed were reportedly twenty-two times higher than those who were breastfed.[75] Whilst the discourses around infant feeding in the nineteenth century suggest parallels with contemporary society, it is worth noting that the choice between breast and bottle was a far riskier one in nineteenth-century Britain, and hand-fed babies were far more likely to contract deadly illnesses as a consequence.

This may go some way towards explaining the valorisation of the breast-feeding mother, and the criticism of those who chose not to nurse their own children. This is evident not only in newspaper discussions and advice literature, but also in some mothers' own accounts. One woman, for example, writing in the early twentieth century, suggests that 'the bottle is the laziest way'.[76] For some, though, there was little choice but to bottle feed when breastfeeding was not possible – particularly for poorer women for whom the cost of hiring a wet nurse was prohibitive. One mother recalls:

> The one great drawback to me was the fact that I was not able to suckle any of my children, owing to my breasts not being properly developed, so that the child could not draw the nipple. In consequence of this my children had to be fed by the bottle, although I am pleased to say they have thriven and are quite healthy children.[77]

This mother's evident relief that her children are healthy despite being bottle fed illustrates the extent to which the practice was associated with poorer outcomes – even in the late nineteenth and early twentieth centuries. It is likely for this reason that – beyond those selling patented infant food and bottles – there are few voices advocating hand feeding in nineteenth-century Britain. However, one exception to this is Jane Ellen Panton, who, in her advice book for mothers, *The Way They Should Go*, suggests bottle feeding as the ideal method of infant feeding, appearing to reflect on her own experience:

> I myself know of no greater misery than nursing a child, the physical collapse caused by which is often at the bottom of the drinking habits of which we hear so much, and I am free to confess see so little, among people of the upper middle-classes. I think too, speaking as usual from my own experience, that a child is far easier got into good habits if it is brought up from its birth by the bottle, than if it be nursed; and though all young mothers are taught to consider themselves inhuman wretches if they decline to nurse their babies, I say they are nothing of the kind […] I most strongly advise any young mother to begin as she means to go on, and to introduce the baby to the bottle as soon as it shows any inclination for food at all.[78]

It is unusual for advice literature to recommend artificial feeding as best practice, partly because of an awareness of the increased health risks, and partly as the act of nursing is typically constructed as both natural and a (sometimes religious) duty in such works. Princess Helena, unlike her sisters Victoria and Alice, also appears to have hand fed at least some of her children. In a letter written in 1873, Queen Victoria reported that Helena's baby – the then 8-month-old Princess Marie-Louise – 'is a splendid child as big as one a year old, almost too fat'. She added, 'She has been entirely brought up by hand and I certainly never saw a finer specimen.'[79] As one article pointed out, though:

> The successful rearing of infants on artificial foods depends not only upon a sound knowledge of the kind of food suitable for infant feeding, but also upon a practical knowledge of its preparation; of the quantity to be administered, of the intervals which ought to elapse between successive feedings; and excessive cleanliness in the most minute details is imperative for success.[80]

For much of the period, there was widespread ignorance around the importance of sterilising infant feeding equipment, and this undoubtedly contributed to the risks posed by hand feeding. The advice of Mrs Beeton regarding the cleaning of infant feeding bottles provides one illustration of this: 'The nipple need never be removed till replaced by a new one, which will hardly be necessary oftener than once a fortnight, though with care one will last for several weeks.'[81] Such practices would have allowed for the build-up of potentially harmful bacteria, which could lead to the development of sometimes-fatal stomach upsets. Another potential danger of hand feeding came from the types of food given to babies. This varied, but could include different types of animal milk, various cereals, sugar, water, bread, as well as patented baby formulas which sometimes contained ingredients unsuitable – and harmful – for infants. Contamination was a significant risk with many of these foods. Sugar was a fairly common addition to the diet of hand-fed infants, and whilst it posed less risk than some other foods, it was nonetheless potentially harmful to emerging infant teeth. This risk, though, was not fully understood: one work on infant feeding suggests 'It is an error to suppose that sugar decays the teeth.'[82] One mother of ten children, a number of whom died in infancy, attributed her losses in part to their diet of 'patent food':

> My first set of children were weakly, and being unable to nurse them, I resorted to patent foods, which I am now firmly convinced did harm and not good, and in my opinion contributed to the convulsions. I found later that weakened milk, afterwards strengthened as the baby got older, was the best and safest food for infants brought up by hand. [...] As a result of my experience, my advice is that mothers unable to suckle their children should shun all patent foods, rusks, etc., as they would shun the devil himself[.][83]

In addition to various (potentially dangerous) foods, babies might also be given soothing syrups or teething powders – numerous examples of which were available in the second half of the nineteenth century in particular, with the increasing commercialisation of motherhood. The ingredients of these products could be even more alarming – including, in some instances, alcohol and opiates. Whilst the advertising of products for consumption by babies, particularly infant formula, is carefully regulated today, in the nineteenth century this was not the case, and mothers were generally entirely reliant on the information which producers chose to give them, much of which was inaccurate at best, and potentially dangerous to the life of the infant at worst. Adverts for Benger's infant food in the late nineteenth century were fairly typical in their inclusion of apparent testimonies from mothers who had used the product:

> I enclose a photo of my little boy, who, this time last year I feared would die before a week passed. Until I tried your Food nothing would stay on his stomach. You will notice what a fine little fellow he now is, and I feel I am indebted to you for the preservation of my child's life.[84]

In contrast to such testimonies, it is likely that some commercial products for infants were responsible for a significant amount of illness and death, either as a result of the ingredients they contained, or due to the manner in which they were administered to children.

In the nineteenth-century debates around infant feeding, and in mothers' experiences of breastfeeding, wet nurses, and hand- or bottle feeding, there are close parallels with the experiences of women today. Infant feeding remains a vexed and contentious subject, with mothers required to negotiate competing discourses alongside their own choices and constraints. These debates continued throughout the twentieth century, with differing and often contrary advice given at different times; breastfeeding rates declined in the middle decades of this period, partly in response to medical advice pointing to bottle feeding as both safe and nutritious. The advice changed around the 1970s, and breastfeeding increased again, although advice on when and how much to feed differed considerably from today: whilst 'feed on demand' is the advice provided to breastfeeding mothers now, when I was born in the late 1970s, my mother was told to feed on a strict four-hour schedule. The shifting advice on infant feeding between the nineteenth and twenty-first centuries highlights some of the common ground shared by mothers then and now, as they negotiate their own desires and capabilities, and the plethora of medical and other advice offered.

Afterword

Birthing Modern Britain

As the nineteenth century and Queen Victoria's reign drew to a close, Sarah Lancaster, a miner's wife in Worsbrough, South Yorkshire, found herself pregnant with her sixth child. Her daughter, who was named Ethel, was born on 27 May 1900. Within a few months of the baby's birth, Queen Victoria was dead, and the era which bears her name at an end. Ethel Lancaster, though, born at the end of a century that had transformed women's maternal experiences, was destined to live through another century of change. When she died on 15 January 2015, at the age of 114, she was the last remaining Briton born in the reign of Queen Victoria. She lived until the early years of the twenty-first century – through a period of rapid and dramatic transformation. One of a large family, she had only one child herself, reflecting the increasing trend for smaller families in the twentieth century. Despite the dramatic changes she witnessed in her lifetime, the continuities between past and present remained evident. Like some of the women discussed in this book, Ethel Lancaster worked in a factory – as a seamstress. She was born at a time when women were still struggling for recognition as midwives, when most babies were still born at home, when maternal and infant mortality remained much higher than today, and when women's maternity rights were extremely limited. By the time her own daughter was born in 1923, she had lived through a world war and witnessed the first momentous step towards female suffrage in Britain (although, as a woman under 30, she would have to wait until 1929 before she could cast a vote herself). The women's rights campaigns fought in part by the Women's Co-operative Guild had achieved much, including the right to a one-off maternity payment of 30 shillings – granted through the 1911 National Insurance Act. By the time Ethel Lancaster turned 100 in 2000, further great strides towards equality had been made, including in relation to women's maternity rights. Maternity leave legislation was introduced in 1975, and further extended in 1980 and 1993. Shared parental leave was introduced in 2015. The introduction of unemployment and sickness benefits, of universal healthcare, and of legislation around abortion also helped address some of the challenges previously faced by nineteenth-century women – particularly poorer women. The experience of pregnancy and childbirth was transformed by developments in medical knowledge and technology: from the early identification of pregnancy which arose with the introduction of reliable pregnancy tests, to the use of ultrasounds to identify the sex of the baby, to the widespread availability of contraception, to the introduction of IVF to help those struggling with infertility. The continuities between Ethel Lancaster's birth and her death over a century later in terms of the maternal experience are found in women's emotional experiences of pregnancy and childbirth, in the cultural pressures exerted on women, and in the wealth of (often contradictory) advice they are offered.

The similarities and differences of the maternal experience – between now and then, rich and poor – are emphasised by the maternal histories of women of the nineteenth century, whose stories emerge from dusty and often largely forgotten newspapers, diaries, letters, and books, to paint a different picture of industrial Britain and the labour behind it. In examining their (sometimes obscure) lived experiences of maternity, we find surprising parallels with the experiences of today's mothers, not least in the complex array of emotions which accompany maternity in all its varied forms, much of which is largely absent from histories of the period. Throughout the nineteenth century, women negotiating motherhood battled with idealised images of femininity which worked to control their behaviours and freedoms and set impossible standards for them to meet. Women struggling with infertility had few options, with limited treatments available and no formal right to adopt. Medical men exercised formidable control over the birthing room, and women underwent sometimes devastating procedures during childbirth, risking theirs and their babies' health and lives. Many women procured illegal abortions, and in some cases faced prosecution, in a country which refused to recognise women's right to terminate a pregnancy. Later in the century, campaigners fought for the right to use contraception, in an attempt to grant women greater freedom over reproduction. At the turn of the twentieth century, the Women's Co-operative Guild campaigned for the maternity rights of working women and highlighted the plight of those women who could not afford adequate maternity care and were forced to return to work in the days and weeks after giving birth. For those experiencing motherhood today, the landscape is very different. In all these respects and more, the transformation of women's maternal experiences in Britain over the last 120 years has been radical.

Perhaps the most significant change came in 1948 with the formation of the National Health Service. The differing experiences of rich and poor are highlighted throughout this book: wealth and social status was a crucial factor in the maternal experience throughout the nineteenth century. Today, women who once would have been forced to give birth in the workhouse, or even in the streets, have undisputed rights to hospital and medical care for them and their babies. The NHS has acted as a social leveller, ensuring all women in Britain have access to medical care throughout their pregnancies, deliveries, and beyond. It is not perfect, but it has transformed maternity and healthcare; the service it provides is invaluable, and its influence on the maternal experience has been, and continues to be, profound. Many of the stories of pregnancy and childbirth from nineteenth-century Britain include tragedy and loss, and whilst these still feature in the maternal experience today, they are far less common than once they were, and many more women achieve the outcomes they want and deserve. These improvements are largely due to developing medical knowledge, a greater emphasis on women's rights, and the access to healthcare provided by the NHS.

Women's experiences of motherhood in nineteenth-century Britain were heavily impacted by a lack of maternal rights: the right to choose if, when, and how often to fall pregnant; the right to decide whether or not to proceed with a pregnancy; the right to maternity leave and pay for working mothers. These rights are now enshrined in law, but in twenty-first-century Britain, women remain subject to social and cultural pressures which are not entirely dissimilar to those which affected their predecessors. Women may choose if and when to have children, but these choices are often subject to intense scrutiny. Those who express a desire not to have children are frequently told they will change their minds. Judgement is also often passed in relation to how many children women have, when they have them, and how they raise them. Women can take maternity leave and return to their careers, but there is significant evidence of a 'motherhood penalty' for working mothers – in terms of pay, promotion, and job security.[1] Maternity care is vastly improved since the nineteenth century, but inequities still remain in recognising and treating women's health problems – in particular in relation to reproductive health. Indeed, it is these inequities which have led the UK government to develop a 'Women's Health Strategy' for England, aimed at tackling 'the gender health gap'.[2] Furthermore, the rights and protections that have been inscribed in law may not be as sacrosanct as we might hope, as the recent overruling of Roe vs Wade by the American Supreme Court indicates. Women in Northern Ireland have only had legal access to abortion services since 2019, and at that time ninety-nine Westminster MPs voted against this change.[3]

In 2011, I gave birth to my first child. I was unmarried and determined to continue my professional career – an unimaginable situation for the nineteenth-century mother. Two more children followed. I kept my job, and benefited from shared parental leave, flexible working, and subsidised childcare. I did, though, face questions about the possible impact on my career, my decision to have a second, and then a third child, my choice to work rather than stay at home during their early years, and in particular my willingness to commute and leave the children in the care of my partner two days a week. This scrutiny fed a sense of guilt and led me to interrogate my own maternal choices. For some in today's society, motherhood still requires a degree of self-sacrifice, a willingness to relinquish all ambition and focus entirely on raising children. We are not as far removed from the attitudes and practices of the nineteenth century as we might think or hope. The maternal experiences of the women of nineteenth-century Britain paved the way for the dramatic improvements that we benefit from today, whilst feminist campaigners helped to reform not only the law but attitudes as well. Nonetheless, the echoes of these earlier experiences of motherhood still resonate.

The birth of Ethel Lancaster at the close of the reign of Queen Victoria marked the end of a century of change, of population explosion driven by industrialisation but made possible by the maternal labours of millions of women. The maternal experience, so often overlooked in histories of the nineteenth century, speaks to a much broader history, encompassing many of the key concerns of the period: class divide, family, work, medicine, law, and more. In the century that birthed modern Britain, the maternal experience played a crucial role.

Works Cited

Allbutt, H. Arthur, *The Wife's Handbook* (London: R. Forder, 1888).

Anon., 'Appendix to the Rules of Gateshead Lying-in Charity'. Available at Northumberland Archives (SANT/BEQ/26/1/4/230). Accessed July 2021.

Anon., 'Appendix to Second Annual Report of the Commissioners Under the Poor Law Amendment Act', *Parliamentary Papers*, Vol. 29, Part I, 495.

Anon., 'A Baby Exchange', *The Review of Reviews* (July 1895), 86.

Anon., 'Chailly and Moreau on Practical Midwifery', *The British and Foreign Medical Review* (April 1845), 419.

Anon., 'Childless Families', *The Lancet* (21 April 1866), 433.

Anon., *The City of London Lying-In Hospital* (London: R. Wilks, 1823).

Anon., *Factories Enquiries Commission: Supplementary Report of the Central Board* (House of Commons, 1834).

Anon., 'Factories and Workshops Bill' (23 July 1891), *Hansard's Parliamentary Debates*, Third Series, Vol. CCCLVI (London: Hansard's Publishing Union, 1891).

Anon., *Forty-Fifth Annual Report of the Registrar-General of Births, Deaths, and Marriages in England (Abstracts of 1882)* (London: Eyre and Spottiswoode, 1884), lxix.

Anon., 'Health of London During the Week', *Weekly Return of Births and Deaths in London* (16 April 1853).

Anon., 'Ignominious Dress for Unchaste Women in Workhouses', Appendix No. 4, *Sixth Annual Report of the Poor Law Commissioners* (1840), 98.

Anon., *Letters to a Mother on the Watchful Care of Her Infant* (London: R. B. Seeley and W. Burnside).

Anon., *The London Practice of Midwifery* (London: James Wallis, 1803).

Anon., Medical Report Book for Newcastle Lying-in Hospital, 1821–1833. Available at Tyne and Wear Archives, Newcastle; ref HO.PM/29.

Anon., 'Midwifery as a Profession for Educated Women', *The Englishwoman's Review* (14 May 1887), 198.

Anon., 'The Milk of Intemperate Mothers' (28 October 1882), *The Lancet*, 715.

Anon., *The Mother's Public Thanksgiving* (London: Wertheim, Macintosh, and Hunt, 1860).

Anon., *The Mother's Thorough Resource Book* (London: Ward and Lock, 1860).

Anon., 'The Prevention of Puerperal Fever', *The Hospital* (3 April 1895), 25–6.

Anon., 'Production of Premature Labour', *The Lancet* (28 October 1843), 112–13.

Anon., 'Provision 60: Concealing the Birth of a Child', Offences Against the Person Act 1861, https://www.legislation.gov.uk/ukpga/Vict/24–25/100/section/60/enacted?view=plain (Accessed April 2022).

Anon., *Public Bills*, Vol. 6 (Parliament, 1901).

Anon., 'Puerperal Mania', *Chambers Encyclopedia*, Vol. VII (1865).

Anon., 'Remarkable Trials', *Annual Register: 1864* (London: Rivingtons, 1865), 223.

Anon., 'Reports on the Nursing and Administration of Provincial Workhouses and Infirmaries', *British Medical Journal* (1894).

Anon., *Report Concerning the Hospital for the Reception of Poor Married Women Lying-In* (Newcastle: T & J Hodgson, 1827), 18.

Anon., 'Startling Craniotomy', *The Lancet* (22 October 1842).

Anon., Advert for 'Swanbill Belts', *Medical Times and Gazette Advertiser* (30 December 1882), viii.

Anon., *Thirty-Eighth Annual Report of the Registrar-General of Births, Deaths, and Marriages in England* (London: George E. Eyre and William Spottiswoode, 1877) xxv.

Anon., 'Turning After Craniotomy', *The Lancet* (4 July 1874), 11.

Anon., 'Women Physicians', *Macmillan's Magazine*, No. 107: Vol. XVIII (September 1868), 375.

Anon., *The Young Mother; or, Affectionate Advice to a Married Daughter* (London: The Religious Tract Society, 1851).

Arnold, Thomas, *Observations on the nature, Kinds, Causes, and Prevention of Insanity*, Vol. 2 (Second edition; London: Richard Phillips, 1806).

Attwood, Philip, ed., *Hard at Work: The Diary of Leonard Wyon*, 1853–1867 (London: Spink & Son, 2014).

Austen, Jane, *Northanger Abbey* (Peterborough: Broadview, 2002).

Frances J. Badger, 'Illuminating Nineteenth-Century English Urban Midwifery', *Women's History Review*, 23:5 (2014).

Baird, Julia, *Victoria the Queen: An Intimate Biography* (London: Blackfriars, 2016).

Ballantyne, J.W., 'Studies in Foetal Pathology and Teratology', *The Transactions of the Edinburgh Obstetrical Society*, Vol. XVII (Edinburgh: Oliver and Boyd, 1892).

Barbauld, Anna Laetitia, 'Elegy', *The Annual Register, or a View of the History, Politics, and Literature, for the Year 1818* (London: Baldwin, Cradock, and Joy, 1819), 612.

Barker, Samuel, *Children and How to Manage Them in Health and Sickness* (London: Robert Hardwicke, 1860).

Beeton, Mrs Isabella, *The Management of Children in Health and Sickness* (London: Ward, Lock & Tyler, 1873).

Begiato, Joanne, 'Breeding a "Little Stranger": Managing Uncertainty in Pregnancy in Later Georgian England' in Jennifer Evans and Ciara Meehan, eds., *Perceptions of Pregnancy from the Seventeenth to the Twentieth Century* (Basingstoke: Palgrave Macmillan, 2017), 13–34.

Bell, Robert, *Sterility* (London: Churchill, 1896).

Bennett, Betty T., ed., *The Letters of Mary Wollstonecraft Shelley* (Baltimore: John Hopkins University Press, 1988).

Benson, Arthur Christopher and Viscount Esher, eds, *The Letters of Queen Victoria*, Vol. I (London: John Murray, 1911).

Berens, Rev. Edward, *An Address upon the Office for the Churching of Women* (3rd edition; Oxford: W. Baxter, 1850).

Bessborough, Earl of, ed., *Lady Charlotte Guest: Extracts From Her Journal, 1833–52* (London: John Murray, 1950).

Black, George, *Household Medicine* (London: Ward, Lock & Co., 1881).

Boos, Florence, *Memoirs of Victorian Working-Class Women* (Basingstoke: Palgrave Macmillan, 2017).

Bowles, Caroline, 'The Dying Mother to her Infant' in *The Birth-Day and Other Poems* (Edinburgh: William Blackwood & Sons, 1836).

Braddon, Mary Elizabeth, *Lady Audley's Secret* (1862; Peterborough: Broadview, 2003).

British Library Newspapers. Gale Primary Resources. https://go.gale.com/ps/publicationSearch.

Brown, Amy, Jaynie Rance, and Paul Bennett, 'Understanding the relationship between breastfeeding and postnatal depression: the role of pain and physical difficulties', *Journal of Advance Nursing*, 72:2 (February 2016), 273–82.

Brudenell Carter, Robert, *On the Influence of Education and Training in Preventing Diseases of the Nervous System* (London: John Churchill, 1855).

Cadogan, William, *An Essay Upon Nursing and the Management of Children* (London: J. Roberts, 1748).

The Carlyle Letters Online (https://carlyleletters.dukeupress.edu/home).

Carpenter, William B., *Principles of Human Physiology* (sixth edition; London: John Churchill, 1864).

Chailly, M., *Practical Treatise on Midwifery*, trans. Gunning S. Bedford (New York: Harper & Brothers, 1854).

Chamberlain, Mary, *Fenwomen: A Portrait of Women in an English Village* (1975; Woodbridge: Full Circle, 2011).

Chapple, John and Alan Shelston, eds, *Further Letters of Mrs Gaskell* (Manchester: Manchester University Press, 2003).

Charlot, Monica, *Victoria: The Young Queen* (Oxford: Blackwell, 1991).

Chase, Alice, *The Memoirs of Alice Maude Chase*, Burnett Archive, Brunel University London.

Chavasse, Pye Henry, *Advice to a Wife on the Management of Her Own Health and on the Treatment of some of the Complaints Incidental to Pregnancy, Labour, and Suckling* (Twelfth Edition; London: J & H Churchill, 1877).

Checkland, S.G. and E.O.A. Checkland, eds, *The Poor Law Report of 1834* (Harmandsworth: Penguin, 1974).

Clapperton, James, 'Maternal Impressions', *British Medical Journal* (6 February 1875).

Clare Bellhouse, Meredith J. Temple-Smith, and Jade E. Bilardi, '"It's just one of those things people don't seem to talk about …": women's experiences of social support following miscarriage: a qualitative study', *BMC Women's Health*, 18: 1 (2018), pp. 1–9.

Clemitt, Pamela, ed., *The Letters of William Godwin, Vol. 1: 1778–1797* (Oxford: Oxford University Press, 2011).

Cockburn, Lord, *Life of Lord Jeffrey, with a Selection From His Correspondence*, Vol. II (Philadelphia: Lippincott, Grambo & Co., 1852).

Cowper, Agnes, *A Backward Glance at Merseyside* (Birkenhead: Willmer Brothers & Co, 1948).

Cox, Jane, ed., *A Singular Marriage: A Labour Love Story in Letters and Diaries* (London: HARRAP, 1988).

Crichton Browne, J., ed., *The West Riding Lunatic Asylum Medical Reports*, Volume 1 (London: J & A Churchill, 1871).

Darwin Correspondence Project, University of Cambridge (https://www. darwinproject.ac.uk).

Dendy, Walter C., *The Book of the Nursery* (London: Whittaker, Treacher, & Co., 1833).

Dickens, Charles, *Oliver Twist* (Peterborough: Broadview, 2005).

---, *Martin Chuzzlewit* (1844; Oxford: Oxford University Press, 1998).

Druitt, Dr R., 'Dr Robert Lee and Craniotomy' (4 May 1861), *Medical Times and Gazette*, 479–80.

Edgeworth, Maria, *Belinda* (1801; London: J. Johnson & Co., 1811).

Eliot, George, *Adam Bede* (New York: Harper & Brothers, 1860).

---, *Middlemarch* (1871; Peterborough, Ontario: Broadview, 2004).

Ellis, Richard H., ed., *The Case Books of John Snow* (London: Wellcome Institute, 1994).

Ellis, Sir William Charles, *A Treatise on the Nature, Symptoms, Causes, and Treatment of Insanity* (London: Samuel Holdsworth, 1838).

Engels, Friedrich, *The Condition of the Working Class in England in 1844* (London: Swan Sonnenschein, 1892).

Feasey, Rebecca, *Infertility and Non-Traditional Family Building* (Basingstoke: Palgrave Macmillan, 2019).

Ferguson, Robert, *Essays on the Most Important Diseases of Women, Part I: Puerperal Fever* (London: John Murray, 1839).

Fisk, Catriona, 'Looking for Maternity: Dress Collections and Embodied Knowledge', *Fashion Theory*, 23:3 (2019), 401–39.

Fox, Sarah, and Margot Brazier, 'The Regulation of Midwives in England, c.1500–1902', *Medical Law International*, 20:4 (December 2020).

Fox, Sarah, *Giving Birth in Eighteenth-Century England* (Institute of Historical Research, 2022).

Fraser, Flora, *Princesses: The Six Daughters of George III*. London: John Murray, 2004.

Fremantle, Anne, ed., *The Wynne Diaries*, Vol. 3, 1798–1820 (London: Oxford University Press, 1940).

Fulford, Roger, ed., *Dearest Child: Letters Between Queen Victoria and the Princess Royal, 1858–1861* (London: Evans Brothers, 1964).

---, ed., *Dearest Mama: Private Correspondence of Queen Victoria and the Crown Princess of Prussia, 1861–1864* (London: Evans Brothers, 1968).

---, ed., *Your Dear Letter: Private Correspondence of Queen Victoria and the Crown Princess of Prussia 1865–1871* (London: Evans Brothers, 1971).

Gaskell, Elizabeth, *The Life of Charlotte Brontë* (1857; London: Penguin, 1997).

---, *Sylvia's Lovers* (1863; London: Smith, Elder, & Co., 1889).

---, *Mary Barton* (1848; Oxford: Oxford University Press, 2008).

Gibson, Kate, *Illegitimacy, Family, and Stigma in England, 1660–1834* (Oxford: Oxford University Press, 2022).

Gilman, Charlotte Perkins, 'The Yellow Wallpaper', *New England Magazine* (1892).

Glynne-Gladstone Archive, Gladstones Library (Hawarden). Ref GG/792.

Godwin, William, *Memoirs of the Author of a Vindication of the Rights of Woman* (London: J. Johnson, 1798).

Gow, William J., 'On the Relation of Heart Disease to Menstruation', *Obstetrical Transactions*, Vol. XXXVI (London: Longmans, Green & Co., 1895).

Graham, Thomas J., *On the Management and Disorders of Infancy and Childhood* (London: Simpkin, Marshall & Co., 1853).

Griffin, Emma, *Breadwinner: An Intimate History of the Victorian Economy* (New Haven: Yale University Press, 2020).

Hardy, Thomas, *Tess of the D'Urbervilles* (1891; Peterborough: Broadview, 1998).

Hare, J.C. Augustus, *The Story of Two Noble Lives*, Vol. III (London: George Allan, 1893).

Harley, David, 'Historians as Demonologists: The Myth of the Midwife-witch', *Social History of Medicine*, 3:1 (April 1990), pp. 1–26.

Hawksley, Lucinda, *Queen Victoria's Mysterious Daughter: A Biography of Princess Louise* (New York: St Martin's Press, 2013).

Hewitt, Margaret, *Wives and Mothers in Victorian Industry* (London: Rockliff, 1958).

Holmes, Vicky, *In Bed with the Victorians: The Life-Cycle of Working-Class Marriage* (Basingstoke: Palgrave Macmillan, 2017).

House, Madeline, Graham Storey, and Kathleen Tillotson, eds, *The Letters of Charles Dickens*, Vol. VI (Oxford: Clarendon Press, 1988).

Jalland, Pat and John Hooper, eds, *Women From Birth to Death: The Female Life Cycle in Britain 1830–1914* (Brighton: The Harvester Press, 1986).

James, David, *Class and Politics in a Northern Industrial Town* (Keele University Press, 1995).

Johnston, Ellen, *Autobiography, Poems, and Songs* (Glasgow: William Love, 1867).

Jones, Hugh R., 'The Perils and Protection of Infant Life', *Journal of the Royal Statistical Society* (March 1894), pp. 21–2.

Kemble, Frances Anne (31 October 1835) in *Records of Later Life*, Vol. 1 (London: Richard Bentley & Son).

Keown, John, *Abortion, Doctors, and the Law* (Cambridge: Cambridge University Press, 1988).

Knight, Paul R. and Douglas R. Bacon, 'An Unexplained Death: Hannah Greener and Chloroform', *Anesthesiology*, Vol. 96 (May 2002), 1250–53.

Kuczynski, R.R., 'Childless Marriages', *Sociological Review* (1938), 130.

Layton, Mrs, 'Memories of Seventy Years' in Margaret Llewellyn Davies, ed., *Life As We Have Known It* (1931; London: Virago, 1977).

Lee, Robert, *Lectures on the Theory and Practice of Midwifery* (London: Longman, Brown, Green, and Longmans, 1844).

---, *Clinical Midwifery* (London: John Churchill, 1842).

---, *Three Hundred Consultations in Midwifery* (London: John Churchill & Sons, 1864).

---, 'Maternal Impressions' (6 February 1875), *British Medical Journal*, 167–8.

Litchfield, Henrietta, ed., *Emma Darwin: A Century of Family Letters*, Vol. II (New York: D. Appleton & Co., 1915).

Llewellyn Davies, Margaret, ed., *Maternity: Letters From Working Women* (1915; London: G. Bell & Sons, Ltd., 1915).

Loudon, Irvine, 'Deaths in Childbed from the Eighteenth Century to 1935', *Medical History*, 30:1 (January 1986).

Lowndes, Fred W., 'Statistics of Stillbirths', *Transactions of the Obstetrical Society of London*, Vol. XIV (London: Longmans, Green & Co., 1873), pp. 283–303.

Luff, Arthur P., *Text-Book of Forensic Medicine and Toxicology*, Vol. II (London: Longmans, Green, & Co., 1895).

Markle, Meghan, 'The Losses We Share', *New York Times* (25 November 2020). Available at: https://www.nytimes.com/2020/11/25/opinion/meghan-markle-miscarriage.html.

Marks, Lara, 'Medical Care for Pauper Mothers and Their Infants', *The Economic History Review*, 46:3 (August 1993), p. 518.

Marland, Hilary, 'Under the Shadow of Maternity: Birth, Death, and Puerperal Insanity in Victorian Britain'. *History of Psychiatry*. 23:1 (2012).

Marrin, Mrs P., Untitled. Burnett Archive, Brunel University London, Ref 1:493.

Marshall, Mrs Julian, ed., *The Life and Letters of Mary Wollstonecraft Shelley*, Vol. 1 (London: Richard Bentley & Son, 1889).

Mayhew, Henry, *London Labour and the London Poor*, Vol. 4 (London: Charles Griffin, 1862).

Millward, Robert and Frances Bell, 'Infant Mortality in Victorian Britain: The Mother as Medium', *Economic History Review*, LIV:4 (2001), pp. 699–733.

Mitchell, Hannah, *The Hard Way Up: The Autobiography of Hannah Mitchell, Suffragette and Rebel*, ed., Geoffrey Mitchell (Faber and Faber 1968).

Mitford, Nancy, ed., *The Ladies of Alderley* (London: Hamish Hamilton, 1967).

---, *The Stanleys of Alderley* (London: Hamish Hamilton, 1969).

Moore, George, *Esther Waters* (London: Walter Scott Ltd, 1894).

Mountcashell, M.J., Countess Dowager [Margaret Jane Moore], *A Grandmother's Advice to Young Mothers on the Physical Education of Children* (London: Baldwin and Cradock, 1835).

Murphy, Edward William, 'The Importance of a Scientific Medical Education to Practitioners in Midwifery', *Association Medical Journal*, 1853.

Napier, Elma, *Life is a Blunder* (London: Jonathan Cape, 1948).

Nayder, Lillian, *The Other Dickens: A Life of Catherine Hogarth* (New York: Cornell University Press, 2011).

Nicholson, Hamlet, *An Autobiographical and Full Historical Account of the Persecution of Hamlet Nicholson in his Opposition to Ritualism at the Rochdale Parish Church* (Manchester: Barber & Farnworth, 1892).

Nightingale, Florence, *Introductory Notes on Lying-In Institutions* (London: Longmans, Green & Co., 1871).

Old Bailey Online: The Proceedings of the Old Bailey, 1674-9-13. https://www. oldbaileyonline.org/

Pakula, Hannah, *An Uncommon Woman* (London: Phoenix Press, 1997).

Pankhurst, E. Sylvia, *The Suffragette Movement: An Intimate Account of Persons and Ideals* (London: Longmans, Green and Co, 1932).

Panton, J.E., *The Way They Should Go: Hints to Young Parents* (London: Downey & Co., 1896).

Pears, Catherine Temple, *The Letters of Catherine Temple Pears*, Durham Archives, Ref ADD.MSS 1700–1749.

Pedley, Mrs Frederick, *Infant Nursing and the Management of Young Children* (London: George Routledge and Sons, 1866).

Pierson, Joan, *The Real Lady Byron* (London: Robert Hale, 1992).

Pooley, Siân, 'Parenthood, child-rearing and fertility in England, 1850–1914', *The History of the Family*, 18:1 (March 2013).

Rappaport, Helen, *Queen Victoria: A Biographical Companion* (Santa Barbara: ABC-CLIO, 2003).

---, 'Charlotte von Siebold: The Pioneering German midwife who delivered the future Queen Victoria' (2018; https://helenrappaport.com/queen-victoria/charlotte-von-siebold-midwife-delivered-queen-victoria/).

Ryan, M., *A Manual of Midwifery* (4th edition; London: W. Wilcockson, 1841).

Radford, Thomas, *Observations on the Caesarean Section, Craniotomy, and Other Obstetric Operations* (London: J. & A. Churchill, 1880), p. 11.

Ray, Donna K., 'A View from the Childwife's Pew: The Development of Rites around Childbirth in the Anglican Communion', *Anglican and Episcopal History*, 69:4 (December 2000), pp. 443–73.

Ray, Gordon N., ed., *The Letters and Private Papers of William Makepeace Thackeray*, Volume I: 1817–1840 (Oxford: Oxford University Press, 1945).

Rive, Richard, ed., *Olive Schreiner Letters*, Vol 1: 1871–1899 (Oxford: Oxford University Press, 1988).

Rogers, Joseph, *Reminiscences of a Workhouse Medical Officer* (London: T. Fisher Unwin, 1889).

Ross, Ellen, 'Rediscovering London's Working-Class Mothers' in Jane Lewis, ed., *Labour and Love: Women's Experience of Home and Family, 1850–1940* (Oxford: Basil Blackwell, 1986).

Routh, C.H.F., 'The moral and physical evil likely to follow if practices intended to act as checks to the population be not strongly discouraged and condemned', *Medical Press and Circular* (1878).

---, *Infant Feeding and its Influence on Life* (1860; London: J. & A. Churchill, 3rd edition, 1876).

Roberts, Wm C., 'Remarks on the Signs of Pregnancy', *The Medical Gazette*, Vol. IV (1870), p. 26.

Russell, Betrand and Patricia Russell, eds, *The Amberley Papers: The Letters and Diaries of Lord and Lady Amberley*, 2 Volumes (London: George Allen & Unwin Ltd, 1937).

Ryan, Michael, *The Philosophy of Marriage in its Social, Moral, and Physical Relations* (London: John Churchill, 1837).

Ryley, J. Beresford, *Sterility in Women: Its Causes and Cure* (2nd edition, 1887).

Saunders Hallaran, William, *Practical Observations on the Causes and Cure of Insanity* (Cork: Edwards and Savage, 1818).

Sheen, Alfred, *The Workhouse and its Medical Officer* (2nd edition; Bristol: John Wright & Co., 1890).

Sherman, James, *Memoir of William Allen* (London: Charles Gilpin, 1851).

Smith, Margaret, ed., *The Letters of Charlotte Brontë*, Volume 3 (Oxford: Oxford University Press, 2004).

Soet, Johanna E., Gregory A. Brack, and Colleen Dilorio, 'Prevalence and Predictors of Women's Experience of Psychological Trauma During Childbirth'. *Birth*. 30:1 (2003).

Sokoll, Thomas, ed., *Essex Pauper Letters 1731–1837* (Oxford University Press), 215.

Spencer, Herbert, *The Principles of Biology*, Vol. II (London: Williams & Norgate, 1867).

Stowe, Harriet Beecher, *Lady Byron Vindicated* (Boston: Fields, Osgood, & Co., 1870).

Teitelbaum, Michael S., *The British Fertility Decline: Demographic Transition in the Crucible of the Industrial Revolution* (Princeton: Princeton University Press, 1984).

Thackeray, William Makepeace, *Vanity Fair* (1848; Oxford: Oxford University Press, 1998).

Thorburn, John, *Female Education from a Physiological Point of View* (Manchester: J. E. Cornish, 1884).

Todd, Janet M., ed., *The Collected Letters of Mary Wollstonecraft* (New York: Columbia University Press, 2003).

Twining, Louisa, *Workhouses and Pauperism* (London: Methuen & Co, 1898), p. 201.

Vanderbilt Balson, Consuelo, *The Glitter and the Gold* (London: Hodder & Stoughton, 1973).

Van Der Kiste, John, *Dearest Vicky, Darling Fritz* (Stroud: Sutton Publishing, 2001).

Victoria, Queen, Queen Victoria's Journals (http://www.queenvictoriasjournals.org/home.do).

Vine, Charles, *Mother and Child* (London: Frederick Warne and Co., 1868).

Von Stockmar, Baron E., *Memoirs of Baron Stockmar*, Volume 1 (London: Longmans, Green, and Co., 1873).

Ward Cousins, J., 'The Midwives Act of 1902' (8 August 1903), *The British Medical Journal*, pp. 293–5.

Weatherly, Lionel A., *The Young Wife's Own Book* (1882; London: Griffith and Farran, n.d.).

Wedgwood, B. & H., *The Wedgwood Circle* (London: Studio Vista, 1980).

Weintraub, Stanley, *Uncrowned King: The Life of Prince Albert* (New York: The Free Press, 1997).

West, Charles, *The Mother's Manual of Children's Diseases* (London: Longmans, Green, & Col, 1885).

Whiteley, Rebecca, 'Spratt's Flaps: Midwifery, Creativity, and Sexuality in Early Nineteenth-Century Visual Culture', *British Art Studies*, p. 19 (February 2021).

Wollstonecraft Godwin, Mary, *Memoirs and Posthumous Works of Mary Wollstonecraft Godwin* (Dublin: Thomas Burnside, 1798).

Wollstonecraft, Mary, *A Vindication of the Rights of Woman* (1792; London: William Strange, 1844).

Woods, Robert, *Death Before Birth: Fetal Health and Mortality in Historical Perspective* (Oxford: Oxford University Press, 2009).

Wordsworth, William, 'Maternal Grief' (1842) in Henry Reed, ed., *The Poetical Works of Wordsworth* (Philadelphia: Troutman Hayes, 1852), 125–6.

Worsley, Lucy, *Queen Victoria: Daughter, Wife, Mother, Widow* (London: Hodder & Stoughton, 2018).

Young, James, 'Case of Puerperal Mania', *Edinburgh Medical Journal*, Vol. 13 (1868), p. 262.

Young Simpson, Sir James, *The Obstetric Memoirs and Contributions of James Y. Simpson*, Vol. 2 (Philadelphia: J. P. Lippincott & Co, 1856).

Zola, Émile, *The Bright Side of Life*. Trans. Andrew Rothwell (Oxford: Oxford University Press, 2018).

---, *How Jolly Life Is!* Trans. Unknown (London: Vizetelly & Co.).

Notes

Introduction

1   Whilst medical limitations and social attitudes negatively impacted many women's experience of childbirth in the nineteenth century, the privileging of the life of the mother in Britain at that time contrasts sharply with recent debates and developments, in particular in America, where women's reproductive rights and control over their own bodies are being increasingly eroded.

2   See Irvine Loudon, 'Deaths in Childbed from the Eighteenth Century to 1935', *Medical History*, 30:1 (January 1986).

3   Childbirth in the nineteenth century was private in so far as it was deemed a topic unsuitable for general discussion, typically occurred in the 'private' space of the home, and was generally attended only by those it was deemed necessary to be there, but of course it did often involve those outside of the family, in the form of medical attendants and/or servants, and the arrival of the child might be considered a more public event, if not the actual birth.

4   There are some exceptions to this: the pauper letters written to parish overseers in the early decades of the period, for example, and the court testimonies which record the words of defendants and witnesses.

5   The use of contraceptive methods, including sponges, condoms made of animal skin, and withdrawal, long pre-dates the nineteenth century, of course, but women's knowledge of and ability to practise contraceptive methods (the latter of which typically required the agreement of their sexual partners) varied considerably, in addition to which there was considerable opposition to the use of contraception in some quarters – an issue I return to later.

6   Florence Boos, in *Memoirs of Victorian Working-Class Women*, suggests that 80 per cent of the Victorian population fit broadly in the category of working class (Basingstoke: Palgrave Macmillan, 2017, 2).

7   For more detailed accounts, see Rozina Visram, *Ayahs, Lascars, and Princes: The Story of Indians in Britain, 1700–1947* (1986; Abingdon: Routledge, 2015), David Olusoga, *Black and British: A Forgotten History* (London: Pan Books, 2017), and Gregor Benton and Edmund Terrence Gomez, *The Chinese in Britain, 1800–Present: Economy, Transnationalism, Identity* (Basingstoke: Palgrave Macmillan, 2007).

8   Legislation such as the 1815 Apothecaries Act and the 1858 Medical Act went some way towards regulating medical practice, by licensing practitioners and establishing a register of approved practitioners respectively, but crucially neither prohibited unlicensed practice, meaning those without training or qualifications remained free to work.

9   The term 'lying-in', now archaic, traditionally refers to the period of rest following childbirth.

10 See *The London Medical Directory* (London: C. Mitchell, 1845), p. 102.

11 These include figures such as Dr Robert Lee and Dr Edward Augustus Cory, both of whom wrote several works on pregnancy and childbirth – some of which material is discussed later in this book.

12 This is evidenced in the various medical directories from the period.

13 Joseph Rogers, MD. *Reminiscences of a Workhouse Medical Officer* (London: T. Fisher Unwin, 1889), p. 10.

14 Ibid., p. 8.

15 Despite these improvements, the maternal mortality rate remained relatively stable, at around 1 in 200, until the early decades of the twentieth century. See Loudon, 'Deaths in Childbed'.

16 On these silences in contemporary culture, see Clare Bellhouse, Meredith J. Temple-Smith, and Jade E. Bilardi, '"It's just one of those things people don't seem to talk about …": women's experiences of social support following miscarriage: a qualitative study', *BMC Women's Health*, 18: 1 (2018), pp. 1–9; Rebecca Feasey, *Infertility and Non-Traditional Family Building* (Basingstoke: Palgrave Macmillan, 2019); Francesca Wallace, 'Why is Abortion Still Taboo?', *Marie Claire* (11 April 2019), https://www.marieclaire.com.au/abortion-taboo. In recent years, there has been an increase in the number of women speaking publicly about these traditionally taboo subjects in an attempt to break the silences around them. See, for example, Hadley Freeman, 'Women aren't meant to talk about miscarriage. But I've never been able to keep a secret', *The Guardian* (13 May 2017), https://www.theguardian.com/lifeandstyle/2017/may/13/hadley-freeman-miscarriage-silence-around-it; Caitlin Moran, 'Let's be upfront about abortion', *The Times* (23 February 2019), https://www.thetimes.co.uk/article/caitlin-moran-lets-be-upfront-about-abortion-9skdvbv86.

Chapter 1

1   Harriet Monroe, 'The Childless Woman' (1914).

2   Cited in Lucinda Hawksley, *Queen Victoria's Mysterious Daughter: A Biography of Princess Louise* (New York: St Martin's Press, 2013), p. 123.

3   These rumours have been fuelled in part by the fact that researchers have been given only limited access to the archive of materials relating to Princess Louise held by the Royal Palaces. See Hawksley, *Queen Victoria's Mysterious Daughter*.

4   Queen Victoria's Journals, 11 December 1839.

5   Cited in Julia Baird, *Victoria the Queen: An Intimate Biography* (London: Blackfriars, 2016), p. 157.

6   Queen Victoria to Victoria, Crown Princess of Prussia (21 April 1858) in Roger Fulford, ed., *Dearest Child: Letters Between Queen Victoria and the Princess Royal, 1858–1861* (London: Evans Brothers, 1964), pp. 93–4.

7   In fact, the engagement took place two years prior to the wedding, when the Princess Royal was only 15 years old, and was delayed at her parents' request. However, her parents desired the marriage, and it may not have been deemed judicious to ask for any further delay.

8   Queen Victoria to Victoria, Crown Princess of Prussia (24 March 1858) in Fulford, ed., *Dearest Child*, 77.

9   Ibid (15 June 1859), p. 195.

10 Consequently, abortion was also used by some women as a means of control over reproduction. See Chapter Five.

11 C. H. F. Routh, 'The moral and physical evil likely to follow if practices intended to act as checks to the population be not strongly discouraged and condemned', *Medical Press and Circular* (1878), p. 8.

12 Ibid, p. 5.

13 Charles Darwin to Charles Bradlaugh (6 June 1877), Darwin Correspondence Project, 'Letter no. 10988,' accessed on 5 April 2022, https://www.darwinproject. ac.uk/letter/?docId=letters/DCP-LETT-10988.xml.

14 Charles Darwin to G. A. Gaskell (15 November 1878), Darwin Correspondence Project, 'Letter no. 11745,' accessed on 5 April 2022, https://www.darwinproject. ac.uk/letter/?docId=letters/DCP-LETT-11745.xml.

15 H. Arthur Albutt, 'An Appeal', in *The Wife's Handbook* (seventh edition; London: R. Forder, 1888), p. 2.

16 Ibid, pp. 47–9.

17 See Helen Rappaport, *Queen Victoria: A Biographical Companion* (Santa Barbara: ABC-Clio, 2003), 340. The original source of this quotation, however, is unclear.

18 Hannah Mitchell, *The Hard Way Up: The Autobiography of Hannah Mitchell, Suffragette and Rebel*, ed., Geoffrey Mitchell (Faber and Faber 1968), p. 65.

19 Pye Henry Chavasse, *Advice to a Wife on the Management of Her Own Health and on the Treatment of some of the Complaints Incidental to Pregnancy, Labour, and Suckling* (Twelfth Edition; London: J & H Churchill, 1877), p. 102.

20 'Childless Families', *The Lancet* (21 April 1866), p. 433.

21 See R. R. Kuczynski, 'Childless Marriages', *Sociological Review* (1938), p. 130.

22 See 'IVF' (2021), https://www.nhs.uk/conditions/ivf/.

23 From approximately 329 per 1,000 in 1800 to 228 per 1,000 in 1900. See https://www.statista.com/statistics/1041714/united-kingdom-all-time-child-mortality-rate/.

24 Margaret Llewellyn Davies, ed., *Maternity: Letters From Working Women* (London: G. Bell and Sons, Ltd., 1915), p. 123.

25 See David James, *Class and Politics in a Northern Industrial Town* (Keele University Press, 1995), p. 29.

26 Robert Lee, *Lectures on the Theory and Practice of Midwifery* (Philadelphia: Ed. Barrington and Geo D. Haswell, 1844), p. 313.

27 Olive Schreiner to W. P. Schreiner (3 June 1884) in Richard Rive, ed., *Olive Schreiner Letters*, Vol 1: 1871–1899 (Oxford: Oxford University Press, 1988), p. 41.

28 Olive Schreiner to Karl Pearson (6 July 1886) in Rive, ed., *Olive Schreiner Letters*, Vol. 1, p. 90.

29 Olive Schreiner to W. T. Stead (March 1892) in Rive, ed., *Olive Schreiner Letters*, Vol. 1, p. 202.

30 Allbutt, *The Wife's Handbook*, p. 45.

31 J. Beresford Ryley, *Sterility in Women: Its Causes and Cure* (2nd edition, 1887), p. 29.

32 Ibid, pp. 30–1.

33 Chavasse, *Advice to a Wife*, p. 2.

34 Ibid, p. 102.

35 Ibid, p. 3.

36 Ibid, p. 2.

37 Ibid, p. xv.

38 Ryley, *Sterility in Women*, p. 72.

39 Chavasse, *Advice to a Wife*, pp. 5–6.

40 Robert Bell, *Sterility* (London: Churchill, 1896), p. 9.

41 Ibid, pp. 15–16.

42 Chavasse, *Advice to a Wife*, p. 84.

43 Ibid, p. 20.

44 Ibid, p. 21.

45 Bell, *Sterility*, p. 20.

46 Ibid, p. 33.

47 Robert Lee, *Clinical Midwifery* (London: John Churchill, 1842), pp. 30–31.

48 See 'Infertility' (2020) https://www.nhs.uk/conditions/infertility/.

49 Lady Waterford to Countess Pembroke (14 August 1889), Augustus J. C. Hare, *The Story of Two Noble Lives*, Vol. III (London: George Allan, 1893), pp. 462–3.

50 Lady Waterford to the Hon. Mrs R. Boyle (11 March 1873) in Hare, *Two Noble Lives*, Vol. III, pp. 317–18.

51 Louisa, Marchioness of Waterford to the Hon. Mrs R. Boyle (31 December 1873) in Hare, *Two Noble Lives*, Vol. III, pp. 331.

52 Queen Victoria to Victoria, Crown Princess of Prussia (18 October 1861) in Fulford, ed., *Dearest Child*, p. 359.

53 Herbert Spencer, *The Principles of Biology*, Vol. II (London: Williams & Norgate, 1867), p. 485.

54 John Thorburn, *Female Education from a Physiological Point of View* (Manchester: J. E. Cornish, 1884), p. 11.

55 Llewellyn Davies, ed., *Maternity*, p. 161.

56 'The Charge Against Lady Gooch', *The Standard* (22 November 1878).

57 'The Charge Against Lady Gooch', *North Wales Chronicle* (14 December 1878).

58 Lady Amberley (8 October 1865), *The Amberley Papers: The Letters and Diaries of Lord and Lady Amberley*, Vol. 1, p. 412.

59   Edward Stanley to Henrietta Stanley (23 September 1847) in Nancy Mitford, ed.,
     The Ladies of Alderley (London: Hamish Hamilton, 1967) p. 139.

60   *Dundee Courier* (12 January 1894), p. 5.

61   'Remarkable Trials', *Annual Register: 1864* (London: Rivingtons, 1865), p. 223.

62   See Kate Gibson, *Illegitimacy, Family, and Stigma in England, 1660–1834* (Oxford:
     Oxford University Press, 2022), p. 130.

63   'Childless Families', *The Lancet* (21 April 1866), p. 433.

64   Llewellyn Davies, ed., *Maternity*, p. 161.

65   'A Baby Exchange', *The Review of Reviews* (July 1895), 86. Whilst Stead's scheme
     was legitimate, similar letters to this one were written by the notorious baby
     killer, Amelia Dyer, and were intended to dupe young women into parting
     with their infants for a fee. Once the money was paid, the infants were then
     murdered and their bodies disposed of. See Old Bailey Proceedings Online (www.
     oldbaileyonline.org, version 8.0, 15 April 2022), May 1896, trial of AMELIA
     ELIZABETH DYER (57) (t18960518–451).

66   'A Baby Exchange', p. 86.

67   Ibid.

68   Maria Josepha Lady Stanley to Lady Henrietta Stanley (15 May 1853) in Mitford,
     ed., *The Stanleys of Alderley*, p. 63.

69   Lady Stanley to Lord Stanley (9 September 1865) in Mitford, ed., *The Stanleys of
     Alderley*, 310.

70   See Siân Pooley, 'Parenthood, child-rearing and fertility in England, 1850–1914',
     The History of the Family, 18:1 (March 2013), n.p.

71   Ibid.

72   Maggy Freyett in Mary Chamberlain, *Fenwomen: A Portrait of Women in an English
     Village* (1975; Woodbridge: Full Circle, 2011), p. 70.

73   Ireene M. Ashby, 'The Birth-Rate and the Mother', in Pat Jalland and John
     Hooper, eds., *Women From Birth to Death: The Female Life Cycle in Britain 1830–1914*
     (Brighton: The Harvester Press, 1986), p. 271.

74   Llewellyn Davies, ed., *Maternity*, p. 95.

75   Ibid, p. 67.

76   Ibid, pp. 48–9.

77   Henrietta Litchfield, ed., *Emma Darwin: A Century of Family Letters*, Vol. II (New
     York: D. Appleton & Co., 1915), p. 45.

78   Charles Darwin to W. D. Fox (7 March 1852), Darwin Correspondence Project,
     'Letter no. 1476,' accessed on 8 April 2022, https://www.darwinproject.ac.uk/
     letter/?docId=letters/DCP-LETT-1476.xml.

79   Lord Francis Jeffrey to Charles Dickens (6 January 1850) in Lord Cockburn,
     Life of Lord Jeffrey, with a Selection From His Correspondence, Vol. II (Philadelphia:
     Lippincott, Grambo & Co., 1852), p. 367 (emphasis in original).

80   Lady Stanley to Henrietta Stanley (6 April 1841) in Mitford, ed., *The Ladies of
     Alderley*, p. 7.

81   Henrietta Stanley to Lady Stanley (6 September 1843) in *The Ladies of Alderley*, p. 58.

82   Access to abortion remains heavily regulated in Britain, but generally speaking at
     least, women here are able to access abortion services.

83 Cited in Margaret Hewitt, *Wives and Mothers in Victorian Industry*, p. 127.

84 *Factories Enquiries Commission: Supplementary Report of the Central Board* (House of Commons, 1834), p. 235.

85 Llewellyn Davies, ed., *Maternity*, p. 34.

86 Ibid, p. 19.

87 Friedrich Engels, *The Condition of the Working Class in England in 1844* (London: Swan Sonnenschein, 1892), p. 161.

88 'The "Queen's Bounty" a Myth', *Daily Gazette for Middlesbrough* (7 February 188).

89 'Triple Birth at Bradford', *York Herald* (22 September 1888).

90 'Triple Births at Little Clacton and Bishop Stortford', *Essex Standard* (23 March 1889).

91 'Triplets Born in a Workhouse', *York Herald* (5 March 1892).

92 'The Queen's Bounty', *Morning Post* (7 July 1877).

93 'A Mother Suspected of Poisoning Her Children', *Nottinghamshire Guardian* (1 December 1871).

94 There is some confusion over the number of children the couple produced: various sources suggest ten; Nancy Mitford, in her published collection of the family letters, lists nine offspring, although she doesn't appear to include at least one who died in very early infancy. However, she subsequently references the couple's twelfth child – born in July 1849. Their children included Kate – later Lady Amberley – whose own maternal experiences are recorded in her diaries (published as *The Amberley Papers*) and referenced in this book.

95 Edward Stanley to Mrs (Henrietta) Stanley (9 November 1847) in Mitford, ed., *The Ladies of Alderley*, p. 142.

96 Mrs (Henrietta) Stanley to Edward Stanley (10 November 1847) in Mitford, ed., *The Ladies of Alderley*, p. 143.

97 See Chapter Five.

98 Mrs (Lucy) Hare to Lady (Henrietta) Eddisbury (August 1849), in Mitford, ed., *The Ladies of Alderley*, p. 203.

Chapter 2

1 Isabella Kelly, 'To an Unborn Infant' (1794).

2 Anna Laetitia Barbauld, 'To a Little Invisible Being Who is Expected Soon to Become Visible' (1825).

3 Lady Lyttelton to Catherine Gladstone (1839–1840), Glynne-Gladstone Archive, ref GG/792.

4 Ellen Johnston, *Autobiography, Poems, and Songs* (Glasgow: William Love, 1867), p. 11.

5 On visual depictions of pregnancy from the sixteenth century to the present day, see Karen Hearn, *Portraying Pregnancy: From Holbein to Social Media* (London: Paul Holberton, 2020).

6 On these images, see Rebecca Whiteley, 'Spratt's Flaps: Midwifery, Creativity, and Sexuality in Early Nineteenth-Century Visual Culture', *British Art Studies*, 19 (February 2021).

7   See Flora Fraser, *Princesses: The Six Daughters of George III* (London: John Murray, 2004), p. 300, p. 318.

8   Lady Charlotte Guest (11 May 1840), in The Earl of Bessborough, ed., *Lady Charlotte Guest: Extracts From Her Journal, 1833–52* (London: John Murray, 1950), p. 111.

9   Charlotte Brontë to Ellen Nussey, 19 January 1855, in Margaret Smith, ed., *The Letters of Charlotte Brontë*, Vol. 3 (Oxford: Oxford University Press, 2004), p. 319.

10 *The Amberley Papers*, Vol. 1, p. 368.

11 Ibid (19 March 1865), p. 385.

12 Eugenia Wynne (11 February 1803), in Anne Fremantle, ed., *The Wynne Diaries*, Vol. 3, 1798–1820 (London: Oxford University Press, 1940), p. 75.

13 Victoria, Crown Princess of Prussia, to Queen Victoria (February 1864) in Roger Fulford, ed., *Dearest Mama: Private Correspondence of Queen Victoria and the Crown Princess of Prussia, 1861–1864* (London: Evans Brothers, 1968), p. 301.

14 *Hard at Work: The Diary of Leonard Wyon*, 1853–1867, ed., Philip Attwood (London: Spink & Son, 2014).

15 Emma Darwin's diary (1842), *Darwin Online*. http://darwin-online.org.uk/content/frameset?keywords=emma%20darwin&pageseq=2&itemID=CUL-DAR242&viewtype=text.

16 Charles Darwin to Charles Babbage (n.d.), Darwin Correspondence Project, 'Letter no. 474,' accessed on 29 April 2022, https://www.darwinproject.ac.uk/letter/?docId=letters/DCP-LETT-474.xml.

17 Charles Darwin to W. D. Fox (24 October 1839). Darwin Correspondence Project, 'Letter no. 541,' accessed on 29 April 2022, https://www.darwinproject.ac.uk/letter/?docId=letters/DCP-LETT-541.xml.

18 Charles Darwin to Caroline Wedgwood (27 October 1839). Darwin Correspondence Project, 'Letter no. 542,' accessed on 29 April 2022, https://www.darwinproject.ac.uk/letter/?docId=letters/DCP-LETT-542.xml.

19 Charles Darwin to W. D. Fox (31 March 1842), Darwin Correspondence Project, 'Letter no. 625,' accessed on 5 April 2022, https://www.darwinproject.ac.uk/letter/?docId=letters/DCP-LETT-625.xml.

20 The Shaw Letters, Cadbury Research Library: Special Collections, University of Birmingham. Quoted in Joanne Begiato, 'Breeding a "Little Stranger": Managing Uncertainty in Pregnancy in Later Georgian England' in Jennifer Evans and Ciara Meehan, eds., *Perceptions of Pregnancy from the Seventeenth to the Twentieth Century* (Basingstoke: Palgrave Macmillan, 2017), p. 14.

21 Ibid, p. 23.

22 Lady Lyttelton to Catherine Gladstone (9 December 1839), Gladstone Archives, Ref GG/792.

23 Ibid (26 [December?] 1839).

24 J. E. Panton, *The Way They Should Go: Hints to Young Parents* (London: Downey & Co., 1896), p. 15.

25 Catherine Temple Pears to Alicia (March 1853), *The Letters of Catherine Temple Pears*, Durham Archives, Ref ADD.MSS 1700–1749.

26 Ibid (7 April 1853).

27 Kate Russell to Georgy [Howard] (2 January 1865) in *The Amberley Papers*, Vol. 1, p. 346.
28 Ibid, p. 347.
29 Kate Amberley to Henrietta Maria Stanley (7 December 1871) in *The Amberley Papers*, Vol. 2, p. 422.
30 Thomas Hardy, *Tess of the D'Urbervilles* (1891; Peterborough: Broadview, 1998), p. 112.
31 Mrs P. Marrin, Untitled, Burnett Archive, Brunel University London, Ref 1:493, p. 1.
32 Llewellyn Davies, ed., *Maternity*, p. 50.
33 Quoted in Emma Griffin, *Breadwinner: An Intimate History of the Victorian Economy* (New Haven: Yale University Press, 2020), p. 100.
34 Llewellyn Davies, ed., *Maternity*, p. 97.
35 Allbutt, *The Wife's Handbook*, p. 9.
36 Llewellyn Davies, ed., *Maternity*, pp. 187–8.
37 Panton, *The Way They Should Go*, p. 18.
38 Queen Victoria to Victoria, Crown Princess of Prussia (19 June 1861) in Fulford, eds., *Dearest Child*, p. 343.
39 Weatherly, *The Young Wife's Own Book*, p. 32. Similar phrasing is found in Pye Henry Chavasse, *Advice to a Wife*, p. 95.
40 Chavasse, *Advice to a Wife*, p. 98.
41 Kate, Lady Amberley, journal (27 October 1867) in *The Amberley Papers*, Vol. II, p. 65.
42 Pregnancy testing of various kinds – mostly unreliable – dates back at least as far as Ancient Egypt, when it was believed a pregnant woman's urine would promote the growth of wheat or barley. Remarkably, recent testing of this approach suggests it is up to 85 per cent reliable in detecting pregnancy (see Erle Henriksen, 'Pregnancy tests of the past and the present', *American Journal of Obstetrics and Gynecology*, p. 49 [1941]).
43 Chavasse, *Advice to a Wife*, p. 99.
44 Allbutt, *The Wife's Handbook*, p. 5, p. 15.
45 Chavasse, *Advice to a Wife*, p. 100.
46 Allbutt, *The Wife's Handbook*, pp. 5–6.
47 Ibid, p. 6.
48 Weatherly, *The Young Wife's Own Book*, 35f; also included in Chavasse, *Advice to a Wife*.
49 Ibid, p. 34.
50 Chavasse, *Advice to a Wife*, p. 103.
51 Ibid.
52 Weatherly, *The Young Wife's Own Book*, p. 40.
53 Ibid, p. 41.
54 Ibid, p. 101.
55 Allbutt, *The Wife's Handbook*, p. 13.
56 Chavasse, *Advice to a Wife*, p. 111. Allbutt also objects to pastry (p. 11).
57 Ibid, p. 100.
58 Weatherly, *The Young Wife's Own Book*, p. 39.
59 Allbutt, *The Wife's Handbook*, p. 11.

60 Ibid.

61 On the history of maternity wear, see Catriona Fisk, 'Looking for Maternity: Dress Collections and Embodied Knowledge', *Fashion Theory*, 23:3 (2019), pp. 401–39.

62 James Clapperton, 'Maternal Impressions', *British Medical Journal* (6 February 1875), p. 169.

63 Henry Mayhew, *London Labour and the London Poor*, Vol. 4 (London: Charles Griffin, 1862), p. 433.

64 Anon., 'Health of London During the Week', *Weekly Return of Births and Deaths in London* (16 April 1853), p. 122.

65 J. Crichton Browne, ed., *The West Riding Lunatic Asylum Medical Reports*, Vol 1, p. 12.

66 *The Autobiography of Joseph Merrick*.

67 Allbutt, *The Wife's Handbook*, p. 16.

68 R. J. Lee, 'Maternal Impressions', *British Medical Journal* (6 February 1875), pp. 167–8.

69 'Shocking Death of Two Durham Miners', *Daily Gazette* for Middlesbrough (9 December 1891).

70 The Shaw Letters, cited in Begiato, 'Breeding a "Little Stranger"', p. 20.

71 Catherine Temple Pears to Alicia Aldous (9 April 1856), The Letters of Catherine Temple Pears 1828–1866 (1853), Durham Archives, ref ADD.MSS 1700–1749, pp. 358–9.

72 Queen Victoria to Victoria, Crown Princess of Prussia (24 March 1858) in Fulford, ed., *Dearest Child*, pp. 77–8.

73 Albert to Victoria, autumn 1856, quoted in Julia Baird, *Victoria: The Queen: An Intimate Biography*, p. 295.

74 Queen Victoria to the King of the Belgians (5 January 1841), in Arthur Christopher Benson and Viscount Esher, eds., *The Letters of Queen Victoria*, Vol. I (London: John Murray, 1911).

75 Queen Victoria to Victoria, Crown Princess of Prussia (11 July 1860) in Fulford, ed., *Dearest Child*, p. 265.

76 Ibid (14 April 1858), p. 90.

77 Ibid (14 April 1858), pp. 89–90.

78 Ibid (26 May 1858), p. 108.

79 Ibid (15 June 1858), p. 115.

80 Ibid (11 June 1858), p. 112.

81 Queen Victoria to the Crown Princess of Prussia (24 February 1864), in *Dearest Mama*, p. 301.

82 Crown Princess of Prussia to Queen Victoria (27 February 1864) in Fulford, ed., *Dearest Mama*, p. 302.

83 Lady Charlotte Guest (3 January 1834), in Bessborough, ed., *Lady Charlotte Guest: Extracts From Her Journal*, p. 42.

84 Charles Darwin to W. D. Fox (24 October 1839), Darwin Correspondence Project.

85 Lord Stanley to Lady Stanley (28 November 1864) in Mitford, ed., *The Stanleys of Alderley*, p. 303.

86 See John Van Der Kiste, *Dearest Vicky, Darling Fritz* (Stroud: Sutton Publishing, 2001), p. 45.

87 Queen Victoria's Journals, 15 March 1857.

88 Ibid (5 April 1857).
89 Ibid (12 April 1857, 13 April 1857).
90 Earl Russell to Lord Amberley (24 January 1865) in *The Amberley Papers*, Vol. 1, p. 351.
91 Ibid (26 January 1865), p. 352.
92 *The Amberley Papers*, Vol. 1, p. 358.
93 Ibid (10 March 1865), p. 378.
94 Ibid (5 April 1865), p. 388.
95 Earl Russell to Lord Amberley (3 June 1865) in *The Amberley Papers*, Vol. 1, p. 393.
96 Ibid (9 June 1865), p. 394.
97 See *The Amberley Papers*, Vol. II, pp. 51–52.
98 *The Amberley Papers* (4 January 1868) Vol. II, p. 82.
99 *The Amberley Papers*, Vol. II, pp. 422–3.
100 Cited in Ellen Ross, 'Rediscovering London's Working-Class Mothers' in Jane Lewis, ed., *Labour and Love: Women's Experience of Home and Family, 1850–1940* (Oxford: Basil Blackwell, 1986), p. 78.
101 Llewellyn Davies, ed., *Maternity*, p. 33.
102 Ibid, p. 22.
103 Ibid, pp. 22–23.
104 Ibid, pp. 18–20.
105 Ibid, p. 99.
106 Ibid, pp. 23–4.
107 Ibid, p. 32.
108 Ibid, p. 29.
109 Allbutt, *The Wife's Handbook*, p. 12.
110 Queen Victoria's Journals, 15 March 1848.
111 Llewellyn Davies, ed., *Maternity*, p. 39.
112 Mitchell, *The Hard Way Up*, pp. 72–3.
113 'Triple Murder and Suicide Near Huddersfield', *Daily News* (8 December 1881).
114 'Distressing Suicide in Birmingham', *Birmingham Daily Post* (5 March 1886).
115 'A Tragedy of Error', *Huddersfield Chronicle* (14 January 1896).
116 'A Farmer's Daughter's Disgrace and Death', *Leicester Chronicle* (9 July 1898).
117 For more on unwanted pregnancies, see Chapter Five.
118 Lord Stanley to Lady Stanley (11 November 1861), in Mitford, ed., *The Stanleys of Alderley*, p. 267.
119 'Distressing Case of Seduction', *Leicester Chronicle* (18 September 1839).
120 'Attempted Suicide by a Young Lady', *Morning Post* (30 December 1840).
121 'Appendix to Second Annual Report of the Commissioners Under the Poor Law Amendment Act', *Parliamentary Papers*, Vol. 29, Part I, p. 495.
122 Anon. 'Ignominious Dress for Unchaste Women in Workhouses', Appendix No. 4, *Sixth Annual Report of the Poor Law Commissioners* (1840), p. 98.
123 *The Standard* (3 January 1839).
124 See 'New Poor Law', *Champion* (10 March 1839).
125 'Ignominious Dress for Unchaste Women in Workhouses', pp. 98–9.
126 See *Royal Cornwall Gazette* (18 March 1842).
127 See 'The Workhouse Scandal at Bedminster', *Bristol Mercury* (27 July 1883).

128 'Government Inquiry at Blaby Workhouse', *Leicester Chronicle* (25 July 1896).
129 'Charge of Immorality Against a Workhouse Official', *Lloyd's Illustrated Newspaper* (8 November 1863).
130 'Charges of Immorality Against the Master of Prescott Workhouse', *Liverpool Mercury* (21 May 1869).
131 See 'Serious Allegations Against a Workhouse Master', *Liverpool Mercury* (2 August 1883).
132 Anon., *The Mother's Thorough Resource Book*, p. 12.

Chapter 3

1   Gerald Massey, *Only a Dream: Craigcrook Castle* (1856).
2   Queen Victoria's Journals, 29 April 1857 (queenvictoriasjournals.org).
3   John Snow (14 April 1857) in Richard H. Ellis, ed., *The Case Books of John Snow* (London: Wellcome Institute, 1994), p. 471.
4   Queen Victoria's Journals, 29 April 1857.
5   'Board of Guardians', *Leeds Times* (2 May 1857), p. 2.
6   'Shocking Affair', *Leeds Times* (25 April 1857), p. 5.
7   Board of Guardians', *Leeds Times* (2 May 1857), p. 2.
8   'Birth of a Child in the Open Street', *Nottinghamshire Guardian* (24 August 1866), p. 3.
9   Crown Princess of Prussia to Queen Victoria (9 January 1864) in Fulford, *Dearest Mama*, p. 288.
10 Queen Victoria to the Crown Princess of Prussia (11 January 1864) in Fulford, ed., *Dearest Mama*, p. 289.
11 Victoria, Crown Princess of Prussia to Queen Victoria (9 January 1864) in Fulford, ed., *Dearest Mama*, p. 288.
12 Queen Victoria to the Crown Princess of Prussia (11 January 1864) in Fulford, ed., *Dearest Mama*, p. 289.
13 Victoria, Crown Princess of Prussia to Queen Victoria (13 January 1864) in Fulford, ed., *Dearest Mama*, p. 290.
14 In fact, although the Prince, named Albert Victor, survived into adulthood, he predeceased both his grandmother, Queen Victoria, and his father, the future Edward VII, dying in 1892 at the age of 28 – a victim of the Asiatic flu pandemic.
15 'The Accouchement of the Princess of Wales', *Huddersfield Chronicle* (16 January 1864).
16 'The Royal Stranger', *Bradford Observer* (14 January 1864).
17 'Inquest on an Infant at Colchester', *Essex Standard* (20 May 1893).
18 Contemporary research on postnatal PTSD cites all of these issues as potential risk factors.
19 Lady Lyttelton to Catherine Gladstone (Undated), Gladstone Archives, Ref GG/792.
20 Agnes Cowper, *A Backward Glance at Merseyside* (Birkenhead: Willmer Brothers & Co, 1948), p. 13.
21 Émile Zola, *The Bright Side of Life*, trans. Andrew Rothwell (Oxford: Oxford University Press, 2018), pp. 275–6.

22 Émile Zola, *How Jolly Life Is!* (London: Vizetelly & Co., 1886), p. 321.
23 Chavasse, *Advice to a Wife*, p. 165.
24 Allbutt, *The Wife's Handbook*, p. 21.
25 Chavasse, *Advice to a Wife* (tenth edition), pp. 182–3.
26 Queen Victoria's Journals, 2 December 1841.
27 Ibid (14 May 1843).
28 Ibid (10 June 1846).
29 Ibid (29 April 1857).
30 Chavasse, *Advice to a Wife*, p. 178.
31 Ibid, p. 179.
32 Allbutt, *The Wife's Handbook*, p. 20.
33 Ibid, 180.This advice is echoed in *The Young Wife's Own Book,* p. 62.
34 Chavasse, *Advice to a Wife*, p. 193.
35 Ibid.
36 Ibid, p. 181.
37 Queen Victoria's Journals, 5 April 1863.
38 Ibid, p. 174.
39 Queen Victoria's Journals, 1 December 1840.
40 Ibid (2 December 1841).
41 Ibid (10 June 1846).
42 Ibid (29 April 1857).
43 Ibid (22 April 1853).
44 *The Amberley Papers*, Vol. 1, p. 406.
45 See, for example, Lee, *Three Hundred Consultations in Midwifery*, p. 200.
46 Chavasse, *The Young Wife's and Mother's Book* (second edition; London: Longman, Brown, Green, and Longmans, 1842), p. 14.
47 Anon., *The Mother's Thorough Resource Book* (1860), p. 14.
48 Ibid, p. 20.
49 Chavasse, *Advice to a Wife* (tenth edition), pp. 176–7.
50 Lionel A. Weatherly, *The Young Wife's Own Book* (1883), pp. 64–5.
51 Allbutt, *The Wife's Handbook*, p. 5.
52 Ibid, p. 17.
53 Llewellyn Davies, ed., *Maternity*, p. 30.
54 Ibid, p. 50.
55 Mary Chamberlain, *Fenwomen* (1975), pp. 69–70. The quote is from a transcript of an oral interview conducted by Chamberlain.
56 Elma Napier, *Life is a Blunder* (London: Jonathan Cape, 1948), p. 36.
57 Lady Lyttelton to Catherine Gladstone (June 1840), Glynne-Gladstone Archive, ref GG/792.
58 See, for example, Johanna E. Soet, Gregory A. Brack, and Colleen Dilorio. 'Prevalence and Predictors of Women's Experience of Psychological Trauma During Childbirth'. *Birth*. 30:1 (2003).
59 Robert Lee, *Lectures on the Theory and Practice of Midwifery* (Philadelphia: Ed Barrington and Geo. D. Haswell, 1844), pp. 28–9.
60 Mitchell, *The Hard Way Up*, p. 75.

61 Ibid.

62 Anne Fremantle, ed., *The Wynne Diaries: The Adventures of Two Sisters in Napoleonic Europe* (Oxford: Oxford University Press, 1982), pp. 411–2.

63 Lady Charlotte Guest (3 July 1834), in Bessborough, ed., *Lady Charlotte Guest: Extracts From Her Journal*, p. 31.

64 Ibid, p. 65.

65 Ibid, pp. 87–8.

66 Lady Henrietta Stanley to Maria Josepha Lady Stanley (24 September 1856) in Mitford, ed., *The Stanleys of Alderley*, p. 161.

67 Queen Victoria to Victoria, Crown Princess of Prussia (11 December 1858), in Fulford, ed., *Dearest Child*, p. 151.

68 Queen Victoria's Journals, 1 December 1840.

69 Ibid (25 August 1844).

70 Ibid (2 April 1848).

71 Ibid (22 April 1853).

72 Ibid.

73 Lady Stanley to Lady Dillon (19 September 1843) in Mitford, ed., *The Ladies of Alderley*, p. 63.

74 *The Amberley Papers*, Vol. 1, p. 402.

75 Probably William Overend Priestly, the celebrated obstetrician.

76 *The Amberley Papers*, Vol. 2, p. 84.

77 Ibid, p. 85.

78 Ibid, p. 490.

79 Lady Stanley to Mrs Stanley (30 June 1841) in Mitford, ed., *The Ladies of Alderley*, pp. 13–14.

80 Mary Wollstonecraft to Ruth Barlow (20 May 1794), in Janet M. Todd, ed., *The Collected Letters of Mary Wollstonecraft* (New York: Columbia University Press, 2003), pp. 252–3.

81 See Nayder, *The Other Dickens: A Life of Catherine Hogarth*, p. 145.

82 Harriet Beecher Stowe, *Lady Byron Vindicated* (Boston: Fields, Osgood, & Co., 1870), pp. 280–1.

83 See Joan Pierson, *The Real Lady Byron* (London: Robert Hale, 1992), p. 88f.

84 Chavasse, *Advice to a Wife* (tenth edition), p. 156.

85 Queen Victoria to Leopold I of Belgium, cited in Monica Charlot, *Victoria: The Young Queen* (Oxford: Blackwell, 1991), p. 192.

86 Queen Victoria's Journals, 1 December 1840.

87 Ibid (2 December 1841).

88 Ibid (15 May 1850).

89 Ibid (29 April 1857).

90 Crown Princess of Prussia to Queen Victoria (20 February 1858) in Fulford, ed., *Dearest Child*, pp. 52–3.

91 Ibid (27 February 1858), pp. 61–2.

92 Queen Victoria's Journals, 5 April 1863.

93 *The Amberley Papers*, Vol, 1, p. 403.

94 Consuelo Vanderbilt Balson, *The Glitter and the Gold* (London: Hodder &

Stoughton, 1973), p. 60.

95 Ibid, p. 105.

96 Lady Maria Josepha Stanley to Edward Stanley (6 March 1842) in Mitford, ed., *The Ladies of Alderley*, pp. 28–9.

97 Lord Stanley to Lady Henrietta Stanley (18 November 1859) in Mitford, ed., *The Stanleys of Alderley*, p. 230.

98 Lord Stanley to Lady Henrietta Stanley (20 July 1865) in Mitford, ed., *The Stanleys of Alderley*, p. 308.

99 Napier, *Life is a Blunder*, p. 35.

100 Cowper, *A Backward Glance at Merseyside*, p. 13.

101 Mrs Layton, 'Memories of Seventy Years', p. 35.

102 See 'Illegitimate Children in Workhouses', *Morning Post* (11 February 1864).

103 'Murderous Attack on a Workhouse Porter', *York Herald* (6 July 1889).

104 Llewellyn Davies, ed., *Maternity*, pp. 114–15.

105 'Fatal Accidents and Sudden Death', *Leeds Times* (25 April 1857), p. 5.

Chapter 4

1 Caroline Bowles, 'The Dying Mother to her Infant' in *The Birth-Day and Other Poems* (Edinburgh: William Blackwood & Sons, 1836), p. 193.

2 *The Times* (6 November 1817), p. 2.

3 'Sad Death of a Domestic Servant', *Huddersfield Chronicle* (13 December 1888), p. 4.

4 'Reports on the Nursing and Administration of Provincial Workhouses and Infirmaries', *British Medical Journal* (1894), p. 764.

5 Ibid.

6 *Thirty-eighth Annual Report of the Registrar-General of Births, Deaths, and Marriages in England* (London: George E. Eyre and William Spottiswoode, 1877), p. 259.

7 Charles Dickens, *Oliver Twist* (Peterborough: Broadview, 2005), p. 2.

8 *The Times*, 7 November 1817, p. 2.

9 Anna Laetitia Barbauld, 'Elegy', *The Annual Register, or a View of the History, Politics, and Literature, for the Year 1818* (London: Baldwin, Cradock, and Joy, 1819), p. 612.

10 *The Times*, 7 November 1817, p. 2.

11 Baron E. Von Stockmar, *Memoirs of Baron Stockmar*, Vol. 1 (London: Longmans, Green, and Co., 1873), p. 67.

12 Alice Chase, *The Memoirs of Alice Maude Chase*, Burnett Archive, Brunel University London.

13 Jane Austen, *Northanger Abbey* (Peterborough: Broadview, 2002), p. 37.

14 Other examples include Charles Dickens' *Oliver Twist* (1838), Emily Brontë's *Wuthering Heights* (1847), Elizabeth Gaskell's *Mary Barton* (1848), Wilkie Collins's *Hide and Seek* (1854) and *No Name* (1862), Mrs Henry Wood's *St Martin's Eve* (1866), and Thomas Hardy's *Far From the Madding Crowd* (1874) and *The Mayor of Casterbridge* (1886).

15 Women bore an average of around five children between 1800 and 1880, but in the latter decades of the century, there was a significant decline in fertility rates, mirrored across Europe and lasting until around the 1930s. For a more detailed discussion of this, see Michael S. Teitelbaum, *The British Fertility Decline: Demographic Transition in the Crucible of the Industrial Revolution* (Princeton: Princeton

University Press, 1984).
16 Anon., *The London Practice of Midwifery* (London: James Wallis, 1803), p. iv.
17 In the late eighteenth century, it may have been as high as 25 in 1,000. See Loudon, 'Deaths in Childbed'.
18 Cited in Begiato, 'Breeding a "Little Stranger"', p. 22.
19 Queen Victoria to Victoria, Crown Princess of Prussia (27 October 1858) in Fulford, ed., *Dearest Child*, p. 141.
20 Kate Amberley's journal (3 August 1865) in *The Amberley Papers*, Vol. I, p. 401.
21 Mitchell, *The Hard Way Up*, p. 74.
22 Lady Charlotte Guest (12 July 1840), in Bessborough, ed., *Lady Charlotte Guest*, p. 115.
23 The traditional association between purification and churching was largely obsolete by the nineteenth century. On the history of the practice of churching, see Donna K. Ray, 'A View from the Childwife's Pew: The Development of Rites around Childbirth in the Anglican Communion', *Anglican and Episcopal History*, 69:4 (December 2000), pp. 443–73.
24 Rev. Edward Berens, *An Address upon the Office for the Churching of Women* (3rd edition; Oxford: W. Baxter, 1850), p. 3.
25 Ibid, 6 (emphasis in original).
26 Anon., *The Mother's Public Thanksgiving* (London: Wertheim, Macintosh, and Hunt, 1860), p. 3.
27 James Sherman, *Memoir of William Allen* (London: Charles Gilpin, 1851), p. 14. In a strange coincidence, Mary Allen's death occurred the day after Mary Wollstonecraft's, and both died giving birth to daughters also named Mary.
28 Ibid, p. 343.
29 Severe bleeding and infections remain two of the main causes of maternal mortality worldwide today. See 'Maternal Mortality', WHO (2019), www.who.int/news-room/fact-sheets/detail/maternal-mortality.
30 Robert Ferguson, M.D. *Essays on the Most Important Diseases of Women, Part I: Puerperal Fever* (London: John Murray, 1839), p. vii.
31 *Thirty-eighth Annual Report of the Registrar-General of Births, Deaths, and Marriages in England*, p. 244.
32 As with Princess Charlotte twenty years later, Wollstonecraft sat for a portrait during her pregnancy, but the resulting work, by John Opie (see figure 7), displays no signs of her condition.
33 William Godwin, *Memoirs of the Author of a Vindication of the Rights of Woman* (London: J. Johnson, 1798), p. 188. Throughout the century, the use of puppies was sometimes recommended in cases where it was deemed necessary for the milk to be drawn and the infant was unable to feed.
34 Elizabeth Fenwick to Evarina Wollstonecraft, 12 September 1797, in Elizabeth Robins Pennell, *Mary Wollstonecraft* (Boston: Roberts Bros, 1890), p. 357.
35 Godwin, *Memoirs of the Author of a Vindication of the Rights of Woman*, p. 188.
36 William Godwin to T. Holcroft (10 September 1797) in Pamela Clemitt, ed., *The Letters of William Godwin, Vol. 1: 1778–1797* (Oxford: Oxford University Press, 2011).
37 Medical Report Book for Newcastle Lying-in Hospital, 1821–1833. Available at Tyne and Wear Archives, Newcastle; ref HO.PM/29.

38 Ibid.

39 'Dr Campbell on Puerperal Fever', *London Medical Gazette* (1832), vol. Ix, p. 354.

40 'A Midwife Convicted of Manslaughter', *Sheffield Daily Telegraph* (27 March 1875), p. 4.

41 'Charge Against a Midwife', *Exeter and Plymouth Gazette* (16 February 1891), p. 7.

42 Robert Lee, *Lectures on the Theory and Practice of Midwifery* (London: Longman, Brown, Green, and Longmans, 1844), p. 267.

43 Robert Lee, *Clinical Midwifery* (Philadelphia: Lee & Blanchard, 1849), p. 11.

44 Robert Lee, *Three Hundred Consultations in Midwifery* (London: John Churchill & Sons, 1864), p. 12.

45 Ibid, p. 177.

46 'Women should leave at least a year between pregnancies'. https://www.nhs.uk/news/pregnancy-and-child/women-should-leave-least-year-between-pregnancies/ (accessed August 2020).

47 Lee, *Three Hundred Consultations in Midwifery*, p. 69.

48 Catherine Dickens' biographer speculates on this. See Nayder, *The Other Dickens*, p. 159.

49 Charlotte Brontë to Ellen Nussey, 19 January 1855, in Margaret Smith, ed., *The Letters of Charlotte Brontë*, Vol.3 (Oxford: Oxford University Press, 2004), p. 319.

50 Elizabeth Gaskell, *The Life of Charlotte Brontë* (London: Penguin, 1997), p. 426.

51 Arthur Bell Nichols to Ellen Nussey, 1 February 1855, in Smith, ed., *The Letters of Charlotte Brontë*, Vol. 3, p. 323.

52 Mrs [Elizabeth] Gaskell, *The Life of Charlotte Brontë* (1857; London: Smith, Elder, & Co, 1889), p. 446.

53 Lee, *Three Hundred Consultations in Midwifery*, p. 19.

54 Ibid, p. 202.

55 Ibid, p. 203.

56 Ibid, p. 155.

57 Ibid, p. 210.

58 'Shocking Death at Beeston', *Nottinghamshire Guardian* (14 April 1865).

59 A report published in the *Pall Mall Gazette* in 1867 suggests the higher than average mortality rate in Queen Charlotte's Hospital between 1857 and 1863 was in part due to 'the great number of single women received there' ('Workhouse Death Rate in Childbirth', *Pall Mall Gazette* [25 January 1867]).

60 'Melancholy Death in Nottingham', *Sheffield Daily Telegraph* (16 January 1874), p. 6.

61 'Lamentable Death in Childbirth', *Western Times* (4 February 1860), p. 1.

62 'Alleged Neglect by a Midwife', *Western Daily Press* (6 August 1864).

63 'Alleged Neglect by a Midwife', *Bristol Mercury* (24 April 1878).

64 'Mortality from Childbirth in the London Workhouses', *Pall Mall Gazette* (27 September 1867), pp. 8–9.

65 See Loudon, 'Deaths in Childbed'.

Chapter 5

1 George Eliot, *Adam Bede* (New York: Harper & Brothers, 1860), pp. 380–1.

2 'A Professional Abortionist Gets Five Years', *Reynolds's Newspaper* (26 January 1896).

3   See 'The Death of Mrs Uzielli' (28 June 1898), *The Standard*; 'Trial of Dr Collins', *Reynolds's Newspaper* (3 July 1898).

4   Whilst the Old Bailey dealt with only 1,356 cases of rape between 1800 and 1900 (see Old Bailey Proceedings Online), it is safe to assume that the vast majority of cases went unreported or did not result in criminal charges. In cases of marital rape, of course, there was no criminal charge to answer.

5   'Report of the Royal Commission on the Poor Laws, 1834', in S. G. Checkland and E. O. A. Checkland, eds., *The Poor Law Report of 1834* (Harmandsworth: Penguin, 1974), p. 482.

6   Mitchell, *The Hard Way Up*, p. 26.

7   Whilst women throughout the UK are now able to access legal terminations (following the repeal of earlier laws criminalising abortion in Northern Ireland in 2019), it remains heavily regulated and subject to possible criminal charges unless carried out under certain conditions. In 2019, the British Medical Association published a position paper calling for the removal of criminal sanctions for abortion in order to render it 'lawful except in exceptional circumstances', rather than 'a crime for which there are some exceptions'. As the law currently stands, abortion remains more heavily regulated than other medical procedures. See 'The removal of criminal sanctions for abortion: BMA position paper', *BMA* (2019), https://www.bma.org.uk/media/1963/bma-removal-of-criminal-sanctions-for-abortion-position-paper-july-2019.pdf.

8   Today in the UK, women can access abortions up to twenty-four weeks of pregnancy, and in certain circumstances (when the mother's life is at risk, for example) beyond this. In Northern Ireland, following the passing of legislation in 2020, women can access abortion up to twelve weeks of pregnancy. For a more detailed examination of abortion law in England, see John Keown, *Abortion, Doctors, and the Law* (Cambridge: Cambridge University Press, 1988).

9   See, for example, Dr R Druitt, 'Dr Robert Lee and Craniotomy', *Medical Times and Gazette* (4 May 1861), pp. 479–80.

10 'Startling Craniotomy', *The Lancet* (22 October 1842), p. 130.

11 Chavasse, *Advice to a Wife* (tenth edition, 1873), p. 98.

12 'On the Propriety of Hanging a Pregnant Female', *Daily News* (19 August 1854) [BLN].

13 Michael Ryan, *The Philosophy of Marriage in its Social, Moral, and Physical Relations* (London: John Churchill, 1837), p. 119.

14 See Sedgh G et al. (2016) 'Abortion incidence between 1990 and 2014: global, regional, and sub regional levels and trends', *The Lancet*, 388:10041 (2016) pp. 258–267.

15 See 'The removal of criminal sanctions for abortion: BMA position paper', p. 2.

16 'A Doctor Charged with Murder', *York Herald* (3 August 1889), p. 8.

17 Old Bailey Proceedings Online (www.oldbaileyonline.org, version 8.0, 11 April 2022), October 1889, trial of FREDERICK MOON (60) (t18891021–875).

18 'Mysterious Death Near Chatham', *Morpeth Herald* (29 August 1891), p. 5.

19 'Doctor Charged with Murder', *Sheffield Daily Telegraph* (3 October 1896), p. 7.

20 'The Charge Against a Swansea Doctor', *Western Daily Press* (23 November 1896), p. 7.

21 Chavasse, *Advice to a Wife* (tenth edition, 1873), p. 142.
22 Diary of Eugenia Wynne (5 March 1806) in Fremantle, ed., *The Wynne Diaries*, Vol 3, p. 251.
23 'Nature's Blood Former' pamphlet, p. 2. Included in Allbutt, *The Wife's Handbook*.
24 See, for example, *Morning Post* (23 February 1803).
25 'Death Occasioned by Seduction', *Morning Post* (3 April 1846).
26 Ibid.
27 Old Bailey Proceedings Online (www.oldbaileyonline.org, version 8.0, 25 August 2021), October 1843, trial of WILLIAM HAYNES (t18431023–2890).
28 Old Bailey Proceedings Online (www.oldbaileyonline.org, version 8.0, 25 August 2021), May 1834, trial of WILLIAM CHILDS (t18340515–47).
29 On the confusion over the number of children the Stanleys produced, see Chapter One.
30 See Nancy Mitford, ed., *The Ladies of Alderley* (London: Hamish Hamilton, 1967), pp. 142–5.
31 Ibid, p. 185.
32 Ibid, p. 202.
33 Anon., *To-Day* (21 December 1895), p. 209.
34 Llewellyn Davies, ed., *Maternity*, p. 15.
35 Ibid, p. 25.
36 Ibid, p. 38.
37 Ibid, p. 45.
38 Ibid, p. 40.
39 Ibid, p. 42.
40 Wm. C. Roberts, 'Remarks on the Signs of Pregnancy', *The Medical Gazette*, Vol. IV (1870), p. 26.
41 Ibid, p. 169.
42 'The Charge of Murder Against a Nurse', *Daily News* (5 January 1899).
43 'Singular Double Birth at Leeds', *Nottinghamshire Guardian* (21 May 1880).
44 'Alleged Abandonment of a Child', *Huddersfield Chronicle* (13 July 1896).
45 'Lunatic Asylum', *Caledonian Mercury* (24 March 1800).
46 'The Foundling Hospital', *The Graphic* (16 September 1893).
47 Ibid.
48 'A Pathetic Incident', *Berrows Worcester Journal* (23 February 1895).
49 'Provision 60: Concealing the Birth of a Child', Offences Against the Person Act 1861, https://www.legislation.gov.uk/ukpga/Vict/24-25/100/section/60/ enacted?view=plain (Accessed April 2022).
50 'Alleged Child Murder', *Northern Star* (11 November 1843).
51 See Thomas Sergeant, ed., *Reports of Cases Argued and Determined in the English Courts of Common Law*, Vol. 24 (Philadelphia: P. H. Nicklin and T. Johnson, 1834), p. 345.
52 'The Alleged Murder at Falmouth', *Royal Cornwall Gazette* (6 February 1868).
53 'The Concealment of Birth at Falmouth', *Royal Cornwall Gazette* (19 March 1868), p. 6.
54 'Horrible Case', *The Standard* (11 April 1829).
55 'Old Bailey Proceedings Online (www.oldbaileyonline.org, version 8.0, 12 April 2022), April 1829, trial of MARTHA BARRETT (t18290409–83).

56 'Body of a Child Found in a Wood', *Leeds Times* (25 April 1857).

57 'Surrey Assizes', *The Times* (3 April 1817), p. 3.

58 Old Bailey Proceedings Online (www.oldbaileyonline.org, version 8.0, 17 September 2021), February 1829, trial of HARRIET FARRELL (t18290219–62).

59 'Suspected Child Murder in Bermondsey', *Morning Post* (3 April 1846).

Chapter 6

1 Florence Nightingale, *Introductory Notes on Lying-In Institutions* (London: Longmans, Green & Co., 1871), p. 72.

2 See 'Disgraceful Management of a Lying-in Hospital', *Lloyds Illustrated Newspaper* (7 March 1852).

3 See John Snow (12 February 1852) in Ellis, ed., *The Case Books of John Snow*, p. 218.

4 See Anon. [T.D.], *The Metropolitan Charities* (London: Sampson Low, 1844), p. 19.

5 See 'Shrewsbury maternity scandal: Better care might have saved 201 babies', BBC News (30 March 2022), https://www.bbc.co.uk/news/uk-60919474.

6 Approximately 2 per cent of births in England and Wales are home births.

7 'Turning' was the external or internal manipulation of the child into a position more favourable for delivery and could be very painful for the mother.

8 Mary Wollstonecraft Godwin, *Memoirs and Posthumous Works of Mary Wollstonecraft Godwin* (Dublin: Thomas Burnside, 1798), p. 105.

9 Émile Zola, *How Jolly Life Is!* (London: Vizetelly & Co.), p. 321.

10 *The Glasgow Herald* (17 November 1862).

11 Anon., 'Women Physicians', *Macmillan's Magazine*, No. 107: Vol. XVIII (September 1868), p. 375.

12 See Sarah Fox and Margot Brazier, 'The Regulation of Midwives in England, c.1500–1902', *Medical Law International*, 20:4 (December 2020).

13 See, for example, Frances J. Badger, 'Illuminating Nineteenth-Century English Urban Midwifery', *Women's History Review*, 23:5 (2014).

14 Mitchell, *The Hard Way Up*, p. 24, p. 31.

15 See David Harley, 'Historians as Demonologists: The Myth of the Midwife-witch', *Social History of Medicine*, 3:1 (April 1990), pp. 1–26.

16 See Badger, 'Illuminating Nineteenth-Century English Urban Midwifery', and for a perspective on eighteenth-century birthing and midwifery, Sarah Fox, *Giving Birth in Eighteenth-Century England* (Institute of Historical Research, 2022).

17 Mitchell, *The Hard Way Up*, p. 32.

18 Badger's 'Illuminating Nineteenth-Century English Urban Midwifery' highlights this – exploring the extensive register of a midwife named Mary Eaves, who worked in Coventry from the 1840s until the 1870s.

19 Charles Dickens, *Martin Chuzzlewit* (1844; Oxford: Oxford University Press, 1998), p. 269.

20 William Cadogan, *An Essay Upon Nursing and the Management of Children* (London: J. Roberts, 1748), p. 3.

21 Edward William Murphy on 'The Importance of a Scientific Medical Education to Practitioners in Midwifery', *Association Medical Journal*, 1853, p. 323.

22 Ibid, p. 324.
23 'District News', *Birmingham Daily Post* (3 December 1860).
24 'Unqualified Midwives', *Lloyds Illustrated Newspaper* (11 March 1866).
25 Ibid.
26 'The Extraordinary Charge Against a Midwife', *Sheffield Independent* (20 January 1883).
27 'Yorkshire Assizes', *Leeds Mercury* (15 February 1883).
28 'Alleged Manslaughter by a Midwife', *York Herald* (1 February 1896).
29 'A Midwife Committed for Manslaughter', *York Herald* (29 July 1893).
30 Old Bailey Proceedings Online (www.oldbaileyonline.org, version 8.0, 8 March 2022), October 1893, trial of HARRIET VINSON (57) (t18931016–930).
31 'Multiple News Items', *Morning Post* (28 October 1836).
32 Llewellyn Davies, ed., *Maternity*, p. 26.
33 See WHO, 'Advice on Caring for a Newborn' (2022), https://www.who.int/tools/advice-for-health-and-wellbeing/life-phase/caring-for-a-newborn.
34 Llewellyn Davies, ed., *Maternity*, p. 31.
35 Ibid, p. 67.
36 Ibid, p. 36.
37 Ibid, p. 186.
38 Ibid, p. 149.
39 See, for example, 'District News' (3 December 1860), *Birmingham Daily Post* and 'Local News' (11 April 1899), *Liverpool Mercury*.
40 'Multum in Parvo', *Liverpool Mercury* (24 April 1846).
41 Samuel White to Mr Joselyne (20 June 1825) in Thomas Sokoll, ed., *Essex Pauper Letters 1731–1837* (Oxford University Press), p. 215.
42 David Rivenall to Joseph Wiffen (19 May 1829) in Sokoll, ed., *Essex Pauper Letters*, p. 286.
43 John Smoothy (19 May 1833) in Sokoll, ed., *Essex Pauper Letters*, p. 140.
44 Marrin, Untitled, p. 1.
45 Llewellyn Davies, ed., *Maternity*, pp. 83–4.
46 See, for example, Llewellyn Davies, ed., *Maternity*, p. 115, pp. 125–6.
47 Inevitably, there were still cases in which midwives faced accusations of neglect or incompetence, and a number of midwives were struck off the register as a consequence. Again, though, these cases were exceptional rather than the rule.
48 Llewellyn Davies, ed., *Maternity*, p. 86.
49 Ibid, pp. 34–5.
50 'Births', *The Examiner* (3 January 1841), p. 45.
51 Anon., 'Midwifery as a Profession for Educated Women', *The Englishwoman's Review* (14 May 1887), p. 198.
52 'The Registration of Midwives', *Morning Post* (1 March 1897).
53 The history of midwifery on the continent differs significantly from Britain, and access to medical training and education was provided much earlier.
54 See Helen Rappaport, 'Charlotte von Siebold: The Pioneering German midwife who delivered the future Queen Victoria' (2018; https://helenrappaport.com/queen-victoria/charlotte-von-siebold-midwife-delivered-queen-victoria/).

55 Old Bailey Proceedings Online (www.oldbaileyonline.org, version 8.0, 8 March 2022), January 1881, trial of SARAH NORMAN (21) (t18810110–201).

56 Nicholson's autobiography is concerned with his opposition to ritualism in the church, but he is better known as inventor of the compound cricket ball.

57 Hamlet Nicholson, *An Autobiographical and Full Historical Account of the Persecution of Hamlet Nicholson in his Opposition to Ritualism at the Rochdale Parish Church* (Manchester: Barber & Farnworth, 1892), p. 3.

58 Mrs Layton, 'Memories of Seventy Years', in Llewellyn, ed., *Life As We Have Known It*, p. 31.

59 See J. Ward Cousins, 'The Midwives Act of 1902' (8 August 1903), *The British Medical Journal*, pp. 293–5.

60 See *Public Bills*, Vol. 6 (Parliament, 1901), p. 4.

61 Mrs Layton, 'Memories of Seventy Years', pp. 43–6.

62 'West Riding Assizes', *Huddersfield Chronicle* (2 August 1892), p. 3.

63 'Murder Charges', *Morning Post* (1 December 1898), p. 3.

64 'The Charge of Murder Against a Nurse', *Daily News* (5 January 1899) [BLN].

65 *Report Concerning the Hospital for the Reception of Poor Married Women Lying-In* (Newcastle: T & J Hodgson, 1827), p. 18.

66 Ibid.

67 Anon., *The City of London Lying-In Hospital* (London: R. Wilks, 1823), p. 9.

68 'Appendix to the Rules of Gateshead Lying-in Charity'. Available at Northumberland Archives (SANT/BEQ/26/1/4/230). Accessed July 2021.

69 See Duncan Kennedy, 'Forced adoption: Birth parents urged to give evidence to inquiry', BBC News (23 September 2021).

70 'British Lying-in Hospital for Married Women', *Morning Post* (3 January 1865), p. 3.

71 See Lara Marks, 'Medical Care for Pauper Mothers and Their Infants', *The Economic History Review*, 46:3 (August 1993), p. 518.

72 Louisa Twining, *Workhouses and Pauperism* (London: Methuen & Co, 1898), p. 201.

73 Medical Report Book for Newcastle Lying-in Hospital, 1821–1833. Available at Tyne and Wear Archives, Newcastle; ref HO.PM/29.

74 Nightingale, *Introductory Notes on Lying-In Institutions*, p. 32.

75 See 'The Prevention of Puerperal Fever', *The Hospital* (1895), pp. 25–6.

76 Sir Robert Peel, 'Domiciliary Midwifery: Peel Report' (1971), The National Archives.

77 Thomas Radford, *Observations on the Caesarean Section, Craniotomy, and Other Obstetric Operations* (London: J. & A. Churchill, 1880), p. 11.

78 M. Chailly, *Practical Treatise on Midwifery*, trans. Gunning S. Bedford (New York: Harper & Brothers, 1854), pp. 314–15.

79 Ibid, pp. 350–1.

80 Ibid, p. 351.

81 Anon., 'Chailly and Moreau on Practical Midwifery', *The British and Foreign Medical Review* (April 1845), p. 419.

82 Robert Lee, *Lectures on the Theory and Practice of Midwifery*, p. 307.

83 Lee, *Clinical Midwifery*, p. 44.

84 Lee, *Three Hundred Consultations in Midwifery*, p. 68.

85 Ibid, p. 200.

86 Lee, *Clinical Midwifery*, pp. 31–2.

87 See Paul R. Knight and Douglas R. Bacon, 'An Unexplained Death: Hannah Greener and Chloroform', *Anesthesiology*, Vol. 96, (May 2002), pp. 1250–53.

88 Lee, *Three Hundred Consultations in Midwifery*, p. 121.

89 Sir James Young Simpson, *The Obstetric Memoirs and Contributions of James Y. Simpson*, Vol.2 (Philadelphia: J. P. Lippincott & Co, 1856), p. 483 (citing Greek philosopher Galen).

90 Frances Anne Kemble (31 October 1835) in *Records of Later Life*, Vol. 1 (London: Richard Bentley & Son), p. 37.

91 Charles Darwin to J. D. Hooker (10 May 1848), Darwin Correspondence Project, 'Letter no. 1174,' accessed on 8 April 2022, https://www.darwinproject.ac.uk/letter/?docId=letters/DCP-LETT-1174.xml.

92 Queen Victoria to Victoria, Crown Princess of Prussia (25 July 1863), in Fulford, ed., *Dearest Mama*, p. 251.

93 Lady Stanley to Lord Stanley (8 November 1852) in Mitford, ed., *The Stanleys of Alderley*, p. 53.

94 Queen Victoria's Journals, 5 April 1863.

95 Olive Schreiner to Mary Sauer (10 May 1895) in Rive, ed., *Olive Schreiner Letters*, Vol. 1, p. 252.

Chapter 7

1 William Wordsworth, 'Maternal Grief' (1842) in Henry Reed, ed., *The Poetical Works of Wordsworth* (Philadelphia: Troutman & Hayes, 1852), p. 125.

2 'The Mirror of Fashion', *Morning Chronicle* (3 January 1821).

3 Ibid (5 March 1821).

4 There were fluctuations in this figure across the course of the period, as well as differences linked to both social status and location. See, for example, Robert Millward and Frances Bell, 'Infant Mortality in Victorian Britain: The Mother as Medium', *Economic History Review*, LIV:4 (2001), pp. 699–733.

5 'The Mirror of Fashion', *Morning Chronicle* (5 March 1821).

6 Ibid.

7 Henry Mayhew, 'Labour and the Poor in the Metropolitan, Rural, and Manufacturing Districts of England and Wales', *Morning Chronicle* (11 January 1850).

8 'Production of Premature Labour', *The Lancet* (28 October 1843), pp. 112–13.

9 'Turning After Craniotomy', *The Lancet* (4 July 1874), p. 11.

10 Llewellyn Davies, ed., *Maternity*, 194–5. These figures are drawn from a relatively small sample of women who gave birth in the late nineteenth and early twentieth centuries, but nonetheless provide some indication of the prevalence of miscarriage, stillbirth, and infant mortality at this time.

11 'Miscarriage', NHS (https://www.nhs.uk/conditions/miscarriage/). Accessed March 2022.

12 'Stillbirth', NHS (https://www.nhs.uk/conditions/stillbirth/). Accessed March 2022.

13 In recent years, survival rates for babies born at twenty-two and twenty-three weeks have improved, but they remain extremely low. See Nick Triggle, 'Babies born at 22 weeks "can now survive"', BBC News (https://www.bbc.co.uk/news/health-50144741). Accessed March 2022.

14 Chavasse, *Advice to a Wife*, p. 140 (emphasis in original).

15 'Miscarriage Statistics', *Tommy's* (https://www.tommys.org/baby-loss-support/miscarriage-information-and-support/miscarriage-statistics). Accessed February 2022.

16 Meghan Markle, 'The Losses We Share', *New York Times* (25 November 2020).

17 In 2020, the Labour MP for Sheffield Hallam, Olivia Blake, spoke about her experience of miscarriage during the Covid pandemic. MP Angela Crawley has campaigned for statutory leave for all those experiencing the loss of a pregnancy at any stage, resulting in the introduction of the Miscarriage Leave Bill in 2022.

18 William J. Gow, 'On the Relation of Heart Disease to Menstruation', *Obstetrical Transactions*, Vol. XXXVI (London: Longmans, Green & Co., 1895), p. 141.

19 J. W. Ballantyne, 'Studies in Foetal Pathology and Teratology', *The Transactions of the Edinburgh Obstetrical Society*, Vol. XVII (Edinburgh: Oliver and Boyd, 1892), p. 56.

20 Chavasse, *Advice to a Wife*, pp. 140–2.

21 George Eliot, *Middlemarch* (1871; Peterborough, Ontario: Broadview, 2004), p. 463.

22 Chavasse, *Advice to a Wife*, pp. 146–7.

23 Ballantyne, 'Studies in Foetal Pathology and Teratology', p. 56.

24 Maria Josepha Lady Stanley to Lady Henrietta Stanley (8 May 1851) in Mitford, ed., *The Stanleys of Alderley*, pp. 6–7.

25 See Thomas Carlyle to Jane Carlyle (22 August 1831), *The Carlyle Letters Online*, (https://carlyleletters.dukeupress.edu/home). Accessed March 2022.

26 See Maggie Cowell-Stepney to Mary Drew (August 1886) in Jalland and Hooper, eds., *Women From Birth to Death*, p. 141.

27 Llewellyn Davies, ed., *Maternity*, p. 62.

28 Ibid, p. 62.

29 Ibid, p. 105.

30 See 'Pregnancy Gap Should be at Least a Year', *BBC News* (30 October 2018), https://www.bbc.co.uk/news/health-46017789.

31 Llewellyn Davies, ed., *Maternity*, p. 86.

32 There is direct evidence of two miscarriages, but gaps between Catherine's pregnancies suggest there may have been more. Lillian Nayder, in her biography of Catherine, notes the gap between her fourth and fifth pregnancies, and suggests the 'interval [...] may have resulted from planning on the Dickenses' part' (*The Other Dickens: A Life of Catherine Hogarth*, 123). However, her husband's expressed antipathy towards the number of pregnancies resulting from their marriage suggests a failure to manage their fertility. The gap may, therefore, be explained by undocumented miscarriage(s).

33 See Nayder, *The Other Dickens: A Life of Catherine Hogarth* (New York: Cornell University Press, 2011), p. 150.
34 Llewellyn Davies, ed., *Maternity*, p. 148.
35 Olive Schreiner to Betty Molteno (2 April 1896) in Rive, ed., *Olive Schreiner Letters*, Vol. 1, p. 251.
36 Olive Schreiner to Frances Schreiner (8 October 1896) in Rive, ed., *Olive Schreiner Letters*, Vol. 1, p. 290.
37 Lady Lyttelton to Catherine Gladstone (Undated), Gladstone Archives, Ref GG/792.
38 *The Life and Letters of Mary Wollstonecraft Shelley*, Vol. I, pp. 114–15.
39 Ibid, Vol. II, p. 3.
40 Llewellyn Davies, ed., *Maternity*, p. 87.
41 See 'Stillbirths and Neo-natal and Infant Mortality', *The Nuffield Trust* (July 2021), https://www.nuffieldtrust.org.uk/resource/infant-and-neonatal-mortality.
42 These include Lily Allen, Amanda Holden, and Gary Barlow, all of whom have spoken publicly about their experience of infant loss and stillbirth.
43 *Thirty-Eighth Annual Report of the Registrar-General of Births, Deaths, and Marriages in England* (London: George E. Eyre and William Spottiswoode, 1877) xxv. For more on nineteenth-century calculations of the stillbirth rate, see Robert Woods, *Death Before Birth: Fetal Health and Mortality in Historical Perspective* (Oxford: Oxford University Press, 2009).
44 Fred W. Lowndes, 'Statistics of Stillbirths', *Transactions of the Obstetrical Society of London*, Vol. XIV (London: Longmans, Green & Co., 1873), pp. 283–303.
45 Ibid, p. 285.
46 Kate was attended by Elizabeth Garrett (later Elizabeth Garrett Anderson) – the first woman to qualify as a doctor in Britain.
47 Lady Amberley's sister, Maude Stanley.
48 The family estate.
49 Lady Amberley's uncle, William Stanley.
50 *The Amberley Papers*, Vol. II, pp. 84–5.
51 Ibid, p. 85.
52 Ibid.
53 Ibid, pp. 568–70.
54 Lady Henrietta Stanley to Lady Maria Stanley (20 November 1853) in Mitford, ed., *The Stanleys of Alderley*, p. 70.
55 Ibid (20 April 1854), p. 80.
56 *Forty-Fifth Annual Report of the Registrar-General of Births, Deaths, and Marriages in England (Abstracts of 1882)* (London: Eyre and Spottiswoode, 1884), p. lxix.
57 *The Life and Letters of Mary Wollstonecraft Shelley*, p. 31.
58 Mary Shelley to Thomas Jefferson Hogg (6 March 1815) in *The Letters of Mary Wollstonecraft Shelley*, ed., Betty T. Bennett (Baltimore: John Hopkins University Press, 1988), pp. 10–11.
59 Ibid (13 March 1815).
60 Ibid (19 March 1815).
61 Emma Wedgwood to Charles Darwin (26 December 1838), Darwin Correspondence Project, 'Letter no. 462,' accessed on 16 April 2022, https://www.darwinproject.ac.uk/letter/?docId=letters/DCP-LETT-462.xml.

62 Ibid (23 January 1839).

63 Emma Darwin's diary for: 1839. CUL-DAR242[.5] Transcribed by Kees Rookmaaker and John van Wyhe (Darwin Online, http://darwin-online.org.uk/).

64 Charles Darwin to W. D. Fox (24 October 1839), Darwin Correspondence Project, 'Letter no. 541,' accessed on 16 April 2022, https://www.darwinproject.ac.uk/letter/?docId=letters/DCP-LETT-541.xml.

65 In *The Wedgwood Circle*, Barbara and Hensleigh Wedgwood suggest that Caroline showed some 'signs of mental disturbance […]. Careless in her appearance and forgetful of the most obvious practical details of managing a house and family, she refused to leave Leith Hill Place, and became an almost complete recluse,' although she subsequently seems to have recovered (B & H Wedgwood, *The Wedgwood Circle* [London: Studio Vista, 1980], p. 263.

66 Quoted in Emma Darwin to Charles Darwin (23 April 1851), Darwin Correspondence Project, 'Letter no. 1411,' accessed on 16 April 2022, https://www.darwinproject.ac.uk/letter/?docId=letters/DCP-LETT-1411.xml.

67 Charles Darwin to Charles Lyell (5–7 October 1842), Darwin Correspondence Project, 'Letter no. 649,' accessed on 5 April 2022, https://www.darwinproject.ac.uk/letter/?docId=letters/DCP-LETT-649.xml.

68 Emma Darwin to Mrs Hensleigh Wedgwood (20 October 1842) in H. E. Litchfield, ed., *Emma Darwin, Wife of Charles Darwin: A Century of Family Letters*, Vol. 2, (Cambridge: Cambridge University Press, 1904), p. 50.

69 Charles Darwin to W. D. Fox (29 April 1851), Darwin Correspondence Project, 'Letter no. 1425,' accessed on 16 April 2022, https://www.darwinproject.ac.uk/letter/?docId=letters/DCP-LETT-1425.xml.

70 Emma Darwin to Charles Darwin (24 April 1851), Darwin Correspondence Project, 'Letter no. 1414,' accessed on 16 April 2022, https://www.darwinproject.ac.uk/letter/?docId=letters/DCP-LETT-1414.xml.

71 Queen Victoria to Victoria, Crown Princess of Prussia (10 April 1861), in Fulford, ed., *Dearest Child*, p. 320.

72 Alice Chase, 'The Memoirs of Alice Maud Chase', Burnett Archive, Brunel University London, pp. 11–25.

73 Lady (Henrietta) Eddisbury to Lord Eddisbury (12/13 August 1849) in Mitford, ed., *The Ladies of Alderley*, p. 205.

74 Ibid, p. 206.

75 Ibid.

76 Ibid (15 August 1849), p. 207.

77 Ibid (13 August 1849), p. 206. For more on Henrietta's unwanted pregnancies, see Chapter Five.

78 Ibid (25 August 1849), p. 208.

79 Victoria, Crown Princess of Prussia to Queen Victoria (19 June 1866) in Fulford, ed., *Your Dear Letter*, p. 77.

80 Queen Victoria to Victoria, Crown Princess of Prussia (28 July 1866) in Fulford, ed., *Your Dear Letter*, p. 82.

81 Victoria, Crown Princess of Prussia to Queen Victoria (31 July 1866) in Fulford, ed., *Your Dear Letter*, p. 83.

82 Olive Schreiner to Ettie Stakesby Lewis (16 May 1895) in Rive, ed., *Olive Schreiner Letters*, Vol. 1, p. 252.

83 Ibid.

84 Anon., 'Margaret Jane', p. 2.

85 Catherine Temple Pears to Mary [?] (11 March 1853), Letters of Catherine Temple Pears (1828–1866), Durham Archives, Ref ADD.MSS 1700-1749.

86 E Sylvia Pankhurst, *The Suffragette Movement: An Intimate Account of Persons and Ideals* (London: Longmans, Green an Co, 1932), p. 88.

87 Anon., 'Margaret Jane', p. 3.

88 Pankhurst, *The Suffragette Movement*, p. 324.

89 Charles Dickens to Catherine Dickens (15 April 1851) in Madeline House, Graham Storey, and Kathleen Tillotson, eds., *The Letters of Charles Dickens*, Vol. VI (Oxford: Clarendon Press, 1988), p. 353.

90 Lavinia Glynne to Catherine Gladstone (April 1850), Glynne-Gladstone Archive, ref GG/792.

91 Elizabeth Gaskell to Harriet Anderson (15 March 1856) in John Chapple and Alan Shelston, eds., *Further Letters of Mrs Gaskell* (Manchester: Manchester University Press, 2003), p. 156.

92 Elizabeth Gaskell, *Mary Barton* (1848; Oxford: Oxford University Press, 2008), p. 75.

93 See Vicky Holmes, *In Bed with the Victorians: The Life-Cycle of Working-Class Marriage* (Basingstoke: Palgrave Macmillan, 2017).

94 Arthur P. Luff, *Text-Book of Forensic Medicine and Toxicology*, Vol. II (London: Longmans, Green, & Co., 1895), p. 146.

95 'Overlaying Case at Syston', *Leicester Chronicle* (30 November 1895), p. 3.

96 Queen Victoria's Journals, 13 January 1845.

Chapter 8

1 Augusta Webster, 'Mother and Daughter', *Sonnet* (1895).

2 Charlotte Perkins Gilman, 'The Yellow Wallpaper', *New England Magazine* (1892).

3 William Makepeace Thackeray to Mrs Carmichael-Smyth (20–21 August 1840), in Gordon N. Ray, ed., *The Letters and Private Papers of William Makepeace Thackeray*, Vol. I: 1817–1840 (Oxford: Oxford University Press, 1945), p. 463.

4 Thackeray to Mrs Carmichael-Smyth (4–5 October 1840), in *The Letters and Private Papers of William Makepeace Thackeray*, Vol. I: 1817–1840, p. 483.

5 Ibid (17 September 1840), p. 474.

6 Ibid (21–23 September 1840), pp. 477–8.

7 Stanley Cobb, 'The Psychiatric Case History of Isabella Shawe Thackeray' in *The Letters and Private Papers of William Makepeace Thackeray*, Vol. I: 1817–1840, 520.

8 Thackeray to Mrs Carmichael-Smyth (12 July 1838), in *The Letters and Private Papers of William Makepeace Thackeray*, Vol. I: 1817–1840, p. 366.

9 Diary of Betsey Wynne (1 August 1800; 5 October 1800) in Fremantle, ed., *The Wynne Diaries*, Vol. 3, p. 20, p. 23.

10 Catherine Dickens to Mary Scott Hogarth (30 May 1837), quoted in Nayder, *The Other Dickens*, p. 76.

11 Lady Lyttelton to Catherine Gladstone (1840), Gladstone Archives, Hawarden, ref. GG/792.

12 Ibid (n.d.).

13 Catherine Temple Pears to Henry Pears (1 October 1858), *The Letters of Catherine Temple Pears*, p. 377.

14 Robert Brudenell Carter, *On the Influence of Education and Training in Preventing Diseases of the Nervous System* (London: John Churchill, 1855), pp. 136–7.

15 Ibid, p. 136.

16 Chavasse, *Advice to a Wife* (Tenth edition), p. 208.

17 Ibid, p. 195.

18 Lady Stanley to Lady Eddisbury (29 August 1850) in Mitford, ed., *The Ladies of Alderley*, p. 242 (emphasis in original).

19 Maria Josepha Lady Stanley to Lady Stanley (21 June 1854) in Mitford, ed., *The Stanleys of Alderley*, p. 81.

20 Alfred Sheen, *The Workhouse and its Medical Officer* (2nd edition; Bristol: John Wright & Co., 1890), p. 36.

21 Llewellyn Davies, ed., *Maternity*, p. 35.

22 Ibid, p. 96.

23 Ibid, p. 20.

24 Cited in 'Factories and Workshops Bill' (23 July 1891), *Hansard's Parliamentary Debates*, Third Series, Vol. CCCLVI (London: Hansard's Publishing Union, 1891), p. 79.

25 Chavasse, *Advice to a Wife*, p. 201. Oatmeal has been used as a means of relieving dry and itchy skin for centuries, which perhaps explains this recommendation.

26 Lee, *Clinical Midwifery*, p. 19.

27 Ibid, p. 64.

28 Ibid, p. 45.

29 Ibid.

30 Ibid, pp. 5–6.

31 Ibid, p. 6.

32 *Three Hundred Consultations in Midwifery*, pp. 53–4.

33 Llewellyn Davies, ed., *Maternity*, p. 70.

34 Ibid, p. 72.

35 Ibid, p. 122.

36 Ibid, p. 119.

37 Chavasse, *Advice to a Wife*, p. 194.

38 Anon., Advert for 'Swanbill Belts', *Medical Times and Gazette Advertiser* (30 December 1882), p. viii.

39 Allbutt, *The Wife's Handbook*, p. 28.

40 Llewellyn Davies, ed., *Maternity*, p. 39.

41 See Overview – Postnatal depression – NHS (www.nhs.uk) and Postpartum psychosis – NHS (www.nhs.uk).

42 Mary Elizabeth Braddon, *Lady Audley's Secret* (1862; Peterborough: Broadview, 2003), p. 358.

43 Ibid, p. 361.

44 Kemble, *Records of Later Life*, Vol. 1 (31 October 1835), p. 41.

45 G. Herbert to Catherine Gladstone (23 August 1857), Gladstone Archive, Hawarden, Ref. GG/1013.

46 Queen Victoria to Victoria, Crown Princess of Prussia (29 January 1859) in Fulford, ed., *Dearest Child*, p. 160.

47 Charles Dickens to Richard Bentley (24 January 1837), Pilgrim 1, p. 223 [quoted Nayder, *The Other Dickens*, p. 72].

48 See Stephanie Liu, 'Breastfeeding Struggles Linked to Postpartum Depression in Mothers' (May 2019), The Conversation, https://theconversation.com/breast-feeding-struggles-linked-to-postpartum-depression-in-mothers-116487.

49 See Nayder, *The Other Dickens*, p. 75.

50 Queen Victoria to Victoria, Crown Princess of Prussia (23 February 1859) in Fulford, ed., *Dearest Child*, p. 162.

51 Queen Victoria's Journals.

52 Queen Victoria to Leopold I (December 1842), quoted in Stanley Weintraub, *Uncrowned King: The Life of Prince Albert* (New York: The Free Press, 1997), p. 137.

53 See Lucy Worsley, *Queen Victoria: Daughter, Wife, Mother, Widow* (London: Hodder & Stoughton, 2018), p. 193.

54 Royal College of Physicians, MS 4973, quoted in Worsley, *Queen Victoria*, p. 193.

55 Queen Victoria's Journals, 25 April 1843.

56 Ibid (9 May 1843).

57 Ibid (13 May 1843).

58 Ibid (15 May 1850).

59 Ibid (22 April 1853).

60 See Rappaport, *Queen Victoria: A Biographical Companion*, p. 340.

61 See Postpartum psychosis – NHS (www.nhs.uk).

62 Anon., 'Puerperal Mania', *Chambers Encyclopedia*, Vol. VII (1865).

63 See James Young M.D., 'Case of Puerperal Mania', *Edinburgh Medical Journal*, Vol. 13 (1868), p. 262.

64 Ibid. See also 'Puerperal Mania', *Chambers Encyclopedia*.

65 Sir William Charles Ellis, *A Treatise on the Nature, Symptoms, Causes, and Treatment of Insanity* (London: Samuel Holdsworth, 1838), p. 90.

66 William Saunders Hallaran, *Practical Observations on the Causes and Cure of Insanity* (Cork: Edwards and Savage, 1818), p. 50.

67 Thomas Arnold, *Observations on the nature, Kinds, Causes, and Prevention of Insanity*, Vol. 2 (Second edition; London: Richard Phillips, 1806), pp. 144–5.

68 Hilary Marland, in her work in this area, suggests that in many institutions, around 10 per cent of female patients were suffering from some form of puerperal insanity by the mid-nineteenth century ('Under the Shadow of Maternity: Birth, Death, and Puerperal Insanity in Victorian Britain'. *History of Psychiatry*. 23:1 [2012]).

69 Ellis, *A Treatise on the Nature, Symptoms, Causes, and Treatment of Insanity*, pp. 92–4.

70 See Johanna E. Soet, Gregory A. Brack, and Colleen Dilorio. 'Prevalence and Predictors of Women's Experience of Psychological Trauma During Childbirth'. *Birth*. 30:1 (2003).

71 Ibid.

72 J. Crichton Browne, ed., *The West Riding Lunatic Asylum Medical Reports*, Vol. 1 (London: J & A Churchill, 1871), p. 171.

73 Young, 'Case of Puerperal Mania', pp. 263–4.

74 Medical Report Book for Newcastle Lying-In Hospital, 1821–1833.

75 Old Bailey Proceedings Online (www.oldbaileyonline.org, version 8.0, 23 April 2022), January 1838, trial of ELIZABETH HODGES (t18380129–499).

76 Ellis, *A Treatise on the Nature, Symptoms, Causes, and Treatment of Insanity*, pp. 90–1.

77 Ibid, pp. 91–2.

78 Hallaran, *Practical Observations on the Causes and Cure of Insanity,* pp. 52–3.

Chapter 9

1 William Wordsworth, *The Prelude*, Book 2 (1850).

2 'Strange Case of Baby Farming', *Lloyds Illustrated Newspaper* (8 August 1869).

3 William Makepeace Thackeray, *Vanity Fair* (1848; Oxford: Oxford University Press, 1998), p. 448.

4 Walter C. Dendy, *The Book of the Nursery* (London: Whittaker, Treacher, & Co., 1833), p. 20.

5 Charles Vine, *Mother and Child* (London: Frederick Warne and Co., 1868), p. 2.

6 Ibid, p. 4.

7 Elizabeth Gaskell, *Sylvia's Lovers* (1863; London: Smith, Elder, & Co., 1889), p. 357.

8 Thackeray, *Vanity Fair*, p. 448.

9 Maria Edgeworth, *Belinda* (1801; London: J. Johnson & Co., 1811), p. 85.

10 George Moore, *Esther Waters* (London: Walter Scott Ltd, 1894), p. 121.

11 Ryan, *The Philosophy of Marriage*, p. 260.

12 George Black, *Household Medicine* (London: Ward, Lock & Co., 1881), p. 768.

13 Ibid.

14 NHS, 'Breastfeeding Challenges' (2022), https://www.nhs.uk/start4life/baby/feeding-your-baby/breastfeeding/breastfeeding-challenges/mastitis.

15 Vine, *Mother and Child*, p. 23.

16 Thomas J. Graham, M.D. *On the Management and Disorders of Infancy and Childhood* (London: Simpkin, Marshall & Co., 1853), p. 194.

17 Robert Brudenell Carter, *On the Influence of Education and Training in Preventing Diseases of the Nervous System* (London: John Churchill, 1855), p. 134.

18 William B. Carpenter, M.D., *Principles of Human Physiology* (sixth edition; London: John Churchill, 1864), pp. 741–2.

19 Braddon, *Lady Audley's Secret*, p. 398.

20 Llewellyn Davies, ed., *Maternity*, p. 175.

21 Mrs Isabella Beeton, *The Management of Children in Health and Sickness* (London: Ward, Lock & Tyler, 1873), p.10.

22 Llewellyn Davies, ed., *Maternity*, p. 52.

23 Ibid, p. 132.
24 See Julie A. Mennella and Gary K. Beauchamp, 'Beer, Breast Feeding, and Folklore', *Developmental Psychobiology* (December 1993), pp. 459–66.
25 Charles West, *The Mother's Manual of Children's Diseases* (London: Longmans, Green, & Col, 1885), p. 57.
26 Anon., 'The Milk of Intemperate Mothers', *The Lancet* (28 October 1882), p. 715.
27 Anon., 'Margaret Jane', The Burnett Archive, Brunel University London, p. 1.
28 Lady Lyttelton to Catherine Gladstone ([June?] 1840), Gladstone Archives, Ref GG/792.
29 Catherine Temple Pears to Alicia (9 October 1858), p. 381.
30 Ryan, *The Philosophy of Marriage*, p. 260.
31 Mary Wollstonecraft, *A Vindication of the Rights of Woman* (1792; London: William Strange, 1844), p. 69.
32 Olive Schreiner to Karl Pearson (12 June 1886) in Rive, ed., *Olive Schreiner Letters*, Vol. 1, p. 82.
33 Allbutt, *The Wife's Handbook*, p. 28.
34 Llewellyn Davies, ed., *Maternity*, p. 82.
35 M. J., Countess Dowager Mountcashell [Margaret Jane Moore], *A Grandmother's Advice to Young Mothers on the Physical Education of Children* (London: Baldwin and Cradock, 1835), p. 29.
36 Lord Amberley, Diary (13–26 August 1865) in *The Amberley Papers*, Vol. 1, pp. 402–05.
37 Kate (Lady) Amberley to Lady Stanley (6 August 1872) in *The Amberley Papers*, Vol. 2, p. 498.
38 Mary Hogarth to Mary Scott Hogarth (26 January 1837), cited in Nayder, *The Other Dickens*, p. 72.
39 See Amy Brown, Jaynie Rance, and Paul Bennett, 'Understanding the relationship between breastfeeding and postnatal depression: the role of pain and physical difficulties', *Journal of Advance Nursing*, 72:2 (February 2016), pp. 273–82.
40 Anon., 'The Provinces'. *The Spectator*. Vol. 17 (13 April 1844), p. 341.
41 Llewellyn Davies, ed., *Maternity*, pp. 81–2.
42 Anon., 'Margaret Jane', p. 4.
43 Chavasse, *Advice to a Wife* (tenth edition), p. 209.
44 See 'Natural Family Planning' (2021), www.nhs.uk/conditions/contraception/natural-family-planning.
45 M. Ryan, *A Manual of Midwifery* (4th edition; London: W. Wilcockson, 1841), p. 260.
46 Llewellyn Davies, ed., *Maternity*, p. 146.
47 'Shocking Tragedy Near Claremont', *Essex Standard* (16 June 1854).
48 Anon., 'A Wet Nurse', *The Temperance Recorder* (August 1842), p. 45.
49 Queen Victoria to Princess Alice, 12 October 1864, quoted in Hannah Pakula, *An Uncommon Woman* (London: Phoenix Press, 1997), p. 221.
50 See Rappaport, *Queen Victoria: A Biographical Companion*, p. 339.
51 Lady Stanley of Alderley to Mrs Edward Stanley (27 January 1841) in Mitford, ed., *The Ladies of Alderley*, p. 4.

52 Mrs Stanley to Lady Stanley (22 September 1843), in Mitford, ed., *The Ladies of Alderley*, p. 65.

53 Ibid, p. 202, p. 205.

54 Anon., *Letters to a Mother on the Watchful Care of Her Infant* (London: R. B. Seeley and W. Burnside), p. 4.

55 Olive Schreiner to Karl Pearson (12 June 1886) in Rive, ed., *Olive Schreiner Letters*, Vol. 1, p. 82.

56 Margaret Gladstone, unrelated to the famous nineteenth-century statesman William Gladstone, was the mother of Margaret Ethel Gladstone, and died shortly after her daughter's birth. Margaret Ethel later married Ramsay MacDonald, who would become the first Labour prime minister.

57 Diary of Elizabeth King [mother of Margaret Gladstone] (August 1870), in Jane Cox, ed., *A Singular Marriage: A Labour Love Story in Letters and Diaries* (London: HARRAP, 1988), p. 26.

58 Medical advice today suggests there is little or no risk to breastfeeding babies from mothers carrying sexually transmitted diseases, although it is recommended that breastfeeding is avoided if there are syphilitic or herpes sores on the breasts themselves.

59 Graham, *On the Management and Disorders of Infancy and Childhood*, p. 191.

60 Anon., *The Young Mother; or, Affectionate Advice to a Married Daughter* (London: The Religious Tract Society, 1851), p. 44.

61 Anon., 'An Infant Poisoned by Two Drops of Laudanum Administered by a Nurse', *London Medical Gazette* (6 November 1846), p. 814.

62 'Coroners Inquests', *The Standard* (31 December 1829), p. 1.

63 'Our Social Habits', *Royal Cornwall Gazette* (20 January 1872), p. 7.

64 Vine, *Mother and Child*, p. 31.

65 Moore, *Esther Waters*, p. 143.

66 'Royal Nursery Gossip', *The Era* (21 November 1841).

67 Lady Eddisbury to Lord Eddisbury (14/15 August 1849) in Mitford, ed., *The Ladies of Alderley*, p. 207.

68 Lord Amberley (28 August 1865), *The Amberley Papers*, Vol. 1, p. 406.

69 Mrs Layton, 'Memories of Seventy Years', p. 7.

70 Vine, *Mother and Child*, p. 26.

71 Samuel Barker, *Children and How to Manage Them in Health and Sickness* (London: Robert Hardwicke, 1860), p. 28.

72 Old Bailey Proceedings Online (www.oldbaileyonline.org, version 8.0, 29 April 2022), November 1836, trial of ELIZA HOLMES (t18361128–131).

73 Old Bailey Proceedings Online (www.oldbaileyonline.org, version 8.0, 29 April 2022), April 1840, trial of CATHERINE MICHAEL (t18400406–1285).

74 C. H. F. Routh, M.D., *Infant Feeding and its Influence on Life* (1860; London: J. & A. Churchill, 3rd edition, 1876), pp. 74–5.

75 Hugh R. Jones, 'The Perils and Protection of Infant Life', *Journal of the Royal Statistical Society* (March 1894), pp. 21–2.

76 Llewellyn Davies, ed., *Maternity*, p. 137.

77 Ibid, p. 136.

78 J. E. Panton, *The Way They Should Go: Hints to Young Parents* (London: Downey & Co, 1896), pp. 43–5.

79 Queen Victoria to Victoria, Crown Princess of Prussia (5 April 1873), in Fulford, ed., *Darling Child*, p. 84.

80 Jones, 'The Perils and Protection of Infant Life', p. 57.

81 Beeton, *The Management of Children in Health and Sickness*, p. 18.

82 Mrs Frederick Pedley, *Infant Nursing and the Management of Young Children* (London: George Routledge and Sons, 1866), p. 104.

83 Llewellyn, ed., *Maternity*, pp. 78–9.

84 Advert for Benger's Food for Infants, Children, and Invalids, 'Multiple Classified Ads' (25 November 1895), *The Standard*, p. 6.

Afterword

1 See Joeli Brearley, *Pregnant Then Screwed: The Truth About the Motherhood Penalty* (London: Gallery Books, 2021).

2 See 'First Women's Health Strategy for England to tackle gender health gap' (22 July 2022), Department of Health and Social Care (https://www.gov.uk/government/news/first-womens-health-strategy-for-england-to-tackle-gender-health-gap).

3 More recently, MPs at Westminster voted to introduce a buffer zone around abortion clinics to prevent the harassment of women using these services, although 110 MPs voted against this measure.

Index

The History Press

The destination for history
www.thehistorypress.co.uk